FINE EDGE NAUTICAL KNO

MW00474584

LOCAL KNOWLEDGE

A SKIPPER'S REFERENCE

Tacoma to Ketchikan

Kevin Monahan

FINE EDGE

Nautical & Recreational Publishing

Important Legal Disclaimer

Both the publisher, Fine Edge, and the author have made every effort to ensure that all the information in this book is accurate. However, errors may exist, due to transposition/typographical errors, and misprints. Values given in various tables may also not be applicable to a particular situation due to variations in actual conditions. The data in this book should be considered a general guide and should be confirmed by actual measurements and/or observations. Neither Fine Edge nor the author warrants this information to be exact and disclaim any liability for errors or omissions or for any loss or damage incurred from using the information in this book.

The tables in this book have been drawn from a number of sources, which are either noted in the Acknowledgements or on the relevant page of *Local Knowledge—A Skipper's Reference*. Other tables have been generated independently from first principles. If I have forgotten to include a reference to any person or organization when giving credit for the tables or any other material, please contact me and proper credit will be given in future editions.

Publisher: Mark J. Bunzel
Book design by Melanie Haage
Copyedited by Pat Hillis and Leslie Bunzel
Original drawings by Kevin Monahan were rendered into digital graphics by Shawn O'Keefe.

Cover photos of the Jeanneau 49 Deck Salon and the American Tug 41 were provided by the exclusive dealer in the Pacific Northwest for both boats, Marine Servicenter, a full-service dealer and repair yard located in Seattle and Anacortes, WA. For more information on these beautiful boats call (206) 323-2405, or see their website at www.marinesc.com.

Address requests for permission to:
Fine Edge
14004 Biz Point Lane
Anacortes, WA 98221
www.FineEdge.com

LIBRARY OF CONGRESS CATALOGING-IN-PUBLICATION DATA

Monahan, Kevin, 1951–
Local knowledge : a skipper's reference : Tacoma to Ketchikan / Kevin Monahan.— 1st ed.
p. cm.
Includes bibliographical references.
ISBN 1-932310-11-8 (alk. paper)
1. Pilot guides—British Columbia. 2. Tides—British Columbia—Tables. 3. Pilot guides—Washington (State) 4. Tides—Washington (State)—Tables. I. Title.
VK945.M66 2005
623.89'22433--dc22 2004029374

Dedication

This book is dedicated to my father, Hugh Monahan, artist, soldier, conservationist and eccentric. He could not stand minutiae, but his oil paintings of waterfowl were intricate and precise; so perhaps it isn't surprising that I honour him with this book. Hugh Monahan taught me to be happy being myself and not to try to satisfy other people's expectations. I can't imagine a greater gift.

The sailing ship on page 14 is from a pen and ink rendering of Sir Francis Drake's *Golden Hinde*, drawn by my father in 1922 at the age of nine.

Acknowledgements

This collection of tables, maps and information could not have been completed without the help of a number of individuals and organizations. In particular I would like to thank: my publisher, Mark Bunzel, and Leslie Bunzel of Fine Edge, for their faith in this project, and their enthusiastic support of my efforts; Nancy Monahan, my wife, who encouraged me to complete this project and who supported me in thousands of small ways; Terry Patten, of Compass Rose Nautical Books; Robert Hale of *The Waggoner Cruising Guide* for his thoughtful suggestions; Jim Rard of Marine Servicenter; Don Odegard; Brian Pemberton of NW Explorations; all of whom reviewed the manuscript, and whose suggestions have made this a much better book. I would also like to thank Tony McCormick of McCormick and Company and Bob Ferguson for their advice and suggestions.

Most of all I would like to thank Nathan Reed, Fisheries Patrol Captain, who inspired me to start making the distance tables many years ago. And, of course, my special thanks to Mark Twain.

All photographs in this book were taken by the author, with the exception of the following:

For the photo of the Ripple Rock explosion in Table 1-14, by Bill Dennet, my thanks to Sandra Parrish of the Museum at Campbell River, Campbell River, BC.

The photo of Triple Island Lighthouse in a storm, in Table 1-25, is provided courtesy of the photographer, Mike Mitchell.

Aerial photograph of Dent Rapids in Table 2, courtesy of Ministry of Environment, Lands and Parks, Geographic Data BC.

Aerial photograph of Deception Pass in Table 2, courtesy of The U.S. Geological Survey and the Microsoft Terraserver Project @ www.terraserver.microsoft.com.

Photos of a fishboat in the Devils's Hole in Table 2 by Réanne Hemingway-Douglass.

Illustrations by Shawn O'Keefe, with the exception of the following:

The cover illustration and the illustration of the sailing ship in Table 1-1 is by Hugh Monahan, c. 1922.

The map in Table 1-2, *A Bird's Eye View of Port Townsend, Puget Sound, Washington Territory 1878,* published by A.L. Bancroft & Co., is courtesy of the Library of Congress Geography and Map Division.

The engravings of "A View of Vancouver Island", in Table 1-9, and of "Captain James Cook" on page 4 are also from the collection of the National Archives of Canada.

The engraving of "The Discovery on the Rocks in Queen Charlotte's Sound" in Table 1-16, is from "A Voyage of Discovery to the North Pacific, and Round the World" by George Vancouver, printed for John Stockdale, 1801, and is held in the collection of the National Archives of Canada.

The drawing of Johnstone Strait in Figure 2-2 is by Kevin Monahan.

The Wind Chill Temperature Index in Table 21, is from the United States National Weather Service.

Environment Canada's "Mariner's Guide" has been provided by Dick Boak, Communications Officer, Environment Canada, Pacific and Yukon Region.

The three-scale Speed/Time/Distance nomogram is taken from the United States Defence Mapping Agency publication 5090 (Maneuvering Board).

Captain James Cook
From the collection of the National Archives of Canada.

According to conventional wisdom, Captain James Cook exemplified the qualities of exceptional navigator and humanist. However, according to Martin Dugan, author of *Farther Than Any Man,* by the time Captain James Cook began his third voyage of exploration in 1776, his taste for power had become an obsession, and the once thoughtful and considerate Cook had become a megalomaniac; his previous gentle paternalism toward natives became confrontational and uncompromising. Arriving in present-day Washington state on March 7, 1778, Cook sailed north, searching for a western entrance to the Northwest Passage, just as Drake had almost 200 years before. He finally gave up, after encountering severe ice on August 29, just 50 miles south of Point Barrow in the Beaufort Sea. With rotting sails and rigging, the *Resolution* limped, leaking, toward the Hawaiian Islands. There, his two ships, appetite for provisions, water and women began to test the patience of the natives. When the *Discovery's* cutter was stolen by natives, Cook led a detachment ashore to seize King Kalniopu as a hostage. On returning to the shore, the party was surrounded by a violent mob. The British killed eight Hawaiians and raked the beach with cannon fire, but to no avail. Cook could not escape; he was captured and dismembered by the mob. Thus ended the career of one of the world's greatest explorers —a flawed, but brilliant man, whose name is remembered throughout the Pacific.

Contents

PART I
Navigation Tables

Table 1 — Distance Tables

Layout of the distance tables

These distance tables make it possible to quickly estimate the distance between any two of over 800 places in the inside waters of Washington State and British Columbia. Over 14,000 separate distance measurements have been tabulated for your convenience in the following 25 tables.

Every measured distance is based on a unique route. Every measured distance represents the actual distance you would have to travel between two places—taking into account the actual conditions which you are likely to encounter, including weather, depth of water, and other hazards.

The tabulated locations have been chosen because they are well known landmarks or because they are logical places from which two voyages may diverge. Some of the selected points may not be familiar to many skippers, so map keys are included with the individual distance tables in order to identify those points.

- The tables are organized into two sections, both of which are made up of a planning table, several detail tables and their accompanying map keys.
- The first table in each section is a primary planning table, showing distances between primary locations along the Inside Passage. The planning table map key shows these primary locations, and also the areas covered by the succeeding detail tables.
- Each of the detail tables shows the distances between locations within specific geographic areas, and also includes the primary locations along the Inside Passage that fall in that geographic area. The associated map key shows the area covered by the table.

All distances greater than 10 nautical miles (Nm) are rounded to the nearest Nm Distances less than 10 Nm are rounded to the nearest 0.5 Nm.

Names of towns, villages, and settlements appear in bold uppercase font. Except in the planning tables, (Tables 1-1 and 1-17) locations that appear in more than one detail table are in bold lowercase font. Since every location in the planning tables appears in other detail tables, none are in bold lowercase font.

Instructions for use of the distance tables

1. To Find the distance between two locations on the same table, simply search for the intersection between the column of one location with the row of the other (See Figure 1-1).

2. In general, the tables show the distance between two locations by the most direct route. However, some tables specify a preferred route. If you wish to follow another route, select an intermediary position along the route and break the voyage into two sections (See Figure 1-2).

Location	Split Head	Boat Bluff	KLEMTU	Begg Point	Legace Point	Jorkins Point	Ramsbotham Islands	Dallain Point	Wingate Point	Wilby Point	Kipp Islet	McInnes Island	Keith Point	Sloop Narrows	Perceval Narrows	Ivory Island	Idol Point	Hyndman Reef	Law Island	Spiller Lagoon	Neekas Cove	Gerald Point	Ellerslie Lagoon	Ingram Bay	Coldwell Point	Troupe Narrows	Dumas Point	BELLA BELLA
Split Head																												
Boat Bluff	2.5																											
KLEMTU	5	3																										
Begg Point (Jackson Passage)	9	6.5	4.5																									
Legace Point (Oscar Passage)	15	12	9	5.5																								
Jorkins Point	15	13	10	7.5	3.5																							
Ramsbotham Islands	24	27	29	34	39	40																						
Dallain Point	17	20	22	27	32	33	7.5																					
Wingate Point	11	14	16	21	26	27	13	6																				
Wilby Point	14	16	19	24	29	30	13	6	3																			
Kipp Islet (West Higgins Passage)	20	22	35	30	35	36	17	12	9	6																		
McInnes Island (Catala Passage)	30	28	25	21	17	14	30	24	22	19	14																	
Keith Point	17	15	12	9	4.5	2	42	36	34	31	26	12																
Sloop Narrows	23	21	18	15	10	7.5	44	38	36	33	28	14	5.5															
Perceval Narrows	25	23	20	17	12	9.5	44	38	36	33	28	14	7.5	2														
Ivory Island	26	24	21	18	14	11	43	37	35	32	27	13	9	7	4.5													
Idol Point	31	29	26	23	19	16	48	42	40	37	32	18	14	12	9.5	5												
Hyndman Reef	32	30	27	24	20	17	54	43	41	38	33	19	15	13	10	6	2											
Law Island	34	32	29	26	22	19	51	45	43	40	35	21	17	15	13	8	4	2										
Spiller Lagoon	38	36	33	30	26	23	55	49	47	44	39	25	21	19	17	12	8	6	7									
Neekas Cove	45	43	40	37	33	30	62	56	54	51	46	32	28	26	24	19	15	13	14	7								
Gerald Point	44	42	39	36	32	29	61	55	53	50	45	31	27	25	23	18	14	13	14	6	3.5							
Ellerslie Lagoon	50	48	45	42	38	35	67	61	59	56	51	37	33	31	29	24	21	19	19	13	9.5	7						
Ingram Bay	56	54	51	48	44	41	73	67	65	62	57	43	39	37	35	30	27	25	25	19	15	13	12					
Coldwell Point	41	39	36	33	29	26	58	52	50	47	42	28	24	22	20	15	11	9	7	14	12	8	15	21				
Troupe Narrows	43	41	38	35	31	28	60	54	52	49	44	30	26	24	22	17	13	11	9	17	15	11	18	24	3			
Dumas Point	38	46	33	30	26	23	55	49	47	44	39	24	21	19	17	12	7	7.5	5.5	13	21	17	24	30	9	6		
BELLA BELLA	40	48	**35**	32	28	25	57	51	49	46	41	27	23	21	18	14	9	9	8	15	24	20	27	35	12	9	3	
Nicholson Island	44	52	39	36	32	29	61	55	53	50	45	31	27	25	22	18	14	12	10	17	18	14	21	27	6	3	9	12

Klemtu column

Distance from Klemtu to Bella Bella

Bella Bella row

Figure 1-1 The distance from Klemtu to Bella Bella is 35 Nm.

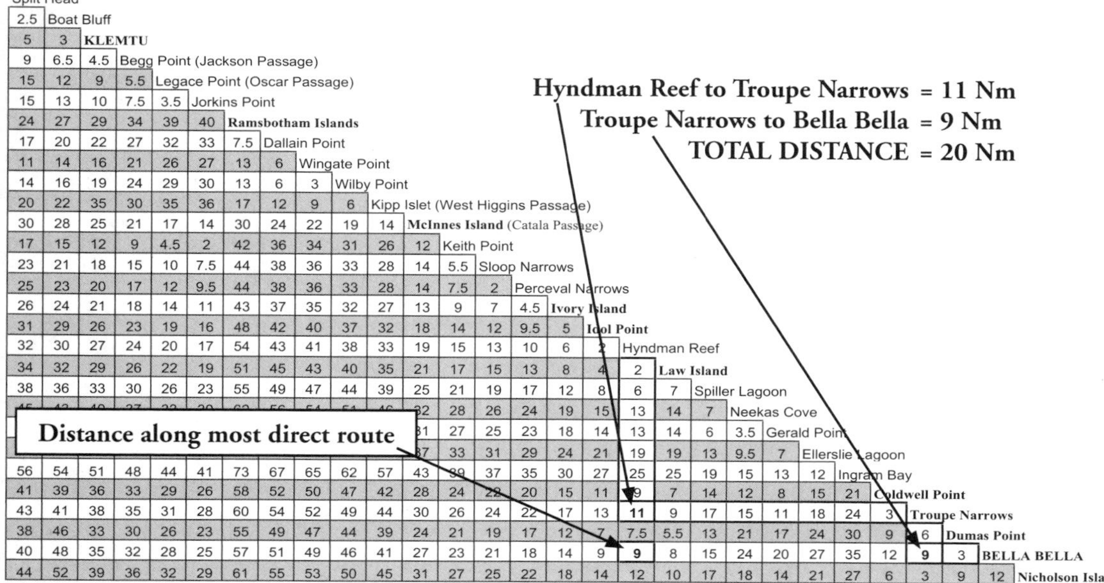
Hyndman Reef to Troupe Narrows = 11 Nm
Troupe Narrows to Bella Bella = 9 Nm
TOTAL DISTANCE = 20 Nm
Distance along most direct route

Location	Split Head	Boat Bluff	KLEMTU	Begg Point	Legace Point	Jorkins Point	Ramsbotham Islands	Dallain Point	Wingate Point	Wilby Point	Kipp Islet	McInnes Island	Keith Point	Sloop Narrows	Perceval Narrows	Ivory Island	Idol Point	Hyndman Reef	Law Island	Spiller Lagoon	Neekas Cove	Gerald Point	Ellerslie Lagoon	Ingram Bay	Coldwell Point	Troupe Narrows	Dumas Point	BELLA BELLA
Split Head																												
Boat Bluff	2.5																											
KLEMTU	5	3																										
Begg Point (Jackson Passage)	9	6.5	4.5																									
Legace Point (Oscar Passage)	15	12	9	5.5																								
Jorkins Point	15	13	10	7.5	3.5																							
Ramsbotham Islands	24	27	29	34	39	40																						
Dallain Point	17	20	22	27	32	33	7.5																					
Wingate Point	11	14	16	21	26	27	13	6																				
Wilby Point	14	16	19	24	29	30	13	6	3																			
Kipp Islet (West Higgins Passage)	20	22	35	30	35	36	17	12	9	6																		
McInnes Island (Catala Passage)	30	28	25	21	17	14	30	24	22	19	14																	
Keith Point	17	15	12	9	4.5	2	42	36	34	31	26	12																
Sloop Narrows	23	21	18	15	10	7.5	44	38	36	33	28	14	5.5															
Perceval Narrows	25	23	20	17	12	9.5	44	38	36	33	28	14	7.5	2														
Ivory Island	26	24	21	18	14	11	43	37	35	32	27	13	9	7	4.5													
Idol Point	31	29	26	23	19	16	48	42	40	37	32	18	14	12	9.5	5												
Hyndman Reef	32	30	27	24	20	17	54	43	41	38	33	19	15	13	10	6	2											
Law Island	34	32	29	26	22	19	51	45	43	40	35	21	17	15	13	8	4	2										
Spiller Lagoon	38	36	33	30	26	23	55	49	47	44	39	25	21	19	17	12	8	6	7									
Neekas Cove												32	28	26	24	19	15	13	14	7								
Gerald Point												31	27	25	23	18	14	13	14	6	3.5							
Ellerslie Lagoon												37	33	31	29	24	21	19	19	13	9.5	7						
Ingram Bay	56	54	51	48	44	41	73	67	65	62	57	43	39	37	35	30	27	25	25	19	15	13	12					
Coldwell Point	41	39	36	33	29	26	58	52	50	47	42	28	24	22	20	15	11	9	7	14	12	8	15	21				
Troupe Narrows	43	41	38	35	31	28	60	54	52	49	44	30	26	24	22	17	13	**11**	9	17	15	11	18	24	3			
Dumas Point	38	46	33	30	26	23	55	49	47	44	39	24	21	19	17	12	7	7.5	5.5	13	21	17	24	30	9	6		
BELLA BELLA	40	48	35	32	28	25	57	51	49	46	41	27	23	21	18	14	9	**9**	8	15	24	20	27	35	12	**9**	3	
Nicholson Island	44	52	39	36	32	29	61	55	53	50	45	31	27	25	22	18	14	12	10	17	18	14	21	27	6	3	9	12

Figure 1-2 To determine the distance from Hyndman Reef to Bella Bella via Troupe Narrows, choose an intermediate position from the map key—in this case, Troupe Narrows.

The distance along the most direct route is 9 Nm The difference between the two routes is 11 Nm In a vessel proceeding at 7 knots, this would mean a difference of more than 1 hour.

3. To determine the distance between two locations on different tables within the same table page (See Figure 1-3).
    - Find the distance from each location to a common intermediate location that is on both tables.
    - Add the two distances to calculate the total distance.
4. To determine the distance between two locations that are on adjacent table pages, simply select a common intermediate location that appears on both table pages. Locations that appear on more than one table page are identified in bold font.
5. To determine the distance between two locations on table pages that are not adjacent, select two intermediate locations that are on the separate table pages and are also primary locations on the **North Coast** or **South Coast** planning tables (**Tables 1-1** or **1-17**) (See Figure 1-4).

Table 1-20 BELLA BELLA TO BUTEDALE

Most Direct Route (Except no routes via Higgins Passage)

Locations in **bold lowercase** appear in other detail tables.

#	Location	1	2	3	4	5	6	7	8	9	10	11	12	13	14	15	16	17	18	19	20	21	22	23	24	25	26	27	28	29	30	31	32	33	34	35
1	**Clifford Bay**																																			
2	Weeteeam Bay	12																																		
3	Prior Passage	13	6																																	
4	**Kingcome Point**	53	63	67																																
5	**Butedale**	64	62	58	11																															
6	Khutze Inlet (Asher Point)	63	56	50	19	8																														
7	Sarah Head	53	44	38	30	20	12																													
8	Split Head	38	31	25	43	33	25	13																												
9	Boat Bluff	41	34	28	47	36	28	16	2.5																											
10	**KLEMTU**	43	36	30	48	37	30	18	5	3																										
11	Begg Point (Jackson Passage)	48	41	35	54	43	**35**	23	9	6.5	4.5																									
12	Legace Point (Oscar Passage)	53	46	40	59	48	40	28	14.5	12	9	5.5																								
13	Jorkins Point	54	47	41	58	47	40	28	15	13	10	7.5	3.5																							
14	**Ramsbotham Islands**	32	25	19	48	59	55	37	24	27	29	34	39	40																						
15	Dallain Point	39	32	26	55	50	42	30	17	20	22	27	32	33	7.5																					
16	Wingate Point	27	18	14	55	44	36	24	11	14	16	21	26	27	13	6																				
17	Wilby Point	44	37	31	58	47	39	27	14	16	19	24	29	30	13	6	3																			
18	Kipp Islet (West Higgins Passage)	21	15	8	64	53	45	33	20	22	35	30	35	36	17	12	9	6																		
19	**McInnes Island** (Catala Passage)	28	21	15	74	63	55	43	30	28	25	21	17	14	30	24	22	19	14																	
20	Keith Point	40	34	27	61	49	42	30	17	15	12	9	4.5	2	42	36	34	31	26	12																
21	Sloop Narrows	42	35	29	67	55	[illegible]	[illegible]	[illegible]	[illegible]	[illegible]	[illegible]	[illegible]	[illegible]	[illegible]	[illegible]	[illegible]	[illegible]	[illegible]	[illegible]	[illegible]															
22	Perceval Narrows	42	35	29	69	57	[illegible]	[illegible]	[illegible]	[illegible]	[illegible]	[illegible]	[illegible]	[illegible]	[illegible]	[illegible]	[illegible]	[illegible]	[illegible]	[illegible]	[illegible]	2														
23	**Ivory Island**	41	34	28	69	59	[illegible]	[illegible]	[illegible]	[illegible]	[illegible]	[illegible]	[illegible]	[illegible]	[illegible]	[illegible]	[illegible]	[illegible]	[illegible]	[illegible]	[illegible]	7	4.5													
24	**Idol Point**	46	39	33	75	63	[illegible]	[illegible]	[illegible]	[illegible]	[illegible]	[illegible]	[illegible]	[illegible]	[illegible]	[illegible]	[illegible]	[illegible]	[illegible]	[illegible]	[illegible]	12	9.5	5												
25	Hyndman Reef	47	40	34	76	64	[illegible]	[illegible]	[illegible]	[illegible]	[illegible]	[illegible]	[illegible]	[illegible]	[illegible]	[illegible]	[illegible]	[illegible]	[illegible]	[illegible]	[illegible]	13	10	6	2											
26	**Law Island**	49	42	36	78	66	[illegible]	[illegible]	[illegible]	[illegible]	[illegible]	[illegible]	[illegible]	[illegible]	[illegible]	[illegible]	[illegible]	[illegible]	[illegible]	[illegible]	[illegible]	15	13	8	4	2										
27	Spiller Lagoon	53	46	40	82	70	[illegible]	[illegible]	[illegible]	[illegible]	[illegible]	[illegible]	[illegible]	[illegible]	[illegible]	[illegible]	[illegible]	[illegible]	[illegible]	[illegible]	21	19	17	12	8	6	7									
28	Neekas Cove	60	53	47	89	77	[illegible]	[illegible]	[illegible]	[illegible]	[illegible]	[illegible]	[illegible]	[illegible]	[illegible]	[illegible]	[illegible]	[illegible]	[illegible]	[illegible]	28	26	24	19	15	13	14	7								
29	Gerald Point	59	52	46	88	76	69	57	44	42	39	36	32	29	61	55	53	50	45	31	27	25	23	18	14	13	14	6	3.5							
30	Ellerslie Lagoon	65	58	52	84	82	75	63	50	48	45	42	38	35	67	61	59	56	51	37	33	31	29	24	21	19	19	13	9.5	7						
31	Ingram Bay	71	64	58	100	88	81	69	56	54	51	48	44	41	73	67	65	62	57	43	39	37	35	30	27	25	25	19	15	13	12					
32	**Coldwell Point**	56	49	43	85	73	66	54	41	39	36	33	29	26	58	52	50	47	42	28	24	22	20	15	11	9	7	14	12	8	15	21				
33	**Troupe Narrows**	58	51	45	87	75	68	56	43	41	38	35	31	28	60	54	52	49	44	30	26	24	22	17	13	11	9	17	15	11	18	24	3			
34	**Dumas Point**	52	45	39	82	70	63	51	38	46	33	30	26	23	55	49	47	44	39	24	21	19	17	12	7	7.5	5.5	13	21	17	24	30	9	6		
35	**BELLA BELLA**	55	48	42	83	73	65	53	40	48	35	32	28	25	57	51	49	46	41	27	23	21	18	14	9	9	8	15	24	20	27	35	12	9	3	
36	**Nicholson Island**	59	52	46	87	77	69	57	44	52	39	36	32	29	61	55	53	50	45	31	27	25	22	18	14	12	10	17	18	14	21	27	6	3	9	12

FJORDLAND--(routes via Finlayson and Mathieson Channels)

Location																			#
Sarah Head	12	9	13	17	16	19	23	28	23	23	31	33	28	31	37	36	38	39	7
Bottleneck Inlet		9.5	14	17	6.5	9	11	17	24	23	31	21	16	20	29	26	28	29	37
Lime Point			5	8.5	14	17	19	25	15	14	23	20	25	28	32	33	35	37	38
Windy Bay				5.5	18	21	23	29	12	11	20	23	27	30	37	38	40	41	39
Mathieson Narrows					22	25	27	32	7	5.5	14	17	21	23	27	32	33	38	40
Boat Bluff						3	6.5	12	28	28	38	17	12	16	21	21	23	24	9
KLEMTU							4.5	9	31	26	36	15	10	18	23	18	20	21	10
Begg Point (Jackson Passage)								5.5	34	22	32	10	5.5	14	**15**	17	18	25	11
Legace Point (Oscar Passage)									39	25	35	13	8.5	5	11	10	12	13	12
Poison Cove (Mussel Inlet)										13	23	25	28	29	33	39	40	45	41
Kynoch Point											10	12	16	18	23	27	28	33	42
Culpepper Narrows (Kynoch Inlet)												22	26	28	33	37	38	43	43
Charles Head													4.5	6.5	11	16	17	22	44
Jackson Narrows														3.5	8.5	13	14	19	45
Buckley Head															5.5	10	11	16	46
Tom Bay																6.5	7	12	47
Sloop Narrows																	2	7	21
Perceval Narrows																		4.5	22
Ivory Island																			23

LAREDO INLET

Location					#
Dallain Point	6	5.5	16	24	15
Wingate Point		3	15	23	16
Quigley Creek			12	19	48
Bay of Plenty				10	49
Arnoup Creek					50

Khutze Inlet to Begg Point = 35 Nm
Begg Point to Tom Bay = 15 Nm
TOTAL DISTANCE = 50 Nm

Figure 1-3 To determine the distance from Khutze Inlet to Tom Bay, choose an intermediate location from the map key—in this case, Begg Point.

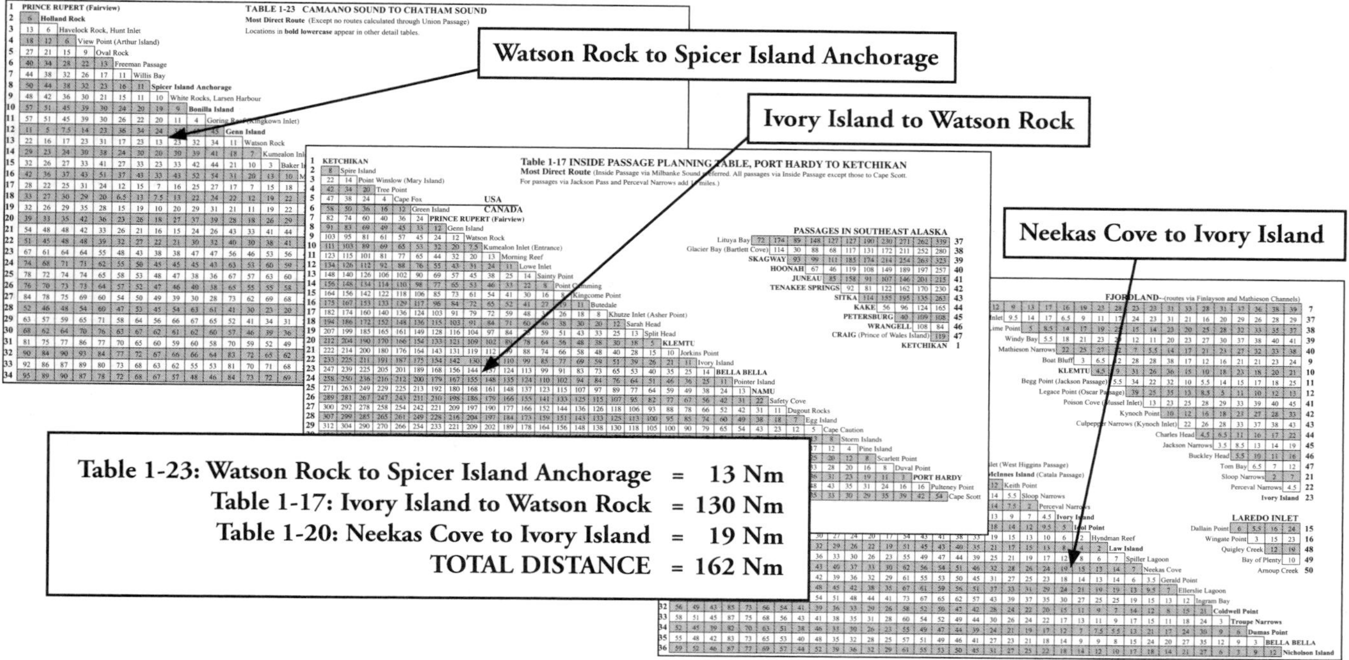
Watson Rock to Spicer Island Anchorage
Ivory Island to Watson Rock
Neekas Cove to Ivory Island
Table 1-23: Watson Rock to Spicer Island Anchorage = 13 Nm
Table 1-17: Ivory Island to Watson Rock = 130 Nm
Table 1-20: Neekas Cove to Ivory Island = 19 Nm
TOTAL DISTANCE = 162 Nm

Figure 1-4 Neekas Cove (Table 1-20) to **Spicer Island Anchorage** (Table 1-23)

In most cases the tabulated distances are accurate to within 1 Nm However, some values in the tables may differ from distances you would measure on a chart. The reasons for the variability in distance measurements are numerous:

- The distance may be measured to a point of land that is not well defined. (See **Point Cumming** in **Table 1-21.**)
- The distance may be measured to an island. Different routes may pass abeam of the island, but because the routes may pass the island at different angles, the point to which they are measured may be different from route to route.
- The routes are constructed allowing a reasonable distance from shore when passing close to a point, island or reef. However, vessels of different drafts will require different margins for error when passing close to land, resulting in different distances traveled. Generally the distance measurements are designed for a vessel with six feet of draft (1.8 meters).
- When passing over shallow areas, the routes require at least six feet (1.8 meters) below the keel at low water.
- The routes are designed for fair weather, but where heavy swells are common in fair weather, the routes require extra depth.
- Most ports and harbours have more than one public marina or anchorage. In general, the route terminates at the primary public wharf or marina. Some harbours, such as **Gorge Harbour**, are so extensive that the route is measured only to the harbour entrance.

Table 1-1 Inside Passage Planning Table, Tacoma to Port Hardy

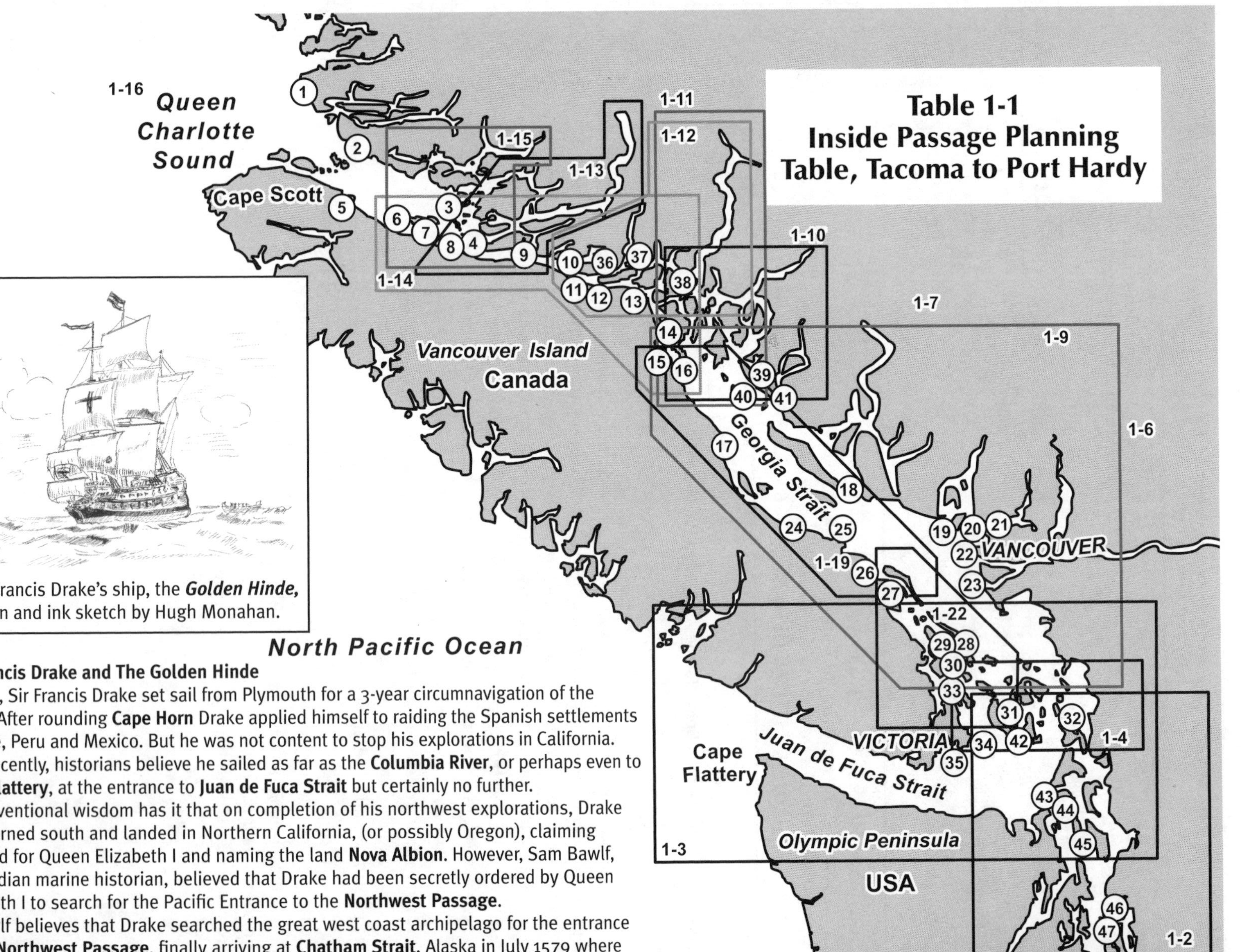
Queen Charlotte Sound
Cape Scott
Vancouver Island
Canada
North Pacific Ocean
Georgia Strait
VANCOUVER
VICTORIA
Juan de Fuca Strait
Cape Flattery
Olympic Peninsula
USA
SEATTLE
TACOMA
1-2
1-3
1-4
1-6
1-7
1-9
1-10
1-11
1-12
1-13
1-14
1-15
1-16
1-19
1-22
1 2 3 4 5 6 7 8 9 10 11 12 13 14 15 16 17 18 19 20 21 22 23 24 25 26 27 28 29 30 31 32 33 34 35 36 37 38 39 40 41 42 43 44 45 46 47 48 49

Sir Francis Drake's ship, the ***Golden Hinde,*** a pen and ink sketch by Hugh Monahan.

Sir Francis Drake and The Golden Hinde

In 1577, Sir Francis Drake set sail from Plymouth for a 3-year circumnavigation of the globe. After rounding **Cape Horn** Drake applied himself to raiding the Spanish settlements in Chile, Peru and Mexico. But he was not content to stop his explorations in California. Until recently, historians believe he sailed as far as the **Columbia River,** or perhaps even to **Cape Flattery,** at the entrance to **Juan de Fuca Strait** but certainly no further.

Conventional wisdom has it that on completion of his northwest explorations, Drake then turned south and landed in Northern California, (or possibly Oregon), claiming the land for Queen Elizabeth I and naming the land **Nova Albion.** However, Sam Bawlf, a Canadian marine historian, believed that Drake had been secretly ordered by Queen Elizabeth I to search for the Pacific Entrance to the **Northwest Passage.**

Bawlf believes that Drake searched the great west coast archipelago for the entrance to the **Northwest Passage,** finally arriving at **Chatham Strait,** Alaska in July 1579 where he was turned back by bitterly cold weather and ice. He further suggests that **Nova Albion** is not in California at all, but is actually the east coast of **Vancouver Island.**

If this theory is correct, it means that Drake sailed Pacific Northwest waters 200 years prior to Captain Cook's epic voyage of discovery, and certainly qualifies Drake as one of the greatest explorers of all time.

Table 1-1 INSIDE PASSAGE PLANNING TABLE, TACOMA TO PORT HARDY

Most Direct Route (Routes cross traffic lanes at nearly right angles. Thus these routes may be longer than the direct line routes.)

No.	Location	1	2	3	4	5	6	7	8	9	10	11	12	13	14	15	16	17	18	19	20	21	22	23	24	25	26	27	28	29	30	31	32	33	34
1	Cape Caution																																		
2	Jeanette Islands	20																																	
3	Numas Island	36	16																																
4	Blackney Pass	56	36	20																															
5	**PORT HARDY** (Duval Point)	29	10	14	34																														
6	Pulteney Point	40	20	10	19	15																													
7	**ALERT BAY**	50	30	20	11	25	10																												
8	Blinkhorne Peninsula	56	36	20	4.5	16	16	6.5																											
9	Broken Islands	75	51	37	17	50	36	26	19																										
10	Fanny Island	88	64	50	30	63	49	39	32	13																									
11	**KELSEY BAY**	90	66	52	32	65	51	41	34	15	4																								
12	Camp Point	95	71	57	37	70	56	46	39	20	9	5																							
13	Chatham Point	111	87	73	53	86	72	62	55	36	25	21	16																						
14	Maude Island (Seymour Narrows)	124	100	86	66	99	85	75	68	49	38	34	29	13																					
15	**CAMPBELL RIVER**	132	108	94	74	107	93	83	76	57	46	42	37	21	8																				
16	Cape Mudge	135	111	97	77	110	96	86	79	60	49	45	40	24	11	3																			
17	Cape Lazo	157	133	119	99	132	118	108	101	82	71	67	62	46	33	25	22																		
18	Point Upwood	183	159	145	125	158	144	134	110	108	97	93	88	72	59	51	31	31																	
19	Cape Roger Curtis	216	192	178	158	191	177	167	160	141	130	126	121	105	92	84	81	60	29																
20	Point Atkinson	222	198	184	164	197	183	173	166	147	136	132	127	111	98	90	87	67	36	7															
21	**VANCOUVER** (First Narrows)	227	203	189	169	202	188	178	171	152	141	137	132	116	103	95	92	72	41	12	5														
22	Point Grey (Fraser River, North Arm)	223	199	185	165	198	184	174	167	148	137	133	128	112	99	91	88	68	37	8	4.5	7.5													
23	Sand Heads (Fraser River, South Arm)	226	202	188	168	201	187	177	170	151	140	136	131	115	102	94	91	71	40	15	14	18	10												
24	**FRENCH CREEK**	186	162	148	128	161	147	137	130	111	100	96	91	75	62	54	51	29	13	36	43	48	43	44											
25	Ballenas Island	193	169	155	135	168	154	144	137	118	107	103	98	82	69	61	58	36	8.5	28	35	40	35	36	8										
26	**NANAIMO**	209	185	171	151	184	170	160	153	134	123	119	114	98	85	77	74	52	24	24	30	35	29	29	24	15									
27	Dodd Narrows	211	187	173	153	186	172	162	155	136	125	121	116	100	87	79	76	54	26	24	30	35	29	28	26	18	5								
28	Nose Point	235	211	197	177	210	196	186	179	160	149	145	140	124	111	103	100	78	50	33	33	36	29	19	50	42	29	24							
29	**GANGES**	239	215	201	181	214	200	190	183	164	153	149	144	128	115	107	104	82	54	37	37	40	33	23	54	46	33	28	4						
30	Yeo Point	238	214	200	180	213	199	189	182	163	152	148	143	127	114	106	103	81	53	36	36	39	31	21	53	45	32	27	3	5.5					
31	**FRIDAY HARBOR**	260	236	222	202	235	221	211	204	185	174	170	165	149	136	128	125	103	75	58	54	57	49	39	75	67	54	49	25	28	22				
32	**ANACORTES**	280	256	242	222	255	241	231	224	205	194	190	185	169	156	148	145	123	95	78	63	66	58	48	95	87	74	69	45	48	42	20			
33	**SIDNEY**	248	224	210	190	223	209	199	192	173	162	158	153	137	124	116	113	91	63	46	44	47	39	29	63	55	42	37	13	16	10	19	38		
34	Discovery Island	268	244	230	210	243	229	219	212	193	182	178	173	157	144	136	133	111	83	60	58	61	53	43	83	75	62	57	27	30	24	20	29	15	
35	**VICTORIA**	275	251	237	217	250	236	226	219	200	189	185	180	164	151	143	140	118	90	73	65	68	60	50	90	82	69	64	40	37	31	29	38	22	9

via CORDERO CHANNEL

Location	No.	36	37	38	39	40	41	17
Fanny Island	9	9	20	34	68	72	81	124
Whirlpool Rapids	36		11	25	59	63	72	115
Green Point Rapids	37			14	48	52	61	104
Dent Rapids	38				34	38	47	90
LUND	39					5	14	57
Mystery Reef	40						8.5	52
WESTVIEW	41							44
Point Upwood	17							

PUGET SOUND

Location	No.	34	31	42	43	44	45	46	47	48	49
VICTORIA	35	8.5	29	19	31	36	46	65	69	91	93
Discovery Island	34		20	12	25	29	39	58	62	84	86
FRIDAY HARBOR	31			7.5	28	32	42	61	65	87	89
Cattle Point	42				21	25	35	54	58	80	82
Point Wilson	43					3.5	14	33	37	60	62
Marrowstone Point	44						10	29	33	56	58
Double Bluff	45							19	23	46	48
BALLARD	46								4.5	28	30
SEATTLE (Smith Cove)	47									25	27
TACOMA	48										8.5
GIG HARBOR	49										

Table 1-2
Anacortes to Tacoma—Including Hood Canal

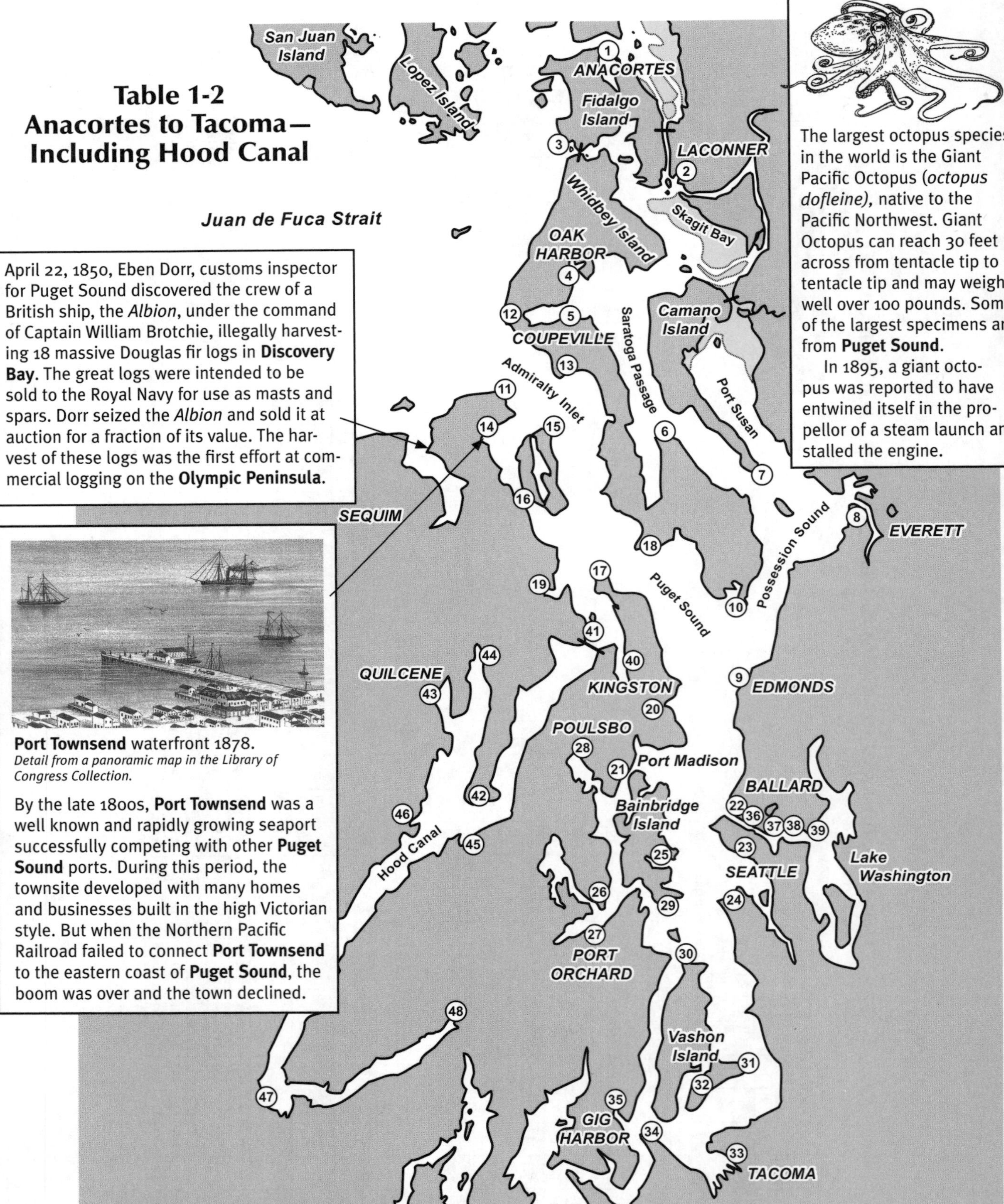

San Juan Island
Lopez Island
ANACORTES
Fidalgo Island
LACONNER
Juan de Fuca Strait
Whidbey Island
Skagit Bay
OAK HARBOR
Camano Island
Saratoga Passage
COUPEVILLE
Admiralty Inlet
Port Susan
SEQUIM
Possession Sound
EVERETT
Puget Sound
QUILCENE
KINGSTON
EDMONDS
POULSBO
Port Madison
BALLARD
Bainbridge Island
Hood Canal
Lake Washington
SEATTLE
PORT ORCHARD
Vashon Island
GIG HARBOR
TACOMA
1
2
3
4
5
6
7
8
9
10
11
12
13
14
15
16
17
18
19
20
21
22
23
24
25
26
27
28
29
30
31
32
33
34
35
36
37
38
39
40
41
42
43
44
45
46
47
48

April 22, 1850, Eben Dorr, customs inspector for Puget Sound discovered the crew of a British ship, the *Albion*, under the command of Captain William Brotchie, illegally harvesting 18 massive Douglas fir logs in **Discovery Bay**. The great logs were intended to be sold to the Royal Navy for use as masts and spars. Dorr seized the *Albion* and sold it at auction for a fraction of its value. The harvest of these logs was the first effort at commercial logging on the **Olympic Peninsula**.

Port Townsend waterfront 1878.
Detail from a panoramic map in the Library of Congress Collection.

By the late 1800s, **Port Townsend** was a well known and rapidly growing seaport successfully competing with other **Puget Sound** ports. During this period, the townsite developed with many homes and businesses built in the high Victorian style. But when the Northern Pacific Railroad failed to connect **Port Townsend** to the eastern coast of **Puget Sound**, the boom was over and the town declined.

The largest octopus species in the world is the Giant Pacific Octopus (*octopus dofleine),* native to the Pacific Northwest. Giant Octopus can reach 30 feet across from tentacle tip to tentacle tip and may weigh well over 100 pounds. Some of the largest specimens are from **Puget Sound**.

In 1895, a giant octopus was reported to have entwined itself in the propellor of a steam launch and stalled the engine.

Table 1-2 ANACORTES TO TACOMA INCLUDING HOOD CANAL

Most Direct Route (Not including passages through Port Townsend Canal)

Locations in **bold lowercase** appear in other detail tables.

No.	Location	1	2	3	4	5	6	7	8	9	10	11	12	13	14	15	16	17	18	19	20	21	22	23	24	25	26	27	28	29	30	31	32	33	34
1	ANACORTES
2	LA CONNER	9.5
3	**Deception Island**	12	10
4	OAK HARBOR	26	16	19
5	COUPEVILLE	28	18	21	5.5
6	Baby Island	31	21	24	13	13
7	Camano Head	37	27	30	20	20	7.5
8	EVERETT	45	35	38	27	27	15	8
9	EDMONDS	51	41	42	33	33	22	15	14
10	Possession Point	46	36	38	28	28	17	10	9	5.5
11	**Point Wilson**	28	27	17	36	38	40	33	32	26	23
12	**Point Partridge**	23	22	12	31	33	35	37	36	30	27	5
13	Admiralty Head	29	28	18	37	39	38	31	30	24	21	3	6
14	PORT TOWNSEND	31	30	20	39	41	40	33	32	26	23	3	8	5
15	Marrowstone Point	31	30	20	39	41	37	30	29	22	20	3.5	9	3	3.5
16	Port Townsend Canal	35	34	24	43	45	34	37	36	20	17	7	12	8.5	5	6.5
17	Foulweather Bluff	42	41	31	38	38	27	20	19	13	10	14	19	14	14	10	7
18	Double Bluff	42	41	31	37	37	26	19	18	12	9	14	19	13	14	10	8.5	3
19	PORT LUDLOW	44	43	33	42	42	31	24	23	17	14	16	21	16	16	12	7	4	6.5
20	KINGSTON	54	45	43	37	37	26	19	18	4.5	9	26	31	26	26	22	19	12	11	16
21	Agate Passage Bridge	61	51	50	43	43	32	25	24	10	15	33	38	33	33	29	26	19	18	23	8
22	BALLARD (Shilsole Bay)	61	50	50	42	42	31	23	22	8.5	14	33	38	33	33	29	26	19	19	23	8.5	7.5
23	SEATTLE (Smith Cove)	65	54	54	46	46	35	28	27	12	18	37	42	36	37	33	30	23	23	27	12	9.5	4.5
24	Duwamish Head	66	55	55	47	47	36	29	28	14	19	38	43	37	38	34	31	24	25	28	13	11	6	2
25	Eagle Harbor	68	57	57	49	49	38	31	30	15	21	40	45	39	40	36	33	26	26	30	13	11	7.5	5.5	6
26	Port Washington Narows Bridge	71	61	60	53	53	42	35	34	20	25	43	48	42	43	39	36	29	28	33	18	10	15	12	11	11
27	PORT ORCHARD	72	62	61	54	54	43	36	35	21	26	44	49	43	44	40	37	30	29	34	19	11	16	13	12	12	1.5
28	POULSBO	66	56	55	48	48	37	30	29	15	20	38	43	37	38	34	31	24	23	28	13	5	13	15	18	16	11	12
29	Bainbridge Reef	68	59	57	51	51	40	33	32	17	23	40	45	39	40	36	33	26	26	30	15	11	9.5	6	5.5	5.5	5.5	6.5	12
30	Point Vashon	71	61	60	53	53	42	35	34	19	25	43	48	42	43	39	36	29	28	33	17	15	11	8	7	7.5	9.5	10.5	16	4
31	Robinson Point	79	68	68	60	60	49	42	41	26	32	51	56	50	51	47	44	37	37	40	26	24	19	16	15	16	19	20	25	13	9
32	DOCKTON (Quartermaster Harbor)	87	76	76	68	68	57	50	49	34	40	59	64	58	59	55	52	45	45	48	34	32	27	24	23	24	27	28	33	21	17	8
33	TACOMA (Hylebos Waterway)	88	77	77	69	69	58	51	50	35	41	60	65	59	60	56	53	46	46	49	35	33	28	25	24	25	27	28	33	21	17	8.5	7.5
34	Point Defiance	88	77	77	69	69	58	51	50	35	41	60	65	59	60	56	53	46	46	49	35	33	28	25	24	25	27	28	33	21	17	8.5	6	6.5
35	GIG HARBOR	90	79	79	71	71	60	53	52	37	43	62	67	61	62	58	55	48	48	51	37	35	30	27	26	27	29	30	35	23	20	11	8	8.5	2

LAKE WASHINGTON SHIP CHANNEL

Location					No.
BALLARD (Shilsole Bay)	1	3.5	4.5	6.5	22
Hiram Chittenden Locks		2.5	3.5	5.5	36
Lake Union (Aurora Bridge)			1.5	3.5	37
University Bascule Bridge				2	38
Lake Washington (Webster Point)					39

HOOD CANAL

Location											No.
Foulweather Bluff	4	6.5	6	20	28	30	22	24	44	54	17
PORT LUDLOW		8	7.5	22	30	32	24	26	46	56	19
Pt Julia (Port Gamble)			2.5	17	25	27	19	21	41	51	40
Hood Canal Bridge				14	22	24	16	18	38	48	41
Oak Head					8	10	2.5	4	25	34	42
QUILCENE Boat Haven						6.5	10	9.5	30	40	43
Tarboo Bay (Long Spit)							12	12	32	42	44
Seabeck Bay								4.5	24	34	45
Pleasant Harbor									22	32	46
Annas Bay										12	47
ALLYN											48

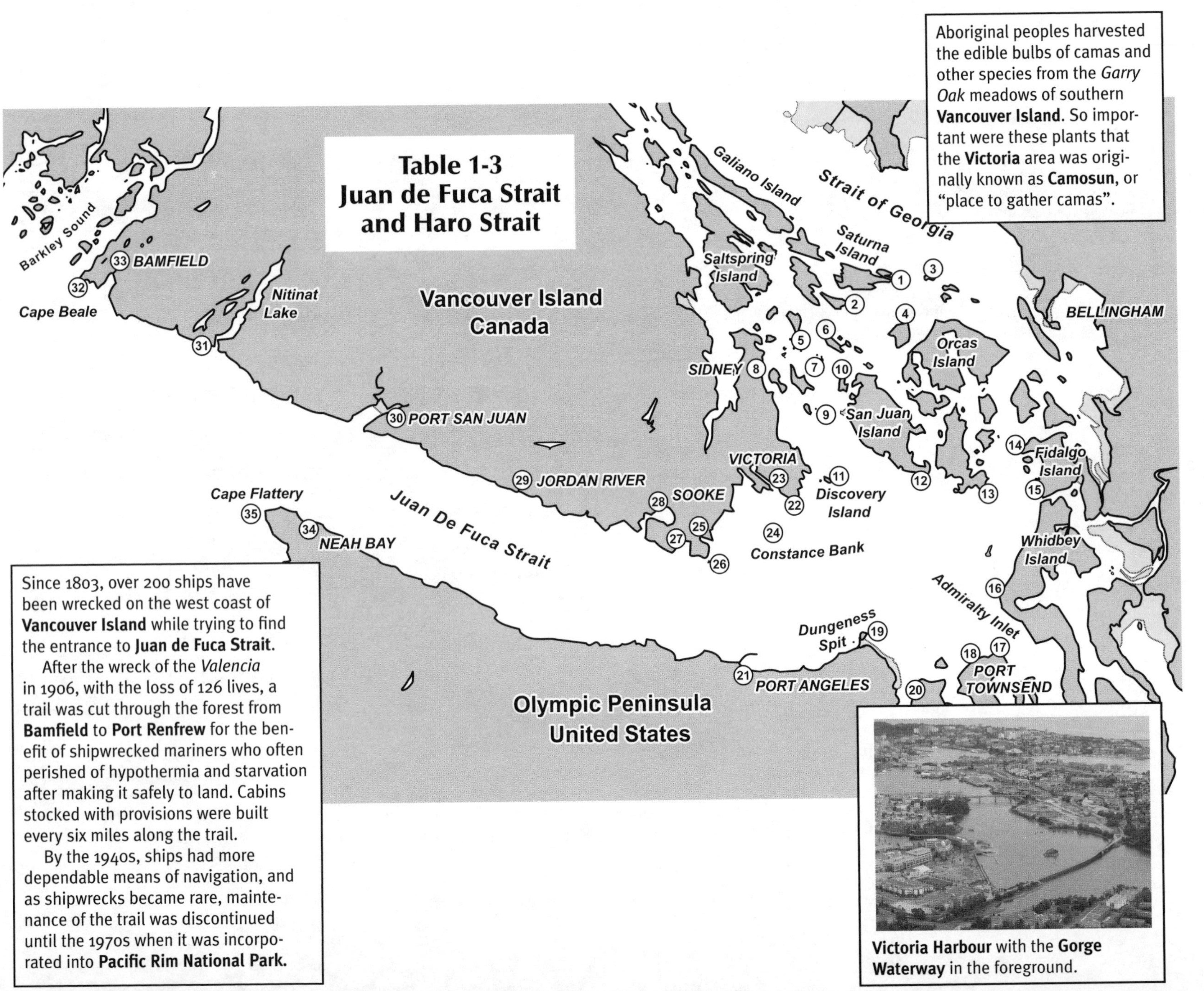
Table 1-3
Juan de Fuca Strait
and Haro Strait
Vancouver Island
Canada
Olympic Peninsula
United States
Barkley Sound
33 BAMFIELD
32
Cape Beale
Nitinat
Lake
31
30 PORT SAN JUAN
29 JORDAN RIVER
Cape Flattery
35
34 NEAH BAY
Juan De Fuca Strait
28 SOOKE
25
27
26
VICTORIA
23
22
24
Constance Bank
11
Discovery
Island
SIDNEY 8
Galiano Island
Strait of Georgia
Saltspring
Island
Saturna
Island
1
2
3
4
5
6
7
10
9 San Juan
Island
12
13
Orcas
Island
BELLINGHAM
14 Fidalgo
Island
15
Whidbey
Island
16
Admiralty Inlet
17
18
PORT
TOWNSEND
20
Dungeness
Spit 19
21 PORT ANGELES

Aboriginal peoples harvested the edible bulbs of camas and other species from the *Garry Oak* meadows of southern **Vancouver Island**. So important were these plants that the **Victoria** area was originally known as **Camosun**, or "place to gather camas".

Since 1803, over 200 ships have been wrecked on the west coast of **Vancouver Island** while trying to find the entrance to **Juan de Fuca Strait**.

After the wreck of the *Valencia* in 1906, with the loss of 126 lives, a trail was cut through the forest from **Bamfield** to **Port Renfrew** for the benefit of shipwrecked mariners who often perished of hypothermia and starvation after making it safely to land. Cabins stocked with provisions were built every six miles along the trail.

By the 1940s, ships had more dependable means of navigation, and as shipwrecks became rare, maintenance of the trail was discontinued until the 1970s when it was incorporated into **Pacific Rim National Park.**

Victoria Harbour with the **Gorge Waterway** in the foreground.

Table 1-3 JUAN DE FUCA STRAIT AND HARO STRAIT

Most Direct Route [For passages via Mayor Channel (Oak Bay) subtract 1.5 Nm]

Locations in **bold lowercase** appear in other detail tables.

No.	Location	1	2	3	4	5	6	7	8	9	10	11	12	13	14	15	16	17	18	19	20	21	22	23	24	25	26	27	28	29	30	31	32	33	34
1	**Tumbo Reef Buoy "U59"** (Boundary Pass)
2	**Blunden Light**	7
3	**Alden Point** (Patos Island)	2.5	8
4	**Skipjack Island**	4	5	4.5
5	**Point Fairfax** (Moresby Island)	14	6	14	10
6	**Turn Point**	11	4.5	12	8	2.5
7	**Gooch Island Light**	13	6.5	14	10	2.5	2
8	**SIDNEY**	19	11	19	13	5	7	5
9	Kelp Reef	20	13	21	17	9.5	8.5	7	9
10	**Battleship Island**	14	8.5	14	10	6.5	4	4	8.5	5
11	**Discovery Island**	26	21	27	22	9.5	16	15	15	7.5	12
12	**Cattle Point**	23	20	22	19	22	22	21	24	14	16	12
13	**Davidson Rock** (Point Colville)	29	26	28	25	27	27	26	28	19	23	16	6
14	**Fidalgo Head**	25	27	23	24	29	28	28	32	25	24	22	13	6.5
15	**Deception Island**	30	32	28	29	33	33	32	34	25	28	22	12	6	5.5
16	**Point Partridge**	39	36	38	35	36	34	33	36	27	31	23	16	11	16	12
17	**Point Wilson**	44	41	43	40	40	39	38	40	31	35	25	21	16	21	17	5
18	Cape George	44	41	43	40	40	38	37	39	30	34	24	21	19	25	20	8.5	7
19	Dungeness Spit	40	37	39	36	32	30	29	30	22	27	15	17	18	24	22	13	14	10
20	Sequim Bay (Travo Spit)	45	42	44	43	39	37	36	37	29	33	22	22	22	28	25	14	13	6	7
21	**PORT ANGELES** (Public)	47	42	48	43	31	37	36	36	29	33	21	28	31	37	36	28	29	25	15	22
22	Trial Island	30	25	31	26	14	20	19	19	12	16	4	15	20	27	26	24	27	24	15	22	18
23	**VICTORIA** (Shoal Point)	35	30	36	31	18	25	24	24	16	21	8.5	19	25	32	31	29	31	28	19	26	20	4.5
24	Constance Bank	34	29	35	30	18	24	23	23	16	20	8	18	22	29	28	25	27	24	14	21	15	3.5	5
25	Pedder Bay	41	36	42	37	25	31	30	30	23	27	15	26	30	37	36	33	35	32	21	28	17	12	10	9
26	Race Rocks	41	36	42	37	25	31	30	30	23	27	15	25	29	36	35	27	33	29	18	26	14	10	9	7	3
27	Becher Bay	45	40	46	41	29	35	34	34	27	31	19	30	34	41	40	32	38	34	23	31	18	15	14	12	7.5	4.5
28	**SOOKE**	51	46	52	47	35	41	40	40	33	37	25	35	39	46	45	37	43	39	28	36	23	20	19	17	13	10	8.5
29	Jordan River	63	58	64	59	47	53	52	52	45	49	37	47	51	58	57	49	55	51	40	48	34	32	31	29	25	22	20	16
30	**PORT RENFREW Public**	84	79	85	80	68	74	73	73	66	70	58	68	72	79	78	70	76	72	61	69	54	53	52	50	46	43	40	37	21
31	Nitinat Narrows	99	94	100	95	83	89	88	88	81	85	73	83	87	94	93	85	91	87	76	84	69	68	67	65	61	58	56	52	36	21
32	Cape Beale	115	110	116	111	99	105	104	104	97	101	89	99	103	110	109	101	107	103	92	100	86	84	83	81	77	74	72	68	52	37	18
33	**BAMFIELD**	121	116	122	117	105	111	110	110	103	107	95	105	109	116	115	107	113	109	98	106	91	90	89	87	83	80	77	73	57	42	23	5
34	**NEAH BAY**	86	81	87	82	70	76	75	75	68	72	60	70	74	81	80	76	77	73	63	70	54	55	54	52	48	45	43	39	24	14	21	36	41
35	Tatoosh Island	90	85	91	86	74	80	79	79	72	76	64	74	78	85	84	81	82	78	68	75	59	59	58	56	52	49	47	43	28	16	17	31	36	7.5

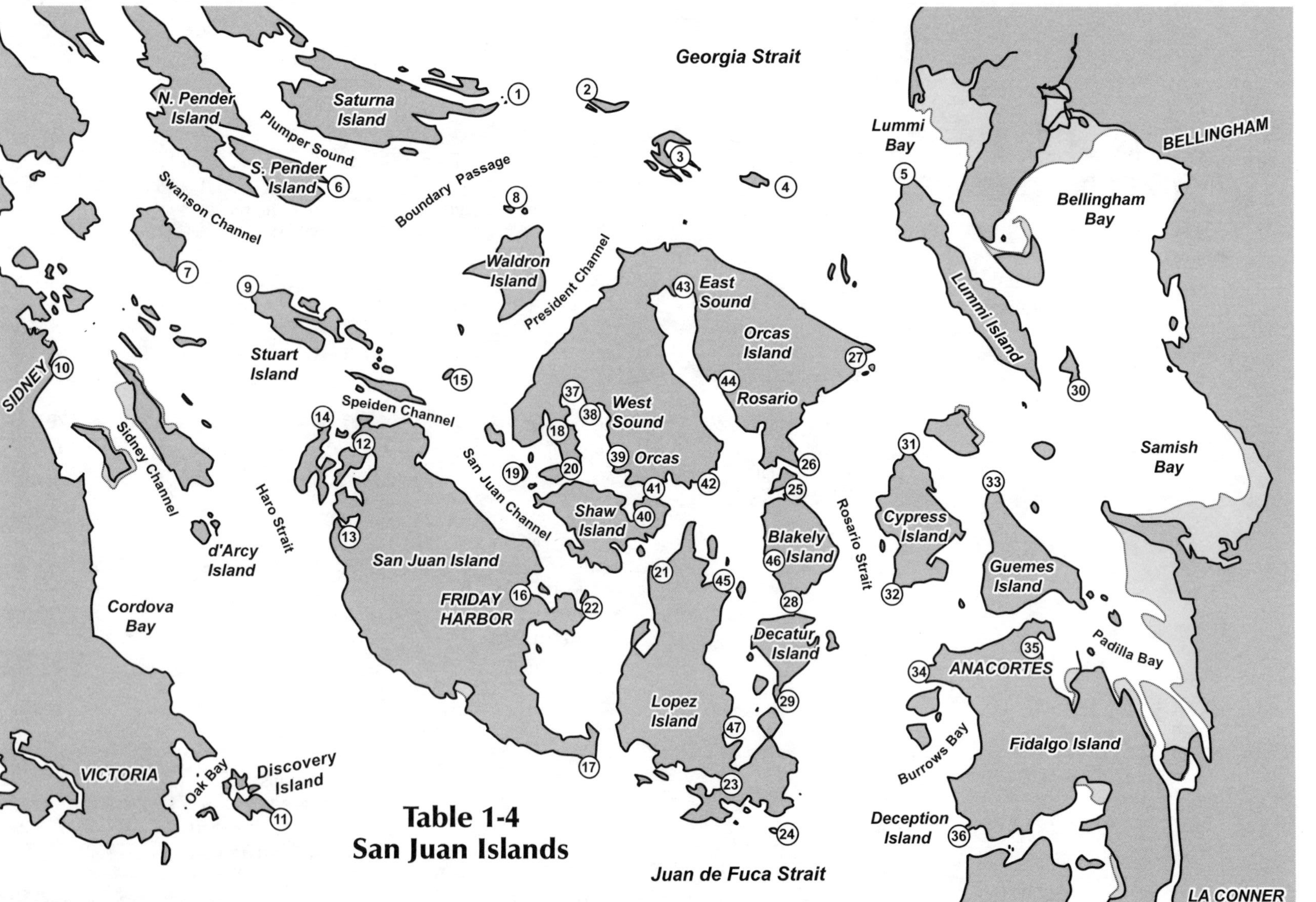
Georgia Strait
N. Pender Island
Saturna Island
Plumper Sound
S. Pender Island
Swanson Channel
Boundary Passage
Waldron Island
President Channel
Stuart Island
SIDNEY
Speiden Channel
Sidney Channel
Haro Strait
d'Arcy Island
San Juan Channel
San Juan Island
FRIDAY HARBOR
Cordova Bay
VICTORIA
Oak Bay
Discovery Island
East Sound
Orcas Island
Rosario
West Sound
Orcas
Shaw Island
Blakely Island
Decatur Island
Lopez Island
Rosario Strait
Juan de Fuca Strait
Lummi Bay
Lummi Island
Bellingham Bay
BELLINGHAM
Samish Bay
Cypress Island
Guemes Island
Padilla Bay
ANACORTES
Fidalgo Island
Burrows Bay
Deception Island
LA CONNER
1
2
3
4
5
6
7
8
9
10
11
12
13
14
15
16
17
18
19
20
21
22
23
24
25
26
27
28
29
30
31
32
33
34
35
36
37
38
39
40
41
42
43
44
45
46
47

Table 1-4
San Juan Islands

In 1846, the international boundary between the Hudson Bay Company lands and the **Oregon Territory** was established by treaty at the 49th parallel and the middle of the **Strait of Juan de Fuca.** Unfortunately the treaty didn't specify whether the boundary should be drawn along **Haro Strait** or **Rosario Strait**, and so both countries claimed the **San Juan Islands.** On June 15, 1859, an American settler, Lyman Cutler, shot a pig belonging to the Hudson Bay Company that was rooting in his garden. This incident set off an armed confrontation between the two countries that lasted for 12 years. Finally in 1871, according to the terms of the Treaty of Washington, the matter was referred to Kaiser Wilhelm I of Germany, who declared the international boundary to be along the center of **Haro Strait,** thus granting the **San Juan Islands** to the United States.

Table 1-4 SAN JUAN ISLANDS

Most Direct Route

Locations in **bold lowercase** appear in other detail tables.

Route	Distance	No.
BELLINGHAM to Point Migley	14	**5**
BELLINGHAM to Eliza Island	7.5	**29**
LACONNER to Deception Island	10	**35**
LACONNER to **ANACORTES**	9.5	**34**
OAK HARBOR to Deception Island	19	**35**
VICTORIA to Discovery Island	8.5	**11**

No.	Location	1	2	3	4	5	6	7	8	9	10	11	12	13	14	15	16	17	18	19	20	21	22	23	24	25	26	27	28	29	30	31	32	33	34	35
1	**Tumbo Reef Buoy "U59"**																																			
2	**Alden Point** (Patos Island)	2.5																																		
3	Echo Bay (Sucia Islands)	8.5	7																																	
4	**Puffin Island Light**	9.5	7.5	4																																
5	**Point Migley** (Lummi Island)	13	11	7.5	4																															
6	**Blunden Islet**	7	8	13	14	18																														
7	**Point Fairfax** (Moresby Island)	14	14	19	20	24	6																													
8	**Skipjack Island**	4	4.5	8.5	9	13	5	10																												
9	**Turn Point**	11	12	17	18	22	4.5	2.5	8																											
10	**SIDNEY**	19	19	24	25	29	11	5	13	7																										
11	**Discovery Island**	26	27	30	30	24	21	9.5	22	16	15																									
12	**ROCHE HARBOR**	15	15	18	18	22	11	8	11	6.5	10	12																								
13	Mitchell Bay	17	17	20	20	24	13	10	13	8.5	11	9.5	3.5																							
14	**Battleship Island**	14	14	16	17	21	8.5	6.5	10	4	8.5	12	1.5	4																						
15	Flattop Island	9.5	10	12	13	16	6.5	9.5	6	7	13	17	5.5	7.5	4.5																					
16	**FRIDAY HARBOR**	17	18	17	18	20	14	16	13	14	19	20	11	12	10	7.5																				
17	**Cattle Point**	23	22	23	24	22	20	22	19	22	24	12	18	15	16	14	7.5																			
18	Deer Harbor	14	13	14	15	18	12	14	10	12	17	24	8.5	11	8	4.5	5.5	12																		
19	Yellow Island	13	12	14	14	17	11	13	9	11	15	22	7.5	9.5	6.5	4	3.5	9.5	2.5																	
20	Bell Island	15	14	15	16	18	13	15	11	13	18	23	10	12	9	6	4.5	11	1.5	2																
21	Flat Point	19	18	19	16	17	16	18	15	16	21	19	13	15	12	9.5	4	6.5	8	6	5.5															
22	Turn Rock	18	17	18	18	18	15	17	14	15	20	17	12	14	11	8.5	2	5	6.5	4.5	5.5	2														
23	Mackaye Harbor	27	26	27	27	27	14	16	13	14	26	14	20	18	20	17	11	4	15	13	14	9.5	8.5													
24	**Davidson Rock** (Point Colville)	29	28	25	21	21	26	27	25	27	28	16	22	20	23	20	14	6	18	16	16	12	11	5.5												
25	Peavine Pass	20	18	15	11	11	21	23	19	21	26	24	18	20	17	15	9	12	8.5	11	7	5	7	18	12											
26	Deer Point (Obstruction Pass)	19	17	14	10	10	22	24	18	22	27	24	19	21	18	15	9.5	12	9	12	7.5	5.5	7.5	18	12	1										
27	Lawrence Point	14	12	9	5.5	5.5	18	28	13	26	31	29	23	25	22	20	14	17	14	16	12	10	12	21	15	5.5	4.5									
28	Thatcher Pass	23	21	18	15	15	22	24	22	22	27	24	19	21	18	16	10	13	10	12	8.5	6	8	14	8	4.5	5.5	9								
29	Lopez Pass	26	24	21	18	18	26	28	25	26	31	21	23	25	22	19	14	11	13	16	12	9.5	12	10	5	8	9.5	12	5							
30	Eliza Rock	21	19	16	13	13	31	33	20	31	36	33	28	30	27	25	19	22	23	21	21	15	17	23	17	10	9.5	7	13	14						
31	Towhead Island	17	15	12	8.5	8.5	25	27	16	25	30	29	22	24	21	19	13	16	17	15	15	9	11	19	13	4	3.5	3	6.5	9.5	6.5					
32	Reef Point	22	20	17	13	13	26	28	21	26	31	25	23	25	22	19	14	16	17.5	15.5	15	9.5	12	14	8.5	5	5	7.5	3.5	5.5	9	5				
33	Clark Point	20	18	15	12	12	28	30	19	28	33	29	25	27	24	22	16	19	20	18	18	12	14	19	13	7	6.5	6	8.5	10	4	3	5			
34	**Fidalgo Head**	25	23	20	17	17	27	29	24	28	32	22	24	26	24	21	15	13	19	17	13	11	13	12	6.5	7.5	7.5	11	5	4.5	11	8	3	6.5		
35	**ANACORTES**	27	25	22	18	19	32	33	26	31	36	29	28	30	27	26	19	22	23	21	18	15	17	19	13	12	12	13	9.5	11	8.5	9.5	6	7	6.5	
36	**Deception Island**	30	28	25	22	22	32	33	29	33	34	22	29	31	28	26	20	12	24	21	18	18	17	12	6	13	13	16	9.5	7.5	17	13	8.5	12	5.5	12

ORCAS AND SHAW ISLANDS AND LOPEZ SOUND

Location	WEST SOUND	Bell Island	ORCAS	Blind Bay	Point Hudson	Shag Rock	EAST SOUND	ROSARIO	Flat Point	Spencer Spit	Peavine Pass	Deer Point (Obstruction Pass)	Thatcher Bay	Thatcher Pass	Lopez Pass	Hunter Bay	No.
Massacre Bay	1.5	3	3.5	4	4	6	13	10	7	9	8.5	9.5	9	10	14	14	**37**
WEST SOUND		2.5	2.5	3	3.5	5.5	12	9	6	8	7.5	8.5	8	9	13	13	**38**
Bell Island			1.5	2	2.5	4.5	11	8	5.5	7	7	7.5	7	8.5	12	12	**20**
ORCAS				1	1	3	9.5	6.5	4	5.5	5.5	6	6	7	11	11	**39**
Blind Bay					1	2.5	9.5	6.5	3.5	5	5	6	5.5	6.5	10	10	**40**
Point Hudson						2	8.5	5.5	3	4.5	4.5	5	5	5.5	9.5	9.5	**41**
Shag Rock							6.5	3.5	3	3.5	2.5	3	3.5	4.5	8	8	**42**
EAST SOUND								3.5	9.5	9.5	7.5	8	9.5	11	14	14	**43**
ROSARIO									6.5	6.5	4.5	4.5	6.5	7.5	11	11	**44**
Flat Point										5	5	5.5	5	6	9.5	10	**21**
Spencer Spit											3.5	4.5	1.5	2	5.5	5.5	**45**
Peavine Pass												1	3	4.5	8	8.5	**25**
Deer Point (Obstruction Pass)													4.5	5.5	9.5	9.5	**26**
Thatcher Bay														1.5	6	6	**46**
Thatcher Pass															5	5	**28**
Lopez Pass																2	**29**
Hunter Bay																	**47**

Table 1-5 Gulf Islands

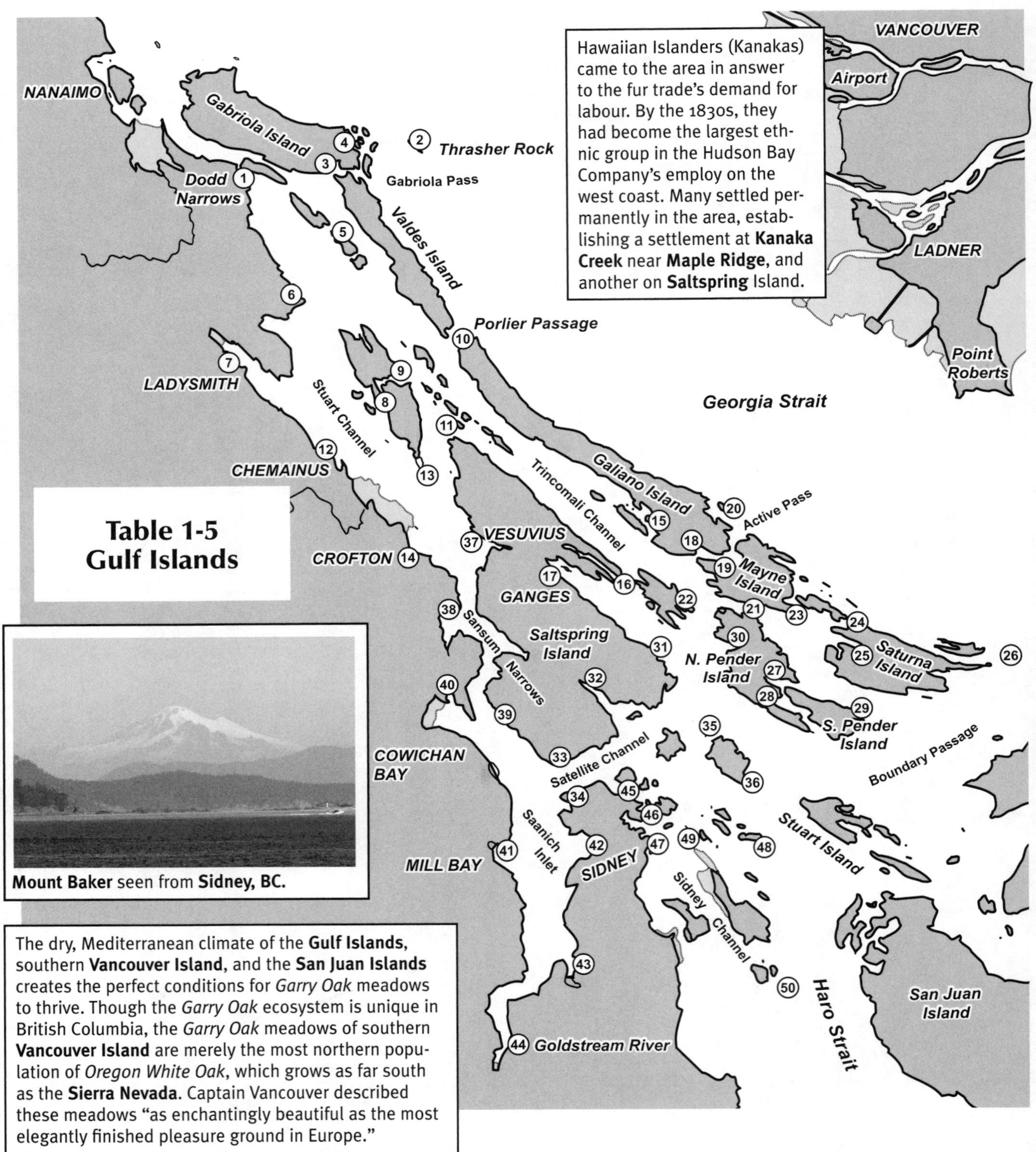

VANCOUVER
Airport
LADNER
Point Roberts
NANAIMO
Gabriola Island
Thrasher Rock
Gabriola Pass
Dodd Narrows
Valdes Island
Porlier Passage
LADYSMITH
Stuart Channel
Georgia Strait
CHEMAINUS
Galiano Island
Trincomali Channel
Active Pass
VESUVIUS
CROFTON
Mayne Island
GANGES
Saltspring Island
Sansum Narrows
Saturna Island
N. Pender Island
S. Pender Island
COWICHAN BAY
Satellite Channel
Boundary Passage
Saanich Inlet
Stuart Island
MILL BAY
SIDNEY
Sidney Channel
Haro Strait
San Juan Island
Goldstream River

Hawaiian Islanders (Kanakas) came to the area in answer to the fur trade's demand for labour. By the 1830s, they had become the largest ethnic group in the Hudson Bay Company's employ on the west coast. Many settled permanently in the area, establishing a settlement at **Kanaka Creek** near **Maple Ridge**, and another on **Saltspring** Island.

Mount Baker seen from **Sidney, BC.**

The dry, Mediterranean climate of the **Gulf Islands**, southern **Vancouver Island**, and the **San Juan Islands** creates the perfect conditions for *Garry Oak* meadows to thrive. Though the *Garry Oak* ecosystem is unique in British Columbia, the *Garry Oak* meadows of southern **Vancouver Island** are merely the most northern population of *Oregon White Oak*, which grows as far south as the **Sierra Nevada.** Captain Vancouver described these meadows "as enchantingly beautiful as the most elegantly finished pleasure ground in Europe."

Table 1-5 GULF ISLANDS

Most Direct Route (Not including passages through "The Gut," Pender Canal, or Boat Passage)

Locations in **bold lowercase** appear in other detail tables.

No.	Location	1	2	3	4	5	6	7	8	9	10	11	12	13	14	15	16	17	18	19	20	21	22	23	24	25	26	27	28	29	30	31	32	33	34	35
1	**Dodd Narrows**																																			
2	**Thrasher Rock**	15																																		
3	Degnen Bay	8	4.5																																	
4	Silva Bay	11	2.5	3.5																																
5	Ruxton Passage	5	6.5	3	5.5																															
6	Yellow Point	6.5	10	6.5	9	3.5																														
7	**LADYSMITH** Public	13	17	13	15	10	6.5																													
8	Telegraph Harbour	13	16	12	15	19	6	7.5																												
9	Clam Bay	12	14	10	13	7.5	5.5	10	9.5																											
10	**Race Point (Porlier Pass)**	12	8.5	9.5	10	7.5	6.5	11	11	3.5																										
11	Jackscrew Island	14	13	13	15	11	8.5	12	7	3.5	4.5																									
12	**CHEMAINUS**	14	19	13	16	10	7	6	3.5	8.5	10	6.5																								
13	Sandstone Rocks	16	18	14	18	13	9	9.5	4.5	4.5	6	2.5	4																							
14	**CROFTON**	19	22	18	21	16	12	12	7.5	8	9.5	6	6.5	3.5																						
15	Montague Harbour	22	25	21	23	18	17	20	15	12	11	8.5	17	10	14																					
16	**Nose Point**	24	26	22	27	19	18	21	16	13	13	9.5	19	12	16	3.5																				
17	**GANGES**	28	30	26	31	23	22	25	20	17	16	13	22	15	19	7	3.5																			
18	Collinson Point	25	24	23	26	20	19	22	18	14	14	11	20	13	17	3.5	3	7																		
19	Miner's Bay	27	23	25	28	22	21	24	20	16	16	13	22	15	19	5.5	5	9	2																	
20	**Gossip Shoals Buoy "U47"**	28	21	22	23	23	22	25	21	14	14	14	23	16	20	6.5	6	10	3	2																
21	Conconi Reef (Navy Channel)	28	28	26	29	24	22	25	21	17	17	14	23	16	20	6.5	5.5	9	3.5	5.5	6.5															
22	Portlock Point	26	26	24	28	22	20	23	19	15	15	12	21	14	18	4.5	3.5	7	2	4	5	2.5														
23	Georgeson Passage	32	26	28	28	28	26	29	25	21	19	18	27	20	24	10	9	13	7	9	5.5	3.5	6													
24	Winter Cove	32	27	29	29	28	26	29	25	21	21	18	27	20	24	11	9.5	13	7.5	9.5	7	4	6.5	1.5												
25	Lyall Harbour Public	32	31	32	33	28	26	29	25	21	21	18	27	20	24	11	9.5	13	7.5	9.5	10	4	6.5	2	2											
26	**Tumbo Reef Buoy "U59"**	38	32	34	34	41	37	37	32	32	26	25	32	28	31	18	17	21	14	19	12	13	15	9.5	11	11										
27	Port Browning	34	34	32	35	30	28	31	27	23	23	20	29	22	26	12	11	15	9	11	12	5.5	8	5	5.5	4	11									
28	Bedwell Harbour Public	35	32	33	38	30	29	32	27	24	24	21	30	23	27	13	11	9.5	11	17	18	11	8.5	9.5	9.5	8	11	8								
29	**Blunden Islet**	35	33	33	36	31	29	32	28	24	24	21	30	23	27	14	13	13	11	13	14	7	10	5.5	6	4.5	7	5	3.5							
30	Hyashi Cove	29	33	27	31	25	23	26	22	18	18	15	24	17	21	7	6	6.5	4.5	9.5	11	4	2.5	7.5	8	8	17	9.5	5	9.5						
31	**Yeo Point**	27	27	25	33	25	24	27	22	19	16	15	25	18	22	6	5.5	3	5	7	8	4.5	3	8	8.5	8.5	17	10	6.5	10	3.5					
32	Fulford Harbour	33	25	34	39	31	29	29	25	25	23	22	24	21	18	13	12	9.5	10	12	13	9.5	8	13	14	14	20	18	5.5	13	7.5	6.5				
33	Cape Keppel	30	29	29	32	26	23	23	19	19	20	17	18	15	12	15	14	12	12	14	15	12	10	16	16	16	21	19	12	14	9.5	8.5	6			
34	Moses Point	31	30	30	33	27	24	24	20	20	21	18	19	16	13	16	14	12	12	14	15	12	11	16	16	16	21	19	13	14	10	9	6.5	1.5		
35	Canoe Rock	31	36	32	37	29	30	30	23	23	21	20	25	22	19	11	10	7.5	7.5	9.5	11	7	5.5	11	11	11	15	13	5.5	7.5	4.5	4.5	5	6.5	7	
36	**Point Fairfax**	34	39	35	40	32	32	32	26	26	24	22	27	24	21	14	13	11	11	13	14	10	8.5	14	14	14	14	11	4.5	6	7.5	7.5	8	8.5	8	3

Access to Tsehum Harbou
from the north via John Passage

SANSUM NARROWS AND SAANICH INLET

Location	CROFTON	VESUVIUS	Maple Bay	MUSGRAVE LANDING	Genoa Bay	Cape Keppel	Moses Point	MILL BAY	Patricia Bay	BRENTWOOD BAY	Goldstream River	No.
Sandstone Rocks	3.5	3	8	11	13	15	16	18	18	22	27	13
CROFTON		2.5	5.5	9	11	12	13	15	16	20	25	14
VESUVIUS			5.5	9	11	12	13	15	16	20	25	37
Maple Bay				6	8	9	10	12	13	17	22	38
MUSGRAVE LANDING					2.5	3	4.5	6.5	7	11	16	39
Genoa Bay						5	6.5	8	8.5	13	18	40
Cape Keppel							1.5	4.5	4.5	9	14	33
Moses Point								3.5	3	7	12	34
MILL BAY									4	6	11	41
Patricia Bay										6	11	42
BRENTWOOD BAY											7	43
Goldstream River												44

VICINITY OF PORT SIDNEY

Location	Point Fairfax	Cape Keppel	Moses Point	Schwartz Bay Public	Tsehum Harbour	SIDNEY	Gooch Island Light	Sidney Spit	Kelp Reef	No.
Canoe Rock	3	6.5	7	4	5	6	5	5	12	32
Point Fairfax		8.5	8	4.5	4.5	5	2.5	4	9.5	36
Cape Keppel			1.5	4.5	6	7.5	10	8	16	33
Moses Point				4	6	7	9.5	7.5	16	34
Schwartz Bay Public					2.5	3	6	4	12	45
Tsehum Harbour						2	5.5	3	11	46
SIDNEY							5	2	9	47
Gooch Island Light								4	7	48
Sidney Spit									8.5	49
Kelp Reef										50

Table 1-6 Fraser River, Burrard Inlet and Howe Sound

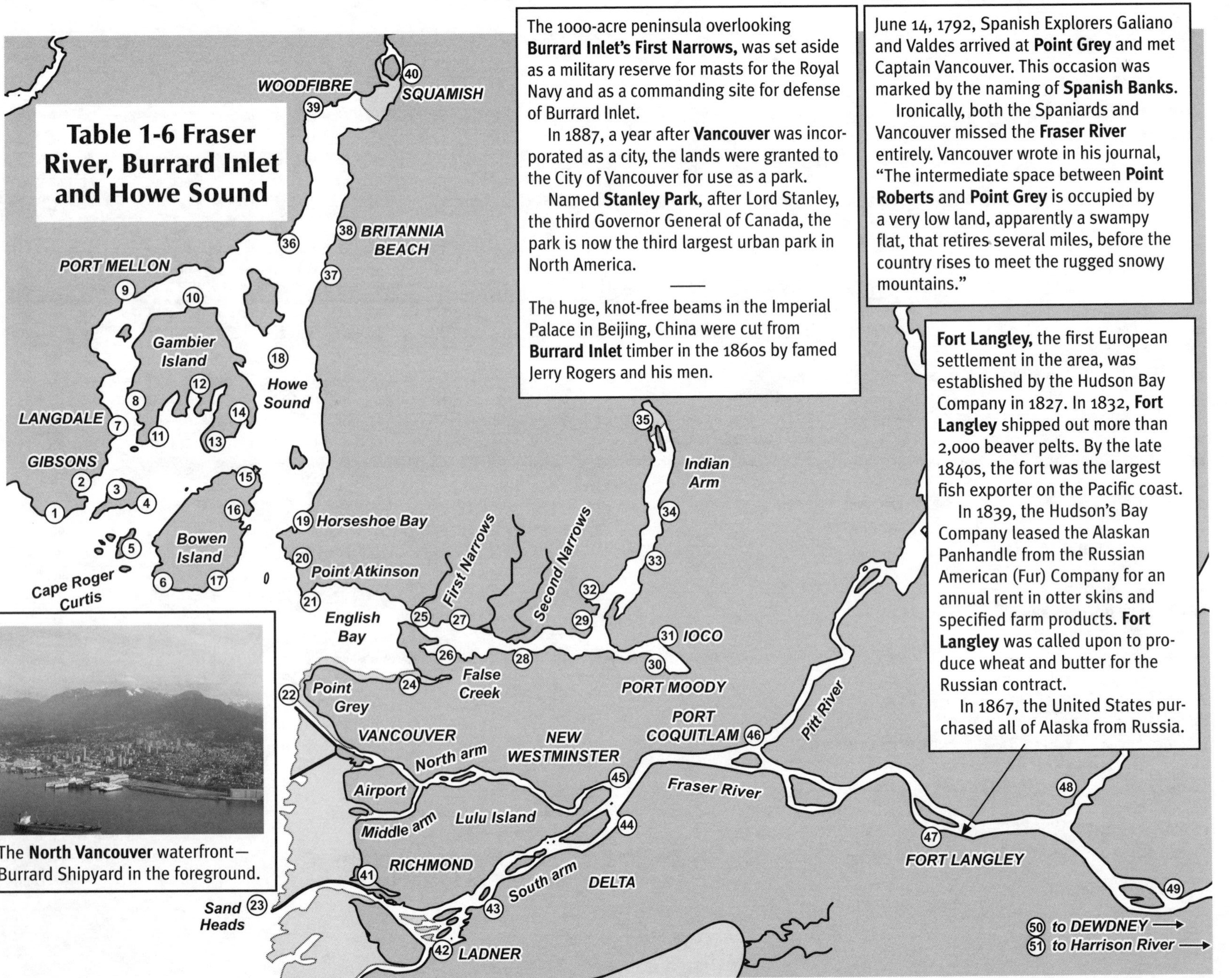
WOODFIBRE
SQUAMISH
BRITANNIA BEACH
PORT MELLON
Gambier Island
Howe Sound
LANGDALE
GIBSONS
Bowen Island
Cape Roger Curtis
Horseshoe Bay
Point Atkinson
English Bay
First Narrows
Second Narrows
Indian Arm
IOCO
False Creek
PORT MOODY
Point Grey
VANCOUVER
PORT COQUITLAM
Pitt River
NEW WESTMINSTER
North arm
Airport
Fraser River
Lulu Island
Middle arm
RICHMOND
South arm
DELTA
FORT LANGLEY
Sand Heads
LADNER
50 to DEWDNEY
51 to Harrison River

The 1000-acre peninsula overlooking **Burrard Inlet's First Narrows,** was set aside as a military reserve for masts for the Royal Navy and as a commanding site for defense of Burrard Inlet.

In 1887, a year after **Vancouver** was incorporated as a city, the lands were granted to the City of Vancouver for use as a park.

Named **Stanley Park**, after Lord Stanley, the third Governor General of Canada, the park is now the third largest urban park in North America.

The huge, knot-free beams in the Imperial Palace in Beijing, China were cut from **Burrard Inlet** timber in the 1860s by famed Jerry Rogers and his men.

June 14, 1792, Spanish Explorers Galiano and Valdes arrived at **Point Grey** and met Captain Vancouver. This occasion was marked by the naming of **Spanish Banks**.

Ironically, both the Spaniards and Vancouver missed the **Fraser River** entirely. Vancouver wrote in his journal, "The intermediate space between **Point Roberts** and **Point Grey** is occupied by a very low land, apparently a swampy flat, that retires several miles, before the country rises to meet the rugged snowy mountains."

Fort Langley, the first European settlement in the area, was established by the Hudson Bay Company in 1827. In 1832, **Fort Langley** shipped out more than 2,000 beaver pelts. By the late 1840s, the fort was the largest fish exporter on the Pacific coast.

In 1839, the Hudson's Bay Company leased the Alaskan Panhandle from the Russian American (Fur) Company for an annual rent in otter skins and specified farm products. **Fort Langley** was called upon to produce wheat and butter for the Russian contract.

In 1867, the United States purchased all of Alaska from Russia.

The **North Vancouver** waterfront—Burrard Shipyard in the foreground.

Table 1-6 FRASER RIVER, BURRARD INLET, AND HOWE SOUND

Most Direct Route (Not including routes through Shoal Channel)

Locations in **bold lowercase** appear in other detail tables.

No.	Location	1	2	3	4	5	6	7	8	9	10	11	12	13	14	15	16	17	18	19	20	21	22	23	24	25	26	27	28	29	30	31	32	33	34
1	**Gower Point**																																		
2	**GIBSONS**	2.5																																	
3	Plumper Cove Marine Park (Keats Island)	3	1.5																																
4	Eastbourne (Keats Island)	4.5	4	3																															
5	Pasley Island	3.5	6	5	2																														
6	**Cape Roger Curtis**	5	7	6	3.5	2																													
7	**LANGDALE**	7.5	2.5	2	3	5	6.5																												
8	New Brighton	8	4	3	4	6	7	1.5																											
9	Port Mellon	12	8	7	8	10	11	5.5	5																										
10	Ekins Point	15	11	10	11	13	14	8	7.5	4																									
11	Gambier Harbour	7	3.5	3	2.5	5	6	2	2.5	7	9.5																								
12	Center Bay Yacht Station	10	7	6	5.5	7.5	8.5	5.5	6	10	12	3.5																							
13	Hope Point	7.5	5.5	4.5	3	5	6	4	4.5	8.5	9	2.5	3																						
14	Halkett Bay Marine Park	10	8	7	5.5	7.5	8.5	6.5	7	11	7.5	5	5.5	2.5																					
15	Smuggler's Cove	9	7	6.5	5	6.5	7.5	6	6.5	11	8.5	4.5	5	2	2.5																				
16	Snug Cove	12	11	10	8.5	10	11	9.5	10	14	11	8	8.5	5.5	5	4																			
17	Point Cowan	8	10	9	6.5	5	3	9.5	10	14	14	9	12	8.5	8	6.5	3.5																		
18	Pam Rocks	12	11	9.5	8	10	11	9	9.5	13	4.5	7.5	8	5	3.5	4.5	7	10																	
19	**HORSESHOE BAY**	13	11	10	8.5	10	8	9.5	10	14	11	8	8.5	5.5	5	4	2.5	5	6.5																
20	Fisherman's Cove	11	13	12	10	8.5	6.5	11	12	16	13	9.5	10	7	6.5	5.5	3	3.5	8.5	3															
21	**Point Atkinson**	12	14	13	11	9	7	12	13	17	14	11	12	8.5	8	7	4.5	3.5	10	4.5	2														
22	**Point Grey** (North Arm Jetty)	13	15	14	12	10	8	15	15	19	18	15	15	12	12	11	8	5.5	14	8.5	6	4.5													
23	**Sand Heads**	19	23	22	19	17	15	22	22	24	28	21	24	21	22	21	18	15	24	18	16	14	10												
24	**FALSE CREEK** (Kitsilano Point)	18	20	19	17	15	13	18	19	23	20	17	18	14	14	13	10	9	16	10	7.5	5.5	7.5	17											
25	First Narrows	17	19	18	16	14	12	17	18	22	19	16	17	14	13	12	10	9	15	9.5	7	5	8	17	3.5										
26	**VANCOUVER** (Coal Harbour)	20	22	21	19	17	15	20	21	25	22	19	20	16	16	15	12	11	18	12	9.5	7.5	11	19	6	2.5									
27	Mosquito Creek Marina	22	24	23	21	19	17	22	23	27	23	21	22	18	20	17	14	13	20	14	12	9.5	13	21	8	2	2								
28	Second Narrows	22	24	23	21	19	17	22	23	27	24	21	22	18	18	17	14	13	20	14	12	9.5	13	21	8	4.5	4	2.5							
29	Roche Point (Cates Park)	24	26	25	23	21	19	24	25	29	26	23	24	21	20	19	17	16	22	17	14	12	16	24	11	7.5	7	5.5	3						
30	**PORT MOODY** (Reed Point)	27	29	28	26	24	22	27	28	32	29	26	27	24	23	22	20	19	25	20	17	15	18	27	13	10	9.5	8	5.5	3					
31	**IOCO**	28	30	29	27	25	23	28	29	33	30	27	28	25	24	23	21	20	26	21	18	16	19	28	14	11	10	8.5	6	3.5	0.5				
32	Deep Cove	27	29	28	26	24	22	27	28	32	29	26	27	24	23	22	20	19	25	20	17	15	18	27	13	10	9.5	8	5.5	2.5	4	4.5			
33	Twin Islands	29	31	30	28	26	24	29	30	34	31	28	29	26	25	24	22	21	27	22	19	17	20	29	15	12	11	9.5	7	4	6	6.5	2.5		
34	Buntzen Bay	31	33	32	30	28	26	31	32	36	33	30	31	28	27	26	24	23	29	24	21	19	22	31	18	14	13	12	9.5	6.5	8.5	9	4.5	2.5	
35	Wigwam Inn	36	38	37	35	33	31	36	37	41	38	35	36	33	32	31	29	28	34	29	26	24	27	36	22	19	18	17	14	11	13	14	9.5	7.5	5

Howe Sound **Burrard Inlet**

SQUAMISH INLET

Location	Ekins Point	Defence Islands	Porteau Cove Marine Park	BRITTANIA BEACH	WOODFIBER	SQUAMISH	No.
Pam Rocks	4.5	5.5	5	9	11	14	18
Ekins Point		5	6	8.5	10	15	10
Defence Islands			1.5	4	5.5	9	36
Porteau Cove Marine Park				4	6	9.5	37
BRITTANIA BEACH					3	6	38
WOODFIBER						4.5	39
SQUAMISH							40

FRASER RIVER

Location	Sand Heads	STEVESTON	LADNER	Deas Slough	Annieville Slough	NEW WESTMINSTER	PORT COQUITLAM	FORT LANGLEY	Stave River	MISSION	DEWDNEY	Harrisson River Bridge	No.
Point Grey (North Arm Jetty)	10	15	20	20	18	16	22	32	38	44	50	63	22
Sand Heads		5	9.5	10	18	20	25	35	41	47	53	66	23
STEVESTON			5.5	5	13	15	20	30	36	42	48	61	41
LADNER				3.5	11	13	18	28	34	40	46	59	42
Deas Slough					8	10	17	26	32	38	44	57	43
Annieville Slough						2	8.5	18	24	30	36	49	44
NEW WESTMINSTER							6.5	16	22	28	34	47	45
PORT COQUITLAM (Pitt River)								10	16	22	28	41	46
FORT LANGLEY									6	12	18	31	47
Stave River										6	12	25	48
MISSION											6	19	49
DEWDNEY (Nicomen Slough)												13	50
Harrisson River Bridge													51

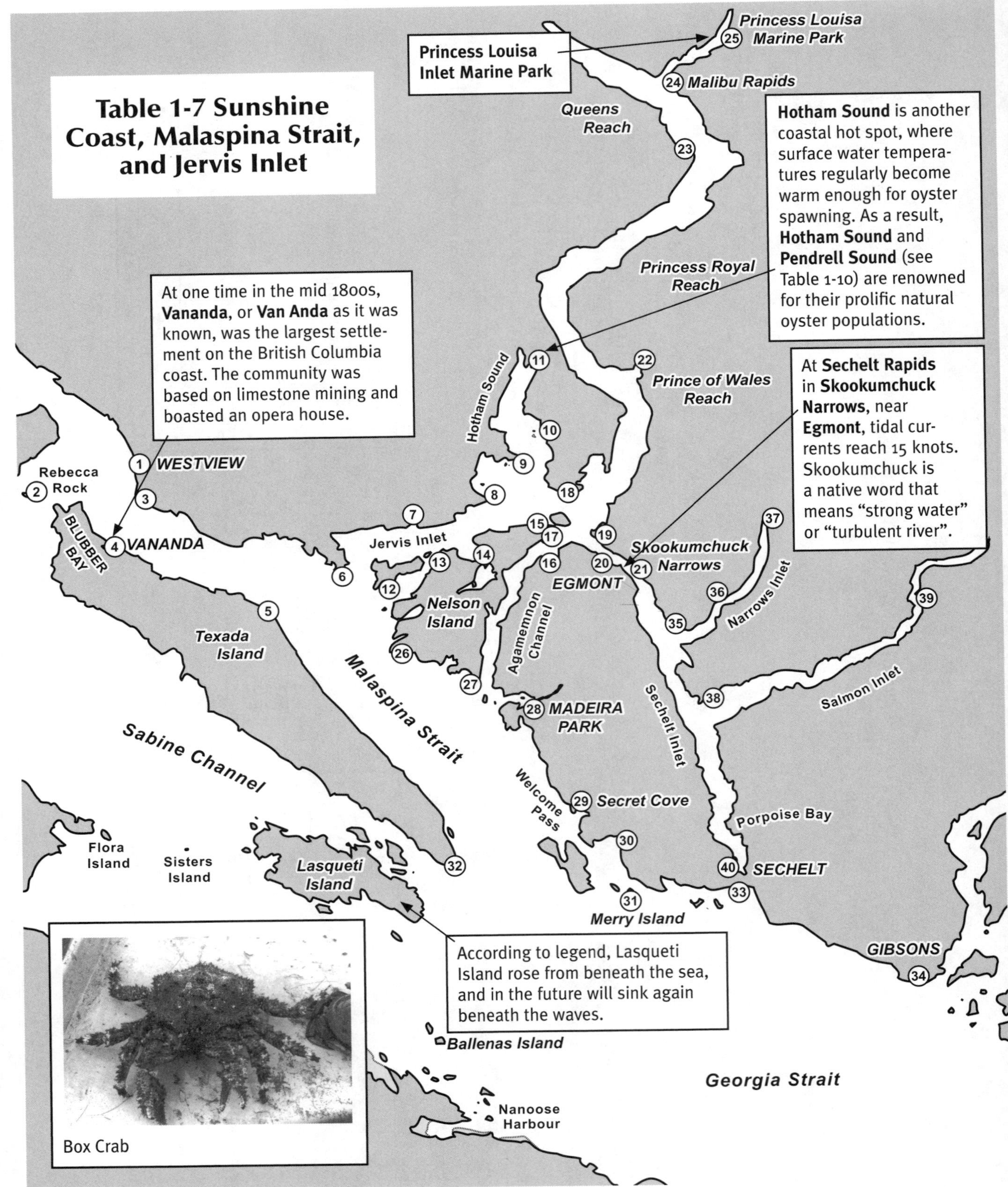

Table 1-7 Sunshine Coast, Malaspina Strait, and Jervis Inlet
Princess Louisa Inlet Marine Park
Princess Louisa Marine Park
Malibu Rapids
Queens Reach
Hotham Sound is another coastal hot spot, where surface water temperatures regularly become warm enough for oyster spawning. As a result, Hotham Sound and Pendrell Sound (see Table 1-10) are renowned for their prolific natural oyster populations.
Princess Royal Reach
At one time in the mid 1800s, Vananda, or Van Anda as it was known, was the largest settlement on the British Columbia coast. The community was based on limestone mining and boasted an opera house.
Hotham Sound
Prince of Wales Reach
At Sechelt Rapids in Skookumchuck Narrows, near Egmont, tidal currents reach 15 knots. Skookumchuck is a native word that means "strong water" or "turbulent river".
WESTVIEW
Rebecca Rock
BLUBBER BAY
VANANDA
Jervis Inlet
Skookumchuck Narrows
EGMONT
Narrows Inlet
Nelson Island
Texada Island
Agamemnon Channel
Malaspina Strait
MADEIRA PARK
Sechelt Inlet
Salmon Inlet
Sabine Channel
Welcome Pass
Secret Cove
Porpoise Bay
Flora Island
Sisters Island
Lasqueti Island
SECHELT
Merry Island
GIBSONS
According to legend, Lasqueti Island rose from beneath the sea, and in the future will sink again beneath the waves.
Ballenas Island
Georgia Strait
Nanoose Harbour

Box Crab

Table 1-7 SUNSHINE COAST, MALASPINA STRAIT, AND JERVIS INLET

Most Direct Route (Not including passages through Telescope Passage)

Locations in **bold lowercase** appear in other detail tables.

#	Location	1	2	3	4	5	6	7	8	9	10	11	12	13	14	15	16	17	18	19	20	21	22	23	24	25	26	27	28	29	30	31	32	33
1	**WESTVIEW**																																	
2	**Rebecca Rock**	5																																
3	Grief Point	2	5																															
4	**VANANDA**	4.5	5.5	3																														
5	**Northeast Point**	11	14	8.5	8.5																													
6	**Scotch Fir Point**	15	18	11	11	4																												
7	**SALTERY BAY**	20	23	16	16	8.5	4.5																											
8	Culloden Point	23	26	19	19	12	8	4.5																										
9	Elephant Point	26	29	22	22	15	11	7	2.5																									
10	Harmony Islands Marine Park	28	31	24	24	17	13	9	4.5	2																								
11	Lena Bay	31	34	27	27	20	16	12	7.5	5	4																							
12	Fox Island (Blind Bay)	17	20	14	14	6	2.5	5	9	12	14	17																						
13	Telescope Pass (Blind Bay)	20	23	17	17	9	5.5	8	12	15	17	20	3																					
14	Vanguard Bay	23	26	19	19	12	7.5	4	3.5	6	8	11	8.5	11																				
15	Agnew Passage	26	29	22	22	15	11	7	3.5	3.5	5.5	9.5	12	15	5.5																			
16	Agamemnon Bay	28	31	24	24	17	13	9	5.5	5.5	7.5	12	14	17	7.5	2																		
17	Nile Point	27	30	23	23	16	12	8	4.5	4.5	6.5	11	13	16	6.5	1	1																	
18	Foley Head	27	30	23	23	16	12	8.5	4	3.5	5	9	13	16	7	2	3	2.5																
19	Egmont Point	28	31	24	24	17	13	9	5.5	5.5	7.5	12	14	17	7.5	2	2.5	1.5	2															
20	**EGMONT**	29	32	25	25	18	14	11	7	7	9	13	15	19	9	3.5	3.5	3	4	2														
21	Sechelt Rapids	31	34	27	27	20	16	12	8	8	10	14	16	20	10	4.5	5	4	5	3	1.5													
22	Vancouver Bay	36	39	32	32	25	21	17	13	12	14	18	22	25	16	11	12	11	8.5	9.5	12	13												
23	Patrick Point	50	53	46	46	39	35	36	31	31	32	36	40	43	34	29	26	25	27	23	25	26	17											
24	Malibu Rapids	55	58	51	51	44	40	41	36	36	37	41	45	48	39	34	31	30	32	28	30	31	22	5										
25	Princess Louisa Marine Park	59	62	55	55	48	44	45	40	40	41	45	49	52	43	38	25	34	36	32	34	35	26	9	4									
26	**Cape Cockburn**	18	21	15	15	6.5	5	8	12	14	16	19	3.5	6.5	11	14	13	13	16	15	17	18	25	38	43	47								
27	**Fearney Point**	22	25	20	20	11	10	13	13	13	14	19	8.5	12	16	9	8	8	11	10	12	13	20	33	38	42	5							
28	**MADIERA PARK**	26	29	23	23	15	13	16	16	16	18	22	12	15	19	12	11	11	14	13	15	16	23	36	41	45	8	3						
29	**Secret Cove**	30	33	28	28	19	18	21	23	23	25	29	17	20	24	19	18	18	21	20	22	23	30	43	48	52	13	9.5	9.5					
30	**HALFMOON BAY**	50	53	47	47	39	37	24	25	25	27	31	20	23	27	21	20	20	23	22	24	25	32	45	50	54	16	12	13	4.5				
31	**Merry Island**	34	37	32	32	23	22	25	26	26	28	32	21	24	28	22	21	21	24	23	25	26	33	46	51	55	17	13	13	5	3			
32	**Point Upwood**	44	47	25	25	16	16	19	23	23	25	29	15	18	22	19	18	18	21	20	22	23	30	43	48	52	11	10	10	8	10	10		
33	**SECHELT**	41	44	38	38	30	29	32	32	32	34	38	28	31	35	28	27	27	30	29	31	32	39	52	57	61	24	19	19	11	9	6	15	
34	**Gower Point**	49	52	47	47	38	37	40	41	41	43	47	36	39	43	37	36	36	39	38	40	41	48	61	66	70	32	28	28	20	18	15	24	11

SECHELT INLET

#	Location	21	35	36	37	38	39	40
20	**EGMONT**	1.5	5.5	9	14	10	23	19
21	Sechelt Rapids		4	7.5	12	8.5	21	17
35	Highland Point			3.5	8.5	4.5	17	13
36	Tzoonie Rapids				5	7.5	20	16
37	Tzoonie River					13	25	21
38	Kunechin Islets						12	9
39	Clowhom River							21
40	Porpoise Bay Public							

Table 1-8 Nanaimo to Cape Mudge and Islands in the Northern Portion of Georgia Strait

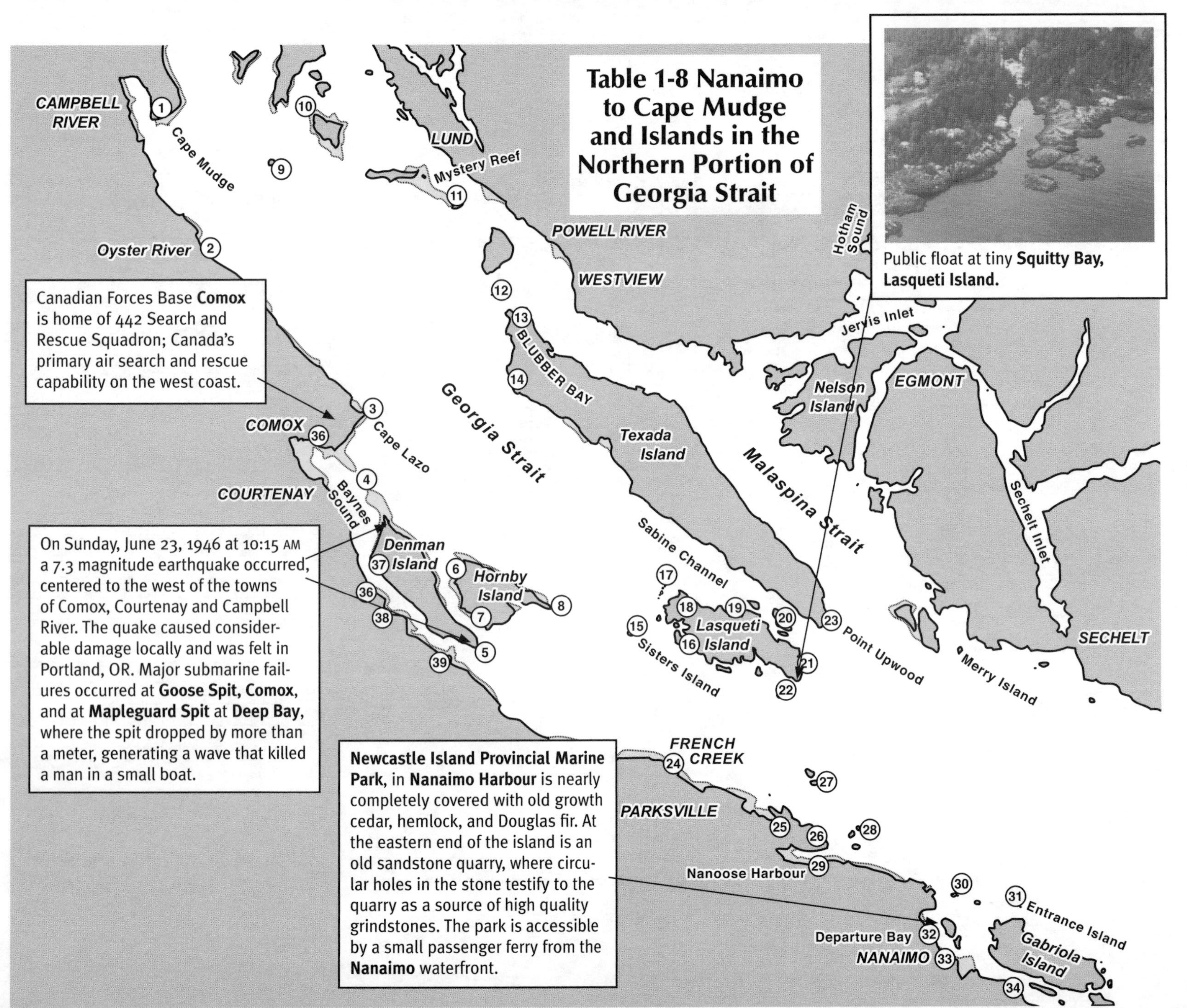
CAMPBELL RIVER
1
Cape Mudge
9
10
LUND
Mystery Reef
11
Oyster River
2
POWELL RIVER
WESTVIEW
12
13
BLUBBER BAY
14
Georgia Strait
3
Cape Lazo
COMOX
36
4
Baynes Sound
COURTENAY
Denman
37 Island
6
Hornby Island
7
8
36
38
5
39
Texada Island
Malaspina Strait
Hotham Sound
Jervis Inlet
Nelson Island
EGMONT
Sechelt Inlet
SECHELT
Merry Island
Point Upwood
23
Sabine Channel
17
18
19
20
Lasqueti
16 Island
15
Sisters Island
21
22
FRENCH CREEK
24
27
PARKSVILLE
25
26
28
29
Nanoose Harbour
30
31
Entrance Island
Departure Bay
32
NANAIMO
33
Gabriola Island
34

Public float at tiny **Squitty Bay, Lasqueti Island.**

Canadian Forces Base **Comox** is home of 442 Search and Rescue Squadron; Canada's primary air search and rescue capability on the west coast.

On Sunday, June 23, 1946 at 10:15 AM a 7.3 magnitude earthquake occurred, centered to the west of the towns of Comox, Courtenay and Campbell River. The quake caused considerable damage locally and was felt in Portland, OR. Major submarine failures occurred at **Goose Spit, Comox,** and at **Mapleguard Spit** at **Deep Bay,** where the spit dropped by more than a meter, generating a wave that killed a man in a small boat.

Newcastle Island Provincial Marine Park, in **Nanaimo Harbour** is nearly completely covered with old growth cedar, hemlock, and Douglas fir. At the eastern end of the island is an old sandstone quarry, where circular holes in the stone testify to the quarry as a source of high quality grindstones. The park is accessible by a small passenger ferry from the **Nanaimo** waterfront.

Table 1-8

NANAIMO TO CAPE MUDGE AND ISLANDS IN THE NORTHERN PORTION OF GEORGIA STRAIT

Most Direct Route (Including passages through Area "WG" but not including passages in Malaspina Strait)

Locations in **bold lowercase** appear in other detail tables.

Caution—Do not transit Area "WG" when active. Contact Winchelsea Control on VHF Channel 10.

No.	Location	1	2	3	4	5	6	7	8	9	10	11	12	13	14	15	16	17	18	19	20	21	22	23	24	25	26	27	28	29	30	31	32	33
1	**Cape Mudge**																																	
2	Oyster River	9																																
3	**Cape Lazo Buoy "PK"**	22	14																															
4	**Comox Bar Buoy "P52"**	25	19	4.5																														
5	**Chrome Island**	36	30	16	14																													
6	Phipps Point	34	26	12	9.5	4.5																												
7	Ford Cove	37	29	15	13	1.5	3																											
8	**Flora Islet**	37	30	16	18	5	8	5																										
9	Mittlenatch Island	8	6	15	20	31	27	30	31																									
10	**Spilsbury Point (Baker Passage)**	10	11	18	23	34	32	35	34	4																								
11	**Mystery Reef**	20	16	13	17	29	23	26	24	12	11																							
12	**Rebecca Rock**	24	18	9.5	12	23	17	20	18	15	18	6.5																						
13	**BLUBBER BAY**	26	20	10	13	22	17	20	19	18	20	8	2																					
14	Favada Point	27	20	8	10	17	12	15	13	19	21	11	5	5.5																				
15	**Sisters Island**	43	35	21	20	10	13	10	5.5	35	38	28	22	22	17																			
16	**FALSE BAY**	46	38	24	23	13	17	14	9	38	40	30	24	25	19	3.5																		
17	Fegan Islets	43	35	21	20	12	14	12	7.5	34	37	27	21	22	16	3.5	3.5																	
18	Scottie Bay	45	37	23	22	14	16	14	9.5	37	39	29	23	24	18	5.5	5.5	2																
19	Tucker Bay	48	40	26	25	17	19	17	12.5	39	41	31	25	26	20	8	8	5	3.5															
20	Jedediah Island (Lang Bay)	50	42	28	27	19	21	19	14.5	41	43	33	27	28	22	10	10	7	5.5	2.5														
21	Squitty Bay	55	45	33	32	21	25	22	18	45	47	37	31	32	26	12	11	10	9	6	4													
22	Sangster Island	53	45	31	30	19	23	20	16	46	48	38	32	33	27	10	9	11	13	8.5	6	2												
23	**Point Upwood**	51	45	31	30	23	26	23	18	44	46	36	30	31	25	14	13	10	8.5	6	4.5	2.5	5											
24	**FRENCH CREEK**	51	43	29	28	14	19	16	13	44	46	37	30	31	26	8.5	9	11	13	15	14	10	8	13										
25	Northwest Bay	58	50	36	35	21	26	23	20	50	53	42	36	36	31	15	14	16	18	17	14	10	8	13	7									
26	Schooner Cove	61	53	39	38	24	29	26	23	54	56	45	39	39	34	17	16	18	20	18	15	12	9.5	13	10	6								
27	**Ballenas Island**	58	50	36	35	22	27	24	20	49	51	41	35	36	31	15	13	15	17	13	11	6.5	4.5	8.5	8	5	4							
28	Winchelsea Island	63	55	41	40	26	31	28	24	53	55	45	39	40	35	19	17	19	21	17	15	11	8.5	12	12	7.5	2	4						
29	Nanoose Harbour	64	56	42	41	31	34	31	27	56	59	49	43	43	38	21	20	22	24	21	19	14	12	16	14	10	4	7.5	3.5					
30	**Five Finger Island**	69	61	47	46	33	39	36	31	60	62	52	46	48	43	26	25	27	29	24	22	18	16	19	19	15	9	11	7.5	9				
31	**Entrance Island**	73	65	51	50	37	43	40	35	64	66	55	50	52	47	30	28	30	32	28	26	22	20	21	23	20	13	15	12	13	4			
32	North End Newcastle Channel	73	65	51	50	36	41	38	34	63	65	55	49	50	45	27	27	29	31	26	24	20	18	20	22	17	11	13	9.5	11	3	6		
33	**NANAIMO Public**	74	66	52	51	37	42	39	35	64	66	56	50	51	46	29	29	31	32	28	26	22	20	21	23	19	13	15	11	13	4.5	6	1.5	
34	**Dodd Narrows**	76	68	54	53	40	45	42	38	67	69	60	53	54	49	33	31	33	35	31	25	25	23	26	26	22	16	18	14	16	7	8	7	5

BAYNES SOUND

Location	COMOX	Buckley Bay	Denman Point	Fanny Bay	DEEP BAY	Chrome Island	No.
Comox Bar Buoy "P52"	3	8	6.5	9.5	14	15	**4**
COMOX		9.5	7.5	11	15	16	**35**
Buckley Bay			1.5	2	6.5	7.5	**36**
Denman Point				3	7.5	9	**37**
Fanny Bay					5	6.5	**38**
DEEP BAY						3	**39**
Chrome Island							**5**

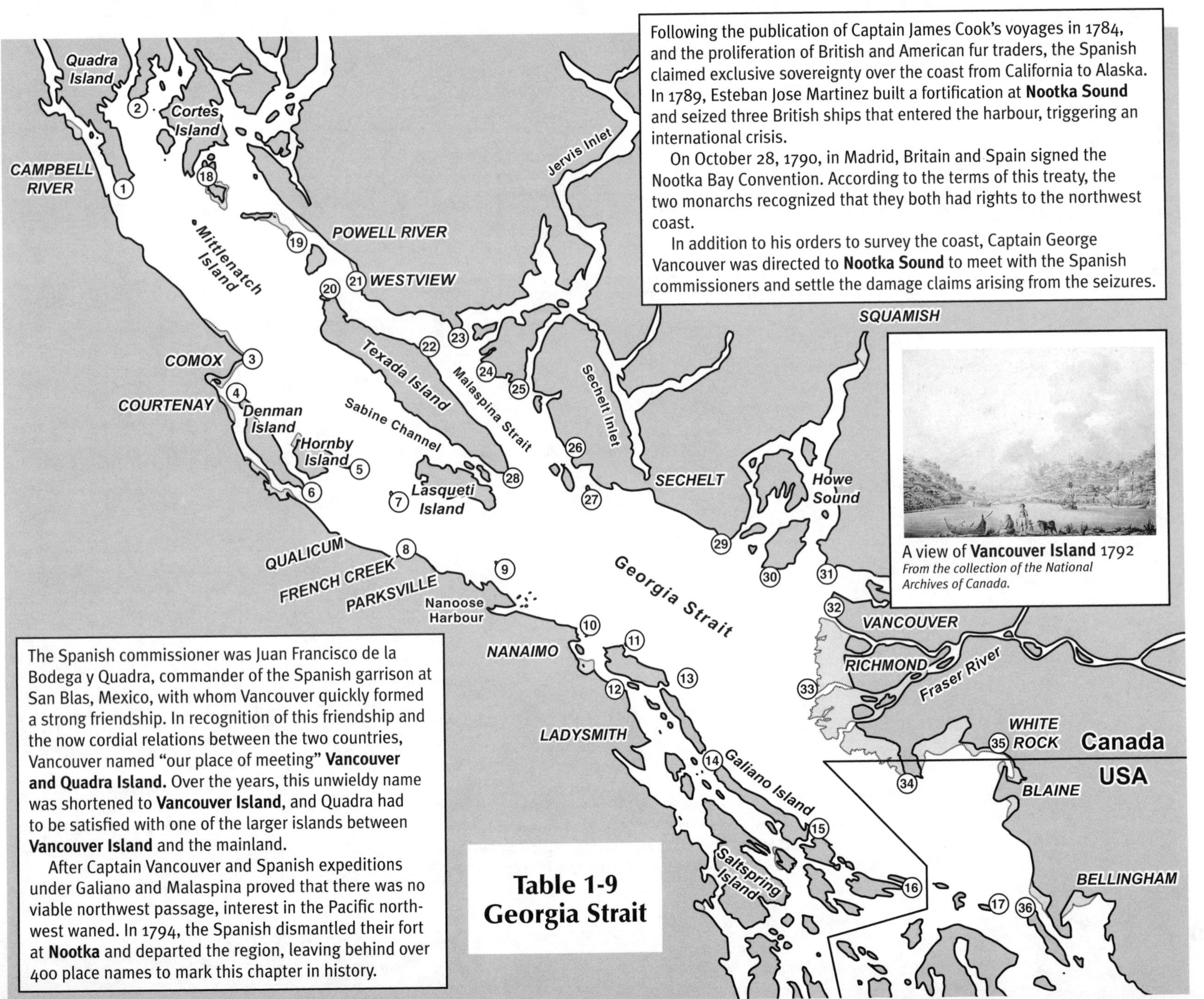
Quadra Island
Cortes Island
CAMPBELL RIVER
Mittlenatch Island
POWELL RIVER
WESTVIEW
Jervis Inlet
COMOX
COURTENAY
Denman Island
Hornby Island
Texada Island
Malaspina Strait
Sabine Channel
Lasqueti Island
Sechelt Inlet
SECHELT
SQUAMISH
Howe Sound
QUALICUM
FRENCH CREEK
PARKSVILLE
Nanoose Harbour
Georgia Strait
NANAIMO
VANCOUVER
RICHMOND
Fraser River
LADYSMITH
WHITE ROCK
Canada
USA
BLAINE
Galiano Island
Saltspring Island
BELLINGHAM
1
2
3
4
5
6
7
8
9
10
11
12
13
14
15
16
17
18
19
20
21
22
23
24
25
26
27
28
29
30
31
32
33
34
35
36

Following the publication of Captain James Cook's voyages in 1784, and the proliferation of British and American fur traders, the Spanish claimed exclusive sovereignty over the coast from California to Alaska. In 1789, Esteban Jose Martinez built a fortification at **Nootka Sound** and seized three British ships that entered the harbour, triggering an international crisis.

On October 28, 1790, in Madrid, Britain and Spain signed the Nootka Bay Convention. According to the terms of this treaty, the two monarchs recognized that they both had rights to the northwest coast.

In addition to his orders to survey the coast, Captain George Vancouver was directed to **Nootka Sound** to meet with the Spanish commissioners and settle the damage claims arising from the seizures.

A view of **Vancouver Island** 1792
From the collection of the National Archives of Canada.

The Spanish commissioner was Juan Francisco de la Bodega y Quadra, commander of the Spanish garrison at San Blas, Mexico, with whom Vancouver quickly formed a strong friendship. In recognition of this friendship and the now cordial relations between the two countries, Vancouver named "our place of meeting" **Vancouver and Quadra Island.** Over the years, this unwieldy name was shortened to **Vancouver Island**, and Quadra had to be satisfied with one of the larger islands between **Vancouver Island** and the mainland.

After Captain Vancouver and Spanish expeditions under Galiano and Malaspina proved that there was no viable northwest passage, interest in the Pacific northwest waned. In 1794, the Spanish dismantled their fort at **Nootka** and departed the region, leaving behind over 400 place names to mark this chapter in history.

Table 1-9
Georgia Strait

Table 1-9 GEORGIA STRAIT

Most Direct Route (Unshaded distances shown in heavy borders represent routes where the clockwise/counter clockwise distances around Texada Island are within five miles of each other. For the purposes of this table, only the clockwise distance is shown.) Locations in **bold lowercase** appear in other detail tables.

No.	Location	1	2	3	4	5	6	7	8	9	10	11	12	13	14	15	16	17	18	19	20	21	22	23	24	25	26	27	28	29	30	31	32	33	34	35
1	**Cape Mudge**																																			
2	**Viner Point (Sutil Channel)**	12																																		
3	**Cape Lazo Buoy "PK"**	22	27																																	
4	**Comox Bar Buoy "P52"**	25	32	4.5																																
5	**Flora Island**	37	42	16	18																															
6	**Chrome Island**	36	43	16	14	5																														
7	**Sisters Island**	43	47	21	20	5.5	10																													
8	**FRENCH CREEK**	51	56	29	28	13	14	8.5																												
9	**Ballenas Island**	58	61	36	35	20	22	15	8																											
10	**Five Finger Island**	69	72	47	46	31	33	26	19	11																										
11	**Entrance Island**	73	76	51	50	35	37	30	23	15	4																									
12	**Dodd Narrows**	76	79	54	53	38	40	33	26	18	7	8																								
13	**Thrasher Rock**	81	84	59	58	53	45	38	31	23	12	7.5	15																							
14	**Race Point (Porlier Passage)**	90	93	68	67	62	54	47	40	32	21	16	12	8.5																						
15	**Gossip Shoals Buoy "U47"**	102	105	80	79	74	66	59	52	44	33	28.5	28	21	14																					
16	**Tumbo Reef Buoy "U59"**	113	116	91	90	85	77	70	63	55	44	39.5	38	32	26	12																				
17	**Puffin Island Light**	122	125	100	99	94	86	79	72	64	53	48.5	47	41	35	21	9																			
18	**Spilsbury Point (Baker Passage)**	10	11	18	23	34	34	38	46	51	62	66	69	74	83	95	106	115																		
19	**Mystery Reef**	20	23	13	17	24	29	28	37	41	53	57	60	65	74	86	97	105	11																	
20	**Rebecca Rock**	24	27	9.5	12	18	23	22	30	35	46	50	53	58	67	79	90	99	18	6.5																
21	**WESTVIEW**	28	31	14	17	22	27	26	34	39	44	48	51	55	64	76	87	96	19	8.5	5															
22	**Northeast Point**	38	41	24	25	30	35	31	29	25	34	37	41	44	53	65	76	85	30	19	14	11														
23	**Scotch Fir Point**	42	45	28	28	32	37	36	29	25	34	36	41	43	51	64	75	84	34	23	18	15	4													
24	**Cape Cockburn**	45	48	31	32	35	35	26	24	20	29	32	36	38	46	59	70	79	37	26	21	18	6.5	5												
25	**Fearney Point (Entrance to Agamemnon Channel)**	49	52	35	36	28	33	24	23	18	27	29	34	39	48	60	76	80	41	30	25	22	11	10	5											
26	**Secret Cove**	57	60	43	38	26	31	22	20	15	19	21	26	31	40	52	68	72	49	38	33	30	19	18	13	9.5										
27	**Merry Island**	61	65	41	39	28	33	24	19	12	14	16	21	26	35	47	63	67	53	42	37	34	23	22	17	13	5									
28	**Point Upwood**	51	55	31	30	18	23	14	13	8.5	19	21	26	28	37	49	60	69	46	52	47	44	16	16	11	10	8	10								
29	**Gower Point**	76	79	55	54	42	45	36	32	24	18	15	23	15	22	31	40	48	70	57	52	49	38	37	32	28	20	15	24							
30	**Cape Roger Curtis**	80	84	60	59	47	50	40	36	28	20	16	24	14	20	28	36	45	75	62	57	54	43	42	37	33	25	20	29	5						
31	**Point Atkinson**	87	91	67	66	54	56	47	43	35	26	22	30	18	23	27	36	44	82	69	64	61	50	49	44	40	32	27	36	12	7					
32	**Point Grey (North Arm Jetty)**	88	92	68	67	55	56	47	43	35	25	21	29	16	19	23	32	40	83	69	64	61	50	49	44	40	32	27	37	13	8	4.5				
33	**Sand Heads**	91	95	71	70	56	59	50	44	36	25	21	28	13	12	13	22	30	86	73	68	66	56	54	49	45	37	32	40	19	15	14	10			
34	Point Roberts	104	108	84	81	77	69	62	55	47	36	32	39	24	20	10	10	17	99	86	81	79	68	67	62	58	50	45	53	32	28	27	23	13		
35	**WHITE ROCK**	117	121	97	94	90	82	75	68	60	49	45	52	37	34	22	15	17	112	99	94	92	81	80	75	71	63	58	66	45	41	40	36	26	13	
36	Point Migley (Lummi Island)	122	127	103	100	96	88	81	74	66	55	51	58	43	38	24	12	3.5	118	105	100	98	87	86	81	77	69	64	72	51	47	46	42	32	19	18

Island Destinations (1–17) — **Mainland Destinations** (18–36)

Route	Distance
CAMPBELL RIVER to Cape Mudge	3
COMOX to Comox Bar	3
COMOX to Chrome Island	16
DEEP BAY to Comox Bar	14
DEEP BAY to Chrome Island	3
NANAIMO to Five Finger Island	4.5
NANAIMO to Entrance Island	6
NANAIMO to Dodd Narrows	5
LUND to Spilsbury Point	7
LUND to Mystery Reef	4
EGMONT to Fearney Point	12
SQUAMISH to Gower Point	27
SQUAMISH to Point Atkinson	24
GIBSONS to Gower Point (via Shoal Channel)	2.5
GIBSONS to Cape Roger Curtis	7
FIRST NARROWS to Point Atkinson	5
FIRST NARROWS to Point Grey	7.5
FALSE CREEK to Point Atkinson	5.5
FALSE CREEK to Point Grey	7
NEW WESTMINSTER to Point Grey	17
NEW WESTMINSTER to Sand Heads	19
STEVESTON to Sand Heads	5
BELLINGHAM to Point Migley	14

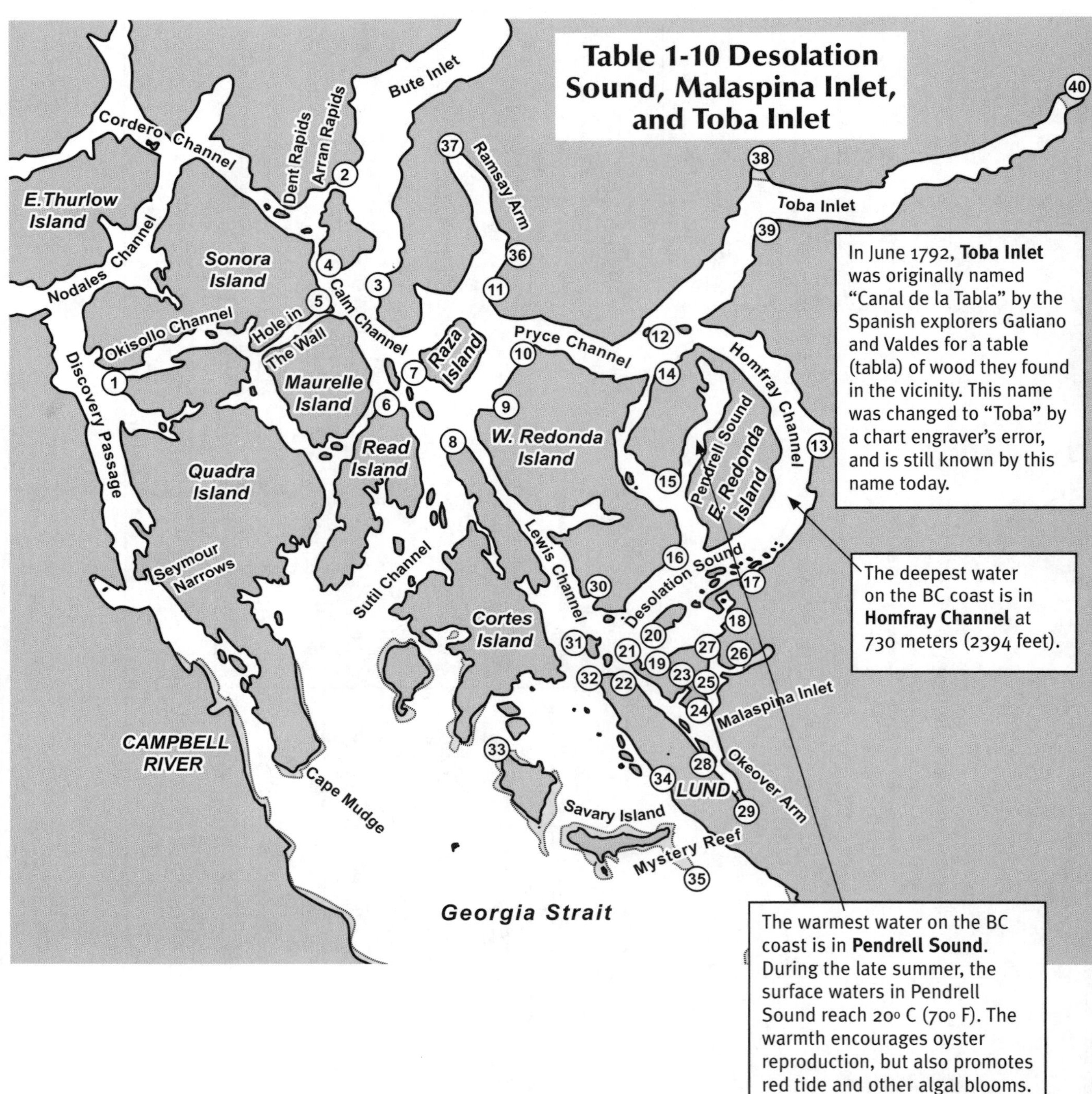
Table 1-10 Desolation Sound, Malaspina Inlet, and Toba Inlet
Cordero Channel
Dent Rapids
Arran Rapids
Bute Inlet
Ramsay Arm
Toba Inlet
E.Thurlow Island
Sonora Island
Nodales Channel
Okisollo Channel
Hole in The Wall
Calm Channel
Raza Island
Pryce Channel
Homfray Channel
Discovery Passage
Maurelle Island
Read Island
W. Redonda Island
Pendrell Sound
E. Redonda Island
Quadra Island
Seymour Narrows
Sutil Channel
Lewis Channel
Desolation Sound
Cortes Island
Malaspina Inlet
Okeover Arm
LUND
CAMPBELL RIVER
Cape Mudge
Savary Island
Mystery Reef
Georgia Strait
1 2 3 4 5 6 7 8 9 10 11 12 13 14 15 16 17 18 19 20 21 22 23 24 25 26 27 28 29 30 31 32 33 34 35 36 37 38 39 40

In June 1792, **Toba Inlet** was originally named "Canal de la Tabla" by the Spanish explorers Galiano and Valdes for a table (tabla) of wood they found in the vicinity. This name was changed to "Toba" by a chart engraver's error, and is still known by this name today.

The deepest water on the BC coast is in **Homfray Channel** at 730 meters (2394 feet).

The warmest water on the BC coast is in **Pendrell Sound**. During the late summer, the surface waters in Pendrell Sound reach 20° C (70° F). The warmth encourages oyster reproduction, but also promotes red tide and other algal blooms.

Table 1-10 DESOLATION SOUND, MALASPINA INLET, AND TOBA INLET

Most Direct Route (Not including routes through Arran or Yaculta Rapids)

Locations in **bold lowercase** appear in other detail tables.

#	Location	1	2	3	4	5	6	7	8	9	10	11	12	13	14	15	16	17	18	19	20	21	22	23	24	25	26	27	28	29	30	31	32	33	34
1	**Granite Point**																																		
2	**Arran Rapids** (Turnback Point)	22																																	
3	**Johnstone Bluff**	13	5.5																																
4	**STUART ISLAND**	13	9	2																															
5	**Basset Point**	11	7	1.5	2																														
6	**Mayes Point**	15	9.5	4.5	6	4																													
7	**Raza Point**	15	9	4.5	5.5	4	2																												
8	**Bullock Bluff**	19	13	7.5	9	7.5	3.5	4																											
9	**Redonda Bay**	19	13	8	9.5	8	5	4	2																										
10	Connis Point	20	14	8.5	10	8.5	6.5	5.5	5	3																									
11	George Head (Ramsay Arm)	18	13	7	8.5	7	7	4	6.5	5	3																								
12	Channel Island (Toba Inlet)	27	21	15	17	15	13	11	12	9.5	6.5	9																							
13	Bohn Point (Forbes Bay)	34	28	23	24	23	21	20	19	17	14	16	7.5																						
14	Dean Point (Waddington Narrows)	25	19	14	15	14	12	11	10	8	5	8	2.5	9.5																					
15	Walter Point (Pendrell Sound)	31	25	20	21	20	18	17	16	14	11	14	8.5	9.5	6																				
16	Marylebone Point (Roscoe Bay)	34	28	23	24	23	19	19	15	17	14	17	11	7.5	8.5	2.5																			
17	Prideaux Haven	36	30	25	26	25	21	21	17	19	16	19	14	6.5	11	5	3																		
18	Tenedos Bay	34	28	23	24	23	19	19	15	17	18	21	15	10	13	6.5	4	4.5																	
19	Galley Bay	32	26	21	22	21	17	17	13	15	18	20	18	12	15	9	6.5	7	5																
20	Mink Island (West)	32	26	21	22	21	17	17	13	15	18	20	16	11	13	7	4.5	5.5	4	2															
21	Zephine Head	31	25	20	21	20	16	16	12	14	17	19	17	12	14	8	5.5	7	5	1	1.5														
22	Josephine Islands	33	27	22	23	22	18	18	14	16	19	21	18	14	16	9.5	7	8.5	6.5	2.5	3	1.5													
23	Grace Harbour	36	30	24	26	24	20	21	17	19	22	24	21	17	19	12	9.5	11	9	5	5.5	4	2.5												
24	Edith Island	36	30	24	26	24	20	21	17	19	22	24	21	17	19	12	9.5	11	9	5	5.5	4	2.5	1.5											
25	Isabel Bay	37	31	26	27	26	22	22	18	20	23	25	22	18	20	14	11	13	11	6.5	7	5.5	4	3	1.5										
26	Galahad Point (Theodosia Inlet)	38	32	27	28	27	23	23	19	21	24	26	23	19	21	15	12	14	12	7.5	8	6.5	5	4	2.5	1.5									
27	Wooton Bay	39	33	27	29	27	23	24	20	22	25	27	24	20	22	15	13	14	12	8	8.5	7	5.5	4.5	3	2	1.5								
28	**OKEOVER**	39	33	27	29	27	23	24	20	22	25	27	24	20	22	15	13	14	12	8	8.5	7	5.5	4.5	3	4.5	6	6							
29	Freke Anchorage	40	34	29	30	29	25	25	21	23	26	28	25	21	23	17	14	16	14	9.5	10	8.5	7	6	4.5	6	7.5	7.5	1.5						
30	**REFUGE COVE**	28	24	18	20	18	14	12	10	12	15	17	18	14	16	9.5	7	9	7	4.5	3.5	3.5	4	6.5	6.5	8	9	9.5	9.5	11					
31	**Kinghorne Rocks**	29	25	19	21	19	15	13	11	13	16	18	17	13	15	8.5	6	8	6.5	3	2	2	3.5	6	6	7.5	8.5	9	9	11	2.5				
32	**Sarah Point**	30	26	20	22	20	16	20	13	15	18	20	18	14	16	9.5	7	8.5	6.5	3	3	1.5	2.5	5	5	6.5	7.5	8	8	9.5	1.5	4			
33	**Spilsbury Point**	30	30	24	26	24	20	19	17	19	22	24	24	20	22	16	13	14	12	8.5	8.5	7	8	11	11	12	13	14	14	15	5.5	8	5.5		
34	**LUND**	36	32	26	28	26	22	21	19	21	24	26	24	20	22	16	13	15	13	9	9	7.5	8.5	11	11	13	14	14	14	16	7.5	10	6	7	
35	**Mystery Reef**	38	37	31	33	31	26	26	24	26	29	31	29	25	27	21	18	20	18	14	14	13	14	17	17	18	19	20	20	21	12	15	11	11	4

RAMSAY ARM

Location	Quatam River	Head of Ramsay Arm	#
George Head (Ramsay Arm)	2.5	7	11
Quatam River		4.5	36
Head of Ramsay Arm			37

TOBA INLET

Location	Brem Bay	Snout Point	Tahumming River	#
Channel Island (Toba Inlet)	8	6.5	19	12
Brem Bay		2	13	38
Snout Point			12	39
Tahumming River				40

Bute Inlet 1862—Alfred Waddington, an entrepreneur from California, began construction of a wagon road from the head of **Bute Inlet** to **Fort Alexandria** in the **Chilcotin** country. In the spring of 1864, a band of Chilcotins, under the direction of Chief Tellot, descended from the interior plateau country and killed 14 of the 17 workers in Waddington's camp. Waddington's plans came to naught after this incident. Five of the killers were later hanged.

Waddington Harbour at the head of Bute Inlet and **Mount Waddington**, the highest mountain in the **Coast Range**, retain his name.

A decade later, **Bute Inlet** was considered as a route for the Canadian Pacific Railway. The plan called for the railway to negotiate the steep sides of the inlet, island hop to **Vancouver Island**, and proceed to a terminus at **Victoria.** However, cooler heads prevailed and **Burrard Inlet** was finally chosen as the terminus.

In the extreme turbulent flows that develop in the tidal rapids in the area, warm fresh surface water and the cold, dense water beneath are aerated and thoroughly mixed, providing ideal conditions for the growth of sea life in the channels between islands.

Arran Rapids is the most turbulent and dangerous of the tidal rapids in the area. Though the official current figures for **Arran Rapids** show maximum currents of nine knots, this is an average speed in the middle of the channel. Locally, the current may reach 14 knots.

Table 1-11 Cape Mudge to Stuart Island

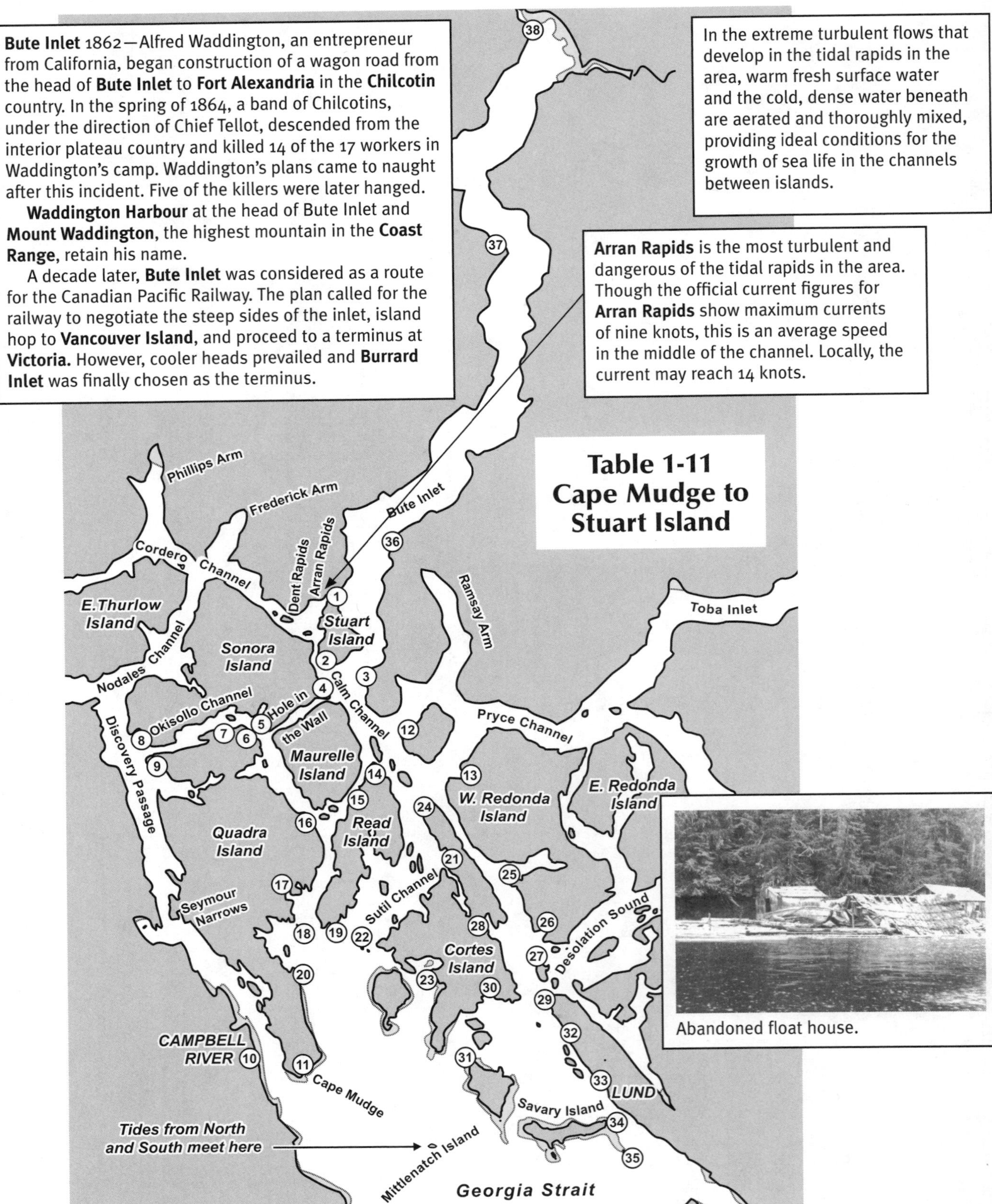

Phillips Arm
Frederick Arm
Bute Inlet
Arran Rapids
Dent Rapids
Cordero Channel
E. Thurlow Island
Stuart Island
Ramsay Arm
Toba Inlet
Sonora Island
Nodales Channel
Calm Channel
Okisollo Channel
Hole in the Wall
Discovery Passage
Maurelle Island
Pryce Channel
W. Redonda Island
E. Redonda Island
Quadra Island
Read Island
Sutil Channel
Desolation Sound
Seymour Narrows
Cortes Island
CAMPBELL RIVER
Cape Mudge
Savary Island
LUND
Tides from North and South meet here
Mittlenatch Island
Georgia Strait
1
2
3
4
5
6
7
8
9
10
11
12
13
14
15
16
17
18
19
20
21
22
23
24
25
26
27
28
29
30
31
32
33
34
35
36
37
38

Abandoned float house.

Table 1-11 CAPE MUDGE TO STUART ISLAND

Most Direct Route (Not including routes through Arran or Yaculta Rapids)

Locations in **bold lowercase** appear in other detail tables.

No.	Location	1	2	3	4	5	6	7	8	9	10	11	12	13	14	15	16	17	18	19	20	21	22	23	24	25	26	27	28	29	30	31	32	33	34
1	**Arran Rapids (Turnback Point)**																																		
2	**STUART ISLAND LANDING**	9																																	
3	**Johnstone Bluff**	5.5	2																																
4	**Basset Point**	7	2	1.5																															
5	West End Hole in the Wall	11	6	5.5	4																														
6	Cooper Point (Okisollo Upper Rapids)	16	7	6.5	5	1																													
7	Okisollo Lower Rapids	17	8	7.5	6	2	1																												
8	**Cinque Islands**	23	14	14	12	8	7	6																											
9	**Granite Point**	22	13	13	11	7	6	5	1																										
10	**CAMPBELL RIVER**	39	30	30	28	24	13	22	18	17																									
11	**Cape Mudge**	36	27	27	25	24	26	25	21	20	3																								
12	**Raza Point**	9	5.5	4.5	4	8	9	10	16	15	26	23																							
13	**Redonda Bay**	13	9.5	8	8	12	13	14	20	19	25	22	4																						
14	**Mayes Point**	9.5	6	4.5	4	8	9	10	16	15	25	22	2	5																					
15	Whiterock Passage	12	7.5	6.5	5.5	7	8	9	15	14	24	21	4.5	7	2																				
16	Surge Narrows (Antonio Point)	14	11	9	8.5	5	5.5	6.5	13	12	22	19	7	9.5	4.5	2.5																			
17	Village Bay	23	18	18	16	12	12	13	19	18	17	14	11	14	8.5	6.5	6.5																		
18	Breton Islands	23	18	18	16	12	13	14	20	19	16	13	12	15	9.5	7.5	7	1.5																	
19	**Viner Point**	24	19	19	17	13	13	14	20	19	15	12	13	16	11	8.5	7.5	3	1.5																
20	Rebecca Spit	25	20	20	18	14	16	17	23	22	15	12	17	14	14	9.5	9	3.5	2	3															
21	Von Donop Inlet	18	13	13	11	15	16	17	23	22	21	18	9.5	5.5	7	9	14	9.5	8	6.5	9.5														
22	Subtle Islands	21	16	16	14	14	15	16	22	21	15	12	13	9.5	10	10	9	4.5	3	1.5	4	6													
23	Gorge Harbour	25	20	20	18	18	19	20	26	25	14	11	17	14	14	14	13	8.5	7	5.5	7.5	9.5	4.5												
24	Bullock Bluff	13	9	8	7.5	13	13	14	20	19	23	20	4	2	3.5	5.5	8	12	10	8.5	12	3.5	7.5	12											
25	Joyce Point (Teakerne Arm)	19	15	13	13	17	17	18	24	23	24	21	8	7.5	9	11	14	17	15	14	18	9	13	18	5.5										
26	**REFUGE COVE**	24	20	18	18	22	22	23	29	28	21	18	12	12	14	16	18	22	20	19	20	14	18	16	10	4.5									
27	**Kinghorne Rocks**	25	21	19	19	23	23	24	30	29	19	16	13	13	15	17	19	23	21	20	18	15	17	13	11	5.5	2.5								
28	**SQUIRREL COVE**	23	19	17	17	21	21	22	28	27	22	19	15	11	13	15	17	21	19	18	21	13	17	16	9	3.5	3	2.5							
29	**Sarah Point**	26	22	20	20	24	24	25	31	30	19	16	20	15	16	18	21	21	19	17	18	18	17	13	13	7	4	1.5	4.5						
30	**Cortes Bay**	28	24	22	23	26	26	27	33	32	15	12	22	17	19	25	23	19	17	16	16	19	14	11	15	9	6.5	4	6.5	3.5					
31	**Spilsbury Point**	30	26	24	24	28	26	27	21	30	13	10	19	19	20	20	19	14	13	11	12	17	11	7.5	17	11	8	5.5	8.5	5.5	4.5				
32	**BLISS LANDING**	29	25	23	23	27	27	28	34	33	18	15	18	18	18	20	24	19	17	16	17	19	16	12	16	10	6.5	4	6.5	2	4.5	4.5			
33	**LUND**	32	28	26	26	30	30	31	37	36	20	17	21	21	22	24	27	22	20	18	19	22	18	15	19	13	10	7.5	10	6	8.5	7	4.5		
34	Mace Point	34	30	28	28	32	32	33	39	38	21	18	23	23	23	25	29	23	21	19	20	24	19	16	21	15	12	9	12	7.5	9.5	8	6	2	
35	**Mystery Reef**	37	33	31	31	35	32	33	39	38	23	20	26	26	26	28	32	26	24	23	23	27	22	19	24	18	15	12	15	11	13	11	9	4	3

BUTE INLET

Location	Fawn Bluff	Boyd Point	Waddington Harbour	No.
Johnstone Bluff	8	25	38	**3**
Fawn Bluff		17	30	**36**
Boyd Point			13	**37**
Waddington Harbour				**38**

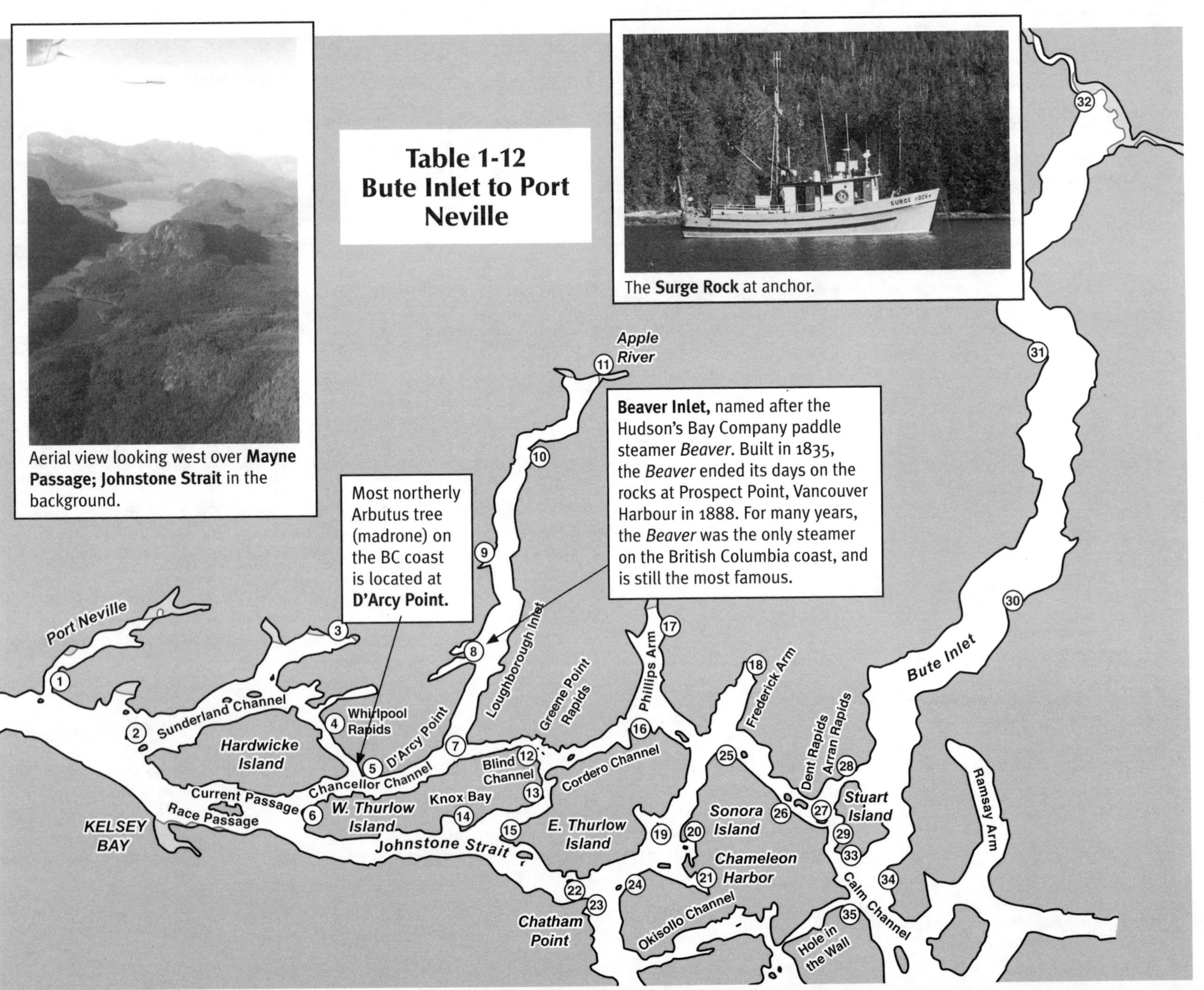
Table 1-12
Bute Inlet to Port Neville
Port Neville
Sunderland Channel
Hardwicke Island
Whirlpool Rapids
D'Arcy Point
Loughborough Inlet
Apple River
Greene Point Rapids
Phillips Arm
Frederick Arm
Dent Rapids
Arran Rapids
Bute Inlet
Ramsay Arm
Stuart Island
Calm Channel
Hole in the Wall
Sonora Island
Chameleon Harbor
Okisollo Channel
E. Thurlow Island
Cordero Channel
Blind Channel
Knox Bay
W. Thurlow Island
Chancellor Channel
Current Passage
Race Passage
KELSEY BAY
Johnstone Strait
Chatham Point
1
2
3
4
5
6
7
8
9
10
11
12
13
14
15
16
17
18
19
20
21
22
23
24
25
26
27
28
29
30
31
32
33
34
35
Most northerly Arbutus tree (madrone) on the BC coast is located at **D'Arcy Point.**
Beaver Inlet, named after the Hudson's Bay Company paddle steamer *Beaver*. Built in 1835, the *Beaver* ended its days on the rocks at Prospect Point, Vancouver Harbour in 1888. For many years, the *Beaver* was the only steamer on the British Columbia coast, and is still the most famous.

Aerial view looking west over **Mayne Passage; Johnstone Strait** in the background.

The **Surge Rock** at anchor.

Table 1-12 BUTE INLET TO PORT NEVILLE

Most Direct Route (Not including routes through Race and Current Passages)

Locations in **bold lowercase** appear in other detail tables.

No.	Location	1	2	3	4	5	6	7	8	9	10	11	12	13	14	15	16	17	18	19	20	21	22	23	24	25	26	27	28	29	30	31	32	33	34
1	**PORT NEVILLE**																																		
2	**Fanny Island**	4.5																																	
3	Haswell Point (Topaze Harbour)	15	11																																
4	**Whirlpool Rapids**	14	9.5	7																															
5	**D'Arcy Point**	17	13	10	3																														
6	**Eden Point**	19	15	13	5	3																													
7	Lyall Islet	22	18	15	7.5	4.5	8																												
8	Mary Point (Beaver Inlet)	26	22	19	12	8.5	12	4.5																											
9	Heydon Bay	30	26	23	16	13	16	9	5																										
10	Towry Head	35	31	28	21	18	21	14	9.5	5.5																									
11	Apple River	40	36	33	26	23	26	18	14	10	4.5																								
12	Green Point Rapids (Cordero Island)	26	22	19	12	9	11	3.5	8	13	18	23																							
13	**BLIND CHANNEL**	28	24	21	14	11	13	5.5	10	15	20	25	2																						
14	Needham Point (Knox Bay)	33	29	26	19	15	18	10	15	20	25	30	6.5	5																					
15	**Edith Point**	32	28	25	18	14	17	8.5	13	18	23	28	5.5	3.5	1.5																				
16	Godwin Point (Shoal Bay)	32	28	25	18	14	17	9	14	19	24	29	5.5	6	11	10																			
17	Dyer Point (Phillips Arm)	36	32	29	22	18	21	13	18	23	28	33	9.5	10	14	13	4																		
18	Estero Rapids (Frederick Arm)	38	34	31	24	21	23	16	20	25	30	35	12	13	18	17	6.5	9.5																	
19	Lee Islands	38	34	31	24	21	23	16	20	25	30	35	12	13	11	9.5	7	10	8																
20	Block Island (Thurston Bay)	39	35	32	25	22	24	17	21	26	31	36	13	14	11	9.5	7.5	11	9	1.4															
21	Cameleon Harbour	41	37	34	27	24	26	19	23	28	33	38	15	14	12	10	9.5	13	11	3	2.5														
22	**Turn Island Light**	43	39	36	29	26	28	21	25	30	35	40	9.5	7.5	5.5	4	12	15	13	5	5.5	6													
23	**Chatham Point**	43	39	36	29	26	28	21	25	30	35	40	11	8.5	6.5	5	11	14	13	4.5	5	5.5	1												
24	**Howe Island (Nodales Channel)**	44	40	30	23	20	29	16	20	25	30	34	12	9.5	7.5	6	10	13	11	3	3.5	4.5	2	1											
25	Hall Point	36	32	29	22	18	21	13	18	23	28	33	9.5	9.5	15	14	3.5	6.5	3.5	4.5	5.5	7.5	9.5	9	7.5										
26	Dent Rapids	39	35	32	25	22	24	17	21	26	31	36	13	14	19	18	8	10	7	8	9	12	13	13	11	3.5									
27	Gillard Passage	41	37	34	27	23	26	18	23	28	33	38	15	15	20	19	9	12	9	10	11	14	15	15	14	6	1.5								
28	**Arran Rapids (Turnback Point)**	43	39	36	29	25	28	20	25	30	35	40	17	17	22	21	11	14	11	12	13	16	17	17	15	7	3.5	2							
29	Yaculta Rapids	42	38	35	28	24	27	19	24	29	34	39	16	16	21	20	10	13	9.5	11	12	15	16	16	15	7	2.5	1	2.5						
30	**Fawn Bluff**	47	43	40	33	30	32	25	29	34	39	44	21	22	27	26	16	18	15	16	17	20	21	21	20	12	8	7	5	7.5					
31	**Boyd Point**	64	60	57	50	47	49	42	46	51	56	61	38	39	44	43	33	35	32	33	34	37	38	38	37	29	25	24	22	25	17				
32	**Waddington Harbour**	77	73	70	63	60	62	55	59	64	69	74	51	52	57	56	46	48	45	46	47	50	51	51	50	42	38	37	35	38	30	13			
33	**STUART ISLAND**	46	42	39	32	29	31	24	28	33	38	43	20	21	26	25	15	17	14	15	16	19	20	20	16	8	7	2.5	4	1.2	9	26	39		
34	**Johnstone Bluff**	48	44	41	34	31	33	26	30	35	40	45	22	23	28	27	17	19	16	17	18	21	22	22	18	10	9	4	6	3	8	25	38	2	
35	**Bassett Point** (Hole in the Wall)	48	44	41	34	31	33	26	30	35	40	45	22	23	28	27	17	19	16	17	18	21	22	22	18	10	9	4	6	3	10	26	40	2	1.5

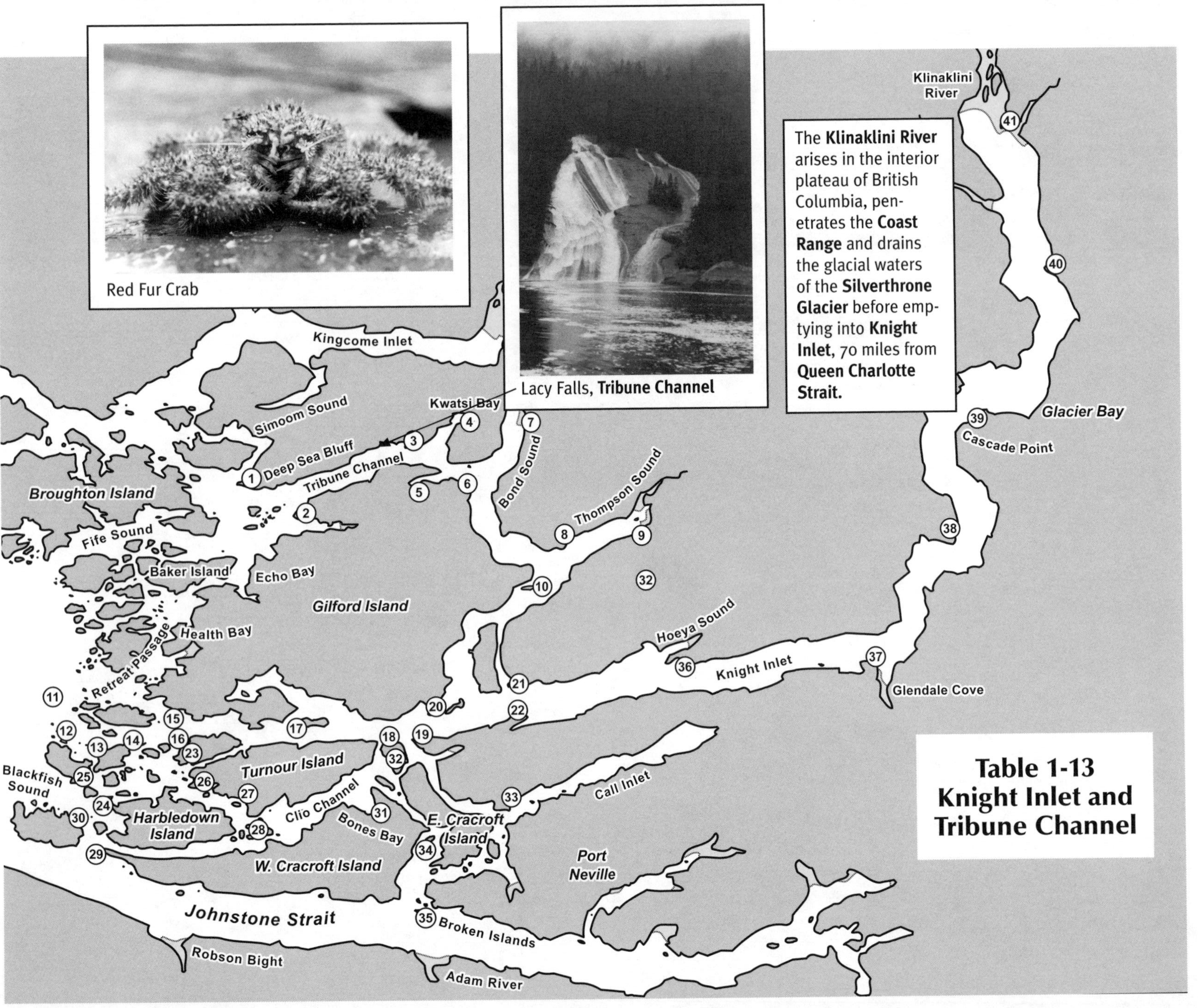
Table 1-13
Knight Inlet and
Tribune Channel
The **Klinaklini River** arises in the interior plateau of British Columbia, penetrates the **Coast Range** and drains the glacial waters of the **Silverthrone Glacier** before emptying into **Knight Inlet**, 70 miles from **Queen Charlotte Strait.**
Red Fur Crab
Lacy Falls, **Tribune Channel**
Klinaklini River
Glacier Bay
Cascade Point
Glendale Cove
Knight Inlet
Hoeya Sound
Thompson Sound
Bond Sound
Kwatsi Bay
Kingcome Inlet
Simoom Sound
Deep Sea Bluff
Tribune Channel
Broughton Island
Fife Sound
Baker Island
Echo Bay
Gilford Island
Health Bay
Retreat Passage
Blackfish Sound
Turnour Island
Harbledown Island
Clio Channel
Bones Bay
E. Cracroft Island
W. Cracroft Island
Call Inlet
Port Neville
Johnstone Strait
Broken Islands
Robson Bight
Adam River

Table 1-13 KNIGHT INLET AND TRIBUNE CHANNEL

Most Direct Route

Locations in **bold lowercase** appear in other detail tables.

No.	Location	1	2	3	4	5	6	7	8	9	10	11	12	13	14	15	16	17	18	19	20	21	22	23	24	25	26	27	28	29	30	31	32	33	34
1	**Deep Sea Bluff**																																		
2	**King Point (Viner Sound)**	3.5																																	
3	Gormely Point	8	6																																
4	Kwatsi Bay Anchorage	11	9.5	3.5																															
5	Wakahna Bay Anchorage	12	9.5	3.5	4.5																														
6	Irvine Point	11	9	3	4	2.5																													
7	Ahta River	15	13	6.5	7.5	6	3.5																												
8	London Point	17	15	9	10	8.5	6	8.5																											
9	Sackville Island	21	19	13	14	12	9.5	13	3.5																										
10	Kumlah Island	17	16	9.5	10	8.7	6.3	9	2.2	6																									
11	**Whitecliff Islet**	15	14	20	24	24	23	27	27	31	25																								
12	**Wedge Island**	16	16	22	26	26	25	29	28	32	26	1.5																							
13	Charles Point	17	16	22	26	26	15	29	25	29	23	3	2																						
14	**Rocky Point**	15	15	21	25	25	24	28	23	27	21	4	3.5	2																					
15	**Ridge Rock**	14	13	19	23	23	22	26	21	25	19	6.5	6	4.5	2																				
16	Warr Bluff	15	14	20	24	24	23	27	21	25	19	6	5.5	4.5	2	1																			
17	Lord Islet	20	20	26	24	23	20	24	16	20	14	11	11	9.5	7	5	5																		
18	White Nob Point	28	26	20	20	19	16	19	12	16	10	15	17	13	11	9	9.5	4																	
19	Littleton Point	27	25	19	19	18	15	18	11	15	9	17	19	15	12	10	11	5.5	1																
20	Doctor Islets	26	24	18	18	17	14	17	10	14	8	17	17	15	13	11	11	6	2	1.5															
21	Steep Head	23	21	15	15	14	12	14	7.5	11	5	21	22	20	17	15	15	10	6	5	4														
22	Protection Point	29	29	23	23	22	19	22	15	19	13	22	21	20	18	16	16	11	6.5	5.5	5	1.5													
23	**MAMALILACULA**	16	15	21	25	25	24	28	22	26	20	6	5.5	4.5	2	1.5	1	6	11	12	12	16	17												
24	**Whitebeach Passage**	21	20	27	31	31	30	31	26	30	24	5	4	2	5.5	6	5	10	15	16	16	20	21	4											
25	West Passage	21	21	27	31	31	31	32	26	30	24	4.5	3.5	1.5	3.5	5.5	5	10	15	16	16	20	21	4.5	1										
26	**Mink Point**	18	18	24	28	28	27	32	25	29	23	7	7	5	3.5	3.5	2.5	8.5	12	14	15	19	19	2	4	4.5									
27	**KARLUKWEES**	35	34	28	28	27	24	27	20	24	18	11	11	8.5	8	7	6	11	8	9	10	14	15	6	7.5	8	3.5								
28	Wilson Passage (North end)	35	34	28	28	27	24	27	20	24	18	11	11	9	8	7	6.5	11	8	9	10	14	15	7	8	8.5	4	1							
29	**Cracroft Point**	23	23	29	33	33	31	34	27	31	25	7	6.5	4.5	9	8.5	7.5	17	15	16	17	21	22	6.5	2.5	3	11	8	7						
30	**Blackney Passage**	22	21	27	31	31	30	33	26	30	24	6	5.5	3.5	8	7.5	6.5	16	14	15	16	20	23	5.5	1.5	2	4	8.5	8	1					
31	**Bones Bay**	31	30	24	24	23	20	23	16	20	14	16	18	14	14	12	12	7	3.5	4.5	6	9.5	10	12	13	14	9	5.5	6	13	14				
32	**MINSTREL ISLAND**	28	27	21	21	20	17	20	13	17	11	19	17	17	13	11	11	5.5	2	1	2.5	6	6.5	12	16	17	12	8	8.5	16	16	3.5			
33	Ray Point	32	31	25	25	24	21	24	17	21	15	23	21	21	17	15	16	10	6.5	5.5	7	11	11	17	20	21	16	13	13	21	21	8	4.5		
34	**Port Harvey**	38	37	31	31	30	27	30	23	27	21	30	28	28	24	22	23	17	13	12	13	17	18	24	20	20	23	20	20	21	18	15	11	6.5	
35	**Broken Islands**	38	37	31	31	30	27	30	23	27	21	29	28	27	24	22	22	17	13	12	13	17	18	23	18	18	22	19	19	15	16	14	11	6	3.5

Route	Distance	No.
Lord Islet to Port Elizabeth Anchorage	4	14
Ray Point to head of Call Inlet	11	31

KNIGHT INLET

Location								No.
Protection Point	1.5	6.5	16	22	29	36	42	22
Steep Head		7.5	18	24	31	38	45	21
Hoeya Head			10	16	23	30	37	36
MacDonald Point (Glendale Cove)				6.5	13	20	27	37
Kwalate Point					6.5	14	21	38
Cascade Point						7	14	39
Wahkash Point							6.5	40
Dutchman Head (Klinaklini River)								41

Table 1-14 Johnstone Strait and Discovery Passage

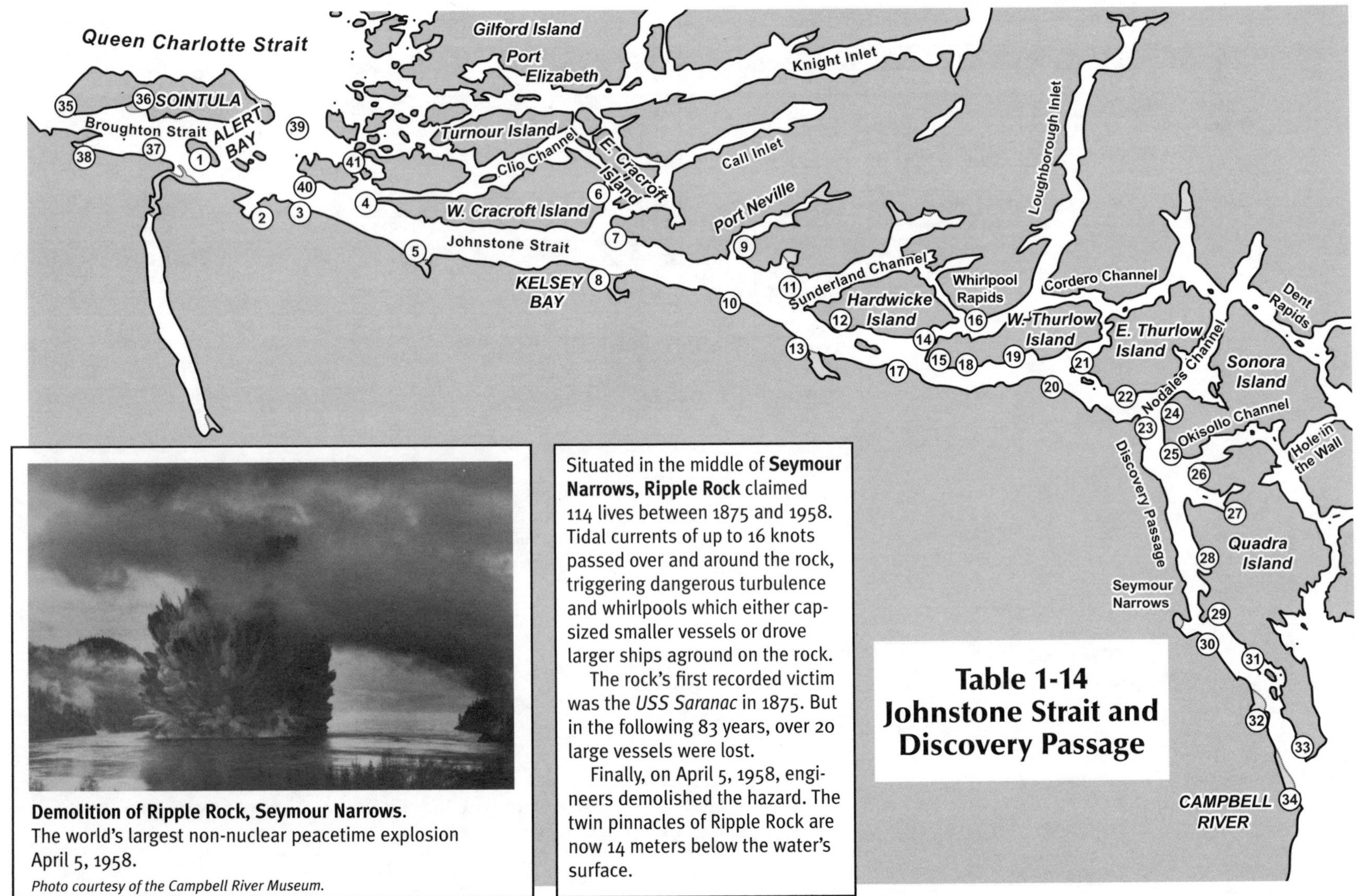
Queen Charlotte Strait
SOINTULA
Broughton Strait
ALERT BAY
Gilford Island
Port Elizabeth
Knight Inlet
Turnour Island
Clio Channel
E. Cracroft Island
Call Inlet
W. Cracroft Island
Johnstone Strait
KELSEY BAY
Port Neville
Loughborough Inlet
Sunderland Channel
Hardwicke Island
Whirlpool Rapids
W. Thurlow Island
Cordero Channel
E. Thurlow Island
Nodales Channel
Dent Rapids
Sonora Island
Okisollo Channel
Hole in the Wall
Discovery Passage
Quadra Island
Seymour Narrows
CAMPBELL RIVER
1
2
3
4
5
6
7
8
9
10
11
12
13
14
15
16
17
18
19
20
21
22
23
24
25
26
27
28
29
30
31
32
33
34
35
36
37
38
39
40
41

Demolition of Ripple Rock, Seymour Narrows.
The world's largest non-nuclear peacetime explosion April 5, 1958.
Photo courtesy of the Campbell River Museum.

Situated in the middle of **Seymour Narrows, Ripple Rock** claimed 114 lives between 1875 and 1958. Tidal currents of up to 16 knots passed over and around the rock, triggering dangerous turbulence and whirlpools which either capsized smaller vessels or drove larger ships aground on the rock.

The rock's first recorded victim was the *USS Saranac* in 1875. But in the following 83 years, over 20 large vessels were lost.

Finally, on April 5, 1958, engineers demolished the hazard. The twin pinnacles of Ripple Rock are now 14 meters below the water's surface.

Table 1-14 JOHNSTONE STRAIT AND DISCOVERY PASSAGE

Most Direct Route (All passages via Race Passage except where underlined)

Locations in **bold lowercase** appear in other detail tables.

No.	Location	1	2	3	4	5	6	7	8	9	10	11	12	13	14	15	16	17	18	19	20	21	22	23	24	25	26	27	28	29	30	31	32	33
1	**ALERT BAY**																																	
2	**TELEGRAPH COVE**	4.5																																
3	**Blinkhorn Peninsula**	6.5	2.5																															
4	**Cracroft Point**	10.5	6.5	4																														
5	Robson Bight	15	11	8	5																													
6	**Port Harvey**	28	24	21	17	14																												
7	**Broken Islands**	26	22	19	15	11	3																											
8	Adam River	27	23	20	17	13	5.5	3																										
9	**PORT NEVILLE**	35	31	28	24	20	13	9	8																									
10	Hickey Point	34	30	27	24	20	12	9	7.5	2.5																								
11	**Fanny Island**	39	35	32	28	24	16	13	11	4.5	3.5																							
12	Earl Ledge	42	38	35	31	27	19	17	15	8.5	7	4																						
13	**KELSEY BAY**	41	37	34	30	26	18	15	14	8	6	4	2																					
14	**Eden Point**	47	43	40	36	32	24	21	20	14	12	9	5	6.5																				
15	Tyee Point	48	44	41	36	32	24	22	20	14	12	9	5	7	1																			
16	**D'Arcy Point**	51	47	44	40	36	28	25	24	17	16	12	8	10	3	4																		
17	Camp Point	46	42	39	35	31	23	20	19	13	11	9	4	5	2	1.5	5																	
18	Vansittart Point	50	46	43	38	34	26	23	22	16	14	11	8	8.5	2.5	2	6	3.5																
19	**Needham Point/Knox Bay**	55	51	48	44	40	32	29	28	21	20	17	14	14	8	7.5	12	9	5.5															
20	Ripple Point	56	52	49	45	41	33	30	29	22	21	18	14	15	9	8.5	14	9.5	6.5	1														
21	**Edith Point (Mayne Passage)**	57	53	50	46	42	34	31	30	24	22	19	15	16	10	9.5	15	10	7.5	1.5	1													
22	**Turn Island Light**	61	57	54	52	48	40	37	36	27	28	24	19	20	15	13	19	14	11	5.5	4.5	4												
23	**Chatham Point**	62	58	55	53	49	41	36	37	28	29	25	20	21	15	15	20	16	12	7.5	6	5	1											
24	**Howe Island (Nodales Channel)**	64	60	57	54	50	42	39	38	29	30	26	21	22	17	15	21	16	13	7.5	6.5	6	2	1										
25	**Cinque Islands**	66	62	59	56	52	44	41	40	31	32	28	23	24	19	17	23	18	15	9.5	8.5	8	4	3	3									
26	**Granite Point (Okisollo Channel)**	67	63	60	57	53	45	42	41	32	33	29	24	25	20	18	24	19	16	11	9.5	9	5	4	4	1								
27	Granite Bay	71	67	64	61	57	49	46	45	36	37	33	28	29	24	22	28	23	20	15	14	13	9	8	8	5	4							
28	Separation Head	72	68	65	63	59	51	46	47	38	39	35	30	31	26	25	30	25	22	17	16	15	11	10	10	7	6	7.5						
29	Maud Island/Seymour Narrows	75	71	68	66	62	54	49	50	41	42	38	33	34	29	28	33	28	25	20	19	18	14	13	13	10	9	11	3					
30	Race Point	78	74	71	68	64	56	53	52	43	44	40	35	36	31	29	35	30	27	22	21	20	16	15	15	12	11	12	4.5	1.5				
31	Steep Islet/Duncan Bay	80	76	73	71	67	59	54	55	46	47	43	38	39	34	33	38	33	30	25	24	28	19	18	18	15	14	16	8	5	3			
32	**CAMPBELL RIVER**	83	79	76	74	70	62	57	58	49	50	46	41	42	37	36	41	36	33	28	27	31	22	21	21	18	17	19	11	8	6	3		
33	**Cape Mudge**	86	82	79	76	72	64	60	60	51	52	49	44	45	39	39	43	38	35	30	30	34	24	23	24	21	20	22	14	11	9	6	3	
34	Willow Point	87	83	80	77	73	65	62	61	52	53	49	44	45	40	38	44	39	36	31	30	29	25	24	25	22	21	23	15	12	10	7	4	1

BROUGHTON STRAIT

Location	No.	36	37	38	1	39	40	2	41	3	4
Pulteney Point	35	5.5	5.5	7	10	14	15	15	19	16	19
SOINTULA	36		1.5	3.5	5	9	10	9	15	11	15
Haddington Island	37			2	3.5	8	9	8	14	10	13
PORT MCNEIL	38				6	10	11	10	16	12	15
ALERT BAY	1					5.5	5.5	4.5	11	6.5	10
Stubbs Island	39						2	3.5	6	4	7
Weynton Island	40							2	5.5	2	5
TELEGRAPH COVE	2								6.5	2.5	6
Blackney Passage	41									4.5	1
Blinkhorn Peninsula	3										4
Cracroft Point	4										

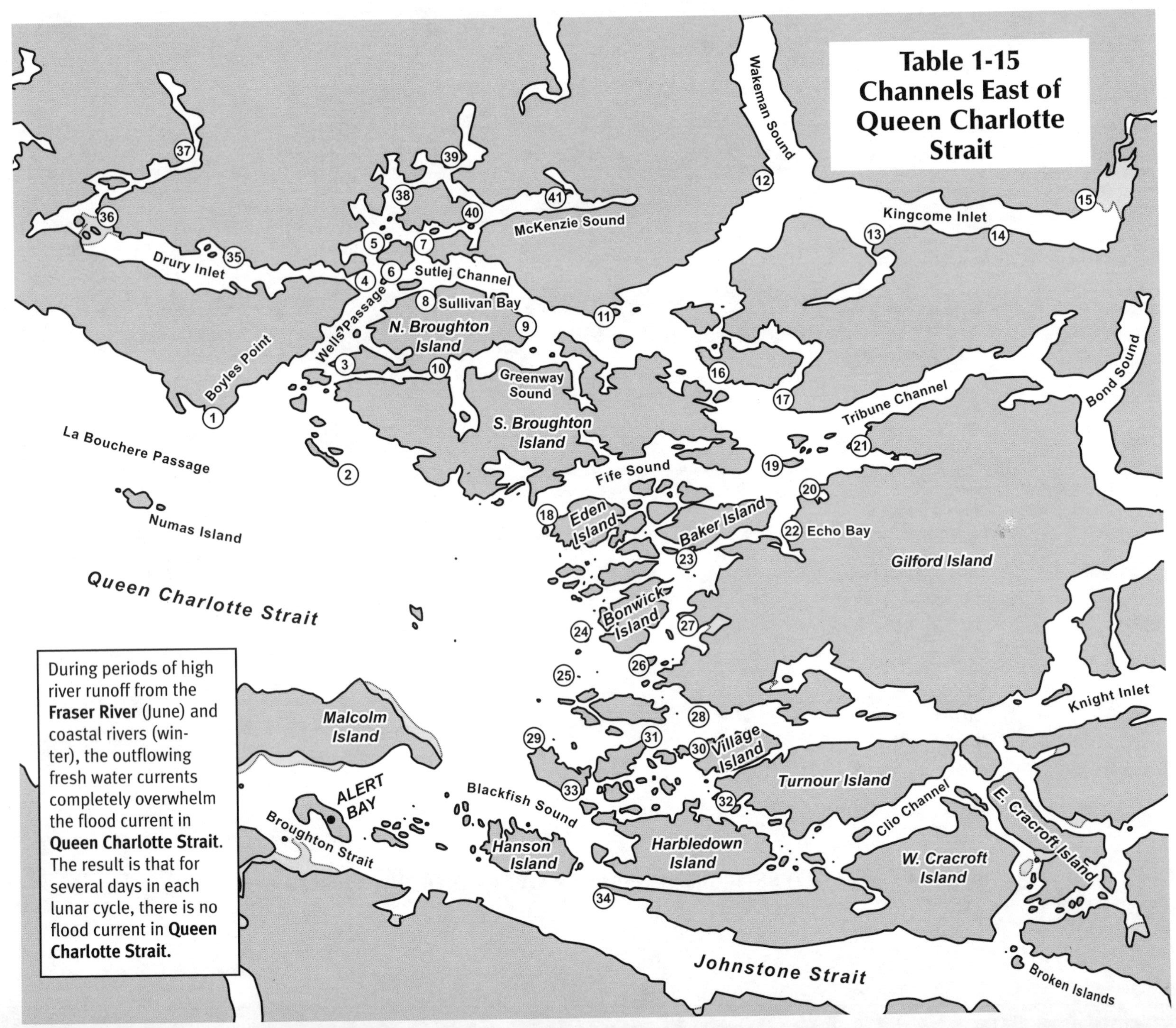
Table 1-15
Channels East of
Queen Charlotte
Strait
Wakeman Sound
Kingcome Inlet
Bond Sound
Tribune Channel
McKenzie Sound
Drury Inlet
Sutlej Channel
Sullivan Bay
N. Broughton Island
Wells Passage
Boyles Point
Greenway Sound
S. Broughton Island
La Bouchere Passage
Numas Island
Fife Sound
Eden Island
Baker Island
Echo Bay
Gilford Island
Queen Charlotte Strait
Bonwick Island
Knight Inlet
Malcolm Island
Village Island
Turnour Island
ALERT BAY
Blackfish Sound
Broughton Strait
Hanson Island
Harbledown Island
Clio Channel
E. Cracroft Island
W. Cracroft Island
Johnstone Strait
Broken Islands
1
2
3
4
5
6
7
8
9
10
11
12
13
14
15
16
17
18
19
20
21
22
23
24
25
26
27
28
29
30
31
32
33
34
35
36
37
38
39
40
41
During periods of high river runoff from the **Fraser River** (June) and coastal rivers (winter), the outflowing fresh water currents completely overwhelm the flood current in **Queen Charlotte Strait**. The result is that for several days in each lunar cycle, there is no flood current in **Queen Charlotte Strait.**

Table 1-15 CHANNELS EAST OF QUEEN CHARLOTTE STRAIT

Most Direct Route

Locations in **bold lowercase** appear in other detail tables.

No.	Location	1	2	3	4	5	6	7	8	9	10	11	12	13	14	15	16	17	18	19	20	21	22	23	24	25	26	27	28	29	30	31	32	33
1	**Boyles Point**																																	
2	**Brig Rock**	5																																
3	Bourmaster Point	3.5	5.5																															
4	Morris Islet (Drury Inlet)	7	9	3																														
5	Kinnaird Rock (Grappler Sound)	8	10	4	1.5																													
6	Surgeon Islets	7	9	3.5	1	1.5																												
7	Cunning Point	9	11	6	3	2	2.5																											
8	**SULLIVAN BAY**	11	13	7.5	3	3	2	2																										
9	Cardale Head	13	15	9.5	7	7	6	5.5	4.5																									
10	Broughton Point	17	19	13	11	11	10	9.5	8.5	4																								
11	Phillip Point	17	17	12	9.5	9.5	8.5	7.5	7	2.5	6																							
12	Upton Point	25	25	20	17	17	16	15	15	10	14	7.5																						
13	Edmund Islet (Belle Isle Sound)	26	26	23	21	21	20	19	18	14	17	11	4																					
14	Halliday Point	30	30	27	25	25	24	23	22	18	21	15	7.5	4.5																				
15	**KINGCOME**	33	33	30	28	28	27	26	25	21	24	18	11	8	4																			
16	Steep Point (Penphrase Passage)	21	19	16	14	14	13	12	11	6.5	10	4	9	12	16	20																		
17	**Deep Sea Bluff**	22	17	19	17	17	16	15	14	9	13	6.5	12	15	21	23	2.5																	
18	**Duff Islet**	12	7	28	26	26	25	24	23	19	22	16	21	24	28	32	12	10																
19	Village Point	20	16	20	18	18	17	16	15	10	14	7.5	13	16	20	24	3.5	2	8.5															
20	Evangeline Rock	21	17	22	19	19	18	17	16	12	15	10	15	18	22	26	6	3.5	10	1.5														
21	**King Point**	23	18	21	20	20	19	18	17	12	16	9.5	15	18	22	26	5.5	3.5	11	2.5	2													
22	**ECHO BAY**	22	17	20	20	20	19	18	17	12	16	9.5	15	18	22	26	5.5	3	10	1	2	3.5												
23	Steep Islet	21	14	20	23	23	22	21	20	16	19	13	18	21	25	29	9	7	7	5	5	7	4											
24	**Fog Islet**	15	10	16	19	20	19	25	14	20	23	17	22	25	29	33	13	11	5	9	9	11	8	4										
25	**House Islet**	15	10	16	19	20	19	21	23	24	27	21	26	29	33	37	17	14	5.5	12	12	14	11	7	2.5									
26	Seabreeze Island	19	14	20	23	24	23	25	24	20	24	17	22	25	29	33	13	11	8	9	9	11	8	4	4	2.5								
27	**HEALTH BAY**	19	15	20	24	24	24	24	23	19	22	16	21	24	28	32	12	9.5	9.5	7.5	7.5	9.5	6.2	2.5	6.5	4	1.5							
28	**Ridge Rock**	20	15	21	24	25	24	26	28	24	27	21	26	29	33	37	17	15	11	13	13	15	12	7.5	8	5	3.5	5.2						
29	**Wedge Island**	16	12	18	21	22	21	23	25	25	28	22	27	30	34	38	18	16	8	14	14	16	13	8.5	5	2.5	4.5	6.5	5.5					
30	**MAMMILILLACULA**	23	18	24	27	28	27	29	29	25	28	22	27	30	34	38	18	16	13	14	14	16	13	8.5	10	6.5	5	6.5	1.5	5.5				
31	**Rocky Point**	20	15	21	24	25	24	26	28	24	27	21	26	29	33	37	17	15	10	13	13	15	12	8	7	7.2	5.5	7	2	3.5	3			
32	**Mink Point**	24	19	25	28	29	28	30	31	27	30	24	29	32	36	40	20	18	15	16	16	18	15	11	10	8.5	7	8.5	3.5	7	1.5	3.5		
33	**Whitebeach Pass**	20	15	21	24	25	24	26	28	29	32	26	31	34	38	42	22	20	12	18	18	20	17	13	9	7	8.5	11	6	9	4	5.5	4	
34	**Cracroft Point**	22	17	23	26	27	26	28	28	32	35	29	34	37	41	45	25	23	13	21	21	23	20	16	11	8.5	11	13	9	6.5	7	8.5	6.5	2.5

DRURY INLET

Location				No.
Morris Islet	5	10.4	15	4
Byron Point (Jennis Bay)		5.5	10	35
Charlotte Point			4.5	36
England Point				37

GRAPPLER SOUND AND MCKENZIE SOUND

Location						No.
Kinnaird Rock	2	4.5	4.5	7	2	5
Watson Point		2.5	4.5	7	2	38
Roaringhole Rapids			2	4.5	4.5	39
Claypole Point				2.5	2.5	40
Stirling Point					5	41
Cunning Point						7

Route	Distance	No.
Upton Point to Wakeman River	5.5	12
Bourmaster Point to Broughton Point	4.5	10

Table 1-16 Queen Charlotte Strait

In heavy weather, mariners should give **Cape Caution** a wide berth. West and Southwest swells are reflected back to sea by the cape and interact with incoming swells, creating confused seas and large standing waves.

Nigei Island, named after a chief of the Nahwitti Tribe.

Bull Harbour, named after the numerous fierce sea lions (known as bulls to the members of the Hudson's Bay Company).

Nahwitti Bar When tidal currents oppose the wind, the shallow waters of Nahwitti Bar become extremely hazardous to vessels of all sizes.

Nakwakto Rapids, at the entrance to **Seymour Inlet**, experiences the strongest tidal currents of any navigable channel in the world.

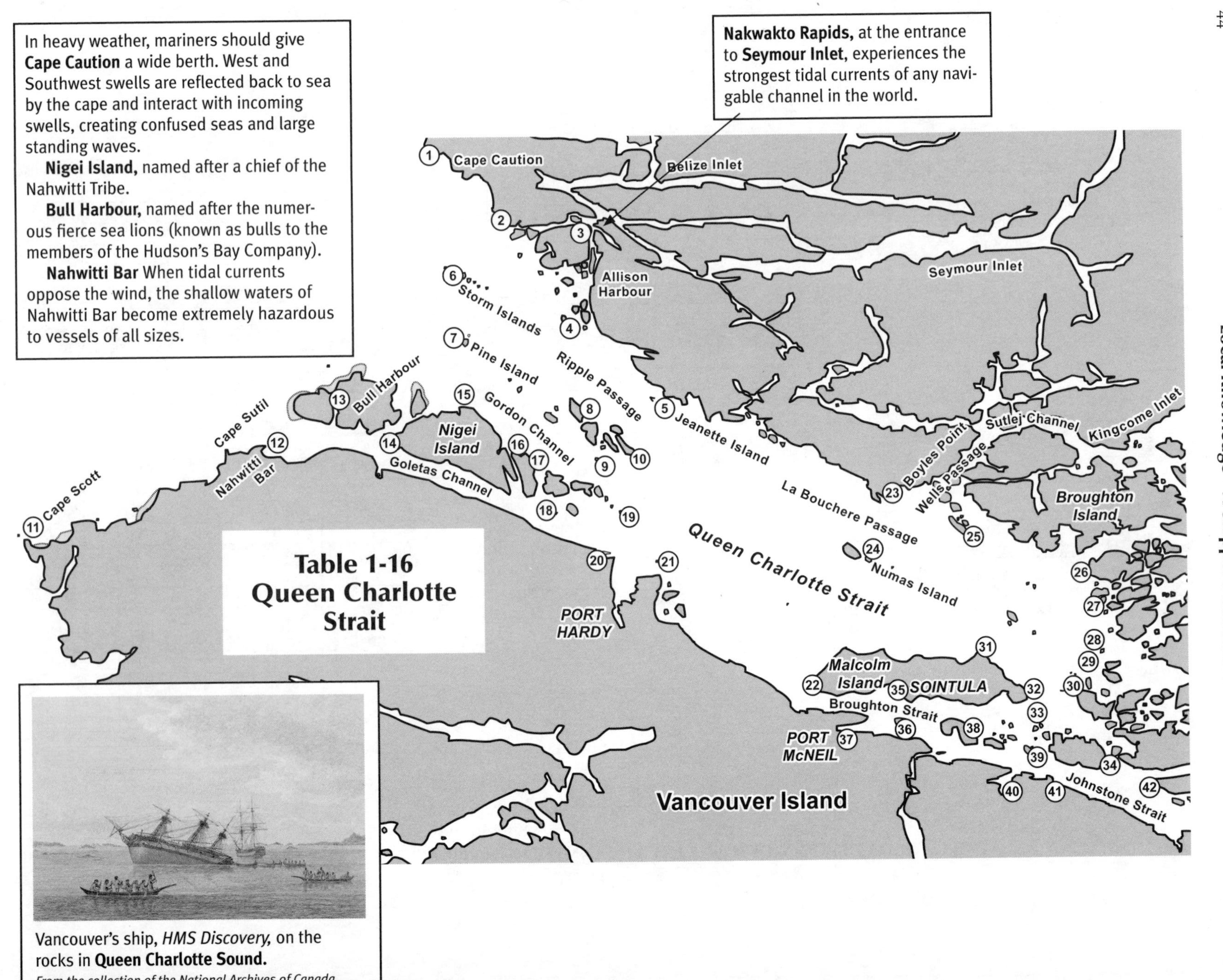
1 Cape Caution
2
3
Belize Inlet
Allison Harbour
Seymour Inlet
4
5 Jeanette Island
6 Storm Islands
7 Pine Island
Ripple Passage
8
9
10
11 Cape Scott
12
Cape Sutil
Nahwitti Bar
13
Bull Harbour
14
15
Nigei Island
Gordon Channel
16
17
18
19
Goletas Channel
20
PORT HARDY
21
Queen Charlotte Strait
La Bouchere Passage
22
Malcolm Island
23
Boyles Point
Wells Passage
24
Numas Island
25
26
27
28
29
30
31
32
33
34
35
SOINTULA
36
37
PORT McNEIL
38
39
40
41
42
Broughton Strait
Johnstone Strait
Sutlej Channel
Kingcome Inlet
Broughton Island
Vancouver Island

Vancouver's ship, *HMS Discovery,* on the rocks in **Queen Charlotte Sound.**

From the collection of the National Archives of Canada.

Table 1-16 QUEEN CHARLOTTE STRAIT

Most Direct Route (Not including passages through Broughton Strait)

Locations in **bold lowercase** appear in other detail tables.

No.	Location	1	2	3	4	5	6	7	8	9	10	11	12	13	14	15	16	17	18	19	20	21	22	23	24	25	26	27	28	29	30	31	32	33
1	**Cape Caution**																																	
2	Lascelles Point	7																																
3	Buttress Island	13	5.5																															
4	Harris Island	13	6	6																														
5	Jeannette Island	20	13	12	7																													
6	West Storm Islands	8	4.5	10	6	15																												
7	**Pine Island**	12	8	14	6	12	3.5																											
8	Walker Anchorage	19	13	13	7	5	12	10																										
9	Davey Rock	23	15	15	9	6	14	11	2																									
10	Castle Point	23	15	15	9	4	16	13	5	3																								
11	**Cape Scott**	34	35	41	35	42	30	30	38	38	41																							
12	**Nahwitti Bar**	19	21	27	19	23	16	13	19	19	22	18																						
13	Bull Harbour	21	20	26	17	22	15	11	18	18	21	21	3																					
14	Willes Island	17	16	22	13	18	11	7	14	14	16	24	5.5	4																				
15	Cholberg Point (Cascade Harbour)	15	12	14	8	13	7	4	9	9	11	29	11	9	5																			
16	Cardigan Rocks	19	13	14	8	10	10	7	5	5	8	33	15	13	9	4																		
17	Scarlett Point	21	14	15	9	10	11	9	4	3.5	6	35	17	15	11	6	2																	
18	Noble Islet	24	17	18	12	13	14	12	6.5	5	6.5	35	17	15	11	11	4.5	2.5																
19	Doyle Island Light	27	19	20	13	7.5	18	15	7	4	4	40	22	20	16	13	9	7	5															
20	Duval Point	29	21	22	16	10	19	17	9	6	6	40	22	20	16	14	10	8	5	2														
21	Masterman Island	30	22	23	16	10	21	18	10	7	7	42	24	22	18	16	12	10	7	3	2.5													
22	**Pulteney Point**	40	33	33	27	20	35	31	22	20	19	56	38	36	31	29	18	23	20	16	15	13												
23	**Boyles Point**	38	31	30	25	18	33	30	23	21	18	58	40	38	34	30	26	24	23	18	19	17	14											
24	Numas Island (East)	36	29	29	23	16	31	29	21	18	16	56	38	36	32	28	34	22	21	16	16	14	10	4										
25	**Brig Rock**	42	35	34	29	22	40	37	27	26	23	62	44	42	38	35	31	29	27	22	22	20	16	5	6.5									
26	**Duff Islet**	49	42	41	36	29	46	43	34	32	29	69	51	49	45	42	37	35	34	29	29	27	21	12	13	7								
27	**Fog Islet**	51	44	43	38	31	48	45	36	34	31	71	53	51	47	44	39	37	36	31	31	29	22	15	15	10	5							
28	**House Islet**	52	45	44	39	32	49	46	37	35	32	70	52	50	46	43	39	37	35	30	30	28	19	15	16	10	5.5	2.5						
29	**White Cliff Islet**	51	44	43	38	31	48	45	36	34	31	69	51	49	45	42	38	36	34	29	29	27	18	15	15	11	6.5	3.5	1.5					
30	**Wedge Islet**	52	45	44	39	32	49	46	37	35	32	70	52	50	46	40	39	37	35	30	30	28	17	16	16	12	8	5	2	2				
31	Lizard Point	46	39	38	33	26	41	37	29	27	24	63	45	43	39	34	32	30	28	23	23	21	13	10	10	7	8	8	7	6	7			
32	Donegal Head	50	43	42	37	30	45	42	32	31	28	67	49	47	43	38	36	34	32	27	27	25	17	14	14	10	9	7	5	4	4	4		
33	**Stubbs Island**	52	45	44	39	32	46	43	35	32	30	69	51	49	45	40	37	35	34	29	28	26	18	16	16	12	10	8	6	4.5	4	5.5	1.5	
34	**Blackney Pass**	56	49	48	43	36	51	47	39	37	35	73	45	43	49	46	42	41	37	33	34	32	23	20	20	16	12	10	7.5	6	5.5	10	6	6.5

BROUGHTON STRAIT

Location	SOINTULA	Haddington Island	PORT MCNEIL	ALERT BAY	Stubbs Island	Weynton Island	TELEGRAPH COVE	Blackney Passage	Blinkhorne Peninsula	Cracroft Point	No.
Pulteney Point	5.5	5.5	7	10	14	15	15	19	16	19	**22**
SOINTULA		1.5	3.5	5	9	10	9	15	11	15	**35**
Haddington Island			2	3.5	8	9	8	14	10	13	**36**
PORT MCNEIL				6	10	11	10	16	12	15	**37**
ALERT BAY					5.5	5.5	4.5	11	6.5	10	**38**
Stubbs Island						2	3.5	6	4	7	**33**
Weynton Island							2	5.5	2	5	**39**
TELEGRAPH COVE								6.5	2.5	6	**40**
Blackney Passage									4.5	1	**34**
Blinkhorne Peninsula										4	**41**
Cracroft Point											**42**

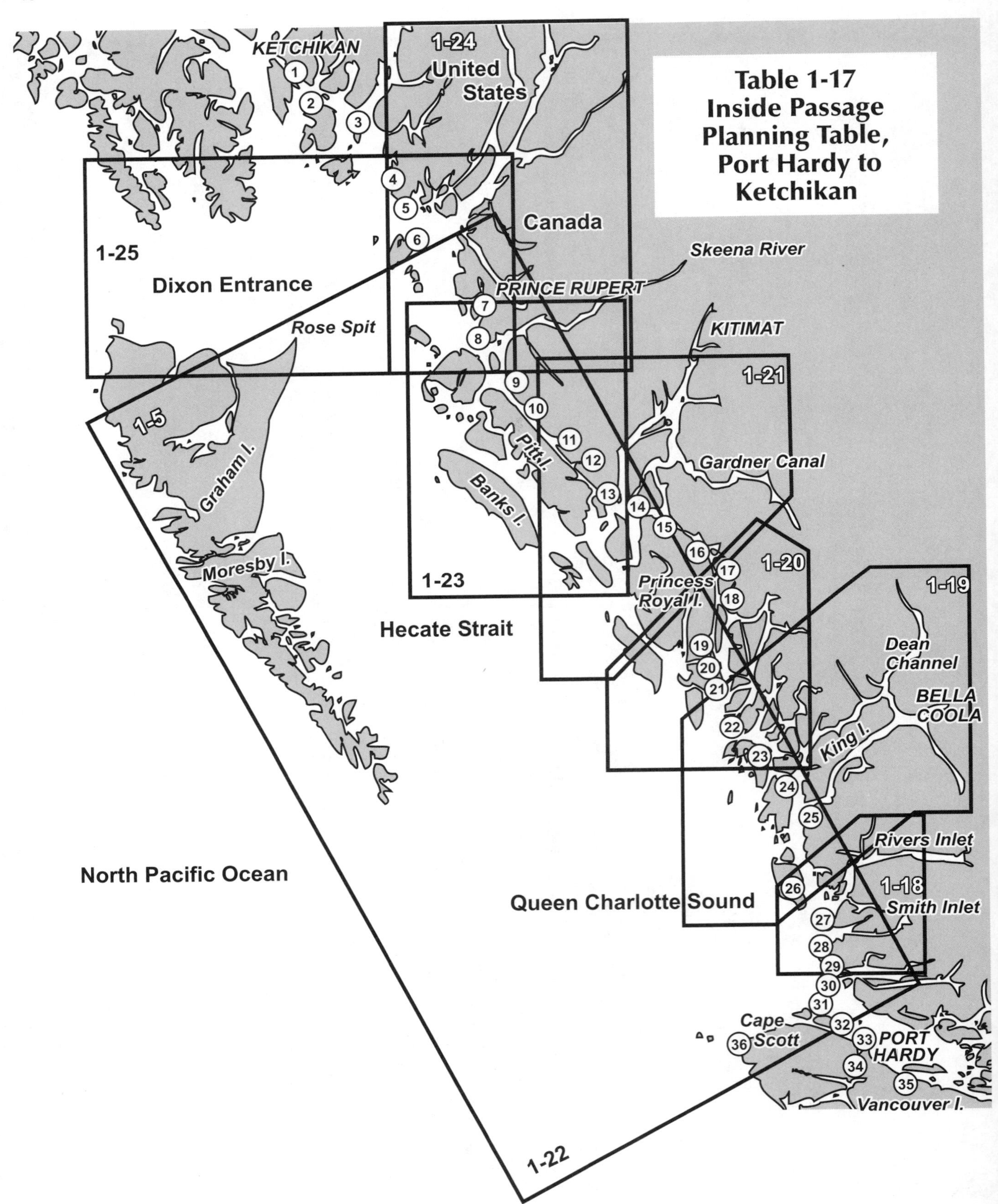

Table 1-17
Inside Passage
Planning Table,
Port Hardy to
Ketchikan
KETCHIKAN
1-24
United States
Canada
1-25
Dixon Entrance
Rose Spit
Skeena River
PRINCE RUPERT
KITIMAT
1-21
1-5
Graham I.
Pitt I.
Banks I.
Gardner Canal
1-20
1-19
1-23
Moresby I.
Princess Royal I.
Hecate Strait
Dean Channel
BELLA COOLA
King I.
Rivers Inlet
1-18
Smith Inlet
North Pacific Ocean
Queen Charlotte Sound
Cape Scott
PORT HARDY
Vancouver I.
1-22
1
2
3
4
5
6
7
8
9
10
11
12
13
14
15
16
17
18
19
20
21
22
23
24
25
26
27
28
29
30
31
32
33
34
35
36

Table 1-17 INSIDE PASSAGE PLANNING TABLE, PORT HARDY TO KETCHIKAN

Most Direct Route (Inside Passage via Milbanke Sound preferred. All passages via Inside Passage except those to Cape Scott. For passages via Jackson Pass and Perceval Narrows add 14 miles.)

USA / CANADA

1	KETCHIKAN																																			
2	8	Spire Island																																		
3	22	14	Point Winslow (Mary Island)																																	
4	42	34	20	Tree Point																																
5	47	38	24	4	Cape Fox																															
6	58	50	36	16	12	Green Island																														
7	82	74	60	40	36	24	PRINCE RUPERT (Fairview)																													
8	91	83	69	49	45	33	12	Genn Island																												
9	103	95	81	61	57	45	24	12	Watson Rock																											
10	111	103	89	69	65	53	32	20	7.5	Kumealon Inlet (Entrance)																										
11	123	115	101	81	77	65	44	32	20	13	Morning Reef																									
12	134	126	112	92	88	76	55	43	31	24	11	Lowe Inlet																								
13	148	140	126	106	102	90	69	57	45	38	25	14	Sainty Point																							
14	156	148	134	114	110	98	77	65	53	46	33	22	8	Point Cumming																						
15	164	156	142	122	118	106	85	73	61	54	41	30	16	8	Kingcome Point																					
16	175	167	153	133	129	117	96	84	72	65	52	41	27	19	11	Butedale																				
17	182	174	160	140	136	124	103	91	79	72	59	48	34	26	18	8	Khutze Inlet (Asher Point)																			
18	194	186	172	152	148	136	115	103	91	84	71	60	46	38	30	20	12	Sarah Head																		
19	207	199	185	165	161	149	128	116	104	97	84	73	59	51	43	33	25	13	Split Head																	
20	212	204	190	170	166	154	133	121	109	102	89	78	64	56	48	38	30	18	5	KLEMTU																
21	222	214	200	180	176	164	143	131	119	112	99	88	74	66	58	48	40	28	15	10	Jorkins Point															
22	233	225	211	191	187	175	154	142	130	123	110	99	85	77	69	59	51	39	26	21	11	Ivory Island														
23	247	239	225	205	201	189	168	156	144	137	124	113	99	91	83	73	65	53	40	35	25	14	BELLA BELLA													
24	258	250	236	216	212	200	179	167	155	148	135	124	110	102	94	84	76	64	51	46	36	25	11	Pointer Island												
25	271	263	249	229	225	213	192	180	168	161	148	137	123	115	107	97	89	77	64	59	49	38	24	13	NAMU											
26	289	281	267	247	243	231	210	198	186	179	166	155	141	133	125	115	107	95	82	77	67	56	42	31	22	Safety Cove										
27	300	292	278	258	254	242	221	209	197	190	177	166	152	144	136	126	118	106	93	88	78	66	52	42	31	11	Dugout Rocks									
28	307	299	285	265	261	249	228	216	204	197	184	173	159	151	143	133	125	113	100	95	85	74	60	49	38	18	7	Egg Island								
29	312	304	290	270	266	254	233	221	209	202	189	178	164	156	148	138	130	118	105	100	90	79	65	54	43	23	12	5	Cape Caution							
30	320	312	298	278	274	262	241	229	217	210	197	186	172	164	156	146	138	126	113	108	98	87	73	62	51	31	20	13	8	Storm Islands						
31	324	316	302	282	278	266	245	233	221	214	201	190	176	168	160	150	142	130	117	112	102	91	77	66	55	35	24	17	12	4	Pine Island					
32	332	324	310	290	286	274	253	241	229	222	209	198	184	176	168	158	150	138	125	120	110	99	85	74	63	43	32	25	20	12	8	Scarlett Point				
33	340	332	318	298	294	282	261	249	237	230	217	206	192	184	176	166	158	146	133	128	118	107	93	82	71	51	40	33	28	20	16	8	Duval Point			
34	343	335	321	301	297	285	264	252	240	233	220	209	195	187	179	169	161	149	136	131	121	110	96	85	74	54	43	36	31	23	19	11	3	PORT HARDY		
35	355	347	333	313	309	297	276	264	252	245	232	221	207	199	191	181	173	161	148	143	133	122	108	97	86	66	55	48	43	35	31	24	16	16	Pulteney Point	
36	321	313	299	279	275	263	242	230	218	211	198	187	173	165	157	147	139	127	114	109	99	91	95	84	72	53	42	35	33	30	29	35	39	42	54	Cape Scott

PASSAGES IN SOUTHEAST ALASKA

Lituya Bay	72	174	89	148	127	127	190	230	271	262	339	37
Glacier Bay (Bartlett Cove)		114	30	88	68	117	131	172	211	252	280	38
SKAGWAY			93	99	111	185	174	214	254	263	323	39
HOONAH				67	46	119	108	149	189	197	257	40
JUNEAU					85	158	91	107	146	201	215	41
TENAKEE SPRINGS						92	81	122	162	170	230	42
SITKA							114	155	195	135	263	43
KAKE								56	96	124	165	44
PETERSBURG									40	109	108	45
WRANGELL										108	84	46
CRAIG (Prince of Wales Island)											119	47
KETCHIKAN												1

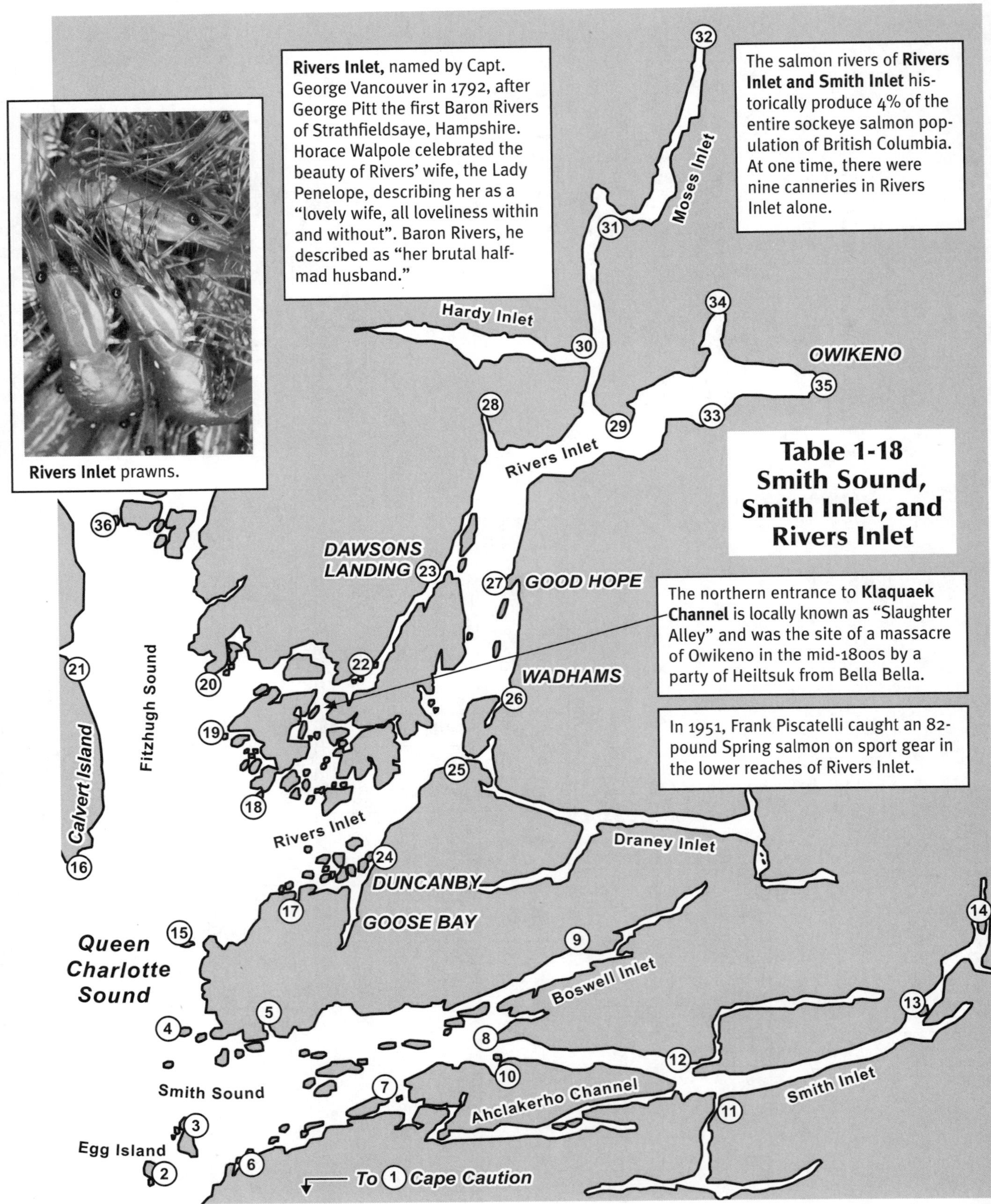
Rivers Inlet, named by Capt. George Vancouver in 1792, after George Pitt the first Baron Rivers of Strathfieldsaye, Hampshire. Horace Walpole celebrated the beauty of Rivers' wife, the Lady Penelope, describing her as a "lovely wife, all loveliness within and without". Baron Rivers, he described as "her brutal half-mad husband."
The salmon rivers of **Rivers Inlet and Smith Inlet** historically produce 4% of the entire sockeye salmon population of British Columbia. At one time, there were nine canneries in Rivers Inlet alone.
Table 1-18 Smith Sound, Smith Inlet, and Rivers Inlet
The northern entrance to **Klaquaek Channel** is locally known as "Slaughter Alley" and was the site of a massacre of Owikeno in the mid-1800s by a party of Heiltsuk from Bella Bella.
In 1951, Frank Piscatelli caught an 82-pound Spring salmon on sport gear in the lower reaches of Rivers Inlet.
Moses Inlet
Hardy Inlet
OWIKENO
Rivers Inlet
DAWSONS LANDING
GOOD HOPE
WADHAMS
Fitzhugh Sound
Calvert Island
Rivers Inlet
Draney Inlet
DUNCANBY
GOOSE BAY
Queen Charlotte Sound
Boswell Inlet
Smith Sound
Ahclakerho Channel
Smith Inlet
Egg Island
To 1 Cape Caution
1 2 3 4 5 6 7 8 9 10 11 12 13 14 15 16 17 18 19 20 21 22 23 24 25 26 27 28 29 30 31 32 33 34 35 36

Rivers Inlet prawns.

TABLE 1-18 SMITH SOUND, SMITH INLET, AND RIVERS INLET

Most Direct Route (Includes routes through Klaquaek Channel)

Locations in **bold lowercase** appear in other detail tables.

No.	Location	1	2	3	4	5	6	7	8	9	10	11	12	13	14	15	16	17	18	19	20	21	22	23	24	25	26	27	28	29	30	31	32	33	34	35
1	**Cape Caution**																																			
2	**Egg Island**	5																																		
3	Table Island Anchorage	7	2.5																																	
4	False Egg Island	10	5	3																																
5	Milbrooke Cove	11	6	4	4.5																															
6	Jones Cove	6.5	2.5	2	5	5																														
7	Takush Harbour, Wakas Point	12	8	6.5	7	4.5	5.5																													
8	Ripon Point	16	12	11	11	7.5	9.5	4																												
9	Security Bay	20	16	14	15	11	13	8	4																											
10	Oblong Island, McBride Bay	16	12	11	11	6.5	9.5	4	1	5																										
11	The Seine Hole, Entrance to Wyclees Lagoon	24	20	19	19	14	17	11	8	12	7.5																									
12	Adelaide Point	23	19	18	18	15	16	10	7	11	6	1.5																								
13	Burnt Island	31	27	26	26	23	24	18	13	19	14	7.5	8																							
14	Nekite River, Jap Island	34	30	29	29	26	27	21	16	22	17	10	11	3																						
	Smith Sound / **Rivers Inlet**																																			
15	Dugout Rock	13	7	6	3	7	8	11	14	18	14	22	21	29	32																					
16	**Cape Calvert**	16	10	9	6.5	11	11	14	18	22	18	25	34	32	36	5																				
17	Home Bay	18	12	11	8	12	13	16	19	23	19	27	26	34	37	5	8.5																			
18	Dimsey Point	19	13	12	9	13	14	17	20	24	20	28	27	35	38	6	7.5	4																		
19	Rouse Reef	20	14	13	10	14	15	18	21	25	21	29	28	36	39	7	7.5	6	2																	
20	**Addenbroke Point**	22	16	15	12	16	17	20	23	27	23	31	30	38	41	9	7	8	4.5	2																
21	**Safety Cove**	24	19	17	14	18	19	21	25	29	25	33	32	40	42	11	9	12	8.5	6.5	5															
22	Darby Narrows	24	18	17	14	18	19	22	25	29	25	33	32	40	43	11	13	8	5	5.5	5	10														
23	**DAWSON'S LANDING**	30	24	23	20	24	25	28	31	35	31	39	38	46	49	17	17	12	10	10	9	14	4													
24	**DUNCANBY LANDING**	20	14	13	10	14	15	18	21	25	21	29	28	36	39	7	11	3	5	7	9	14	8	12												
25	Draney Narrows	25	19	18	15	19	20	22	26	30	26	34	33	41	44	12	14	7.5	7	10	12	17	10	7	5.5											
26	**WADHAMS**	27	21	20	17	21	22	25	28	32	28	36	35	43	46	14	17	11	10	12	12	17	9	4.5	9	3.5										
27	**GOOD HOPE** (Ida Island)	31	25	24	21	25	26	29	32	36	32	40	39	47	50	18	19	14	13	13	12	17	7	3	12	6	3.5									
28	Sandell Bay	36	30	29	26	30	31	34	37	41	37	45	44	52	55	23	24	20	15	15	14	19	9	5	17	12	9	5.5								
29	McAllister Point	38	32	31	28	32	33	36	39	43	39	47	46	54	57	25	26	21	20	18	17	22	12	8	19	13	11	7	5							
30	Ralph Point	39	33	32	29	33	34	37	40	44	40	48	47	55	58	26	27	22	21	19	18	23	13	9	20	14	12	8	6	2.5						
31	Nelson Narrows	45	39	38	35	39	40	43	46	50	46	54	53	61	64	32	33	28	27	25	24	29	19	15	26	20	17	14	12	8.5	6					
32	Head of Moses Inlet	52	46	45	42	46	47	50	53	57	53	61	60	68	71	39	39	35	34	31	29	34	25	21	32	26	24	20	18	15	12	7				
33	Shotbolt Bay	41	35	34	31	35	36	39	42	46	42	50	49	57	60	28	29	24	23	21	20	25	15	11	22	16	13	10	8	3	5.5	12	18			
34	Kilbella River	42	36	35	32	36	37	40	43	47	43	51	50	58	61	29	30	25	24	22	21	26	16	12	23	17	14	11	9.5	4	6.5	13	19	2.5		
35	Wannock River	45	39	38	35	39	40	43	46	50	46	54	53	61	64	32	32	28	27	25	24	29	19	15	26	20	18	14	11	6.5	9	15	22	4	3	
36	**Addenbroke Island**	26	20	19	16	20	21	24	27	31	27	35	34	42	45	13	13	14	11	8	6	5	11	15	15	18	18	18	20	23	24	30	35	26	27	30

Route	Distance	No.
Seine Hole to Docee River	3.5	**11**
Draney Narrows to Allard Bay	10	**25**

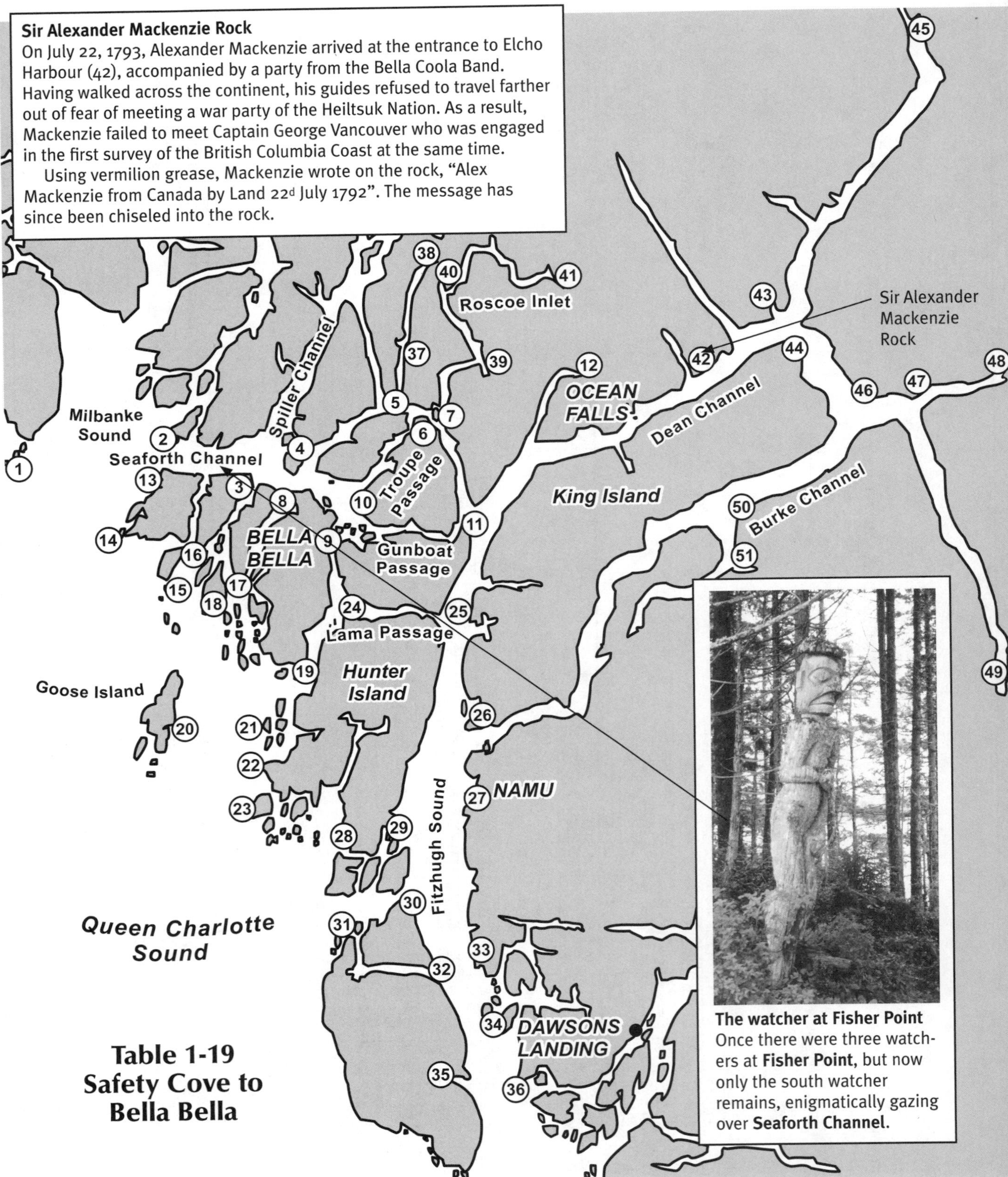
Sir Alexander Mackenzie Rock
Milbanke Sound
Seaforth Channel
Spiller Channel
Roscoe Inlet
OCEAN FALLS
Dean Channel
Troupe Passage
King Island
Burke Channel
BELLA BELLA
Gunboat Passage
Lama Passage
Goose Island
Hunter Island
NAMU
Fitzhugh Sound
Queen Charlotte Sound
DAWSONS LANDING
1
2
3
4
5
6
7
8
9
10
11
12
13
14
15
16
17
18
19
20
21
22
23
24
25
26
27
28
29
30
31
32
33
34
35
36
37
38
39
40
41
42
43
44
45
46
47
48
49
50
51

Sir Alexander Mackenzie Rock

On July 22, 1793, Alexander Mackenzie arrived at the entrance to Elcho Harbour (42), accompanied by a party from the Bella Coola Band. Having walked across the continent, his guides refused to travel farther out of fear of meeting a war party of the Heiltsuk Nation. As a result, Mackenzie failed to meet Captain George Vancouver who was engaged in the first survey of the British Columbia Coast at the same time.

Using vermilion grease, Mackenzie wrote on the rock, "Alex Mackenzie from Canada by Land 22d July 1792". The message has since been chiseled into the rock.

The watcher at Fisher Point
Once there were three watchers at **Fisher Point**, but now only the south watcher remains, enigmatically gazing over **Seaforth Channel**.

Table 1-19 Safety Cove to Bella Bella

Table 1-19 SAFETY COVE TO BELLA BELLA

Most Direct Route

Locations in **bold lowercase** appear in other detail tables.

No.	Location	1	2	3	4	5	6	7	8	9	10	11	12	13	14	15	16	17	18	19	20	21	22	23	24	25	26	27	28	29	30	31	32	33	34	35
1	**McInnes Island** (Catala Passage)																																			
2	**Ivory Island**	13																																		
3	**Idol Point**	17	5																																	
4	**Law Island**	21	8	4																																
5	**Coldwell Point**	28	15	11	7																															
6	**Troupe Narrows**	30	17	12	9	3																														
7	**Nicholson Island**	31	18	14	10	3	3																													
8	Kintail Point	21	8.5	3.5	3.5	9.5	9	12																												
9	**BELLA BELLA**	27	14	9	8	12	9	12	5.5																											
10	**Dumas Point**	24	12	7	5.5	9	6	9	3.5	3																										
11	Teal Island	33	21	16	15	10	10	7.5	13	11	9.5																									
12	**OCEAN FALLS**	46	34	29	28	23	23	20	26	23	23	13																								
13	Cape Swain	12	2	6	9	16	18	21	9.5	15	13	22	35																							
14	Cape Mark	10	9	13	16	23	25	28	20	22	20	29	42	7																						
15	Houghton Islands (North Anchorage)	15	14	18	18	25	25	28	15	21	19	28	41	12	5																					
16	Cree Point (Thompson Bay)	19	18	18	20	27	27	30	17	23	21	30	43	15	8	3																				
17	Clarie Island	22	21	9	11	17	17	20	7.5	13	11	21	34	19	12	7.5	9																			
18	Codfish Passage (Alleyne Island)	20	19	12	13	20	20	23	10	16	14	23	36	17	10	5	7	2.5																		
19	Stubbs Point	27	25	18	20	23	20	23	16	11	14	22	33	24	17	12	13	8.5	7.5																	
20	Goose Island Anchorage	25	24	21	23	30	30	33	20	21	23	31	41	22	15	12	14	12	10	9																
21	Purple Bluff	25	31	20	22	29	29	29	18	17	20	28	38	24	17	13	15	11	9	5.5	4.5															
22	Superstition Point	30	29	24	26	30	27	30	22	18	21	29	40	27	20	16	18	15	12	8	7	3.5														
23	Breadner Point	31	33	26	28	34	31	34	25	22	25	33	42	30	23	19	21	17	15	11	8	6	3													
24	Beak Point	32	19	14	13	17	14	17	11	5	8	16	26	20	24	18	20	15	13	6.5	15	12	14	16												
25	Pointer Island	38	25	20	19	18	18	16	17	11	14	9	20	26	30	24	26	22	21	13	22	19	21	23	6.5											
26	Walker Point	47	34	29	28	27	27	24	26	20	23	16	29	35	39	34	35	31	30	22	28	27	22	22	15	9										
27	**NAMU**	51	38	33	32	31	31	28	30	24	27	20	33	39	43	38	39	35	34	26	27	27	21	21	19	13	4									
28	West Entrance Nalau Passage	41	41	34	36	41	41	44	32	29	32	31	39	40	33	29	30	25	25	18	16	16	10	9	26	20	12	11								
29	Hergest Point	41	41	36	35	34	34	31	31	27	30	23	35	45	38	34	35	30	30	23	21	21	15	14	22	16	7.5	6.5	4.5							
30	Kelpie Point	48	45	40	39	44	40	37	37	32	34	26	41	47	41	35	38	32	31	25	23	22	17	16	26	20	10	9	7	5						
31	Odlum Point	45	44	42	43	42	42	40	36	32	35	32	44	42	35	31	32	29	27	22	19	18	14	12	30	24	16	14	6	8.5	5					
32	Experiment Point	53	52	44	43	42	42	40	41	35	38	32	44	50	43	39	40	37	35	30	27	26	22	19	31	24	16	13	12	10	5	8				
33	Kwakume Point	56	55	43	42	41	41	38	40	34	37	30	43	54	47	43	44	41	39	34	31	30	26	21	29	23	14	11	22	8.5	5	12	3.5			
34	**Addenbroke Island**	58	57	49	48	47	47	43	46	40	43	35	49	55	48	44	45	42	40	35	32	31	27	24	35	29	18	17	17	14	9.5	13	4.5	6		
35	**Safety Cove**	63	62	51	50	49	49	49	48	42	45	41	51	73	66	62	63	60	58	40	37	36	32	28	37	31	23	22	21	19	14	18	9.5	11	5	
36	**Addenbroke Point**	64	63	55	54	53	53	50	52	46	49	42	55	74	67	63	62	59	57	41	38	37	33	30	41	35	24	23	22	20	15	19	11	12	6	5

BRIGGS INLET AND ROSCOE INLET

Location	Troupe Narrows	Briggs Narrows	Briggs Lagoon	Nicholson Island	Clatse Bay	Roscoe Narrows	Roscoe Bay	No.
Coldwell Point	3	3	10	6	13	16	26	5
Troupe Narrows		10	13	3	9	13	23	6
Briggs Narrows			7	10	11	14	24	37
Briggs Lagoon				13	18	21	31	38
Nicholson Island					6.5	9.5	20	7
Clatse Bay						7.5	18	39
Roscoe Narrows							10	40
Roscoe Bay								41

FITZHUGH SOUND TO BELLA COOLA

Location	OCEAN FALLS	Elcho Point	Eucott Bay	Edwards Point	Kimsquit Narrows	Mesachie Nose	Loyentsi Point	BELLA COOLA	Bentinck Narrows	Cathedral Point	Kwatna Bay	Haaskvold Point	Walker Point	No.
Teal Island	13	20	28	28	55	36	43	51	63	41	44	24	16	11
OCEAN FALLS		20	27	27	54	35	42	50	62	53	59	38	29	12
Elcho Point			8.5	11	35	18	25	33	45	32	39	42	36	42
Eucott Bay				2.5	29	10	17	25	37	24	31	41	45	43
Edwards Point					27	7.5	15	22	35	21	28	39	46	44
Kimsquit Narrows						33	40	48	60	47	54	64	72	45
Mesachie Nose							7	15	27	14	21	31	39	46
Loyentsi Point								8	22	21	28	38	46	47
BELLA COOLA									29	29	36	46	54	48
Bentinck Narrows										41	48	58	66	49
Cathedral Point											6.5	17	25	50
Kwatna Bay												20	28	51
Haaskvold Point													7.5	52
Walker Point														26

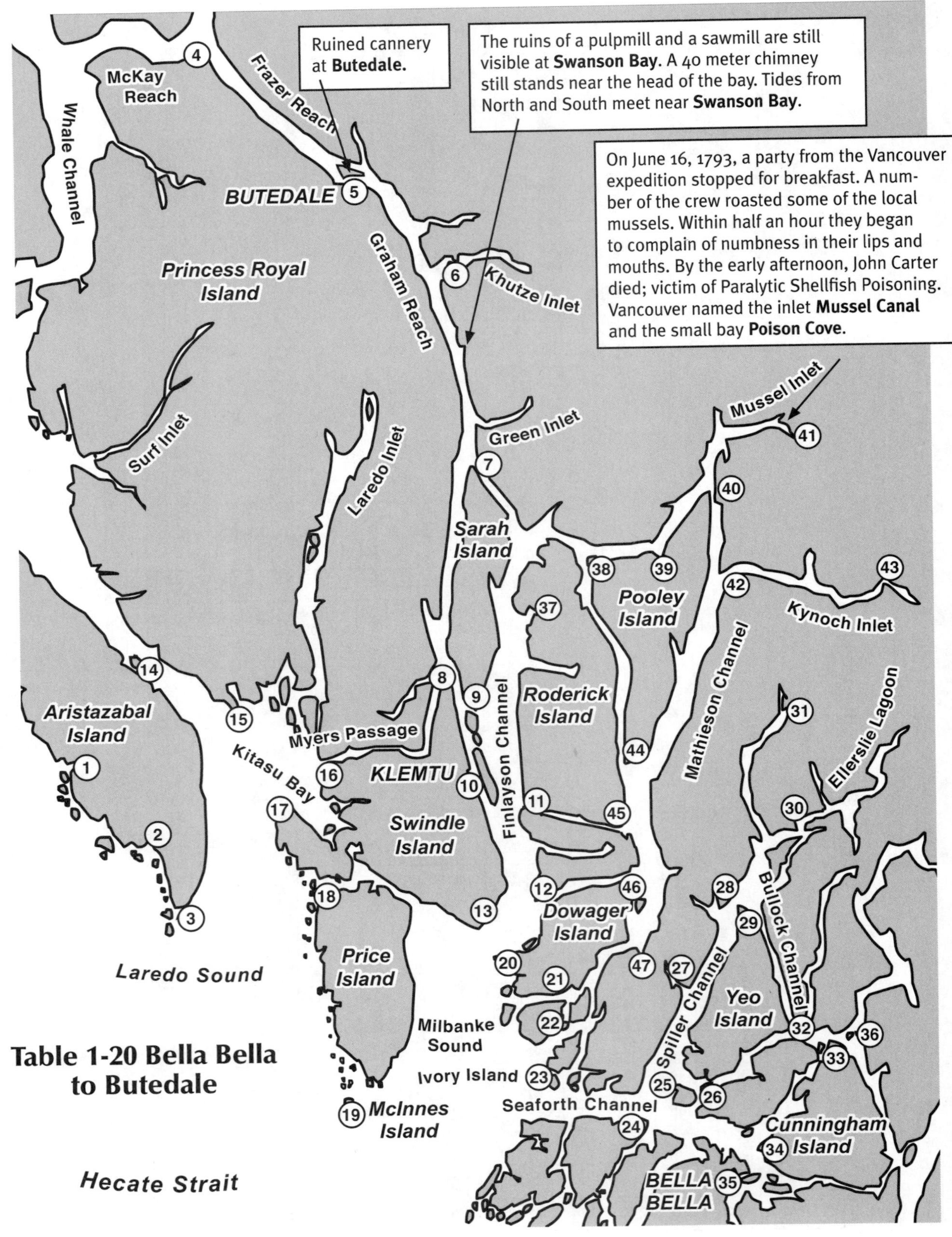
Ruined cannery at **Butedale.**
The ruins of a pulpmill and a sawmill are still visible at **Swanson Bay**. A 40 meter chimney still stands near the head of the bay. Tides from North and South meet near **Swanson Bay**.
On June 16, 1793, a party from the Vancouver expedition stopped for breakfast. A number of the crew roasted some of the local mussels. Within half an hour they began to complain of numbness in their lips and mouths. By the early afternoon, John Carter died; victim of Paralytic Shellfish Poisoning. Vancouver named the inlet **Mussel Canal** and the small bay **Poison Cove**.
McKay Reach
Frazer Reach
Whale Channel
BUTEDALE
Princess Royal Island
Graham Reach
Khutze Inlet
Surf Inlet
Laredo Inlet
Green Inlet
Mussel Inlet
Sarah Island
Pooley Island
Kynoch Inlet
Aristazabal Island
Myers Passage
Kitasu Bay
KLEMTU
Finlayson Channel
Roderick Island
Mathieson Channel
Ellerslie Lagoon
Swindle Island
Dowager Island
Bullock Channel
Laredo Sound
Price Island
Spiller Channel
Yeo Island
Milbanke Sound
Ivory Island
Seaforth Channel
McInnes Island
Cunningham Island
BELLA BELLA
Hecate Strait

Table 1-20 Bella Bella to Butedale

Table 1-20 BELLA BELLA TO BUTEDALE

Most Direct Route (Except no routes via Higgins Passage)

Locations in **bold lowercase** appear in other detail tables.

No.	Location	1	2	3	4	5	6	7	8	9	10	11	12	13	14	15	16	17	18	19	20	21	22	23	24	25	26	27	28	29	30	31	32	33	34	35
1	**Clifford Bay**																																		
2	Weeteeam Bay	12																																	
3	Prior Passage	13	6																																
4	**Kingcome Point**	53	63	67																															
5	**Butedale**	64	62	58	11																														
6	**Khutze Inlet** (Asher Point)	63	56	50	19	8																													
7	**Sarah Head**	53	44	38	30	20	12																												
8	**Split Head**	38	31	25	43	33	25	13																											
9	Boat Bluff	41	34	28	47	36	28	16	2.5																										
10	**KLEMTU**	43	36	30	48	37	30	18	5	3																									
11	Begg Point (Jackson Passage)	48	41	35	54	43	35	23	9	6.5	4.5																								
12	Legace Point (Oscar Passage)	53	46	40	59	48	40	28	14.5	12	9	5.5																							
13	**Jorkins Point**	54	47	41	58	47	40	28	15	13	10	7.5	3.5																						
14	**Ramsbotham Islands**	32	25	19	48	59	55	37	24	27	29	34	39	40																					
15	Dallain Point	39	32	26	55	50	42	30	17	20	22	27	32	33	7.5																				
16	Wingate Point	27	18	14	55	44	36	24	11	14	16	21	26	27	13	6																			
17	Wilby Point	44	37	31	58	47	39	27	14	16	19	24	29	30	13	6	3																		
18	Kipp Islet (West Higgins Passage)	21	15	8	64	53	45	33	20	22	35	30	35	36	17	12	9	6																	
19	**McInnes Island** (Catala Passage)	28	21	15	74	63	55	43	30	28	25	21	17	14	30	24	22	19	14																
20	Keith Point	40	34	27	61	49	42	30	17	15	12	9	4.5	2	42	36	34	31	26	12															
21	Sloop Narrows	42	35	29	67	55	48	36	23	21	18	15	10	7.5	44	38	36	33	28	14	5.5														
22	Perceval Narrows	42	35	29	69	57	50	38	25	23	20	17	12	9.5	44	38	36	33	28	14	7.5	2													
23	**Ivory Island**	41	34	28	69	59	51	39	26	24	21	18	14	11	43	37	35	32	27	13	9	7	4.5												
24	**Idol Point**	46	39	33	75	63	56	44	31	29	26	23	19	16	48	42	40	37	32	18	14	12	9.5	5											
25	Hyndman Reef	47	40	34	76	64	57	45	32	30	27	24	20	17	54	43	41	38	33	19	15	13	10	6	2										
26	**Law Island**	49	42	36	78	66	59	47	34	32	29	26	22	19	51	45	43	40	35	21	17	15	13	8	4	2									
27	Spiller Lagoon	53	46	40	82	70	63	51	38	36	33	30	26	23	55	49	47	44	39	25	21	19	17	12	8	6	7								
28	Neekas Cove	60	53	47	89	77	70	58	45	43	40	37	33	30	62	56	54	51	46	32	28	26	24	19	15	13	14	7							
29	Gerald Point	59	52	46	88	76	69	57	44	42	39	36	32	29	61	55	53	50	45	31	27	25	23	18	14	13	14	6	3.5						
30	Ellerslie Lagoon	65	58	52	84	82	75	63	50	48	45	42	38	35	67	61	59	56	51	37	33	31	29	24	21	19	19	13	9.5	7					
31	Ingram Bay	71	64	58	100	88	81	69	56	54	51	48	44	41	73	67	65	62	57	43	39	37	35	30	27	25	25	19	15	13	12				
32	**Coldwell Point**	56	49	43	85	73	66	54	41	39	36	33	29	26	58	52	50	47	42	28	24	22	20	15	11	9	7	14	12	8	15	21			
33	**Troupe Narrows**	58	51	45	87	75	68	56	43	41	38	35	31	28	60	54	52	49	44	30	26	24	22	17	13	11	9	17	15	11	18	24	3		
34	**Dumas Point**	52	45	39	82	70	63	51	38	46	33	30	26	23	55	49	47	44	39	24	21	19	17	12	7	7.5	5.5	13	21	17	24	30	9	6	
35	**BELLA BELLA**	55	48	42	83	73	65	53	40	48	35	32	28	25	57	51	49	46	41	27	23	21	18	14	9	9	8	15	24	20	27	35	12	9	3
36	**Nicholson Island**	59	52	46	87	77	69	57	44	52	39	36	32	29	61	55	53	50	45	31	27	25	22	18	14	12	10	17	18	14	21	27	6	3	9	12

FJORDLAND--(routes via Finlayson and Mathieson Channels)

Location	37	38	39	40	9	10	11	12	41	42	43	44	45	46	47	21	22	23	No.
Sarah Head	12	9	13	17	16	19	23	28	23	23	31	33	28	31	37	36	38	39	7
Bottleneck Inlet		9.5	14	17	6.5	9	11	17	24	23	31	21	16	20	29	26	28	29	37
Lime Point			5	8.5	14	17	19	25	15	14	23	20	25	28	32	33	35	37	38
Windy Bay				5.5	18	21	23	29	12	11	20	23	27	30	37	38	40	41	39
Mathieson Narrows					22	25	27	32	7	5.5	14	17	21	23	27	32	33	38	40
Boat Bluff						3	6.5	12	28	28	38	17	12	16	21	21	23	24	9
KLEMTU							4.5	9	31	26	36	15	10	18	23	18	20	21	10
Begg Point (Jackson Passage)								5.5	34	22	32	10	5.5	14	15	17	18	25	11
Legace Point (Oscar Passage)									39	25	35	13	8.5	5	11	10	12	13	12
Poison Cove (Mussel Inlet)										13	23	25	28	29	33	39	40	45	41
Kynoch Point											10	12	16	18	23	27	28	33	42
Culpepper Narrows (Kynoch Inlet)												22	26	28	33	37	38	43	43
Charles Head													4.5	6.5	11	16	17	22	44
Jackson Narrows														3.5	8.5	13	14	19	45
Buckley Head															5.5	10	11	16	46
Tom Bay																6.5	7	12	47
Sloop Narrows																	2	7	21
Perceval Narrows																		4.5	22
Ivory Island																			23

LAREDO INLET

Location	16	48	49	50	No.
Dallain Point	6	5.5	16	24	15
Wingate Point		3	15	23	16
Quigley Creek			12	19	48
Bay of Plenty				10	49
Arnoup Creek					50

Table 1-21 Caamano Sound, Wright Sound, and Douglas Channel

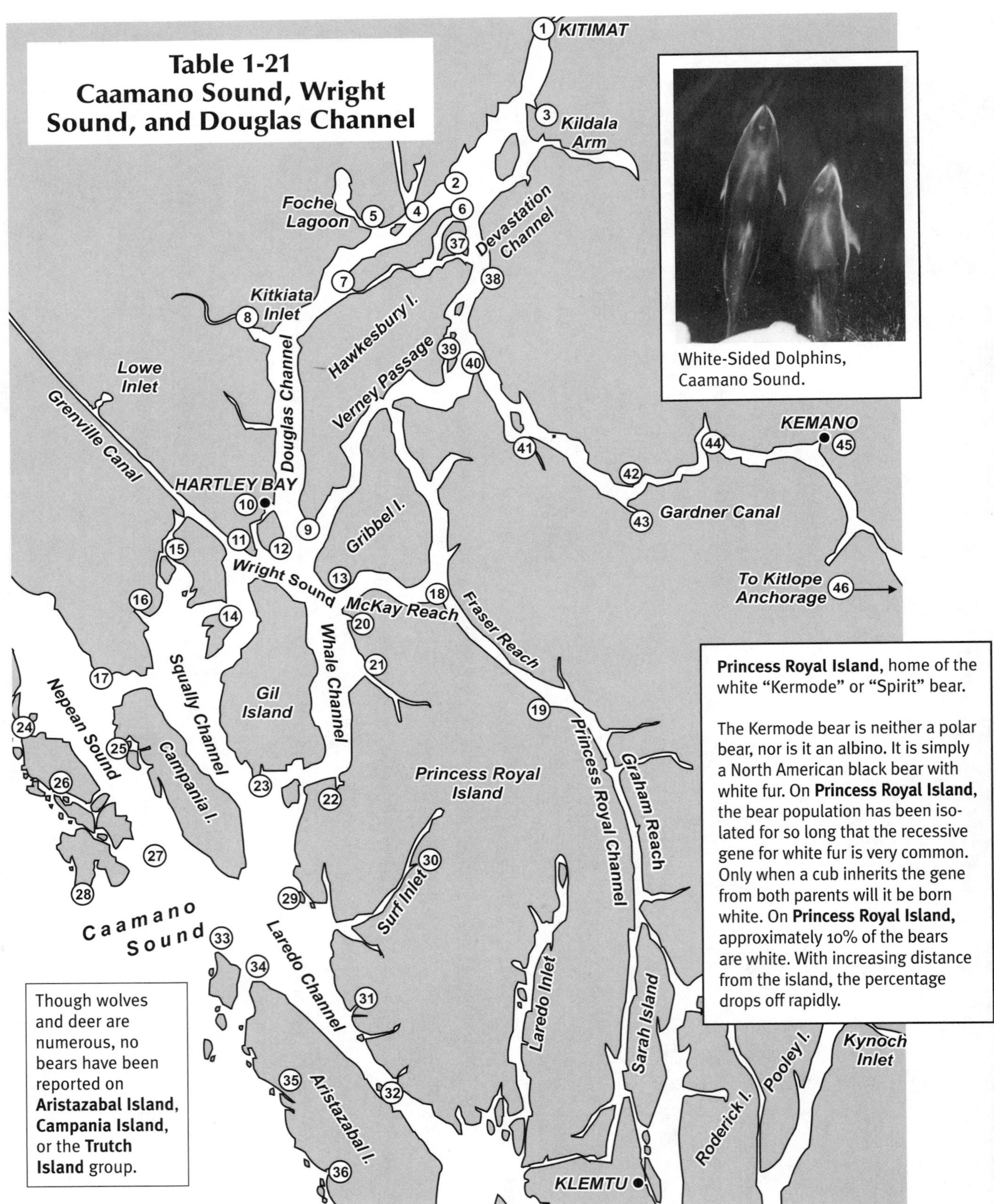

1 KITIMAT
3 Kildala Arm
2
4
5 Foche Lagoon
6
37
Devastation Channel
38
7
8 Kitkiata Inlet
Hawkesbury I.
Verney Passage
39
40
Lowe Inlet
Grenville Canal
Douglas Channel
HARTLEY BAY 10
9
Gribbel I.
11
12
15
13
Wright Sound
16
14
McKay Reach
18
20
Fraser Reach
21
Whale Channel
17
Gil Island
Squally Channel
Nepean Sound
24
25
Campania I.
23
22
Princess Royal Island
19
Princess Royal Channel
Graham Reach
26
27
28
30
Surf Inlet
29
Caamano Sound
33
34
Laredo Channel
31
Laredo Inlet
Sarah Island
35
Aristazabal I.
32
36
KLEMTU
41
42
43
Gardner Canal
44
KEMANO 45
To Kitlope Anchorage 46
Roderick I.
Pooley I.
Kynoch Inlet

White-Sided Dolphins, Caamano Sound.

Princess Royal Island, home of the white "Kermode" or "Spirit" bear.

The Kermode bear is neither a polar bear, nor is it an albino. It is simply a North American black bear with white fur. On **Princess Royal Island**, the bear population has been isolated for so long that the recessive gene for white fur is very common. Only when a cub inherits the gene from both parents will it be born white. On **Princess Royal Island,** approximately 10% of the bears are white. With increasing distance from the island, the percentage drops off rapidly.

Though wolves and deer are numerous, no bears have been reported on **Aristazabal Island**, **Campania Island**, or the **Trutch Island** group.

Table 1-21 CAMAANO SOUND, WRIGHT SOUND, AND DOUGLAS CHANNEL

Most Direct Route

Locations in **bold lowercase** appear in other detail tables.

No.	Location	1	2	3	4	5	6	7	8	9	10	11	12	13	14	15	16	17	18	19	20	21	22	23	24	25	26	27	28	29	30	31	32	33	34	35
1	**KITIMAT**																																			
2	Nanakwa Shoal	11																																		
3	Gobeil Bay (Kildala Arm)	8.5	6.5																																	
4	Point Ashton (Giltoyees Inlet)	17	6	12																																
5	Foche Lagoon (Narrows)	21	9.5	15	3.5																															
6	Kersey Point	14	3.5	9	3.5	6.5																														
7	Grant Point (Sue Channel)	24	13	19	7	5	10																													
8	Kitkiata (Old Town) Anchorage	32	19	26	15	13	18	7.5																												
9	Money Point	44	33	39	27	25	30	20	15																											
10	**HARTLEY BAY**	43	33	37	25	23	28	18	13	3.5																										
11	**Sainty Point**	49	38	43	31	29	34	24	19	6	6																									
12	Cape Farwell	45	34	40	28	26	31	21	16	2.5	4.5	3																								
13	**Point Cumming**	50	39	44	32	30	35	25	20	4.5	8	8	4.5																							
14	Curlew Bay (Fin Island)	51	40	46	34	32	37	27	22	8.5	9.5	5.5	6	9																						
15	**Peters Narrows**	56	45	51	39	37	42	32	26	14	13	8	11	19	9.5																					
16	**Tuwartz Narrows**	60	49	56	44	42	47	37	30	16	17	13	16	17	9	9																				
17	**Fleischman Point** (Otter Channel)	62	51	57	45	43	48	38	33	19	20	16	17	20	12	14	9.5																			
18	**Kingcome Point**	62	51	52	40	38	43	33	33	13	17	16	13	8	17	24	24	28																		
19	**Butedale**	73	62	63	51	49	54	44	44	24	28	27	24	19	28	33	33	39	11																	
20	Home Bay	53	42	47	35	33	38	28	23	7	11	10	7	3	12	18	19	22	9	20																
21	Cornwall Inlet	57	46	51	39	37	42	32	27	11	15	13	11	7	15	21	22	25	12	23	4.5															
22	**Barnard Harbour**	66	55	59	47	45	50	39	34	19	23	21	18	15	22	26	24	21	21	32	13	10														
23	Fawcett Point	64	53	59	47	45	50	40	35	22	25	19	19	18	15	19	17	14	24	35	16	13	7													
24	**Man Islet** (Otter Passage)	71	60	66	54	52	57	47	41	28	28	24	26	28	20	22	18	9	36	47	37	34	29	21												
25	Dunn Passage (Weinberg Inlet)	67	56	62	50	48	53	43	38	25	26	22	22	26	18	19	14	7	34	45	28	31	27	23	9.5											
26	Ethelda Bay	73	62	68	56	54	59	49	44	31	31	27	28	31	23	25	21	13	39	50	34	36	28	24	13	8.5										
27	**Dupont Island**	76	65	71	59	57	62	52	47	33	35	31	31	28	26	29	25	17	34	45	27	24	17	13	18	12	13									
28	**Jacinto Island**	86	75	81	69	67	72	62	57	43	45	41	41	38	36	39	35	27	44	55	37	34	27	23	13	15	16	6.5								
29	Duckers Islands	72	61	67	55	53	58	48	45	28	32	28	27	24	24	28	25	23	34	45	22	19	12	10	26	19	21	8.5	15							
30	Penn Harbour (Surf Inlet)	84	73	79	67	65	70	60	57	40	44	40	39	38	36	40	37	35	46	57	34	31	24	22	38	31	32	20	26	12						
31	Evinrude Inlet	81	70	76	64	62	67	57	54	37	41	37	36	35	33	37	34	32	43	54	31	28	21	19	33	27	29	16	21	19	16					
32	**Ramsbotham Islands**	87	76	82	70	68	73	63	60	43	47	43	42	40	39	43	40	38	48	59	37	34	27	25	39	32	34	20	26	15	21	6				
33	**Oswald Point (Renison Island)**	77	66	72	60	58	63	53	48	32	36	32	32	30	27	32	29	23	35	46	27	25	18	14	24	18	19	5.5	11	7	17	11	15			
34	**Ulric Point**	79	68	74	62	60	65	55	52	35	39	35	34	31	31	35	32	26	36	47	28	26	18	15	28	21	22	9	15	6.5	15	7.5	11	3.5		
35	Kettle Inlet	87	76	82	70	68	73	63	59	43	46	42	42	40	39	42	39	35	46	57	38	36	27	25	34	30	31	18	21	15	25	16	21	12	10	
36	**Clifford Bay**	98	87	93	81	79	84	74	71	54	58	54	53	50	50	54	51	42	53	64	45	43	35	32	40	37	38	25	27	26	32	25	28	19	17	12

VERNEY PASSAGE, DEVASTATION CHANNEL AND GARDINER CANAL

Location	7	37	38	39	40	41	42	43	44	45	46	47	48	9	18	No.
Kersey Point	10	5	5.5	11	11	20	25	27	33	42	56	18	29	30	33	6
Grant Point (Sue Channel)		9.5	12	17	18	27	32	34	40	49	63	25	36	37	40	7
Loretta Anchorage			3.5	8.5	9	18	23	25	31	40	54	17	27	28	31	37
Weewanie Hot Springs				6.5	7	16	21	23	29	38	52	14	25	26	29	38
Kitsaway Anchorage					4	13	18	20	26	35	49	11	22	23	26	39
Staniforth Bank						9	14	16	22	31	45	8	18	19	22	40
Triumph Bay							10	12	18	27	41	16	25	27	30	41
Europa Point								2	8	17	31	20	30	31	34	42
Kiltuish Inlet									8.5	18	32	22	32	33	37	43
Cornwall Point										9	23	28	38	39	42	44
KEMANO											17	37	47	48	51	45
Kitlope Anchorage												51	61	62	65	46
Amy Point													10	11	15	47
Bishop Bay (Hot Springs)														22	12	48
Money Point															13	9
Kingcome Point																18

In the vicinity of capes and headlands in **Hecate Strait**, the water is almost always rough. In heavy weather, these areas can be extremely hazardous. Among the most dangerous of these are **Scudder Point, Cape St. James**, the vicinity of **Bonnila Island**, the south ends of both **Aristazabal** and **Price Islands, Cape Scott, Cape Calvert**, and the western entrance to **Hakai Passage.**

In 1787, the **Queen Charlotte Islands** were named by Captain George Dixon after his ship, the *Queen Charlotte*. In 1789, Captain Gray, an American fur trader named them after his own sloop, the *Washington*. For some years both names were used, but eventually the American name fell out of usage.

In 1786, **Queen Charlotte Sound** was named by Mr. S. Wedgeborough, commander of the *Experiment*, after Queen Charlotte Sophia, wife of George III of England.

Queen Charlotte Channel, Howe Sound, was named by Captain Richards of *HMS Plumper* after *HMS Queen Charlotte*, flagship of Lord Howe at the battle of the "Glorious First of June" in 1794.

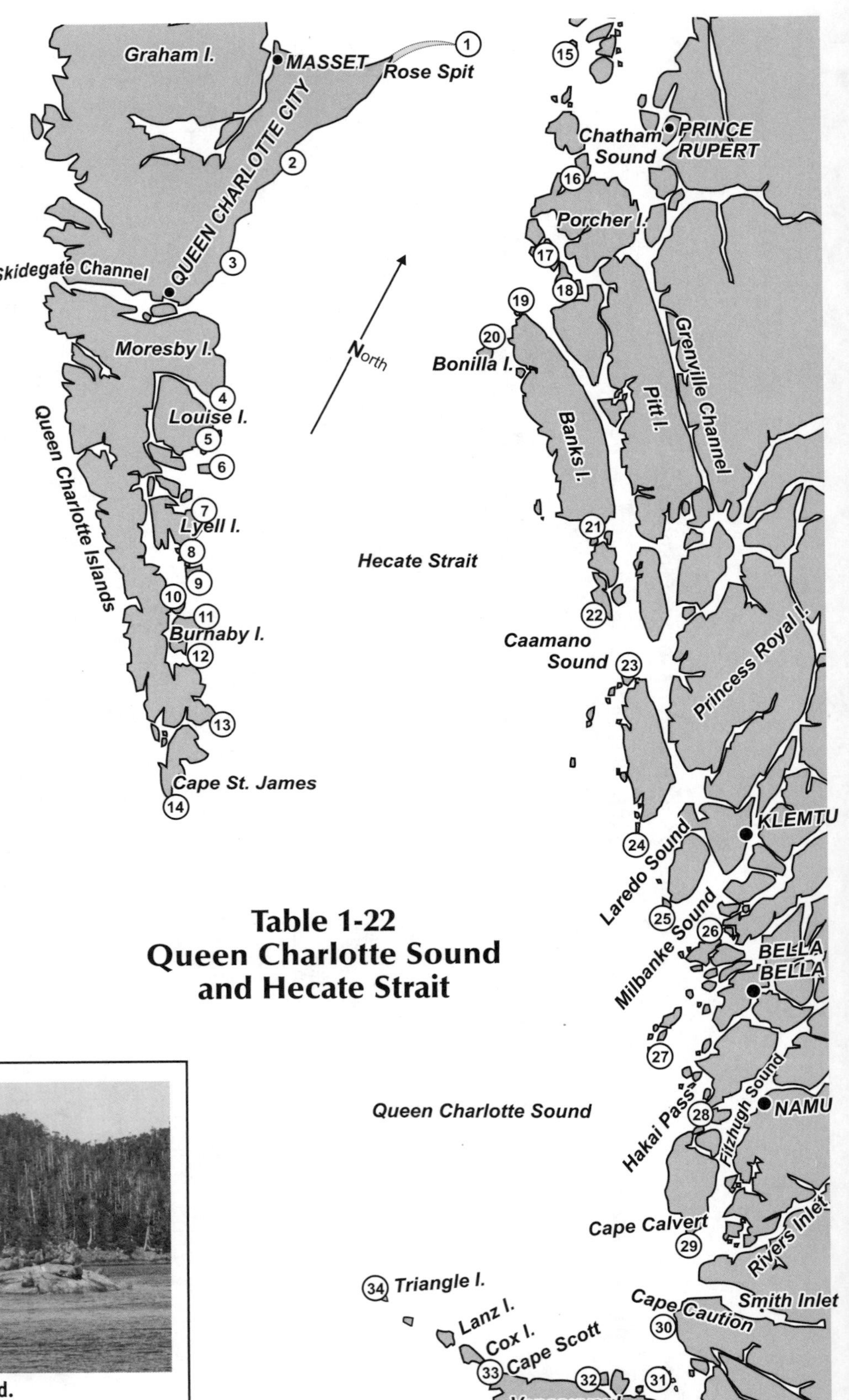
Graham I.
MASSET
Rose Spit
QUEEN CHARLOTTE CITY
Skidegate Channel
Moresby I.
Louise I.
Lyell I.
Burnaby I.
Cape St. James
Queen Charlotte Islands
North
Hecate Strait
Chatham Sound
PRINCE RUPERT
Porcher I.
Bonilla I.
Banks I.
Pitt I.
Grenville Channel
Caamano Sound
Princess Royal I.
KLEMTU
Laredo Sound
Milbanke Sound
BELLA BELLA
Queen Charlotte Sound
Hakai Pass
Fitzhugh Sound
NAMU
Cape Calvert
Rivers Inlet
Smith Inlet
Cape Caution
Triangle I.
Lanz I.
Cox I.
Cape Scott
Vancouver I.

Table 1-22
Queen Charlotte Sound and Hecate Strait

Sea Lion Rookery, **Caamano Sound.**

TABLE 1-22 QUEEN CHARLOTTE SOUND AND HECATE STRAIT

Most Direct Route

Locations in **bold lowercase** appear in other detail tables.

1	**Rose Spit (Overfall Shoal Green Whistle Buoy)**																																	
2	Cape Ball	35																																
3	Lawn Point	52	17																															
4	Cumshewa Head	80	45	28																														
5	Skedans Island	84	49	32	4																													
6	Reef Island	91	56	39	11	7																												
7	Dodge Point	99	64	47	19	15	8																											
8	Hot Springs Island	110	75	58	30	26	19	11																										
9	Tatsung Rock (Ramsay Island)	114	79	62	34	30	23	15	6																									
10	All Alone Stone	116	81	64	36	32	25	17	6	4																								
11	Scudder Point	119	84	67	39	35	28	20	11	7	6																							
12	Copper Island East	125	90	73	45	41	34	26	17	13	12	6																						
13	Garcin Rocks	137	102	85	57	53	46	38	29	25	24	18	12																					
14	Cape St James	154	119	102	74	70	63	55	46	42	41	35	29	17																				
15	**Triple Island**	23	48	67	82	86	91	97	108	109	113	115	109	130	147																			
16	View Point (Edye Pass)	34	49	59	73	77	80	87	97	98	102	103	120	117	134	19																		
17	**Freeman Pass**	43	44	52	61	64	67	73	83	83	87	88	92	103	119	35	22																	
18	**Spicer Anchorage**	60	54	61	62	64	68	74	85	83	87	87	91	98	114	45	32	16																
19	White Rocks	49	44	51	52	54	58	64	75	73	77	77	81	88	104	43	30	15	10															
20	**Bonilla Island**	54	44	45	44	47	51	55	63	62	66	66	71	79	95	52	39	24	19	9														
21	**Man Island (Otter Pass)**	99	83	80	67	67	64	67	70	67	71	67	69	71	87	90	74	58	48	47	38													
22	**Jacinto Island**	107	92	88	73	72	70	69	72	68	71	66	67	66	80	100	87	72	67	57	48	13												
23	**Rennison Island (Oswald Point)**	118	102	97	83	81	78	79	79	76	78	72	73	71	83	110	98	83	78	68	59	24	10											
24	Nab Rock	151	133	125	105	103	98	95	93	88	90	83	83	75	80	141	128	113	108	98	89	54	41	33										
25	**McInnes Island**	163	143	137	117	115	109	105	103	97	99	93	91	83	89	153	140	125	120	110	101	66	53	45	12									
26	**Ivory Island**	175	156	150	130	128	122	118	116	110	112	106	104	96	100	166	153	138	133	123	114	79	66	58	25	13								
27	Currie Light (Goose Group)	184	165	156	136	131	127	123	119	115	115	108	107	98	96	180	167	152	140	137	128	93	80	72	38	28	29							
28	**Hakai Pass (Odlum Point)**	199	180	173	151	146	142	138	134	130	130	123	121	111	110	196	183	168	163	153	144	109	96	90	53	45	46	15						
29	**Cape Calvert**	219	199	190	167	163	159	154	149	144	144	138	137	125	122	214	201	186	181	171	162	127	114	107	75	65	66	36	24					
30	**Cape Caution**	234	212	202	180	176	172	167	162	157	157	151	148	137	131	229	216	201	196	186	177	142	129	120	86	78	80	49	41	17				
31	**Pine Island**	242	224	214	189	185	180	175	169	164	165	158	156	143	138	243	230	215	210	200	191	156	140	131	99	88	90	60	51	27	12			
32	Nahwitti Bar	237	219	209	183	180	175	170	164	159	159	152	149	137	130	241	228	213	208	198	189	155	137	130	98	89	92	61	50	32	18	14		
33	Triangle island	221	212	184	158	155	150	144	138	131	131	124	121	107	97	221	208	193	188	178	169	140	125	122	90	85	89	63	61	55	50	51	41	
34	**Cape Scott**	233	197	202	176	174	168	162	155	150	150	143	139	127	118	232	219	204	199	189	180	151	137	132	98	90	92	65	56	42	32	33	20	25

MASSET to Rose Spit	36
QUEEN CHARLOTTE to Lawn Point	15
PRINCE RUPERT to Triple Island	20
KLEMTU to Nab Rock	31
BELLA BELLA to Ivory Island	14
PORT HARDY to Pine Island	19

Table 1-23 Caamano Sound to Chatham Sound

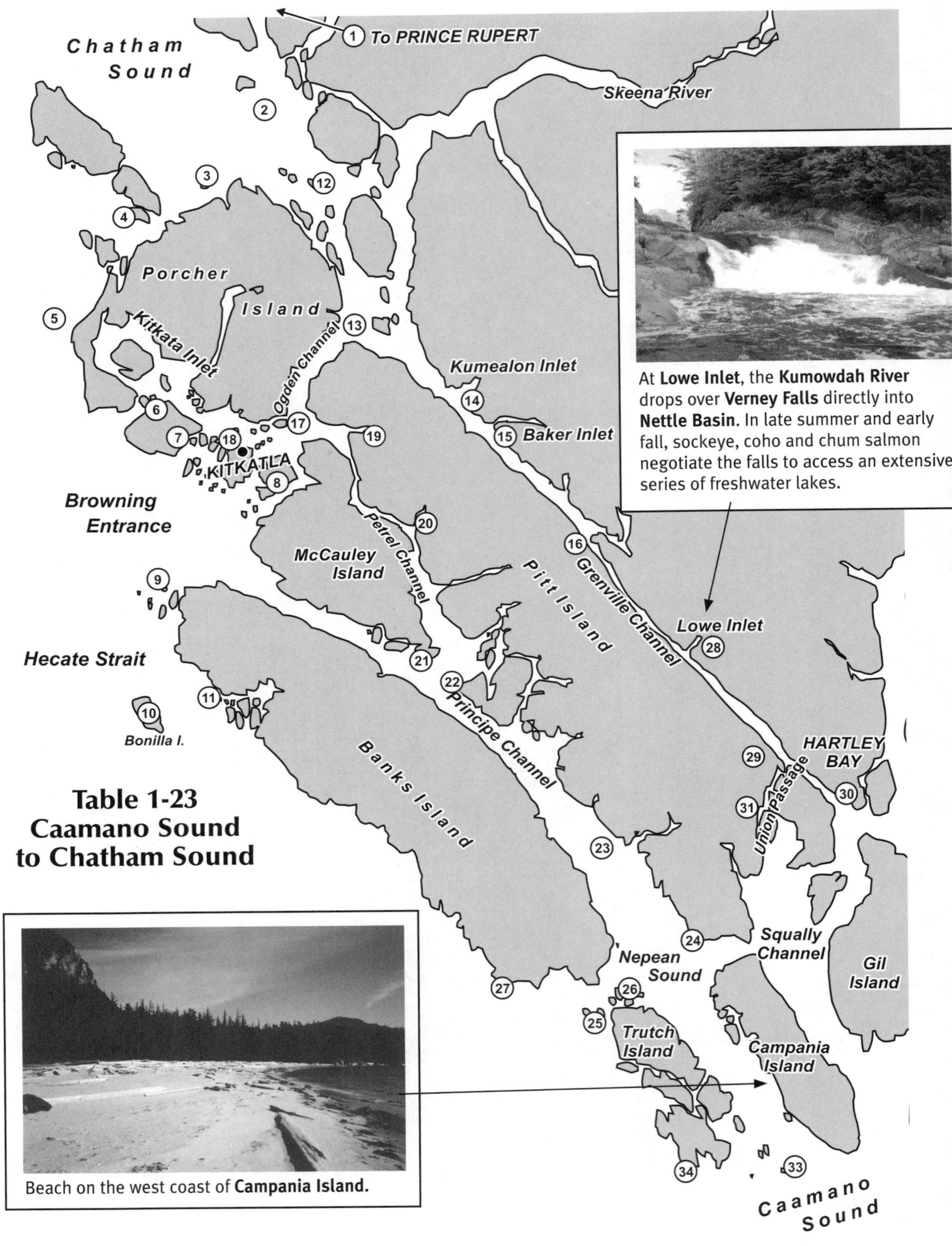

Chatham Sound
1 To PRINCE RUPERT
Skeena River
2
3
4
12
Porcher Island
5
Kitkata Inlet
Ogden Channel
13
Kumealon Inlet
14
15 Baker Inlet
6
7
18
17
19
KITKATLA
8
Browning Entrance
Petrel Channel
20
16
McCauley Island
Pitt Island
Grenville Channel
9
Lowe Inlet
28
Hecate Strait
21
22
11
10
Bonilla I.
Principe Channel
Banks Island
HARTLEY BAY
29
30
31
Union Passage
23
24
Squally Channel
Nepean Sound
Gil Island
27
26
25
Trutch Island
Campania Island
34
33
Caamano Sound

At **Lowe Inlet**, the **Kumowdah River** drops over **Verney Falls** directly into **Nettle Basin.** In late summer and early fall, sockeye, coho and chum salmon negotiate the falls to access an extensive series of freshwater lakes.

Beach on the west coast of **Campania Island.**

TABLE 1-23 CAMAANO SOUND TO CHATHAM SOUND

Most Direct Route (Except no routes calculated through Union Passage)

Locations in **bold lowercase** appear in other detail tables.

#	Location	1	2	3	4	5	6	7	8	9	10	11	12	13	14	15	16	17	18	19	20	21	22	23	24	25	26	27	28	29	30	31	32	33
1	**PRINCE RUPERT (Fairview)**																																	
2	**Holland Rock**	6																																
3	Havelock Rock, Hunt Inlet	13	6																															
4	View Point (Arthur Island)	18	12	6																														
5	Oval Rock	27	21	15	9																													
6	Freeman Passage	40	34	28	22	13																												
7	Willis Bay	44	38	32	26	17	11																											
8	**Spicer Island Anchorage**	50	44	38	32	23	16	11																										
9	White Rocks, Larsen Harbour	48	42	36	30	21	15	11	10																									
10	**Bonilla Island**	57	51	45	39	30	24	20	19	9																								
11	Goring Reef (Kingkown Inlet)	57	51	45	39	30	26	22	20	11	4																							
12	**Genn Island**	11	5	7.5	14	23	36	34	24	34	43	45																						
13	Watson Rock	22	16	17	23	31	17	23	13	23	32	34	11																					
14	Kumealon Inlet	29	23	24	30	38	24	30	20	30	39	41	18	7																				
15	Baker Inlet	32	26	27	33	41	27	33	23	33	42	44	21	10	3																			
16	Morning Reef	42	36	37	43	51	37	43	33	43	52	54	31	20	13	10																		
17	Comrie Head (Ogden Channel)	28	22	25	31	24	12	15	7	16	25	27	17	7	15	18	28																	
18	**KITKATLA**	33	27	30	29	20	6.5	13	7.5	13	22	24	22	12	19	22	32	5																
19	Captain Cove Anchorage	32	26	29	35	28	15	19	10	20	29	31	21	11	19	22	32	4	9															
20	Newcombe Harbour Entrance	39	33	35	42	36	23	26	18	27	37	39	28	18	26	29	39	11	16	11														
21	Dixon Island	54	48	48	42	33	26	21	16	15	24	26	43	33	41	44	54	22	20	25	15													
22	Foul Point (Anger Island)	51	45	48	48	39	32	27	22	21	30	32	40	30	38	41	51	23	26	23	12	6.5												
23	Moncton Inlet, Gale Point	67	61	64	64	55	48	43	38	38	47	47	56	46	53	56	49	39	44	39	28	23	16											
24	**Fleishman Point (Otter Channel)**	74	68	71	71	62	55	50	45	45	45	43	63	53	60	59	49	46	51	46	35	30	23	7										
25	**Man Islet (Otter Passage)**	78	72	74	74	65	58	53	48	47	38	36	67	57	63	60	50	50	55	50	39	32	26	11	7.5									
26	**Block Islet (Otter Passage)**	76	70	73	73	64	57	52	47	46	40	38	65	55	55	58	48	48	53	48	37	31	25	9	5.5	2								
27	Terror Point	84	78	75	69	60	54	50	49	39	30	28	73	62	69	68	58	55	63	58	47	40	34	19	15	8	10							
28	Tom Islet	52	46	48	54	60	47	53	45	54	63	61	41	30	23	20	10	38	42	42	49	61	55	39	32	40	38	48						
29	Hawkins Narrows	63	57	59	65	71	58	64	56	66	67	65	52	41	34	31	21	49	53	53	56	51	44	28	21	29	27	37	11					
30	**Sainty Point**	68	62	64	70	76	63	67	62	61	62	60	57	46	39	36	26	53	58	57	52	46	40	23	16	24	22	32	15	4.5				
31	**Peters Narrows**	81	75	77	86	77	70	65	60	59	60	58	70	59	52	49	39	58	63	58	47	44	37	21	14	22	20	30	28	2.5	13			
32	**Barnard Harbour**	90	84	90	93	84	77	72	67	66	66	64	83	72	65	62	52	67	72	67	56	51	44	28	21	28	26	36	41	31	26	27		
33	**Dupont Island**	92	86	87	89	80	73	68	63	62	55	53	81	70	71	68	58	63	68	63	52	47	40	24	17	19	18	25	47	36	32	29	16	
34	**Jacinto Island**	95	89	90	87	78	72	68	67	57	48	46	84	73	72	69	59	66	71	66	55	50	43	27	20	13	15	18	49	39	34	31	22	6

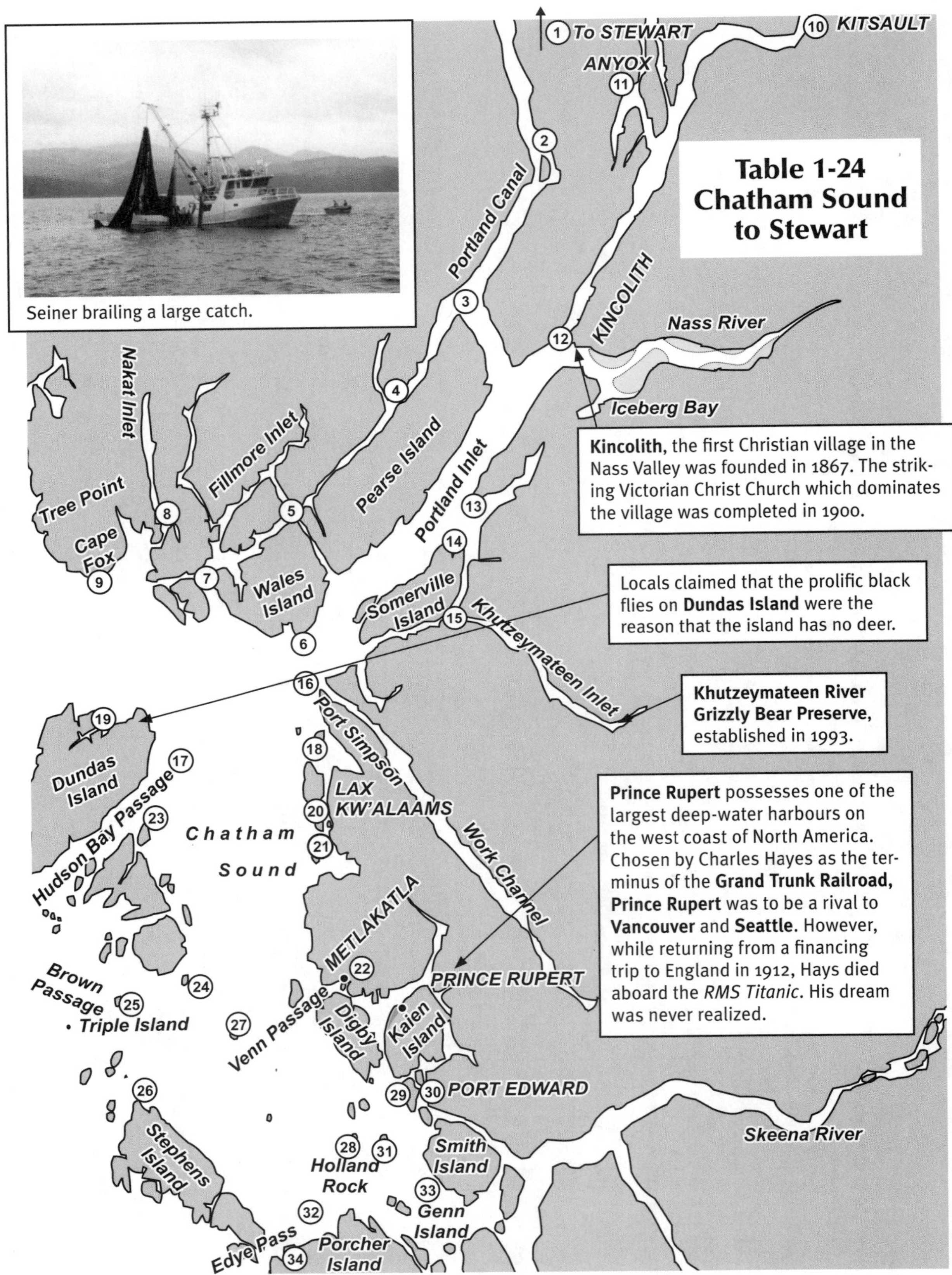

Table 1-24
Chatham Sound to Stewart
1 To STEWART
10 KITSAULT
ANYOX
11
2
Portland Canal
3
KINCOLITH
12
Nass River
Iceberg Bay
4
Nakat Inlet
Fillmore Inlet
Pearse Island
Portland Inlet
13
14
Tree Point
8
5
Cape Fox
9
7
Wales Island
6
Somerville Island
15
Khutzeymateen Inlet
16
Port Simpson
19
18
Dundas Island
17
LAX KW'ALAAMS
20
Hudson Bay Passage
23
Chatham Sound
21
Work Channel
METLAKATLA
22
Brown Passage
24
25
Triple Island
27
Venn Passage
Digby Island
Kaien Island
PRINCE RUPERT
29
30 PORT EDWARD
26
Stephens Island
28
31
Holland Rock
Smith Island
Skeena River
33
32
Genn Island
Edye Pass
Porcher Island
34
Kincolith, the first Christian village in the Nass Valley was founded in 1867. The striking Victorian Christ Church which dominates the village was completed in 1900.
Locals claimed that the prolific black flies on Dundas Island were the reason that the island has no deer.
Khutzeymateen River Grizzly Bear Preserve, established in 1993.
Prince Rupert possesses one of the largest deep-water harbours on the west coast of North America. Chosen by Charles Hayes as the terminus of the Grand Trunk Railroad, Prince Rupert was to be a rival to Vancouver and Seattle. However, while returning from a financing trip to England in 1912, Hays died aboard the RMS Titanic. His dream was never realized.

Seiner brailing a large catch.

TABLE 1-24 CHATHAM SOUND TO STEWART

Most Direct Route

Locations in **bold lowercase** appear in other detail tables.

No.	Location	1	2	3	4	5	6	7	8	9	10	11	12	13	14	15	16	17	18	19	20	21	22	23	24	25	26	27	28	29	30	31	32	33
1	**STEWART**																																	
2	Hattie Island	40																																
3	**Tree Point**	57	17																															
4	Gwent Cove (Hidden Inlet)	65	23	8																														
5	Akeku Point	74	32	17	9																													
6	Wales Point	81	41	24	18	9																												
7	Bartlett Point	79	39	24	16	7	8																											
8	Nakat Harbour	90	50	33	25	14	16	7																										
9	**Cape Fox**	89	49	32	24	15	14	8	6																									
10	**KITSAULT**	99	59	42	50	60	59	67	75	73																								
11	**ANYOX**	90	50	33	41	51	50	58	66	64	16																							
12	**KINKOLITH** (Nass Point)	65	25	8.5	16	26	25	33	41	39	34	25																						
13	Trefusis Point	70	30	13	21	15	14	22	30	28	45	36	11																					
14	Start Point (Sommerville Bay)	73	33	16	21	12	11	19	27	25	48	39	14	3																				
15	Spakels Point	78	38	21	24	15	9	17	25	23	53	43	18	7	5																			
16	Maskelyne Point	91	51	34	21	12	3	10	17	15	61	52	27	16	13	9																		
17	Green Islet	92	52	35	29	20	11	12	16	12	71	62	37	26	23	19	10																	
18	**PORT SIMPSON** (Birnie Island)	96	56	39	33	15	7	13	20	17	65	56	31	20	17	13	4	9																
19	**Brundige Inlet** (Prospector Point)	93	51	36	28	19	14	12	14	9	73	64	39	29	27	22	14	7	14															
20	Flat Top Islands (Pearl Harbour)	100	60	43	30	21	20	17	25	21	70	61	36	25	22	18	9	19	5	16														
21	Escape Reefs (Big Bay)	103	63	46	33	24	23	20	27	22	73	64	39	28	25	21	12	10	8	17	3													
22	**METLAKATLA**	113	73	56	43	34	30	30	37	31	83	74	49	38	35	31	15	9	11	26	13	10												
23	**White Sand Island**	104	64	47	34	25	17	15	19	15	74	65	40	29	26	44	13	3	12	10	10	10	16											
24	**Beaver Rock**	112	72	55	42	33	23	26	33	26	82	73	48	37	24	30	21	14	17	21	13	11	10	11										
25	Hanmer Rocks	116	76	59	46	37	27	30	37	30	86	77	52	41	28	34	25	18	25	25	17	15	14	15	4									
26	**Qlawdzeet Anchorage**	120	80	63	50	41	31	34	41	34	90	81	56	45	32	38	29	22	25	29	21	19	14	19	8	7								
27	Lucy Island	114	74	57	44	35	27	29	33	36	84	75	50	39	36	32	23	17	20	24	15	11	7	15	4.5	7	8							
28	Greentop Island	122	82	65	52	43	36	38	42	45	92	83	58	47	44	40	31	26	28	33	22	20	12	25	15	17	13	10						
29	Ridley Island	123	83	66	53	44	37	39	43	46	93	84	59	48	45	41	32	27	29	34	23	20	13	26	16	18	15	11	4					
30	**PORT EDWARD**	126	86	69	56	47	39	41	46	48	96	87	62	51	48	44	35	30	32	37	26	23	16	29	19	21	19	14	6	4				
31	**Holland Rock**	124	84	67	54	45	38	40	44	47	94	85	60	49	46	42	33	28	30	35	24	21	13	27	17	18	15	12	2	3	5			
32	Havelock Rock	125	85	68	55	46	40	42	46	49	95	86	61	50	47	43	34	30	32	37	26	24	16	28	18	18	13	13	5	9	12	6		
33	**Genn Island**	123	83	66	58	49	42	43	50	46	99	90	65	54	51	47	39	33	35	40	29	26	18	31	21	23	19	16	6	8	10	5	7	
34	Refuge Bay	130	90	73	60	51	41	43	47	50	97	88	63	52	49	45	37	32	34	39	29	25	19	31	21	19	12	16	8	12	15	9.5	3	10

PRINCE RUPERT HARBOUR

Location								No.
PORT EDWARD	4	8.5	11	13	16	15	13	30
Ridley Island		4.5	7	8.5	12	10.5	9	29
PRINCE RUPERT (Fairview)			2.5	4	7.5	6	4.5	35
PRINCE RUPERT (Rushbrooke)				1.5	5	3.5	5.5	36
Seal Cove					4	2	7	37
Tuck Narrows						6	10	38
Butze Rapids							9	39
METLAKATLA								22

Route	Distance	No.
Maskelyne Point to Head of Work Channel	27	16
ANYOX to Head of Hastings Arm	20	11
Spakels Point to Khutzeymateen River	14	15

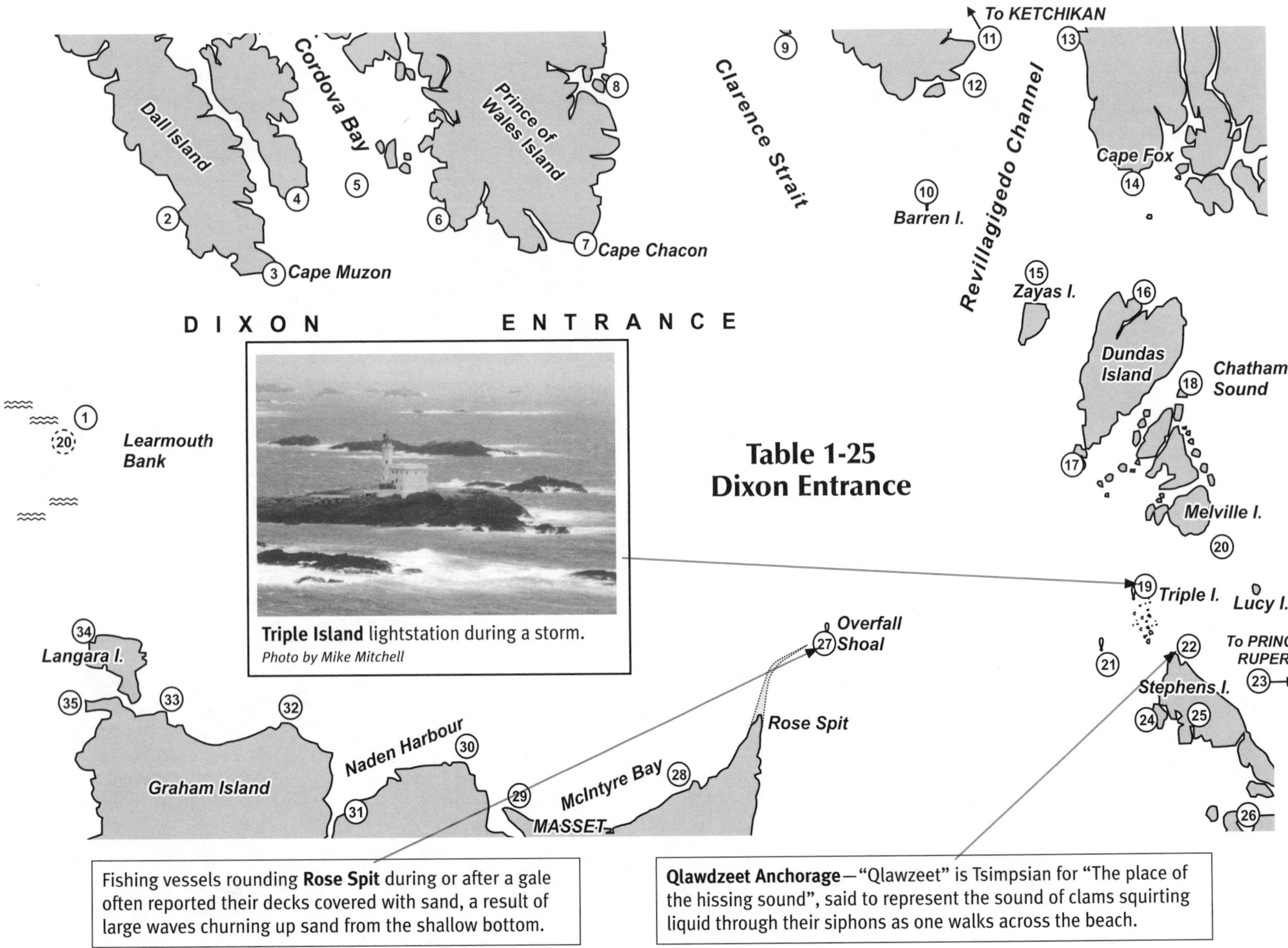
To KETCHIKAN
Dall Island
Cordova Bay
Prince of Wales Island
Clarence Strait
Revillagigedo Channel
Barren I.
Cape Fox
Cape Muzon
Cape Chacon
Zayas I.
DIXON ENTRANCE
Dundas Island
Chatham Sound
Learmouth Bank
Melville I.
Triple I.
Lucy I.
Overfall Shoal
To PRINCE RUPERT
Stephens I.
Langara I.
Rose Spit
Naden Harbour
McIntyre Bay
Graham Island
MASSET
1
2
3
4
5
6
7
8
9
10
11
12
13
14
15
16
17
18
19
20
21
22
23
24
25
26
27
28
29
30
31
32
33
34
35

Table 1-25
Dixon Entrance

Triple Island lightstation during a storm.
Photo by Mike Mitchell

Fishing vessels rounding **Rose Spit** during or after a gale often reported their decks covered with sand, a result of large waves churning up sand from the shallow bottom.

Qlawdzeet Anchorage—"Qlawzeet" is Tsimpsian for "The place of the hissing sound", said to represent the sound of clams squirting liquid through their siphons as one walks across the beach.

TABLE 1-25 DIXON ENTRANCE

Most Direct Route (Including routes through Venn Passage to Prince Rupert)

Locations in **bold lowercase** appear in other detail tables.

Entry Point to **MASSET**	3
Entry Point to Port Clements	25
Entry Point to Juskatla Narrows	27

USA

CANADA

#	Location	1	2	3	4	5	6	7	8	9	10	11	12	13	14	15	16	17	18	19	20	21	22	23	24	25	26	27	28	29	30	31	32	33	34
1	Learmouth Bank (20 Meter Shoal)																																		
2	Point Cornwallis	15																																	
3	Cape Muzon	17	7																																
4	Kaigani Point	24	14	6.5																															
5	Round Islands	27	17	10	5.5																														
6	Point Marsh	29	22	14	12	8.5																													
7	Cape Chacon	40	31	24	24	20	12																												
8	Kendrick Islands	51	43	36	36	32	24	12																											
9	Percy Islands	59	51	44	44	40	32	20	12																										
10	Barren Island	61	55	48	47	44	35	24	23	16																									
11	**KETCHIKAN**	83	75	68	67	64	56	43	33	25	42																								
12	East Island	72	61	54	54	50	42	30	29	19	9	36																							
13	Foggy Point	78	69	62	62	58	50	38	36	26	16	35	7.5																						
14	**Cape Fox**	79	72	65	65	61	53	41	40	31	19	47	14	13																					
15	East Devil Rock (Zayas Island)	70	64	57	57	53	45	33	33	25	10	48	14	26	10																				
16	Prospector Point (Brundige Inlet)	82	76	69	69	65	57	45	45	37	22	53	21	21	9.5	12																			
17	Chearnley Islet/Prince Leboo Island	72	69	62	62	58	50	40	45	40	22	63	28	29	20	15	16																		
18	**Whitesand Islet**	89	79	72	72	68	60	50	52	44	30	61	28	27	16	19	10	10																	
19	**Triple Island**	77	74	67	68	64	56	46	51	47	32	72	37	38	29	24	25	9	18																
20	**Beaver Rock**	84	81	74	75	71	63	53	58	54	39	72	41	42	33	28	21	13	11	7															
21	Butterworth Rocks	74	72	65	66	62	54	45	51	49	34	75	41	42	33	28	29	13	23	5	12														
22	Qlawdzeet Anchorage	84	81	74	75	71	63	53	58	54	39	80	43	44	35	30	31	15	19	7	8	9													
23	**PRINCE RUPERT (Fairview)**	97	94	87	88	84	76	66	71	67	52	82	51	50	39	49	31	28	21	20	15	29	20												
24	China Islet/Phillips Island	80	80	73	74	70	62	53	69	57	42	83	47	48	39	34	35	19	25	10	14	7.5	7	27											
25	Skiakl Bay	84	84	79	78	74	66	57	73	61	44	87	51	52	43	38	39	23	29	14	18	12	11	31	4										
26	View Point/Welcome Harbour	93	89	82	83	82	71	62	78	66	51	95	56	57	48	43	44	28	34	19	23	17	16	19	9	9									
27	Overfall Shoal (Rose Spit Green Whistle Buoy)	55	55	48	49	48	39	31	41	43	31	67	40	45	40	32	36	22	32	23	29	19	27	43	25	29	34								
28	Yakan Point	49	52	46	49	48	41	36	48	52	43	77	56	57	54	47	51	39	39	40	46	36	44	60	42	46	51	17							
29	**MASSET (Entry Point)**	40	47	40	45	44	40	39	51	54	52	81	66	68	66	57	63	49	59	50	56	46	54	70	52	56	55	27	14						
30	Wiah Point	34	40	34	39	40	35	34	47	55	50	79	63	66	63	54	65	50	62	53	59	49	57	73	55	59	64	30	17	6.5					
31	Alexandra Narrows	33	42	38	43	44	40	42	65	63	59	86	73	76	73	65	76	61	73	64	70	60	68	84	66	70	75	41	28	18	4				
32	Klashwun Point (Shag Rock)	24	34	29	35	37	35	38	51	57	57	82	70	74	72	63	76	62	74	65	71	61	69	85	67	71	76	42	29	19	12	9			
33	Gunia Point	19	32	30	36	39	39	44	57	65	65	88	78	81	81	72	84	71	84	75	81	71	79	95	77	81	86	52	39	29	23	19	10		
34	Langara Point	13	27	27	33	37	38	44	57	65	60	89	75	82	83	74	87	73	87	78	84	74	82	98	80	84	88	55	45	35	28	25	16	9	
35	Cape Knox	17	31	31	37	41	43	49	61	71	70	94	79	86	87	78	90	77	90	81	87	77	85	101	83	87	92	58	45	35	28	25	16	6	4

Table 2 Managing Tidal Rapids

Table 2-1 — General Principles for Managing Tidal Rapids

Laminar Flow

When a body of water moves rapidly along a relatively smooth channel or canal, the sides and bottom of the channel don't restrict the movement of the water. The result is that the water flows smoothly, without turbulence, and consequently, small vessels may navigate in relative comfort. This type of smooth water flow is known as **laminar flow**.

Most navigable rivers exhibit laminar flow. Chatham Channel, in BC's central coast, and Myers Passage in the north, are both excellent examples of small channels with laminar flow. Though Chatham Channel flows at up to seven knots, it does so relatively smoothly even at maximum current. Conditions dangerous to small craft develop only when strong to gale force winds oppose the peak current.

Fig 2-1 Laminar Flow in a smooth sided canal

Turbulent Flow in Tidal Rapids

Pronounced irregularities in the sides or bottom of a channel deflect some of the current in a different direction than the rest of the stream. A single irregularity causes a single standing wave with localized turbulence. However, numerous irregularities or obstructions interfering with

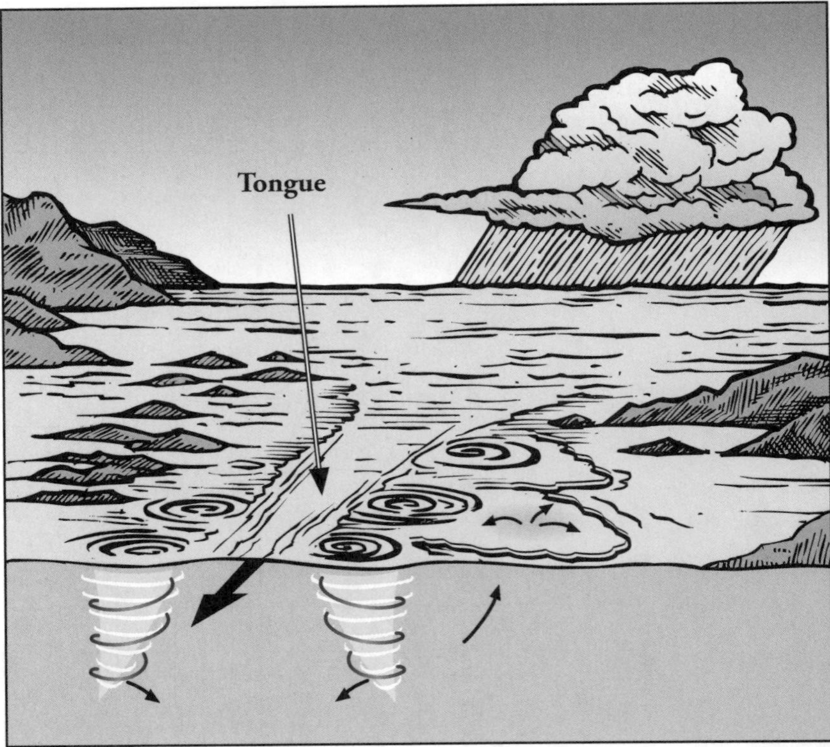
Tongue

Fig 2-2 Subsidence (Whirlpools) and Upwelling (Boils) in a Tidal Rapids.

At the interface between the laminar flowing tongue and the surrounding water, a series of whirlpools and boils develops. Water subsiding in whirlpools is circulated to the surface in boils (upwellings). Anything lost in a whirlpool (including small boats) will surface again in a boil, sometimes a long distance away.

the flow of the current cause extensive turbulence—usually filling the channel from one side to the other and for a distance downstream. Where a restriction in a channel significantly interferes with the flow of water in a tidal channel, the result is a tidal rapids. These rapids have many common characteristics.

From the upstream to the downstream side of the rapids, the water level flows down a slope. (If there were no difference in level there would be no tidal current.) A tongue of relatively smooth water flows through the opening, defined by curved zones of turbulence on either side that extend from the point of restriction and curve downstream toward the middle of the channel. Forming the boundary between the merely turbulent surrounding water and the relatively smooth tongue you will find a series of whirlpools (subsidence) and boils (upwelling). This area may be very hazardous to small craft, and is usually lower than the tongue.

The tongue extends downstream until it loses its identity in the general turbulence. This turbulence often extends downstream for several hundred meters. In Seymour Narrows the turbulence from the flood current extends past Race Point, more than 1.5 Nm downstream (2800 m).

Pass Island
Tongue

Fig 2-3
Deception Pass during a Flood

To the west of Pass Island, the tongue is defined on the north by the curved zone of turbulence generated by Lighthouse Point. The tongue flows toward Pass Island, then along the south side of the island as it passes under the highway bridge. Once past the island, the relatively smooth flowing currents in the tongue disappear into a highly tubulent stream which extends to Strawberry Island and beyond. Note that the boat in the upper right is maneuvering to avoid the worst of the turbulence by entering the tongue just to the east of Pass Island.

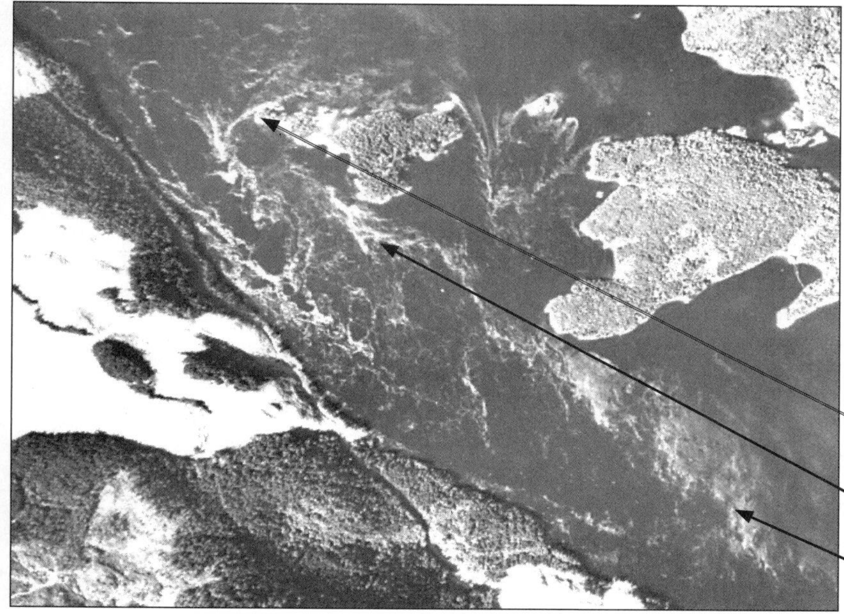

Fig 2-4
Dent Rapids During a Large Flood

At the time of the photograph, the current in Dent Rapids was running near maximum. At this time Dent Rapids is extremely dangerous and should not be attempted by vessels of any size.

Note:
—Dent Point on Little Dent Island spawns a curved series of whirlpools extending downstream along the side of the tongue.
—A large, dangerous whirlpool forms in the Devil's Hole during peak current.
— The upwelling turbulence extends more than three times the length of the tongue.

Fig 2-5 Heading Upstream

General Rules

Though specific strategies for certain rapids on the Inside Passage appear in Tables 2-2 and 2-3, the principles for navigating a tidal channel are the same everywhere.

- When you first transit any rapids, do so at slack water.
- If you wish to challenge a tidal rapids the first time you do so should be shortly before slack water. If you get into difficulties, the current will be abating, not increasing. Never challenge a flood or ebb current for the first time on a large tide; the rapids may approach maximum current shortly after slack water.
- With the experience you have gained you will then be able to challenge the rapids a longer time before slack water. As you gain confidence you can increase the time before (or after) slack water.
- Always calculate the velocity of the current each time you challenge a rapids. But remember that the predicted speed is the average speed in the middle of the tongue. Localized areas of the rapids may be moving much faster than this average speed.
- The degree of turbulence is not directly proportional to the current speed. When the current is running at twice the speed, it may be three or four times more turbulent.
- Never attempt to transit the rapids if the current speed is more than one half your vessel's maximum speed. You must always have a reserve of speed available.
- Certain rapids must never be attempted at any time other than slack water (Arran Rapids). Others may be transited at moderate speeds (Greene Point Rapids). Local knowledge is the key.
- If possible, observe a rapids from the shore to learn about its characteristics.
- Duration of slack water is usually just a few minutes. In certain high-velocity rapids the change of direction may be virtually instantaneous. Make sure you are in position to take advantage of the slack when it occurs.
- Interfaces between boils (upwellings) may actually be subsidence zones. Small open boats have been sucked down and capsized on encountering these zones. Stay well clear if at all possible.
- Planing hulls operating "on step" are least influenced by turbulence because only a small portion of their hulls is immersed. However, sudden shocks and cavitation caused by passing between packets of water moving in different directions, can stress drive trains.

When heading upstream

- You may encounter large areas of turbulence downstream of the tongue. Attempt to approach the tongue from the side that is least affected by turbulence. Do not attempt to approach the tongue from directly downstream; the turbulence is generally worse directly downstream from the end of the tongue.
- Enter the tongue near its end. Look for an area least affected by boils, and as far from whirlpools as possible.
- When crossing the boundary into a boil, the water in the boil will probably be in motion either to port or starboard. As soon as the bow of your vessel crosses into the boil, your bow will be pushed in the direction the upwelling water is moving, so you should steer in the opposite direction in order to maintain your heading. Don't wait for the cross current to take effect on your bow. Steer to anticipate the movement, otherwise you will not be able to compensate in time. Once your vessel has crossed the interface, straighten out your rudder or you will find the vessel taking a rapid sheer in the other direction.
- Once you have entered the tongue, make every effort to remain in the middle of the tongue until finally past the rapids.

When heading downstream

- Remain in the middle of the tongue until near its end.
- Then look for the best place to exit. Look for an area least affected by boils, and as far from whirlpools as possible.
- When exiting the tongue, be careful you don't enter an eddy that is setting rapidly toward the shore.

Table 2-2 — Johnstone Strait and Adjacent Tidal Rapids

The biggest barrier to cruising the central coast of British Columbia isn't the distance, or the wet weather, or the cost of fuel. The biggest barriers are the capricious (and confusing) tides and rapids north of Campbell River. Unpredictable tidal currents always seem to be working against you; either pushing your boat along faster than you wish, or retarding its progress. If you miss the slack current at the next set of rapids, you will either have to wait for the next tide or you may have to tackle the rapids when the current is running.

It is apparently impossible to plan a trip or meet deadlines—and that creates anxiety. The result is that most folks are happy to cruise to Desolation Sound or the southern Gulf Islands, but are seriously reluctant to travel north of Seymour Narrows or Stuart Island.

Fig 2-6
Helmcken Island seen from near Ripple Shoal.

You need not be anxious. Planning a trip north of Campbell River is not as difficult as you might think—Johnstone Strait is a complex system, but it is predictable. By understanding the dynamics of the tidal flow in Johnstone Strait, you can easily develop strategies for managing a passage through the tidal narrows and rapids. The secret lies in taking advantage of the characteristics of the tidal flow.

Net outward flow
Fresh water mixes with salt water
River current

Fig 2-7 Fresh water mixing in Georgia Strait and Johnstone Strait

---

It's all in the Timing!!

In the 1980s, I worked on a fish packer, transporting farmed salmon from western Johnstone Strait and Knight Inlet to Campbell River and Vancouver. Almost every day we transited Johnstone Strait, on every stage of the tide. Every day I recorded the time in transit and the state of the current, and after a while, using this information, I was able to predict the transit time from Broken Islands to Seymour Narrows, a distance of 49 Nm. I was seldom in error by more than a few minutes.

By paying close attention to the Tide and Current Tables, I planned a trip from Discovery Channel to Vancouver's Second Narrows via Okisollo Rapids and Hole in the Wall. The trip took more than 12 hours, but my estimated time was off by only five minutes.

Characteristics of the System

Johnstone Strait and adjacent channels connect the northern portion of Georgia Strait with Queen Charlotte Sound. In response to the rise and fall of the tide, Pacific Ocean water flows into and out of Georgia Strait via Johnstone Strait. Where the channels are constricted by topography, turbulent rapids and whirlpools develop (Seymour Narrows and Race Passage).

Fresh water discharged into Georgia Strait by mainland rivers (primarily the Fraser and Homathko Rivers) mixes with the heavier sea water. The resulting brackish mixture floats on top of denser sea water and flows toward the open ocean at an average of approximately 0.5 Knots. This continuous outward flow enhances the tidal current flowing out of Georgia Strait (ebb) and partially counteracts the flood.

During the smallest tides of a Lunar cycle (Neap tides), river outflow may completely overwhelm the weaker flood current on the surface (though the tide still rises and falls). During every lunar cycle, for several days there are no surface flood currents at the Johnstone Strait Current Station, (located 1.5 Nm southwest of Port Neville), though there may be a flood current at depth.

At Seymour Narrows, the deep flood current is deflected to the surface by the underwater topography. Consequently, the surface current ebbs and flows in a normal manner, ***even on days when there is no surface flood current at Johnstone Strait Central.***

The effect of fresh water discharge is strongest in early summer when rivers are in freshet. However, whenever there is a large amount of runoff into the Georgia Basin, this effect will also be apparent (ie. during heavy winter rainstorms). As a result, ***current values may differ from those published in the tide tables.***

In the open ocean, continuous strong to gale force winds generate wind-driven currents of up to 3% of the wind speed. In the confines of Johnstone Strait, wind-driven currents may enhance or retard flood and ebb currents by up to one knot. Continuous westerly winds may even generate a small flood current when there is none predicted. Continuous south-easterlies may enhance the ebb current to the point where it completely overwhelms a small flood.

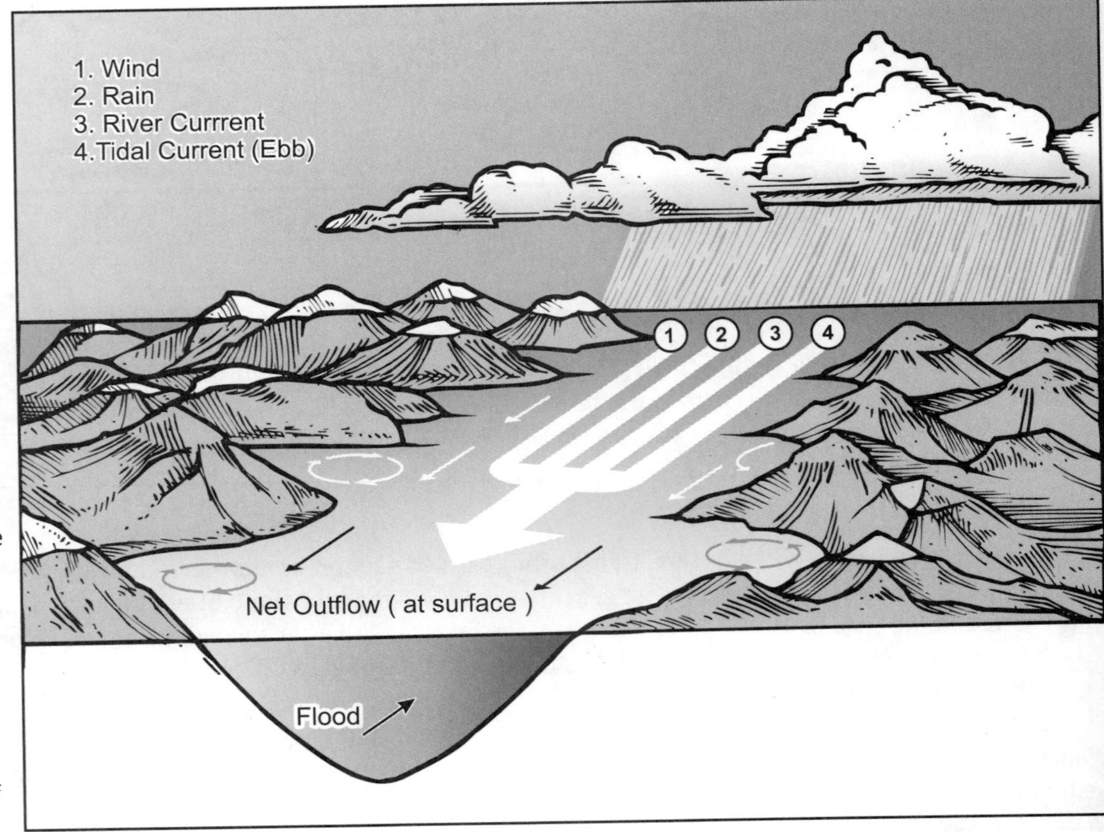
1. Wind
2. Rain
3. River Currrent
4.Tidal Current (Ebb)
1
2
3
4
Net Outflow (at surface)
Flood

Fig 2-8
The direction and strength of the surface current in Johnstone Strait is the sum of the various forces acting upon the tidal flow. In this example, heavy local rains, continuous southeasterly winds, and river currents enhance the natural ebb at the surface. At depth there may be a small flood where there is no outflowing fresh water.

The net outflow current generates back eddies along the shore between headlands. These eddies flow along the shore opposite to the main flow of the current.

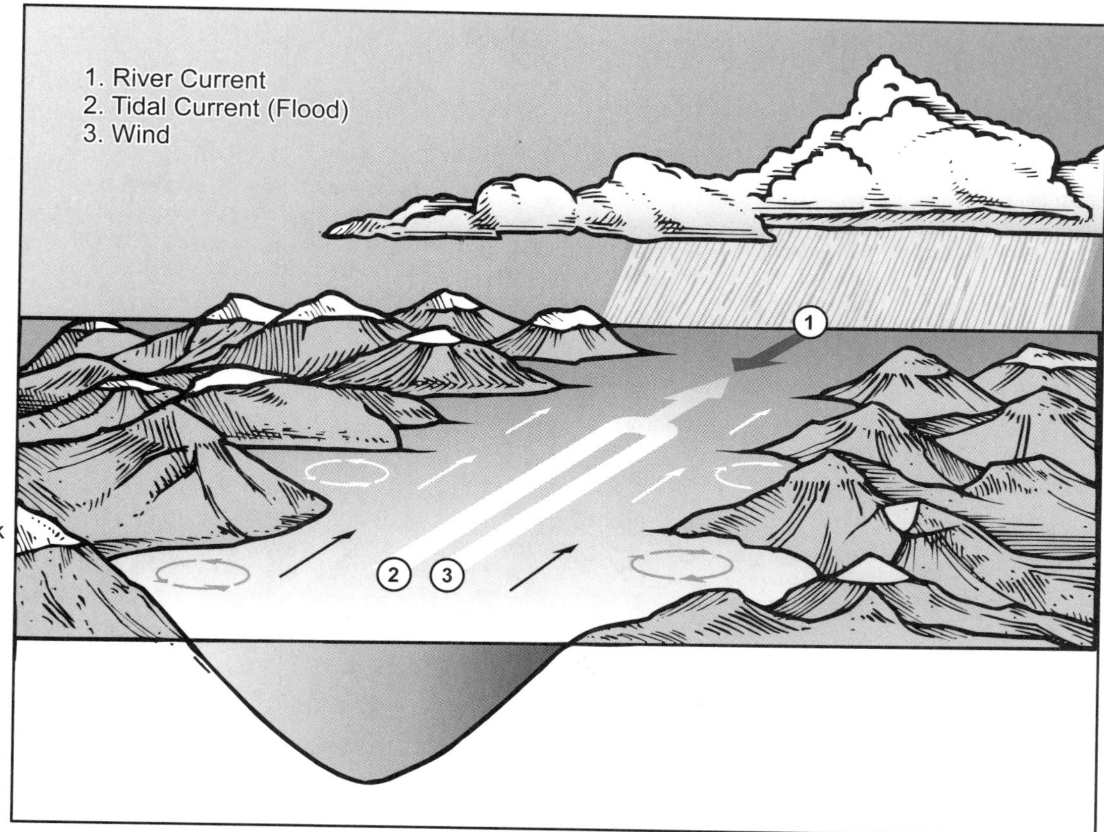
1. River Current
2. Tidal Current (Flood)
3. Wind
1
2
3

Fig 2-9
In this example, the flood is enhanced by continuous westerly winds, and is strong enough to result in a net inflow current. Back eddies now rotate in the opposite direction.

During Neap tides, when the moon and sun act out of phase, the flood may disappear (at least at the surface) for several days at a time.

The World's Largest Tides

Location	Tide	Location	Tide
Minas Basin, Bay of Fundy, Nova Scotia	38.4 feet	Herring Cove, Bay of Fundy, New Brunswick	28.3 feet
Cumberland Basin, Bay of Fundy, Nova Scotia	35.6 feet	Granville, France	28.2 feet
Petitcodiac River, Bay of Fundy, New Brunswick	33.2 feet	Cardiff, Bristol Channel, England	28.1 feet
Joggins, Bay of Fundy, Nova Scotia	33.2 feet	Banco Direccion, Magellan Strait, Chile	28.0 feet
Leaf Lake, Ungava Bay, Quebec	32.0 feet	Cancale, France	27.8 feet
Port of Bristol (Avonmount), England	31.5 feet	Bahia Posesion, Magellan Strait, Chile	27.5 feet
Spencer Island, Bay of Fundy, Nova Scotia	30.5 feet	Ile Haute, Bay of Fundy, Nova Scotia	27.5 feet
Newport, Bristol Channel, England	30.3 feet	Barry, Bristol Channel, England	27.1 feet
Sunrise, Turnagain Arm, Cook Inlet, Alaska	30.3 feet	Hopes Advance Bay, Ungava Bay, Quebec	27.0 feet
Burnham, Parrett River, England	29.9 feet	Spicer Cove, Chignecto Bay, Nova Scotia	27.0 feet
Weston-super-Mare, Bristol Channel	29.5 feet	Iles Chausey, English Channel Islands	26.9 feet
Rio Gallegos (Reduccion Beacon), Argentina	29.0 feet	Port George, Bay of Fundy, Nova Scotia	26.7 feet
Koksoak River entrance, Hudson Bay, Greenland	28.5 feet	Watchet, Bristol Channel, England	26.6 feet

Local Effects – Ebb

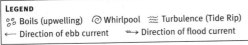

Legend
Boils (upwelling) Whirlpool Turbulence (Tide Rip)
← Direction of ebb current ⇝ Direction of flood current

West of Port Neville, the ebb begins along the mainland shore and takes almost two hours to completely cover the strait from one side to the other.

Turn to flood occurs in Sunderland Channel 1h 40m before Johnstone Strait Central and 1h 20m before Camp Point.

To avoid heavy weather in Johnstone Strait (especially when wind opposes currents) Sunderland, Wellbore and Cordero Channels offer calmer conditions.

Current Passage turns to ebb 50m after Johnstone Strait Central, but 1h 15m before Camp Point.

Turn to ebb at Vansittart Point occurs up to 30m before Current Passage, almost two hours before Camp Point.

Freshet conditions in mainland rivers may encourage a premature turn to ebb in the vicinity of Mayne Passage.

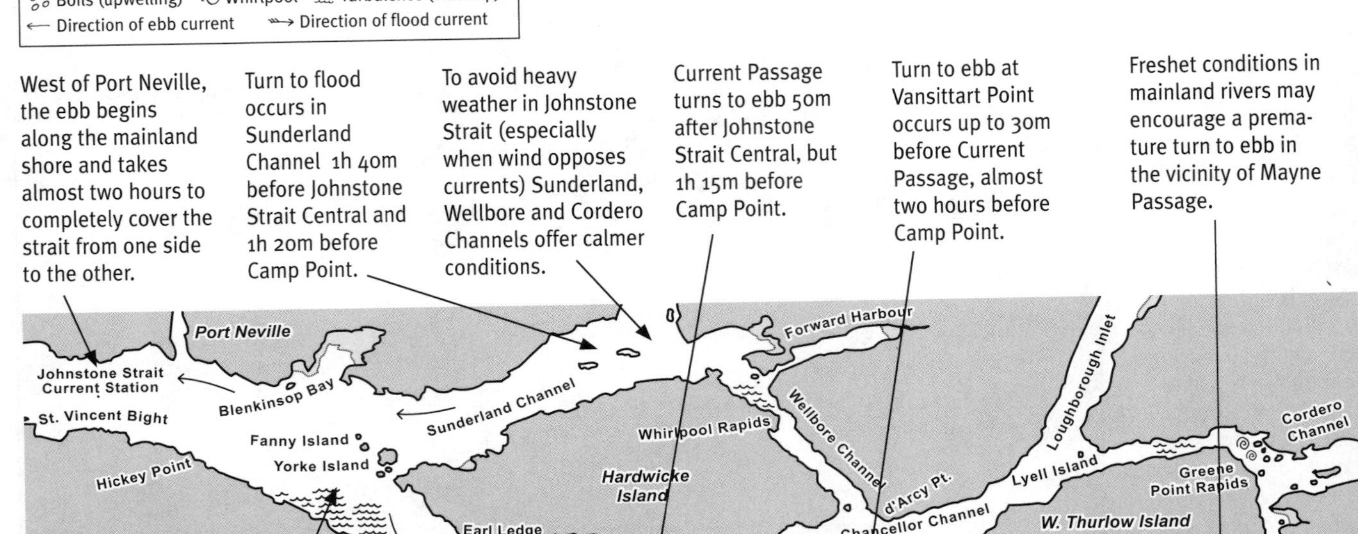
Port Neville
Johnstone Strait Current Station
St. Vincent Bight
Blenkinsop Bay
Sunderland Channel
Fanny Island
Yorke Island
Hickey Point
Forward Harbour
Wellbore Channel
Whirlpool Rapids
Hardwicke Island
Loughborough Inlet
Cordero Channel
Lyell Island
d'Arcy Pt.
Greene Point Rapids
Chancellor Channel
W. Thurlow Island
Blind Channel
Earl Ledge
Current Passage
Ripple Shoal
Eden Pt.
Knox Bay
Mayne Passage
E. Thurlow Island
EBB
Kelsey Bay
Race Passage
Camp Pt.
Tyee Pt.
Vansittart Pt.
Johnstone Strait
Ripple Pt.

When waves from gale force westerlies oppose a strong ebb current, large seas propagating southward are generated in this area. In this case, smaller boats should seek shelter at Port Neville or enter the harbour at Kelsey Bay and wait for the contrary current to moderate.

Tide rips and conditions dangerous to small craft are generated in this area during large tides, especially when strong westerlies oppose the ebb current.

Immediately adjacent to the shore, back eddies may run in the opposite direction to the main flow. However, at headlands between back eddies, the ebb current is strong right up to the shore.

A steep underwater ridge extends southward from Earl Ledge across the channel to the Vancouver Island shore. Deep tidal currents meet this steep topography and are deflected to the surface, causing extreme turbulence west of Helmcken Island during large tides.

Stay clear of Ripple Shoal. Dangerous whirlpools form to the west of the shoal during the ebb.

Tide rips and turbulent conditions are generated in this area during large tides, especially when strong westerly winds oppose the ebb current.

Slack water is a time of weak or insignificant current that occurs when the tidal current changes direction. When the current turns from ebb to flood, (**Turn to Flood—TTF**) it is **low water slack**; from flood to ebb, (**Turn to Ebb—TTE**) it is **high water slack.** Slack water may last only an instant, or it may last for 15 minutes or more. Usually slack water lasts longer when the tides (and thus current speeds) are smaller.

Local Effects – Flood

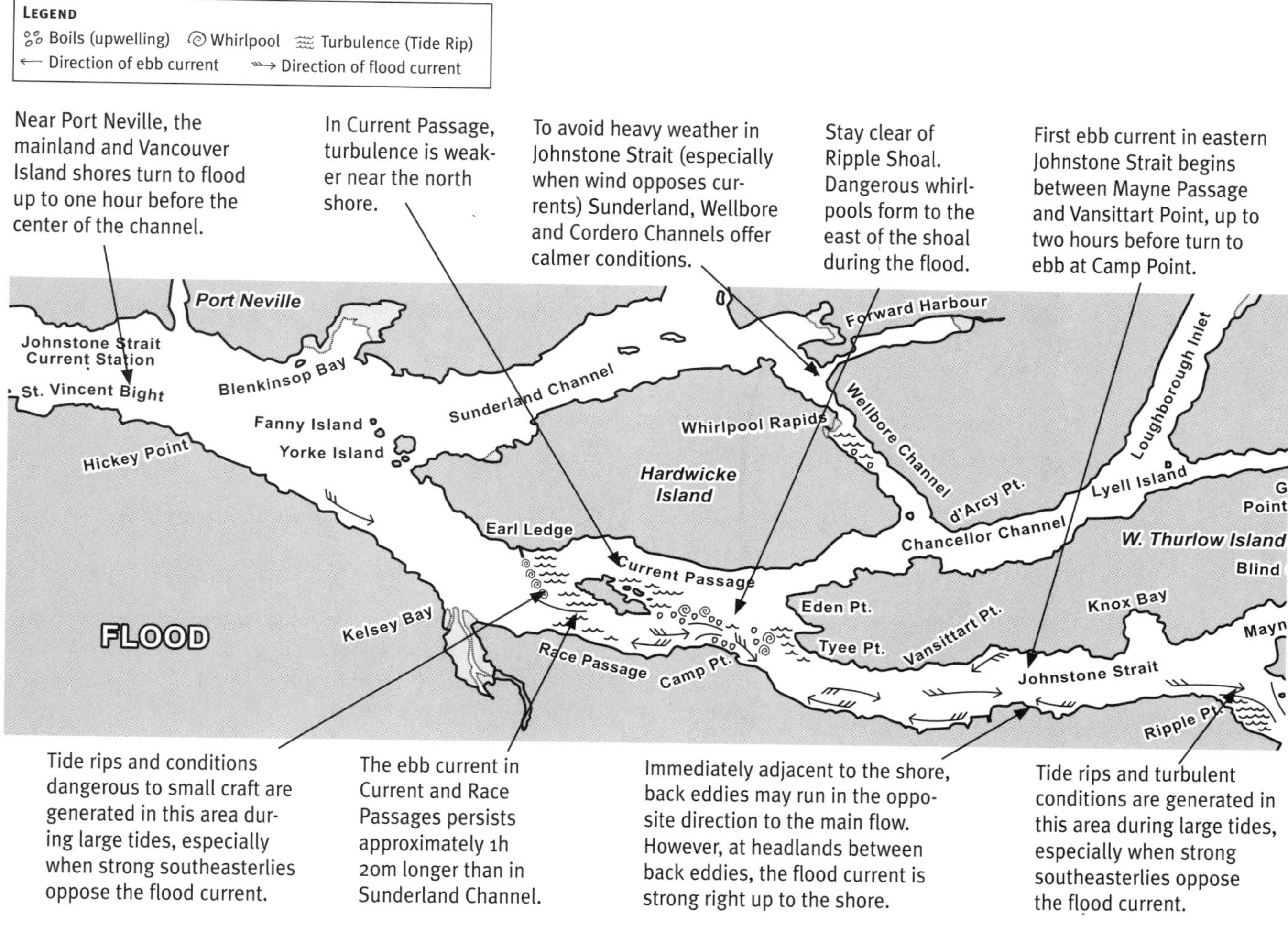
LEGEND
Boils (upwelling)
Whirlpool
Turbulence (Tide Rip)
Direction of ebb current
Direction of flood current
Near Port Neville, the mainland and Vancouver Island shores turn to flood up to one hour before the center of the channel.
In Current Passage, turbulence is weaker near the north shore.
To avoid heavy weather in Johnstone Strait (especially when wind opposes currents) Sunderland, Wellbore and Cordero Channels offer calmer conditions.
Stay clear of Ripple Shoal. Dangerous whirlpools form to the east of the shoal during the flood.
First ebb current in eastern Johnstone Strait begins between Mayne Passage and Vansittart Point, up to two hours before turn to ebb at Camp Point.
Port Neville
Johnstone Strait Current Station
St. Vincent Bight
Blenkinsop Bay
Forward Harbour
Sunderland Channel
Fanny Island
Yorke Island
Hickey Point
Whirlpool Rapids
Wellbore Channel
Loughborough Inlet
Hardwicke Island
d'Arcy Pt.
Lyell Island
Point
Earl Ledge
Chancellor Channel
W. Thurlow Island
Current Passage
Blind
Eden Pt.
Knox Bay
FLOOD
Kelsey Bay
Tyee Pt.
Vansittart Pt.
Mayn
Race Passage
Camp Pt.
Johnstone Strait
Ripple Pt.
Tide rips and conditions dangerous to small craft are generated in this area during large tides, especially when strong southeasterlies oppose the flood current.
The ebb current in Current and Race Passages persists approximately 1h 20m longer than in Sunderland Channel.
Immediately adjacent to the shore, back eddies may run in the opposite direction to the main flow. However, at headlands between back eddies, the flood current is strong right up to the shore.
Tide rips and turbulent conditions are generated in this area during large tides, especially when strong southeasterlies oppose the flood current.

The difference between the height of high water and low water on any given tidal cycle is the range of that tide.

- A large tide is a tide, either rising or falling, that has a large range compared to other tides at that location.
- A mean tide is a tide that is close to the average range for that location.
- A small tide at any location has a relatively small range. In the tables that follow the terms small tide and mean tide can be used interchangeably.

Tables 1 and 2 of the CHS Tide and Current Tables give the ranges of large and mean tides at every reference or secondary port.

Most locations in the Pacific Northwest experience a mixed semi-diurnal tide, meaning that there are two complete tidal oscillations per day. Normally one of the daily tidal oscillations has a significantly larger range than the other. As the phase of the moon progresses, the higher high water of the day becomes higher, and the lower low water gets lower, until at or near the new moon and the full moon the tidal range reaches its maximum value.

The large tides that occur near the full and new moons are known as spring tides. The smaller tides that occur between spring tides are known as neap tides.

Not all small tides are neap tides. During spring tides, only one of the daily tidal oscillations is a large tide; the other may be relatively small.

Important Narrows and Rapids on the Inside Passage

Refer to the *Sailing Directions* and to *Exploring the South Coast of British Columbia*, by Don Douglass and Réanne Hemmingway-Douglass to learn more about the narrows discussed below.

Seymour Narrows	Seymour Narrows reaches 16 knots on the flood and 14 knots on the ebb. The channel is exposed to southeasterly and northerly winds. When these winds reach gale force and oppose the current, Seymour Narrows can be a very dangerous place. In general, small vessels should transit Seymour Narrows only near slack water. According to the *Sailing Directions*, a vessel transiting in the first hour before or after slack water on a large tide should be capable of a minimum of 13 knots. If you must challenge the narrows, do so in small increments either side of slack water until you develop experience. Unless you have significant experience, do not attempt Seymour Narrows more than one hour either side of slack water. Seymour Narrows can be quite deceptive. Through the greater portion of the narrows the current flow is laminar, but on a flood tide extremely turbulent conditions develop south of Maude Island, near Race Point. If a southeasterly wind is blowing at the time, the conditions can be extremely dangerous.
Arran Rapids	Attempt these rapids only at slack water. Better yet, ***stay out of Arran Rapids completely.*** Numerous lives have been lost in Arran Rapids.
Dent Rapids, Gillard Passage and Yuculta Rapids ***In the Devil's Hole, south of Little Dent Island and west of Dent Island, a large, dangerous whirlpool forms during the peak of the current.***	You may see small fishing boats, zipping back and forth through the rapids on any stage of the tide, ***but don't allow yourself to believe you can perform the same feats.*** These boats are operated by experts, who are intimately familiar with every nuance of the rapids; their vessels are designed for the environment; and their motors are in peak condition. Otherwise, they don't survive. Never challenge Dent Rapids by more than 30 minutes during large tides or one hour on small tides. At maximum flow, Dent and Yuculta Rapids are extremely dangerous, filled with violent whirlpools and eddies, and should not be attempted by vessels of any size.
Greene Point Rapids	Greene Point Rapids reaches seven knots on maximum flood and ebb. However, if you are experienced, you can challenge the rapids up to 1½ hours before or after slack water (less on large tides).
Whirlpool Rapids	Though Whirlpool Rapids sets up whirlpools and eddies adjacent to Carterer Point, the tongue is well defined and the rapids can be transited up to 1½ hours either side of slack water even on large tides. However, low powered boats or open boats with low freeboard should exercise extreme caution.
Chatham Channel	The laminar flow of Chatham Channel makes this channel safe to transit during all current conditions, so long as you have a reserve of two knots or more above the speed of the current. However, when gale force westerlies oppose the ebb current, large standing waves form. Small vessels should not attempt the channel under these conditions.
Blackney Passage	Maximum current in Blackney Passage is four knots on both flood and ebb. You can transit Blackney Passage at almost any time. However, when gale to storm force southeasterlies oppose the flood, or northwesterlies oppose the ebb, it is dangerous for small craft to transit the passage.

Dent Rapids

As the *Bella Nova* steamed westward through Gillard Passage toward Dent Island, the water was like satin, and ahead, only a faint line of white showed the beginning of the flood current, so I chose to push my seven-knot fishboat through, definitely a mistake. By the time I realized the state of the current, I discovered just how turbulent Dent Rapids can be, and also just how limited my options had become. Dent Point was spitting out whirlpools 30 feet across, and between two of these whirlpools, the *Bella Nova* chugged up a three-foot overfall.

I couldn't turn my boat around because to do so would have put me smack in the middle of one or another of these violent eddies. *Bella Nova,* whirlpools and all were propelled laterally across the channel at a horrifying speed, and I feared being dashed into the shore of Sonora Island. Slowly, slowly I could see that we were creeping ahead of the point, and after a few minutes, we were once again in smooth water, making a couple of knots over the ground.

It turned out that I had planned to arrive at Yuculta Rapids at the time of slack water in Gillard Pass, but I had actually arrived a half-hour late. As a result, when I arrived at Yuculta Rapids it was slack water—1/2 hour after slack at Gillard Pass. The miscalculation, plus the steaming time between Yuculta Rapids and Dent Island, placed me in Dent Rapids an hour after slack water, and upon reading the tide tables a little more closely, I discovered that I had done this on the second largest tide of the year!

I resolved in future to pay a little more attention to detail. Though displacement boats can manage Dent Rapids shortly before or after slack, it is best not to do so. I now transit Dent Rapids as close to slack as possible—especially on large tides. If I am going to challenge any rapids in the area, I would prefer to challenge Yuculta Rapids or Gillard Passage, not Dent Rapids.

Fig 2-10
A fishboat in a moderate current in the Devil's Hole, Dent Rapids.

Table 2-3 Table of Specific Strategies for Managing Tidal Rapids on the Inside Passage

Strategies for Transiting Johnstone Strait

The strategies below are designed to help you transit Johnstone Strait between Seymour Narrows and Broughton Strait in a single day. If you want to take more than a single day, you can proceed at your own pace and travel only when the current is in your favour. At speeds over 12 knots, the relative effects of a following or contrary current are minimal, and consequently these strategies are not necessary.

The strategies assume that you will transit Seymour Narrows at or near slack water.

General Strategy

Coriolis force (due to the rotation of the earth) weakens flood currents near the north shore and ebb currents near the south shore. This means that unless conditions dictate otherwise, you should always head west along the north shore and east along the south shore.

Strategies for Transiting Johnstone Strait *(cont'd)*

North/West bound

- The ideal time to transit Seymour Narrows is at a morning low water slack (turn to flood) after which you have an entire day to navigate Johnstone Strait. If there is no convenient slack water in the morning, then you should transit the narrows the previous evening and spend the night at Brown Bay or Plumper Bay. You can then proceed early in the morning without having to wait for slack water.
- In general the flood is weaker in Current Passage than in Race Passage. As a result, you should always use Current Passage when heading against the flood current (unless you intend to stop at Kelsey Bay).

Via Seymour Narrows at Low Water Slack (Turn to Flood)	Via Seymour Narrows at High Water Slack (Turn to Ebb)
• You will experience an opposing flood current in Discovery Passage that will reach maximum shortly after you reach Chatham Point. • Once past Chatham Point, stay near the north shore of the Strait. As the turn to ebb approaches, the opposing current will diminish first on the north side of the channel. • Arrive between Mayne Passage and Vansittart Point close to the time of turn to ebb at Johnstone Strait Central. This is at least two hours before the turn to ebb at Camp Point and Seymour Narrows. • The turn to ebb begins in Mayne Passage and near Vansittart Point before any other location in eastern Johnstone Strait. While the current begins to ebb along the north shore, the south shore continues to flood. • Remain on the north side of the channel, pass to the north of Ripple Shoal, and Helmcken Island and stay on the north side of Current Passage. You will arrive at Earl Ledge while the current is still flooding in Race Passage. • On approach to Earl Ledge, move well out into the channel to avoid the whirlpools and boils set up by the underwater ridge. • West of Fanny Island, stay near the north shore in order to take advantage of the beginning of the ebb current.	• You will be assisted by the ebb current and will reach Helmcken Island near maximum ebb. • At Chatham Point and Turn Island stay near mid channel in order to avoid the heaviest turbulence which is along the shore. • If there is no major oncoming traffic in Race Passage, you can use Race Passage. Stay 0.15 Nm (300 m) from Camp Point. This will provide space for other vessels heading south/east and will also keep you away from the worst turbulence along the shore and west of Ripple Shoal. • Pass close to the south shore of Helmcken Island and then favour the north side of the channel to the west of Earl Ledge.

South/East bound

- Because there is often no flood current to the west of Helmcken Island, (even though there may be a flood current to the east), there is no correlation between the times of turn to flood and turn to ebb at Johnstone Strait Central and Seymour Narrows. The result is that you must base your timing on the turns of the current at Seymour Narrows taking into account the state of the current in Johnstone Strait Central.
- When south/east bound, you must plan for a transit of Seymour Narrows at or near slack water. This means that you must plan for arrival at Camp Point and Chatham Point with specific amounts of time remaining, depending on your vessel's speed.
- Ideally you should plan for an evening transit of Seymour Narrows, securing at Campbell River overnight. However, if there is no convenient evening slack, then you should spend the night at Brown Bay or Plumper Bay and transit the narrows the following morning.
- When strong westerly winds oppose a large ebb current, dangerous conditions are generated in the southern portion of the strait between Hickey Point and Helmcken Island. In this case, smaller boats should:
  a) take shelter at Port Neville and wait for the contrary current to moderate, or
  b) enter Sunderland Channel and follow the alternate route through Wellbore Channel and Cordero Channel.

Strategies for Transiting Johnstone Strait *(cont'd)*

South/East bound

Via Whirlpool Rapids and Dent Rapids

Plan to arrive near Port Neville approximately two hours before the turn to flood at Johnstone Strait Central. Sunderland Channel turns to flood up to 1h 20m before Race and Current Passages, so you can take advantage of this early flood current.

Via Seymour Narrows at Low Water Slack (Turn to Flood)

General Notes for TTF

- You will experience contrary currents in Race Passage and in the eastern strait and Discovery Passage prior to the turn to flood.
- West of Kelsey Bay, the currents seldom exceed one knot, so you can easily estimate your time of arrival at Kelsey Bay. Arrange to arrive at or near Kelsey Bay at the appropriate time.
- If you are transiting Johnstone Strait against a large ebb, intending to transit Seymour Narrows at low water slack, allow more time at each major point.

-at 6 knots

- Kelsey Bay—Six hours before turn to flood at Seymour Narrows. Depending on the duration of the current, you will pass Kelsey Bay near turn to ebb. Stay near the south shore as the ebb current begins in order to take advantage of back eddies and weaker currents.
- Camp Pt—Five hrs before turn to flood at Seymour Narrows. By this time the contrary ebb current will be well established.
- In the vicinity of Camp Point, there is no back eddy and the strongest current is directly by the shore. Pass Camp Point between 0.1 Nm and 0.2 Nm from shore (200 m to 400 m) to ensure you stay clear of Ripple Shoal.
- Once past Camp Point, stay close to the south shore to take advantage of back eddies and weaker currents. But do not approach the shore closer than 0.05 Nm (100 meters).
- When rounding the points between back eddies, (Bear Pt., Ripple Pt., Rock Pt., and Chatham Pt.), move away from the shore to avoid the strong ebb currents near the points.
- Chatham Point—Two hours before turn to flood at Seymour Narrows. After rounding Chatham Point, remain in the western portion of the channel (away from shore), and make maximum speed for Seymour Narrows.

-at 9 knots

- Hickey Point—Six hours before turn to flood at Seymour Narrows. Depending on the duration of the flood current, you will pass Hickey Pt. near turn to ebb.
- Kelsey Bay—Five hours before turn to flood at Seymour Narrows.
- Chatham Pt—1h 30m before turn to flood at Seymour Narrows.

Via Seymour Narrows at High Water Slack (Turn to Ebb)

General Notes for TTE

- If the duration of the flood current at Johnstone Strait Central is less than three hours, add one hour to estimated times at Kelsey Bay, and use opposing current procedures until the flood begins.
- Even if the flood is limited (or non-existent) west of Helmcken Island, there will still be a significant flood to the east, so you can still take advantage of the flood current for a few hours before the turn to ebb.
- Between St. Vincent Bight and Kelsey Bay, stay near the south shore. The ebb current is weakest along this shore. As the turn to flood approaches, you will be able to take advantage of the first of the flood (if any) along this shore.
- Once the flood current is established, stay at least 0.1 Nm (200 m) from shore so you are not slowed down by opposing back eddies. However, you may pass close to prominent points and take advantage of the main current directly by the shore.

-at 6 knots

- Kelsey Bay—Four hours before turn to ebb at Seymour Narrows.
- Pass close to Camp Point—3h 20m before turn to ebb at Seymour Narrows.
- Chatham Point—1h 20m before turn to ebb at Seymour Narrows. You will transit Seymour Narrows at slack water or on the tail end of the flood.

-at 9 knots

- Kelsey Bay—Three hours before turn to ebb at Seymour Narrows.
- Pass close to Camp Point—Three hours before turn to ebb at Seymour Narrows.
- Chatham Point—1h 15m before turn to ebb at Seymour Narrows.

Strategies for Transiting Yuculta Rapids, Gillard Passage and Dent Rapids

Under most circumstances you can transit Yuculta Rapids, Gillard Passage and Dent Rapids on the same tide.

Since Dent Rapids are more violent than Gillard Passage or Yuculta Rapids, it is more important to transit Dent Rapids at slack water than either of the other passages. Arrange to arrive at Dent Rapids at slack water.

Dent Rapids turns to flood 15 minutes before Gillard Passage and turns to ebb 25 minutes before.
Yuculta Rapids turns to flood 15 minutes after Gillard Passage and turns to ebb five minutes after.

	Southbound	
	At Low Water Slack (Turn to Flood)	**At High Water Slack (Turn to Ebb)**
On Any Size Tide	**-at 6 knots**—Arrive at Dent Rapids at slack water (15 minutes before Gillard Passage). By the time you reach Gillard Passage and Yuculta Rapids, they will also be at slack water. **-at 9 knots**—Faster vessels should arrive at Dent Rapids at slack water, then either reduce speed to arrive at Gillard Passage at slack water or simply pass through Gillard Passage early, on the end of the ebb current.	**at 6 knots**—Arrive at Dent Rapids at slack water (25 minutes before Gillard Passage). The end of the flood will carry you through Gillard Passage. By the time you enter Yuculta Rapids, it will be slack water there. **-at 9 knots**—Faster vessels should transit Dent Rapids at slack, then either reduce speed to arrive at Yuculta Rapids at slack, or maintain speed to pass through Yuculta Rapids on the end of the flood.
	Northbound	
	At Low Water Slack (Turn to Flood)	**At High Water Slack (Turn to Ebb)**
On Any Size Tide	**-at 6 knots**—Arrive at Yuculta Rapids 30 minutes before slack water at Gillard Passage. The last of the ebb will carry you through Yuculta and Gillard Passage. By the time you reach Dent Rapids, it should be slack water. **-at 9 knots**—Faster vessels may transit Yuculta Rapids a little earlier in order to arrive at Dent Rapids at slack water.	**-at 6 knots**—Arrive at Yuculta Rapids 30 minutes before slack water at Gillard Passage). You will have to stem the last of the flood in Yuculta Rapids (and maybe Gillard Passage as well), but you should arrive at Dent Rapids shortly after the turn to ebb. The beginning of the ebb will carry you through. **-at 9 knots**—Faster vessels should transit Yuculta Rapids 30 minutes before slack water at Gillard Passage, then maintain speed to arrive at Dent Rapids as near to slack water as possible.

Strategies for Transiting Cordero Channel from Greene Point Rapids to Stuart Island

It is sometimes possible, to transit Greene Point Rapids on the same tide as Dent Rapids. ***The distance between the two is 12.6 Nm.*** If you are late for slack water at Greene Point Rapids, or if there is not enough time between slack water at Dent Rapids and Greene Point Rapids, you can tie up at Shoal Bay on the northern end of East Thurlow Island and wait for the next favourable tide.

The times of slack water at Greene Point Rapids are referenced to Seymour Narrows, whereas the time of slack water at Dent Rapids is referenced to Gillard Pass. Since Gillard Pass and Seymour Narrows do not have a constant relationship (especially on small tides), estimates of timing between Greene Point Rapids and Dent Rapids must remain estimates at best.

Before you attempt to transit Cordero Channel, familiarize yourself with the chart of the area, and study the current tables for the day. Use the worksheet at the end of this table to find the times of Turn To Flood and Turn To Ebb at Greene Point Rapids, Dent Rapids and Yuculta Rapids, and write the times directly on your chart (in pencil) near the respective rapids.

To judge whether you are dealing with a large tide or a small tide, refer to the Canadian Hydrographic Service Current Tables for Seymour Narrows. If the maximum current following the **Turn to Flood** (or **Ebb**) you are interested in exceeds 9 knots, follow the strategy for a large tide. *(Note—a large tide is usually a Spring tide but a small tide may not necessarily be a Neap tide. It may just be the smaller of two tidal cycles in a given day.)*

Always double-check these strategies against the actual times of slack water at Gillard Pass and Seymour Narrows for the day of travel (see worksheet below).

Strategies for Transiting Cordero Channel from Greene Point Rapids to Stuart Island *(cont'd)*

Also remember that this table is referenced against the size of the tide following slack water. However, you may be transiting Greene Point Rapids on the last of a large ebb prior to a small flood. Under these circumstances, Greene Point Rapids may be extremely turbulent.

Caution—On large tides Greene Point Rapids is very turbulent. Unless you are very comfortable managing your boat in turbulent rapids you should not attempt to pass through Greene Point Rapids at this time.

	Southbound	
	At Low Water Slack (Turn to Flood)	**At High Water Slack (Turn to Ebb)**
On Large Tides	***Slack water at Green Point is very predictable, occurring approximately 30 minutes before slack water at Dent Rapids.*** ***Note***—When travelling against the ebb current in Chancellor Channel, in order to catch the **Turn To Flood** at Dent Rapids, allow plenty of time to travel from Loughborough Inlet to Greene Point against the current. **-at 6 knots** In order to arrive at Dent Rapids near slack water, you must transit Greene Point Rapids at least two hours before slack water. However, the currents against you will be so strong that you will make very little headway. ***Do not try to transit both Greene Point Rapids and Dent Rapids on the same Turn to Flood (large tides).*** **-at 9 knots** Transit Greene Point Rapids one hour before slack water. On emerging from the rapids you will have 1½ hours to travel 12.6 Nm against the last of the ebb. You may actually arrive at Dent Rapids a little early, in which case you can slow down as you approach Dent Rapids. At vessel speeds greater than nine knots, you can transit Greene Point Rapids closer to slack water.	***Slack water at Green Point is very predictable, occurring approximately 30 minutes before slack water at Dent Rapids.*** **-at 6 knots** In order to arrive at Dent Rapids near slack water, you must transit Greene Point Rapids at least one hour before slack. On emerging from the rapids you will have 1½ hours to travel 12.6 Nm assisted by the last of the flood. You will arrive at Dent Rapids near slack water. **-at 9 knots** Transit Greene Point Rapids 30 minutes before slack water. On emerging from the rapids you will have one hour to travel 12.6 Nm assisted by the last of the flood. You will arrive at Dent Rapids near slack. At vessel speeds greater than nine knots, you can transit Greene Point Rapids closer to slack water. ***Caution***—On large tides Greene Point Rapids is very turbulent. Unless you are very comfortable managing your boat in turbulent rapids you should not attempt to pass through Greene Point Rapids at this time.
On Small Tides	***Slack water at Greene Point occurs from 15 minutes to 1 hour before Dent Rapids.*** There is no predictable relationship between Dent Rapids and Greene Point Rapids on small tides. Consequently you should use the worksheet below, and then estimate if you can transit both Dent Rapids and Greene Point Rapids on the same **Turn To Flood**. **-at 6 knots** In order to arrive at Dent Rapids near slack water, you would have to transit Greene Point Rapids at least two hours before slack water at Dent Rapids. If the time difference between slack water at Dent Island and Greene Point Rapids is 30 minutes or more, you can transit Greene Point Rapids 1¼ hours before slack water and still arrive at Dent Rapids shortly after slack, as the current begins to flood. The beginning of the flood will carry you through Gillard Passage and Yuculta Rapids.	***Slack water at Greene Point occurs from 15 minutes to 45 minutes before Dent Rapids.*** There is no predictable relationship between Dent Rapids and Greene Point Rapids on small tides. Use the worksheet below in order to estimate the time to transit Greene Point Rapids. **-at 6 knots** In order to arrive at Dent Rapids near slack water, you must transit Greene Point Rapids at least 1½ hours before slack water at Dent Rapids. If the time difference between slack water at Dent island and Greene Point Rapids is 30 minutes or more, transit Greene Point Rapids one hour before slack water. On emerging from the rapids you will have 1½ hours to travel 12.6 Nm assisted by the last of the flood. You will arrive at Dent Rapids near slack. If the difference is less than 30 minutes, transit Greene Point Rapids 1¼ hours before slack, and you should still be able to arrive at Dent Rapids near slack.

<table>
<tr><th colspan="3">Strategies for Transiting Cordero Channel from Greene Point Rapids to Stuart Island (cont'd)</th></tr>
<tr><th colspan="3">Southbound</th></tr>
<tr><th></th><th>At Low Water Slack (Turn to Flood)</th><th>At High Water Slack (Turn to Ebb)</th></tr>
<tr><td>On Small Tides (cont'd)</td><td>If the difference is less than 30 minutes, it is unlikely you will be able to arrive at Dent Rapids within the first hour of the flood. The best strategy is to transit Greene Point Rapids at slack water and then wait for the next slack water at Dent Rapids.
-at 9 knots
If the time difference between slack water at Dent Rapids and Greene Point Rapids is more than 30 minutes, transit Greene Point Rapids one hour before slack water. You will arrive at Dent Rapids near slack water. If the difference is less than 30 minutes, transit Greene Point Rapids 1¼ hours before slack water. You will arrive at Dent Rapids shortly after slack water, as the current begins to flood. The beginning of the flood will carry you through Gillard Passage and Yuculta Rapids.</td><td>If the difference is less than 30 minutes, transit Greene Point Rapids 1¼ hours before slack water, and you should still be able to arrive at Dent Rapids near slack water.
-at 9 knots
If the time difference between slack water at Dent Rapids and Greene Point Rapids is more than 30 minutes, transit Dent Rapids 30 minutes before slack water. You will arrive at Dent rapids near slack water.
If the difference is less than 30 minutes, transit Greene Point Rapids 45 minutes before slack water. The last of the flood should carry you to Dent Rapids at or near slack water.</td></tr>
<tr><th colspan="3">Northbound</th></tr>
<tr><th></th><th>At Low Water Slack (Turn to Flood)</th><th>At High Water Slack (Turn to Ebb)</th></tr>
<tr><td>On Any Size Tide</td><td>Since you must transit Dent Rapids at slack water, as you proceed from there toward Greene Point Rapids, you will be facing a steadily increasing flood current. Unless your vessel is capable of negotiating the full force of the flood current in Greene Point Rapids, you should not attempt to transit Greene Point Rapids on the same tide. Instead, tie up at Shoal Bay and wait until the next slack water (Turn To Ebb).</td><td>Since you must transit Dent Rapids at slack water, as you proceed from there toward Greene Point Rapids, you will be assisted by a steadily increasing ebb current.
By the time you reach Greene Point Rapids it will be 1½ hours after Turn To Ebb. If you cannot maintain six knots through the water (or eight knots by GPS assisted by the current) you should not try to transit Greene Point Rapids at this time.
Caution—On large tides Greene Point Rapids is very turbulent. Unless you are very comfortable managing your boat in turbulent rapids you should not attempt to pass through Greene Point Rapids more than 1½ hours after Turn To Ebb.</td></tr>
</table>

Reading the Current Tables

The Canadian Hydrographic Service's (CHS) *Tide and Current Tables* contain a wealth of information. But they are without value if you don't know how to read them. First make sure you have the correct volume. There are three volumes for the Pacific Coast:

- Volume V Juan de Fuca Strait and Strait of Georgia
- Volume VI Discovery Passage and West Coast of Vancouver Island
- Volume VII Queen Charlotte Sound to Dixon Entrance

Reference and Secondary Current Stations

(Refer to Table 4 in the Canadian Hydrographic Service *Tide and Current Tables)*

Daily current predictions are tabulated only for certain **reference current stations**. If the channel you are interested in is a **reference station**, you need simply read off the times the current turns and the times and speed (rate) of maximum flow.

Other tidal channels are considered **secondary stations**; the time the current turns and the time of maximum flow are shown as time differences from a specific **reference station**.

Note the **Direction of Flood,** as some tidal channels flood and ebb in a direction that is not obvious.

Caution—Two neighbouring secondary stations (such as Dent Rapids and Greene Point Rapids) may be referenced to different reference stations.

The Daily Tables

Each line refers to a single ebb or flood current. To determine if the line refers to a flood or ebb current, refer to Column four. (***Ports and Passes,*** a popular tide table book, has a slightly different presentation, but the columns provide the same information as the CHS tables.)

First Column—Date and day of the week.

Second Column—Time the current turns (**slack water**). Note that the CHS tables must be adjusted for daylight time; when daylight time is in effect add 1 hour to all tabulated times. (***Ports and Passes*** has added the hour for you.)

Third Column—The time of maximum speed (rate) for the cycle following the **slack water** in Column one.

Fourth Column—Maximum current speed is given directly in Knots, followed by either a plus sign (+) for flood, or a minus sign (-) for ebb. This will indicate whether the **slack water** in Column one is **TTE (high water slack)** or **TTF (low water slack)**.

To calculate approximate intermediate current speeds; once you have determined the time of slack water and the time of maximum flow, refer to the "Rule of Thirds" below or the Canadian Hydrographic Service's *Pacific Current Atlas. (http://gp2.chs-shc.dfo-mpo.gc.ca/atlas/)*

Worksheet for Calculating Time Differences between Tidal Rapids in Cordero Channel

Turn to Flood

		Time	Speed		
Seymour Narrows (from Current Tables)					
Greene Point Rapids (calculated)	-1:25 =				
Gillard Passage (from Current Tables)					Time Difference between Slack Water at Seymour Narrows and Gillard Passage
Dent Rapids (calculated)	-0:15 =				Time Difference between Slack Water at Greene Point Rapids and Dent Rapids
Yuculta Rapids (calculated)	+0:25 =				

Turn to Ebb

		Time	Speed		
Seymour Narrows (from Current Tables)					
Greene Point Rapids (calculated)	-1:35 =				
Gillard Passage (from Current Tables)					Time Difference between Slack Water at Seymour Narrows and Gillard Passage
Dent Rapids (calculated)	-0:25 =				Time Difference between Slack Water at Greene Point Rapids and Dent Rapids
Yuculta Rapids (calculated)	+0:05 =				

The "Rule of Thirds" for Estimating Intermediate Current Speeds

You cannot use tide tables to predict tidal currents; instead you must use current tables. In fact, a tidal current may continue to ebb long after low water or flood long after high water.

The "Rule of Thirds" assumes that maximum current strength occurs halfway between the ***turns*** of the current. You can obtain the time of the ***turn*** of the current from "Current Tables". The time of increasing (or decreasing) current is then divided into thirds. For a six-hour current cycle, estimate as follows.

Hour zero	0%	of maximum speed (slack water)			
End of 1st hour	50%	of maximum speed	**End of 4th hour**	90%	of maximum speed
End of 2nd hour	90%	of maximum speed	**End of 5th hour**	50%	of maximum speed
End of 3rd hour	100%	of maximum speed	**End of 6th hour**	0%	of maximum speed (slack water)

If the duration of the current is more (or less) than six hours, adjust the estimate accordingly.

Table 3 — Time, Speed, and Distance

Table 3-1 — To Determine Time When Speed and Distance Are Known

Time in Minutes

Speed in Knots	0.25	0.5	0.75	1.0	1.25	1.5	1.75	2.0	2.25	2.5	2.75	3.0	3.25	3.5	3.75	4.0
	Nautical Miles															
5	3:00	6:00	9:00	12:00	15:00	18:00	21:00	24:00	27:00	30:00	33:00	36:00	39:00	42:00	45:00	48:00
6	2:30	5:00	7:30	10:00	12:30	15:00	17:30	20:00	22:30	25:00	27:30	30:00	32:30	35:00	37:30	40:00
7	2:08	4:17	6:24	8:34	10:43	12:48	15:00	17:08	19:17	21:26	23:34	25:42	27:51	30:00	32:09	34:17
8	1:52	3:45	5:36	7:30	9:23	11:12	13:08	15:00	16:53	18:45	20:38	22:30	24:23	26:15	28:07	30:00
9	1:40	3:20	5:00	6:40	8:20	10:00	11:40	13:20	15:00	16:40	18:20	20:00	21:40	23:20	25:00	26:40
10	1:30	3:00	4:30	6:00	7:30	9:00	10:30	12:00	13:30	15:00	16:30	18:00	19:30	21:00	22:30	24:00
11	1:21	2:43	4:05	5:27	6:49	8:10	9:33	10:54	12:16	13:38	15:00	16:21	17:44	19:06	20:27	21:49
12	1:15	2:30	3:45	5:00	6:15	7:30	8:45	10:00	11:15	12:30	13:45	15:00	16:15	17:30	18:45	20:00
13	1:09	2:18	3:27	4:36	5:46	6:54	8:05	9:13	10:23	11:32	12:42	13:50	15:00	16:09	17:18	18:27
14	1:04	2:08	3:12	4:17	5:22	6:24	7:30	8:34	9:39	10:43	11:47	12:51	13:56	15:00	16:04	17:08
15	1:00	2:00	3:00	4:00	5:00	6:00	7:00	8:00	9:00	10:00	11:00	12:00	13:00	14:00	15:00	16:00
16	0:56	1:52	2:48	3:45	4:41	5:36	6:34	7:30	8:26	9:23	10:19	11:15	12:11	13:08	14:04	15:00
18	0:49	1:39	2:29	3:19	4:10	4:58	5:50	6:39	7:30	8:20	9:10	9:59	10:50	11:40	12:30	13:19
20	0:45	1:30	2:15	3:00	3:45	4:30	5:15	6:00	6:45	7:30	8:15	9:00	9:45	10:30	11:15	12:00

Time in Minutes

Speed in Knots	4.25	4.5	4.75	5.0	5.5	6.0	6.5	7.0	7.5	8.0	8.5	9.0	9.5	10.0
	Nautical Miles													
5	51:00	54:00	57:00	60:00	66:00	72:00	78:00	84:00	90:00	96:00	102:00	108:00	114:00	120:00
6	42:30	45:00	47:30	50:00	55:00	60:00	65:00	70:00	75:00	80:00	85:00	90:00	95:00	100:00
7	36:26	38:34	40:43	42:51	47:09	51:24	55:43	60:00	64:17	68:34	72:51	77:09	81:26	85:43
8	31:53	33:45	35:37	37:30	41:15	45:00	48:45	52:30	56:15	60:00	63:45	67:30	71:15	75:00
9	28:20	30:00	31:40	33:20	36:40	40:00	43:20	46:40	50:00	53:20	56:40	60:00	63:20	66:40
10	25:30	27:00	28:30	30:00	33:00	36:00	39:00	42:00	45:00	48:00	51:00	54:00	57:00	60:00
11	23:11	24:33	25:55	27:16	30:00	32:42	35:27	38:11	40:55	43:38	46:22	49:06	51:49	54:33
12	21:15	22:30	23:45	25:00	27:30	30:00	32:30	35:00	37:30	40:00	42:40	45:00	47:30	50:00
13	19:37	20:46	21:55	23:04	25:23	27:40	30:00	32:18	34:37	36:55	39:14	41:32	43:51	46:09
14	18:13	19:17	20:21	21:25	23:34	25:42	27:51	30:00	32:09	34:17	36:26	38:34	40:43	42:51
15	17:00	18:00	19:00	20:00	22:00	24:00	26:00	28:00	30:00	32:00	34:00	36:00	38:00	40:00
16	15:56	16:53	17:49	18:45	20:38	22:30	24:23	26:15	28:08	30:00	31:53	33:45	35:38	37:20
18	14:10	15:00	15:50	16:39	18:20	19:58	21:40	23:20	25:00	26:40	28:20	30:00	31:40	33:20
20	12:45	13:30	14:15	15:00	16:30	18:00	19:30	21:00	22:30	24:00	25:30	27:00	28:30	30:00

ELAPSED TIME Use this table to determine elapsed time for dead reckoning purposes. Interpolate as necessary

Table 3-2 — Time, Speed, and Distance Nomogram

To solve for vessel time and route, find the time in the appropriate distance column that most closely matches the elapsed time, and read the speed off the speed scale.

If the elapsed time is less than the smallest value in that distance column, divide the distance by two and double the solution from the speed scale.

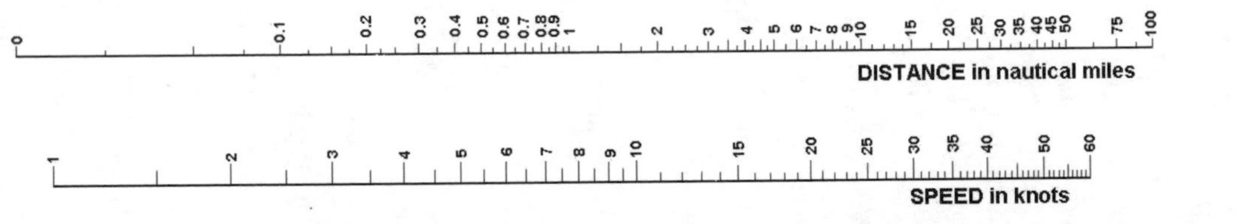
TIME in minutes
DISTANCE in nautical miles
SPEED in knots

Use of Three Scale Nomogram

Given any two of three values (time, speed or distance) solve for the third by ruling a line through the known values on their respective scales, then read the third value where the line intersects with the third scale.

Table 3-3 — To Determine Speed When Time and Distance Are Known

Distance in Nm / Speed in Knots

More than 50 knots

Time in Minutes	0.25	0.5	0.75	1.0	1.25	1.5	1.75	2.0	2.25	2.5	2.75	3.0	3.25	3.5	3.75	4.0	4.25	4.5	4.75	5.0	6.0	7.0	8.0	9.0	10.0
1:00	15.0	30.0	45.0																						
2:00	7.5	15.0	22.5	30.0	37.5	45.0																			
3:00	5.0	10.0	15.0	20.0	25.0	30.0	35.0	40.0	45.0	50.0															
4:00	3.8	7.5	11.3	15.0	18.8	22.5	26.3	30.0	33.8	37.5	41.3	45.0	48.8												
5:00	3.0	6.0	9.0	12.0	15.0	18.0	21.0	24.0	27.0	30.0	33.0	36.0	39.0	42.0	45.0	48.0									
6:00	2.5	5.0	7.5	10.0	12.5	15.0	17.5	20.0	22.5	25.0	27.5	30.0	32.5	35.0	37.5	40.0	42.5	45.0	47.5	50.0					
7:00	2.1	4.3	6.4	8.6	10.7	12.9	15.0	17.1	19.3	21.4	23.6	25.7	27.9	30.0	32.1	34.3	36.4	38.6	40.7	42.9					
8:00	1.9	3.8	5.6	7.5	9.4	11.3	13.1	15.0	16.9	18.8	20.6	22.5	24.4	26.3	28.1	30.0	31.9	33.8	35.6	37.5	45.0				
9:00	1.7	3.3	5.0	6.7	8.3	10.0	11.7	13.3	15.0	16.7	18.3	20.0	21.7	23.3	25.0	26.7	28.3	30.0	31.7	33.3	40.0	46.7			
10:00	1.5	3.0	4.5	6.0	7.5	9.0	10.5	12.0	13.5	15.0	16.5	18.0	19.5	21.0	22.5	24.0	25.5	27.0	28.5	30.0	36.0	42.0	48.0		
11:00	1.4	2.7	4.1	5.5	6.8	8.2	9.5	10.9	12.3	13.6	15.0	16.4	17.7	19.1	20.5	21.8	23.2	24.5	25.9	27.3	32.7	38.2	43.6	49.1	
12:00	1.3	2.5	3.8	5.0	6.3	7.5	8.8	10.0	11.3	12.5	13.8	15.0	16.3	17.5	18.8	20.0	21.3	22.5	23.8	25.0	30.0	35.0	40.0	45.0	50.0
13:00	1.2	2.3	3.5	4.6	5.8	6.9	8.1	9.2	10.4	11.5	12.7	13.8	15.0	16.2	17.3	18.5	19.6	20.8	21.9	23.1	27.7	32.3	36.9	41.5	46.2
14:00	1.1	2.1	3.2	4.3	5.4	6.4	7.5	8.6	9.6	10.7	11.8	12.9	13.9	15.0	16.1	17.1	18.2	19.3	20.4	21.4	25.7	30.0	34.3	38.6	42.9
15:00	1.0	2.0	3.0	4.0	5.0	6.0	7.0	8.0	9.0	10.0	11.0	12.0	13.0	14.0	15.0	16.0	17.0	18.0	19.0	20.0	24.0	28.0	32.0	36.0	40.0
16:00	0.9	1.9	2.8	3.8	4.7	5.6	6.6	7.5	8.4	9.4	10.3	11.3	12.2	13.1	14.1	15.0	15.9	16.9	17.8	18.8	22.5	26.3	30.0	33.8	37.5
17:00	0.9	1.8	2.6	3.5	4.4	5.3	6.2	7.1	7.9	8.8	9.7	10.6	11.5	12.4	13.2	14.1	15.0	15.9	16.8	17.6	21.2	24.7	28.2	31.8	35.3
18:00	0.8	1.7	2.5	3.3	4.2	5.0	5.8	6.7	7.5	8.3	9.2	10.0	10.8	11.7	12.5	13.3	14.2	15.0	15.8	16.7	20.0	23.3	26.7	30.0	33.3
19:00	0.8	1.6	2.4	3.2	3.9	4.7	5.5	6.3	7.1	7.9	8.7	9.5	10.3	11.1	11.8	12.6	13.4	14.2	15.0	15.8	18.9	22.1	25.3	28.4	31.6
20:00	0.8	1.5	2.3	3.0	3.8	4.5	5.3	6.0	6.8	7.5	8.3	9.0	9.8	10.5	11.3	12.0	12.8	13.5	14.3	15.0	18.0	21.0	24.0	27.0	30.0
21:00	0.7	1.4	2.1	2.9	3.6	4.3	5.0	5.7	6.4	7.1	7.9	8.6	9.3	10.0	10.7	11.4	12.1	12.9	13.6	14.3	17.1	20.0	22.9	25.7	28.6
22:00	0.7	1.4	2.0	2.7	3.4	4.1	4.8	5.5	6.1	6.8	7.5	8.2	8.9	9.5	10.2	10.9	11.6	12.3	13.0	13.6	16.4	19.1	21.8	24.5	27.3
23:00	0.7	1.3	2.0	2.6	3.3	3.9	4.6	5.2	5.9	6.5	7.2	7.8	8.5	9.1	9.8	10.4	11.1	11.7	12.4	13.0	15.7	18.3	20.9	23.5	26.1
24:00	0.6	1.3	1.9	2.5	3.1	3.8	4.4	5.0	5.6	6.3	6.9	7.5	8.1	8.8	9.4	10.0	10.6	11.3	11.9	12.5	15.0	17.5	20.0	22.5	25.0
25:00	0.6	1.2	1.8	2.4	3.0	3.6	4.2	4.8	5.4	6.0	6.6	7.2	7.8	8.4	9.0	9.6	10.2	10.8	11.4	12.0	14.4	16.8	19.2	21.6	24.0
26:00	0.6	1.2	1.7	2.3	2.9	3.5	4.0	4.6	5.2	5.8	6.3	6.9	7.5	8.1	8.7	9.2	9.8	10.4	11.0	11.5	13.8	16.2	18.5	20.8	23.1
27:00	0.6	1.1	1.7	2.2	2.8	3.3	3.9	4.4	5.0	5.6	6.1	6.7	7.2	7.8	8.3	8.9	9.4	10.0	10.6	11.1	13.3	15.6	17.8	20.0	22.2
28:00	0.5	1.1	1.6	2.1	2.7	3.2	3.8	4.3	4.8	5.4	5.9	6.4	7.0	7.5	8.0	8.6	9.1	9.6	10.2	10.7	12.9	15.0	17.1	19.3	21.4
29:00	0.5	1.0	1.6	2.1	2.6	3.1	3.6	4.1	4.7	5.2	5.7	6.2	6.7	7.2	7.8	8.3	8.8	9.3	9.8	10.3	12.4	14.5	16.6	18.6	20.7
30:00	0.5	1.0	1.5	2.0	2.5	3.0	3.5	4.0	4.5	5.0	5.5	6.0	6.5	7.0	7.5	8.0	8.5	9.0	9.5	10.0	12.0	14.0	16.0	18.0	20.0
31:00	0.5	1.0	1.5	1.9	2.4	2.9	3.4	3.9	4.4	4.8	5.3	5.8	6.3	6.8	7.3	7.7	8.2	8.7	9.2	9.7	11.6	13.5	15.5	17.4	19.4
32:00	0.5	0.9	1.4	1.9	2.3	2.8	3.3	3.8	4.2	4.7	5.2	5.6	6.1	6.6	7.0	7.5	8.0	8.4	8.9	9.4	11.3	13.1	15.0	16.9	18.8
33:00	0.5	0.9	1.4	1.8	2.3	2.7	3.2	3.6	4.1	4.5	5.0	5.5	5.9	6.4	6.8	7.3	7.7	8.2	8.6	9.1	10.9	12.7	14.5	16.4	18.2
34:00	0.4	0.9	1.3	1.8	2.2	2.6	3.1	3.5	4.0	4.4	4.9	5.3	5.7	6.2	6.6	7.1	7.5	7.9	8.4	8.8	10.6	12.4	14.1	15.9	17.6
35:00	0.4	0.9	1.3	1.7	2.1	2.6	3.0	3.4	3.9	4.3	4.7	5.1	5.6	6.0	6.4	6.9	7.3	7.7	8.1	8.6	10.3	12.0	13.7	15.4	17.1
36:00	0.4	0.8	1.3	1.7	2.1	2.5	2.9	3.3	3.8	4.2	4.6	5.0	5.4	5.8	6.3	6.7	7.1	7.5	7.9	8.3	10.0	11.7	13.3	15.0	16.7
37:00	0.4	0.8	1.2	1.6	2.0	2.4	2.8	3.2	3.6	4.1	4.5	4.9	5.3	5.7	6.1	6.5	6.9	7.3	7.7	8.1	9.7	11.4	13.0	14.6	16.2
38:00	0.4	0.8	1.2	1.6	2.0	2.4	2.8	3.2	3.6	3.9	4.3	4.7	5.1	5.5	5.9	6.3	6.7	7.1	7.5	7.9	9.5	11.1	12.6	14.2	15.8
39:00	0.4	0.8	1.2	1.5	1.9	2.3	2.7	3.1	3.5	3.8	4.2	4.6	5.0	5.4	5.8	6.2	6.5	6.9	7.3	7.7	9.2	10.8	12.3	13.8	15.4
40:00	0.4	0.8	1.1	1.5	1.9	2.3	2.6	3.0	3.4	3.8	4.1	4.5	4.9	5.3	5.6	6.0	6.4	6.8	7.1	7.5	9.0	10.5	12.0	13.5	15.0

Formula for Speed/Time/Distance

$$\text{Speed (knots)} = \frac{\text{Distance (nautical miles)} \times 60}{\text{Time (minutes)}}$$

$$\text{Time (minutes)} = \frac{\text{Distance (nautical miles)} \times 60}{\text{Speed (knots)}}$$

$$\text{Distance} = \frac{\text{Speed (knots)} \times \text{Time (minutes)}}{60}$$

Table 4 — Tidal Change over Time To Find Approximate Intermediate
Tidal Height (Mixed Semi-Diurnal Tide)

Instructions

1. From the Tide Guide, calculate the duration and range of the current tide and the time elapsed since the last high or low tide.

   Duration—the number of hours from the last high or low tide to the next low or high tide.

   Range—the difference in height (meters or feet) between the last high or low tide and the next low or high tide.

   Example: To calculate the tide height at 0330….

Time	Height/Feet	Height/Meters
0045	2.7	0.8
0630	14.2	4.3
1255	5.6	1.7
1910	9.8	3.0

   Range = 14.2 – 2.7 = 11.5
   Duration = 6h 30m – 0h 45m = 5h 45m
   Elapsed time = 3h 30m – 0h 45m = 2h 45m

2. Find the point on the left side of the lower scale that equals a duration of 5h 45m It will be between the 5.5 and the 6.0 in the **Duration** scale at the lower left.

3. Follow a line horizontally to intersect the curved line representing the elapsed time (**Hours Since Last High or Low Water**). For 2h 45m this line will lie midway between the curves representing 2.5 and 3.0 hours (Point **A**).

4. For a rising tide, follow a line vertically from **A** to a point on the rising tide curve (Point **B**). From Point **B**, follow a horizontal line to the "**Percent of Tidal Range**" scale (in this case, 45%).

5. Multiply the **Range** by this value (45%) and add to the height of the previous low tide.
   45% of 11.5 ft = 5.2 ft
   Current height of tide = 5.2 ft + 2.7 ft = 7.9 ft

For a **falling tide**, follow the line vertically from Point **A** to point **B** on the falling tide curve. Then project a horizontal line from Point **B** to the "**Percent of Tidal Range**" scale. Multiply the **Range** by this value and add to the height of the following low tide.

The chart can also be worked backwards to find the time a tide will be at a given height.

1. First, calculate the percent of tidal range for that height of tide.

2. From the percent value on the left, follow a horizontal line to the rising or falling tide curve (Point **B**).

3. From Point **B**, drop a vertical line to the scale in the lower portion of the chart. Find Point **A** by drawing a horizontal line from the indicated **Duration**. Where the vertical and horizontal lines intersect, that is Point **A**.

4. Follow the curve from Point **A** to the bottom of the chart to find the **Hours Since Last High or Low Water**.

5. Add this value to the time of the last tide to find the time the tide will be at the given height.

> Tidal Datum (and Chart Datum) is the plane from which tidal heights (and charted depths) are measured. In Canada Tide Datum is the plane of Lowest Normal Tides (below which the tide very seldom falls) but in the US, Tide Datum is mean Lower Low Water (MLLW) and negative tides are much more common.

Table 4 — Tidal Change Over Time

To Find Approximate Intermediate Tidal Height

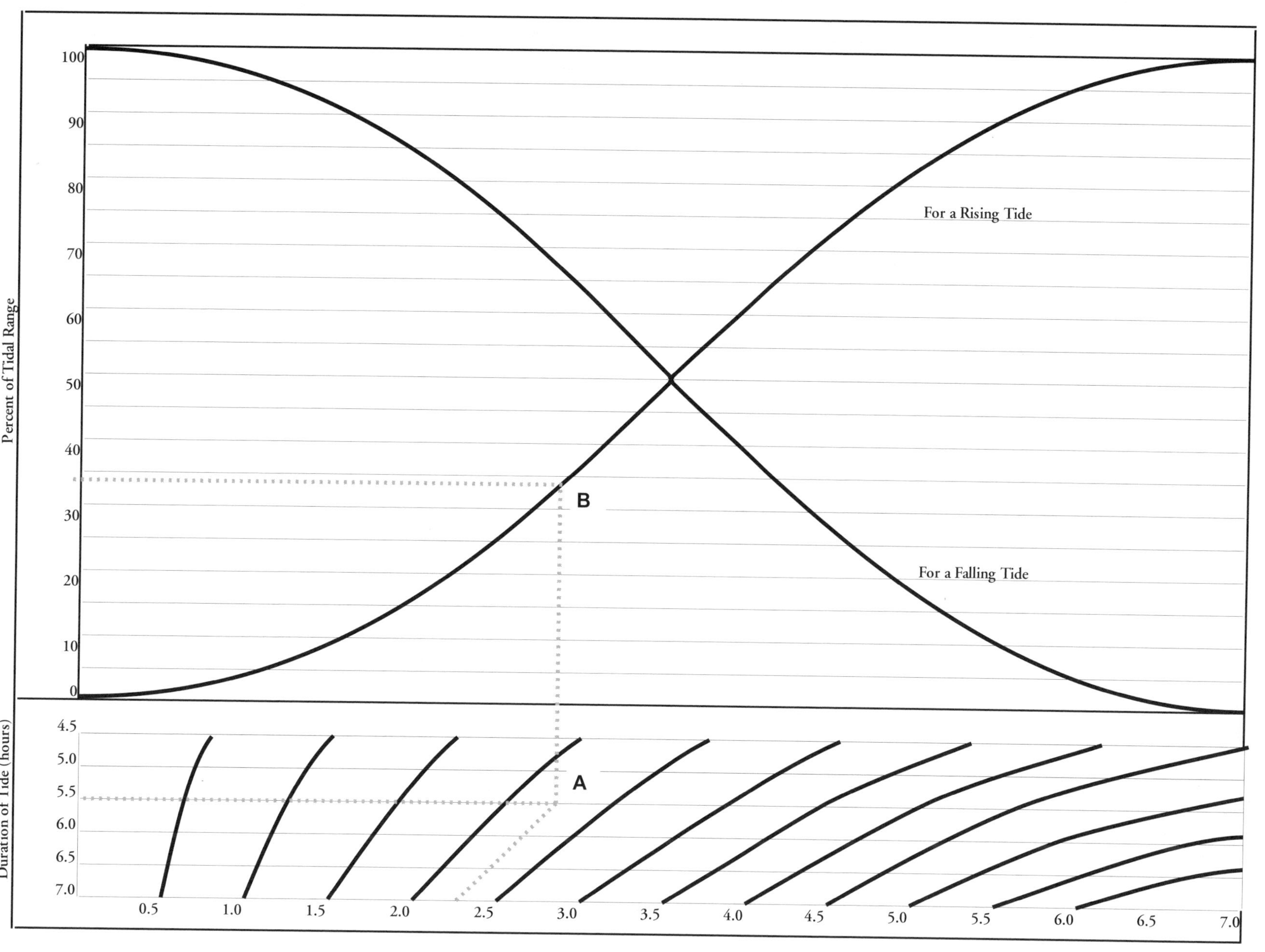
Percent of Tidal Range
100
90
80
70
60
50
40
30
20
10
0
For a Rising Tide
For a Falling Tide
B
A
Duration of Tide (hours)
4.5
5.0
5.5
6.0
6.5
7.0
0.5
1.0
1.5
2.0
2.5
3.0
3.5
4.0
4.5
5.0
5.5
6.0
6.5
7.0
Hours Since Last High or Low Water

Table 5 — Estimating Distance

To Estimate Distance from Shore by the Appearance of Shoreline Vegetation

Distance	On an Overcast Day with at Least Five Miles Visibility	On a Sunny Day
0.05 Mile 304 Feet 93 Meters	Differing types of bushes clearly distinguishable Ferns identifiable. Texture of tree trunks can be seen clearly. Blades of grass can be seen.	Differing types of bushes clearly distinguishable. Ferns identifiable. Texture of tree trunks can be seen clearly. Blades of grass can be seen.
0.1 Mile 608 Feet 185 Meters	Individual leaves visible on deciduous trees and bushes. Coniferous branchlets visible. Different types of vegetation not distinguishable. Grass appears fuzzy.	Individual leaves visible on trees and bushes. Coniferous branchlets visible. Different types of vegetation not distinguishable. Grass appears fuzzy.
0.2 Miles 1215 Feet 370 Meters	Conifers—small branches appear.	Conifers—small branches appear.
1/2 Mile 3038 Feet 926 Meters	Conifers—large branches clear and distinct. Texture of deciduous bushes apparent, showing lighter green than conifers.	Conifers—large branches clear and distinct. Dead branches on conifers visible.
3/4 Mile 4557 Feet 1389 Meters	Conifers—large branches becoming distinct.	Conifers—large branches becoming distinct. Texture of deciduous bushes apparent, showing lighter green than conifers.
1 Mile 6076 Feet 1852 Meters	Conifers—large branches barely visible. Deciduous—large branches distinct.	Conifers—large branches barely visible. Deciduous—large branches distinct.
2 Miles	Deciduous—texture of branches and leaves clear, but individual large branches not visible.	Individual conifers clearly visible. Deciduous—texture of branches and leaves clear, but individual large branches not visible.
2.5 Miles	Trees dull green. Individual trees just visible.	Individual dead conifers just visible. Individual trees just visible.
3 Miles	Deciduous trees apparent by cloudy texture and lighter colour. In winter they appear like smoke.	Coniferous forest has a textured appearance. Individual trees barely distinguishable except on the skyline. Deciduous trees apparent by cloudy texture and lighter colour.
4 Miles	Trees take on a bluish appearance. Individual trees not distinguishable except on skyline, but texture of forested areas is apparent.	Individual trees not distinguishable except on the skyline.
5 Miles	Texture of forested areas is just visible.	Trees a dull green. Individual trees not distinguishable except on skyline, but texture of forested areas is apparent.
more than 5 Miles	Texture of forest not readily apparent. Objects at sea level are below the horizon to an observer on a small boat. Individual trees on skyline not detectable.	Texture of forest not readily apparent. Objects at sea level are below the horizon to an observer on a small boat. Individual trees on skyline not detectable.

This table applies only to observers with good eyesight when atmospheric conditions are favourable. The distances quoted are estimates only and the criteria are quite subjective. Use the table with caution.

Table 6 — Angular Measure

Table 6-1 — Rule of Thumb for Measuring Horizontal Angles

This table is based on persons with average build and bone structure when viewing their hands at arms length. Persons with especially large (or small) hands for their size should modify the table accordingly. (The degree scale in this table is accurate when viewed from a distance of 36 inches.)

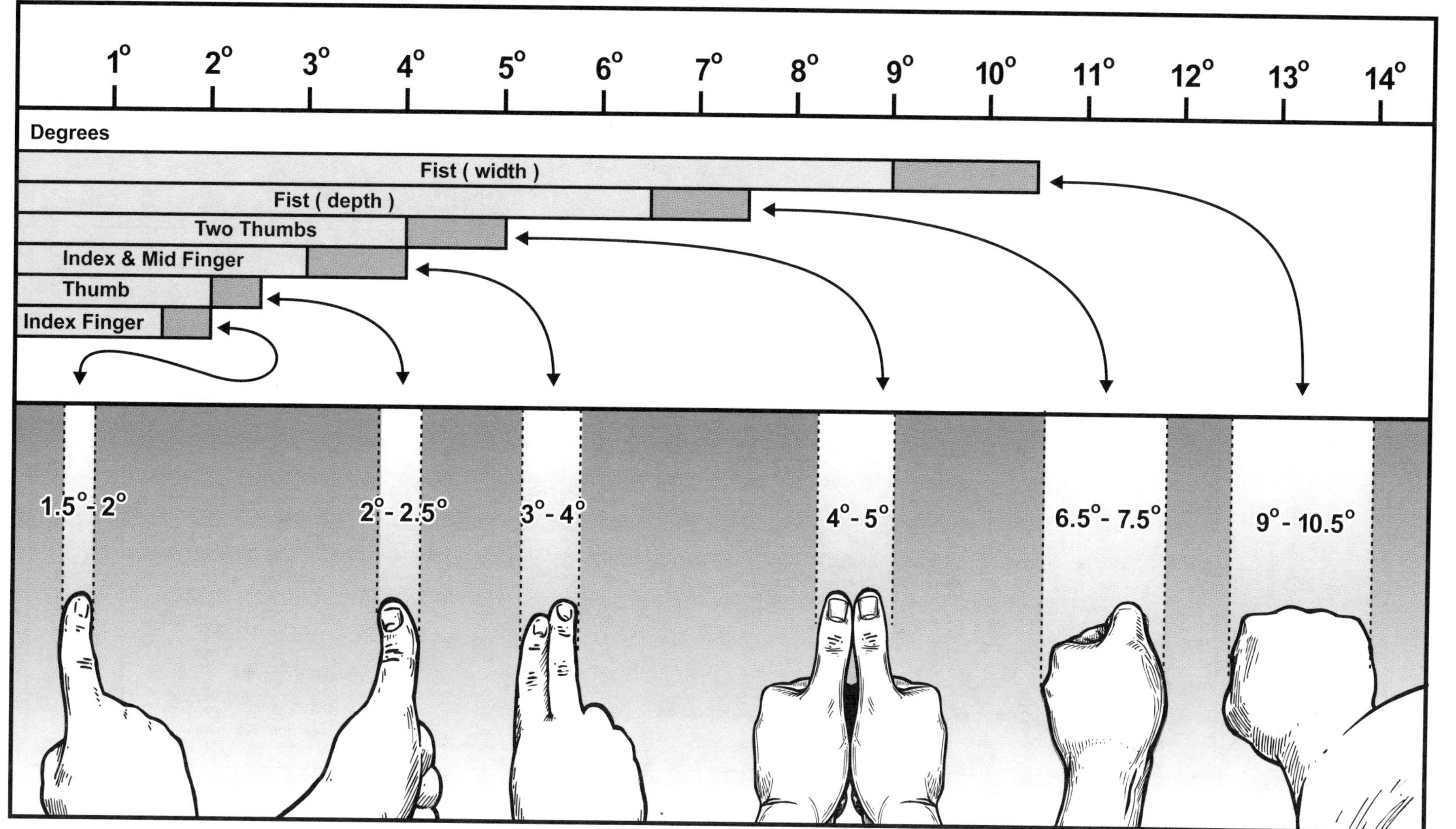
1° 2° 3° 4° 5° 6° 7° 8° 9° 10° 11° 12° 13° 14°
Degrees
Fist (width)
Fist (depth)
Two Thumbs
Index & Mid Finger
Thumb
Index Finger
1.5°- 2°
2°- 2.5°
3°- 4°
4°- 5°
6.5°- 7.5°
9°- 10.5°

Table 6-2 — To Determine the Angular Separation when the Range is Known

Angle a -- Angular Separation in Degrees (Beam-width); B -- Range in Nautical Miles

Angle a	0.1	0.2	0.3	0.4	0.5	0.6	0.7	0.8	0.9	1.0	1.25	1.5	1.75	2.0	2.25	2.5	3.0	3.5	4.0	4.5	5.0	6.0	7.0	8.0	9.0	10
1	Range in Meters									32	40	48	57	65	73	81	97	113	129	145	162	194	226	259	291	323
2	(over 900 meters in nautical miles)							52	58	65	81	97	113	129	146	162	194	226	259	291	323	388	453	517	582	647
3						58	68	78	87	97	121	146	170	194	218	243	291	340	388	437	485	582	679	776	873	*0.52*
4				52	65	78	91	104	117	129	162	194	227	259	291	324	388	453	518	583	647	777	906	*0.56*	*0.63*	*0.70*
5				65	81	97	113	130	146	162	203	243	284	324	365	405	486	567	648	729	810	*0.52*	*0.61*	*0.70*	*0.79*	*0.87*
6			58	78	97	117	136	156	175	195	243	292	341	389	438	487	584	681	779	876	*0.53*	*0.63*	*0.74*	*0.84*	*0.95*	*1.05*
7			68	91	114	136	159	182	205	227	284	341	398	455	512	568	682	796	910	*0.55*	*0.61*	*0.74*	*0.86*	*0.98*	*1.10*	*1.23*
8		52	78	104	130	156	182	208	234	260	325	390	455	521	586	651	781	911	*0.56*	*0.63*	*0.70*	*0.84*	*0.98*	*1.12*	*1.26*	*1.41*
9		59	88	117	147	176	205	235	264	293	367	440	513	587	660	733	880	*0.55*	*0.63*	*0.71*	*0.79*	*0.95*	*1.11*	*1.27*	*1.43*	*1.58*
10	33	65	98	131	163	196	229	261	294	327	408	490	571	653	735	816	*0.53*	*0.62*	*0.71*	*0.79*	*0.88*	*1.06*	*1.23*	*1.41*	*1.59*	*1.76*
11	36	72	108	144	180	216	252	288	324	360	450	540	630	720	810	900	*0.58*	*0.68*	*0.78*	*0.87*	*0.97*	*1.17*	*1.36*	*1.55*	*1.75*	*1.94*
12	39	79	118	157	197	236	276	315	354	394	492	590	689	787	886	*0.53*	*0.64*	*0.74*	*0.85*	*0.96*	*1.06*	*1.28*	*1.49*	*1.70*	*1.91*	*2.13*
13	43	86	128	171	214	257	299	342	385	428	534	641	748	855	*0.52*	*0.58*	*0.69*	*0.81*	*0.92*	*1.04*	*1.15*	*1.39*	*1.62*	*1.85*	*2.08*	*2.31*
14	46	92	139	185	231	277	323	369	416	462	577	693	808	*0.50*	*0.56*	*0.62*	*0.75*	*0.87*	*1.00*	*1.12*	*1.25*	*1.50*	*1.75*	*1.99*	*2.24*	*2.49*
15	50	99	149	198	248	298	347	397	447	496	620	744	868	*0.54*	*0.60*	*0.67*	*0.80*	*0.94*	*1.07*	*1.21*	*1.34*	*1.61*	*1.88*	*2.14*	*2.41*	*2.68*
16	53	106	159	212	266	319	372	425	478	531	664	797	*0.50*	*0.57*	*0.65*	*0.72*	*0.86*	*1.00*	*1.15*	*1.29*	*1.43*	*1.72*	*2.01*	*2.29*	*2.58*	*2.87*
17	57	113	170	226	283	340	396	453	510	566	708	849	*0.53*	*0.61*	*0.69*	*0.76*	*0.92*	*1.07*	*1.22*	*1.38*	*1.53*	*1.83*	*2.14*	*2.45*	*2.75*	*3.06*
18	60	120	181	241	301	361	421	481	542	602	752	903	*0.57*	*0.65*	*0.73*	*0.81*	*0.97*	*1.14*	*1.30*	*1.46*	*1.62*	*1.95*	*2.27*	*2.60*	*2.92*	*3.25*
19	64	128	191	255	319	383	446	510	574	638	797	*0.52*	*0.60*	*0.69*	*0.77*	*0.86*	*1.03*	*1.21*	*1.38*	*1.55*	*1.72*	*2.07*	*2.41*	*2.75*	*3.10*	*3.44*
20	67	135	202	270	337	404	472	539	607	674	843	*0.55*	*0.64*	*0.73*	*0.82*	*0.91*	*1.09*	*1.27*	*1.46*	*1.64*	*1.82*	*2.18*	*2.55*	*2.91*	*3.28*	*3.64*
21	71	142	213	284	355	427	498	569	640	711	889	*0.58*	*0.67*	*0.77*	*0.86*	*0.96*	*1.15*	*1.34*	*1.54*	*1.73*	*1.92*	*2.30*	*2.69*	*3.07*	*3.45*	*3.84*
22	75	150	224	299	374	449	524	599	673	748	*0.50*	*0.61*	*0.71*	*0.81*	*0.91*	*1.01*	*1.21*	*1.41*	*1.62*	*1.82*	*2.02*	*2.42*	*2.83*	*3.23*	*3.64*	*4.04*
23	79	157	236	314	393	472	550	629	707	786	*0.53*	*0.64*	*0.74*	*0.85*	*0.95*	*1.06*	*1.27*	*1.49*	*1.70*	*1.91*	*2.12*	*2.55*	*2.97*	*3.40*	*3.82*	*4.24*
24	82	165	247	330	412	495	577	660	742	824	*0.56*	*0.67*	*0.78*	*0.89*	*1.00*	*1.11*	*1.34*	*1.56*	*1.78*	*2.00*	*2.23*	*2.67*	*3.12*	*3.56*	*4.01*	*4.45*
25	86	173	259	345	432	518	604	691	777	864	*0.58*	*0.70*	*0.82*	*0.93*	*1.05*	*1.17*	*1.40*	*1.63*	*1.87*	*2.10*	*2.33*	*2.80*	*3.26*	*3.73*	*4.20*	*4.66*
26	90	181	271	361	452	542	632	723	813	903	*0.61*	*0.73*	*0.85*	*0.98*	*1.10*	*1.22*	*1.46*	*1.71*	*1.95*	*2.19*	*2.44*	*2.93*	*3.41*	*3.90*	*4.39*	*4.88*
27	94	189	283	377	472	566	660	755	849	944	*0.64*	*0.76*	*0.89*	*1.02*	*1.15*	*1.27*	*1.53*	*1.78*	*2.04*	*2.29*	*2.55*	*3.06*	*3.57*	*4.08*	*4.59*	*5.09*
28	98	197	295	394	492	591	689	788	886	*0.53*	*0.66*	*0.80*	*0.93*	*1.06*	*1.20*	*1.33*	*1.59*	*1.86*	*2.13*	*2.39*	*2.66*	*3.19*	*3.72*	*4.25*	*4.78*	*5.32*
29	103	205	308	411	513	616	719	821	*0.50*	*0.55*	*0.69*	*0.83*	*0.97*	*1.11*	*1.25*	*1.39*	*1.66*	*1.94*	*2.22*	*2.49*	*2.77*	*3.33*	*3.88*	*4.43*	*4.99*	*5.54*
30	107	214	321	428	535	641	748	855	*0.52*	*0.58*	*0.72*	*0.87*	*1.01*	*1.15*	*1.30*	*1.44*	*1.73*	*2.02*	*2.31*	*2.60*	*2.89*	*3.46*	*4.04*	*4.62*	*5.20*	*5.77*

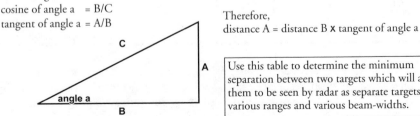

One-in-Sixty Rule

A difference in bearing (angle) at close range represents a small distance, but a difference in bearing (angle) at long range represents a much longer distance. Simply put, **the one in sixty rule** states that a difference in bearing of one degree represents a distance of one mile at a distance of sixty miles. A difference in bearing of five degrees represents a distance of five miles at a distance of sixty miles, and so on.

Trignometric Functions
In any right angle triangle
sine of angle a = A/C
cosine of angle a = B/C
tangent of angle a = A/B

If angle a and distance B are known, then

$\frac{\text{distance A}}{\text{distance B}}$ = tangent of angle a

Therefore,
distance A = distance B x tangent of angle a

Use this table to determine the minimum separation between two targets which will allow them to be seen by radar as separate targets at various ranges and various beam-widths.

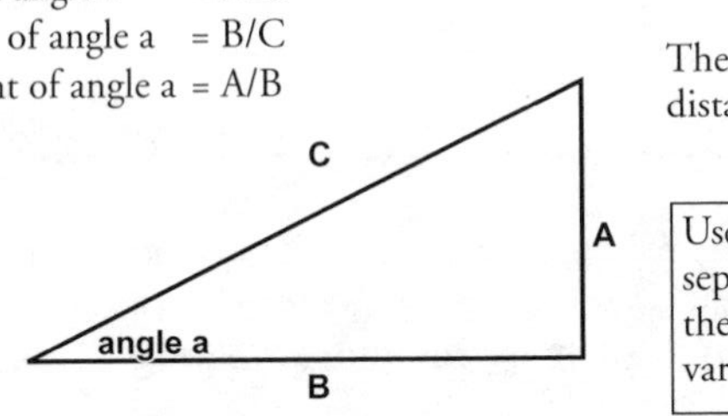

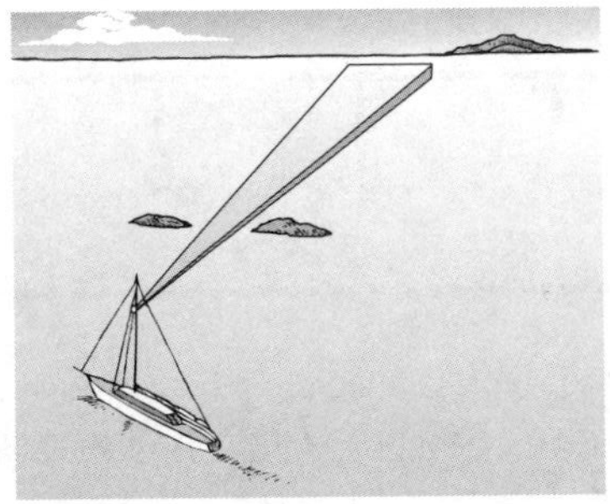

Radar Beam Width

The minimum angular separation for two targets to be seen as separate targets is dependent on the horizontal beam width, which is dictated by the length of the scanner radiating surface.

72-inch scanner	1.2°
48-inch scanner	1.9°
36-inch scanner	2.5°
24-inch scanner	3.9°
18-inch scanner	>5°

Table 6-3 — To Determine the Range When the Angular Separation is Known

Angle a— Angular Separation in Degrees (Beam width)	Angular Separation (A) in Meters *(over 900 meters in nautical miles)*																													
	5	10	15	20	25	30	35	40	45	50	55	60	65	70	75	80	85	90	95	100	110	120	130	140	150	160	170	180	190	200
0.25	*0.62*	*1.24*	*1.86*	*2.48*	*3.09*	*3.71*	*4.33*	*4.95*	*5.57*	*6.19*	*6.81*	*7.43*	*8.04*	*8.66*	*9.28*	*9.90*	*10.5*	*11.1*	*11.8*	*12.4*	*13.6*	*14.9*	*16.1*	*17.3*	*18.6*	*19.8*	*21.0*	*22.3*	*23.5*	*24.8*
0.50	573	*0.62*	*0.93*	*1.24*	*1.55*	*1.86*	*2.17*	*2.48*	*2.78*	*3.09*	*3.40*	*3.71*	*4.02*	*4.33*	*4.64*	*4.95*	*5.26*	*5.57*	*5.88*	*6.19*	*6.81*	*7.43*	*8.04*	*8.66*	*9.28*	*9.90*	*10.5*	*11.1*	*11.8*	*12.4*
0.75	382	764	*0.62*	*0.83*	*1.03*	*1.24*	*1.44*	*1.65*	*1.86*	*2.06*	*2.27*	*2.48*	*2.68*	*2.89*	*3.09*	*3.30*	*3.51*	*3.71*	*3.92*	*4.13*	*4.54*	*4.95*	*5.36*	*5.78*	*6.19*	*6.60*	*7.01*	*7.43*	*7.84*	*8.25*
1.0	286	573	859	*0.62*	*0.77*	*0.93*	*1.08*	*1.24*	*1.39*	*1.55*	*1.70*	*1.86*	*2.01*	*2.17*	*2.32*	*2.47*	*2.63*	*2.78*	*2.94*	*3.09*	*3.40*	*3.71*	*4.02*	*4.33*	*4.64*	*4.95*	*5.26*	*5.57*	*5.88*	*6.19*
1.5	191	382	573	764	*0.52*	*0.62*	*0.72*	*0.82*	*0.93*	*1.03*	*1.13*	*1.24*	*1.34*	*1.44*	*1.55*	*1.65*	*1.75*	*1.86*	*1.96*	*2.06*	*2.27*	*2.47*	*2.68*	*2.89*	*3.09*	*3.30*	*3.51*	*3.71*	*3.92*	*4.12*
2.0	143	286	430	573	716	859	*0.54*	*0.62*	*0.70*	*0.77*	*0.85*	*0.93*	*1.01*	*1.08*	*1.16*	*1.24*	*1.31*	*1.39*	*1.47*	*1.55*	*1.70*	*1.86*	*2.01*	*2.16*	*2.32*	*2.47*	*2.63*	*2.78*	*2.94*	*3.09*
2.5	115	229	344	458	573	687	802	*0.49*	*0.56*	*0.62*	*0.68*	*0.74*	*0.80*	*0.87*	*0.93*	*0.99*	*1.05*	*1.11*	*1.17*	*1.24*	*1.36*	*1.48*	*1.61*	*1.73*	*1.86*	*1.98*	*2.10*	*2.23*	*2.35*	*2.47*
3.0		191	286	382	477	572	668	763	859	*0.52*	*0.57*	*0.62*	*0.67*	*0.72*	*0.77*	*0.82*	*0.88*	*0.93*	*0.98*	*1.03*	*1.13*	*1.24*	*1.34*	*1.44*	*1.55*	*1.65*	*1.75*	*1.85*	*1.96*	*2.06*
3.5		164	245	327	409	491	572	654	736	818	899	*0.53*	*0.57*	*0.62*	*0.66*	*0.71*	*0.75*	*0.79*	*0.84*	*0.88*	*0.97*	*1.06*	*1.15*	*1.24*	*1.32*	*1.41*	*1.50*	*1.59*	*1.68*	*1.77*
4.0		143	215	286	358	429	501	572	644	715	787	858	*0.50*	*0.54*	*0.58*	*0.62*	*0.66*	*0.70*	*0.73*	*0.77*	*0.85*	*0.93*	*1.00*	*1.08*	*1.16*	*1.24*	*1.31*	*1.39*	*1.47*	*1.54*
4.5		127	191	254	318	381	445	508	572	635	699	762	826	890	*0.51*	*0.55*	*0.58*	*0.62*	*0.65*	*0.69*	*0.75*	*0.82*	*0.89*	*0.96*	*1.03*	*1.10*	*1.17*	*1.24*	*1.30*	*1.37*
5.0		114	171	229	286	343	400	457	514	572	629	686	743	800	857	*0.49*	*0.52*	*0.56*	*0.59*	*0.62*	*0.68*	*0.74*	*0.80*	*0.86*	*0.93*	*0.99*	*1.05*	*1.11*	*1.17*	*1.23*
6.0			143	190	238	285	333	381	428	476	523	571	618	666	714	761	809	856	*0.49*	*0.51*	*0.57*	*0.62*	*0.67*	*0.72*	*0.77*	*0.82*	*0.87*	*0.92*	*0.98*	*1.03*
7.0			122	163	204	244	285	326	367	407	448	489	529	570	611	652	692	733	774	814	896	*0.53*	*0.57*	*0.62*	*0.66*	*0.70*	*0.75*	*0.79*	*0.84*	*0.88*
8.0			107	142	178	213	249	285	320	356	391	427	463	498	534	569	605	640	676	712	783	854	*0.50*	*0.54*	*0.58*	*0.61*	*0.65*	*0.69*	*0.73*	*0.77*
9.0				126	158	189	221	253	284	316	347	379	410	442	474	505	537	568	600	631	695	758	821	884	*0.51*	*0.55*	*0.58*	*0.61*	*0.65*	*0.68*
10				113	142	170	199	227	255	284	312	340	369	397	425	454	482	510	539	567	624	681	737	794	851	*0.49*	*0.52*	*0.55*	*0.58*	*0.61*
11				103	129	154	180	206	232	257	283	309	334	360	386	412	437	463	489	514	566	617	669	720	772	823	875	*0.50*	*0.53*	*0.56*
12					118	141	165	188	212	235	259	282	306	329	353	376	400	423	447	470	518	565	612	659	706	753	800	847	894	*0.51*
13					108	130	152	173	195	217	238	260	282	303	325	347	368	390	412	433	476	520	563	606	650	693	736	780	823	866
14					100	120	140	160	180	201	221	241	261	281	301	321	341	361	381	401	441	481	521	562	602	642	682	722	762	802
15						112	131	149	168	187	205	224	243	261	280	299	317	336	355	373	411	448	485	523	560	597	634	672	709	746
16						105	122	140	157	174	192	209	227	244	262	279	296	314	331	349	384	419	453	488	523	558	593	628	663	698
17							114	131	147	164	180	196	213	229	245	262	278	294	311	327	360	393	425	458	491	523	556	589	622	654
18							108	123	139	154	169	185	200	215	231	246	262	277	292	308	339	369	400	431	462	492	523	554	585	616
19							102	116	131	145	160	174	189	203	218	232	247	261	276	290	319	349	378	407	436	465	494	523	552	581
20								110	124	137	151	165	179	192	206	220	234	247	261	275	302	330	357	385	412	440	467	495	522	550
25										107	118	129	139	150	161	172	182	193	204	214	236	257	279	300	322	343	365	386	407	429
30												104	113	121	130	139	147	156	165	173	191	208	225	243	260	277	294	312	329	346
35														100	107	114	121	129	136	143	157	171	186	200	214	229	243	257	271	286

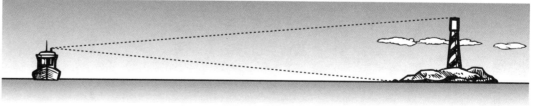

If **angle a** and **distance C** are known, then

distance A / **distance B** = **tangent of angle a**

Therefore

distance B = **distance A** / **tangent of angle a**

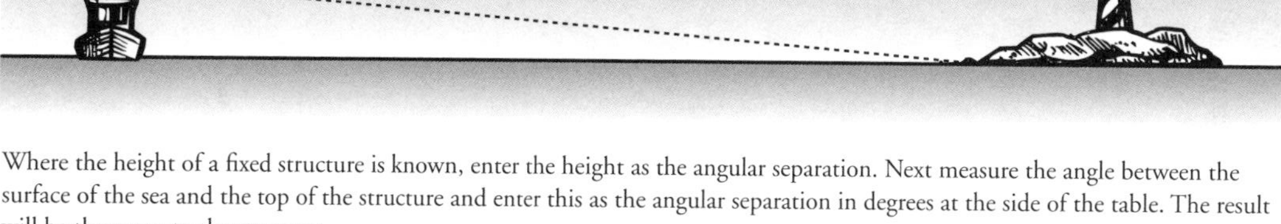

Where the height of a fixed structure is known, enter the height as the angular separation. Next measure the angle between the surface of the sea and the top of the structure and enter this as the angular separation in degrees at the side of the table. The result will be the range to the structure.

This table will accomodate any height up to 200 meters.

Table 7 — Estimating Distance of Ships

Table 7-1 — Ship Lengh in Meters (Feet)

Distances less than 0.5 Nm given in *meters (bold italics)*.

Measured Angular Length of Vessel in Degrees

Index Finger	1½° – 2°
Thumb	2° – 2½°
Index and Mid Finger	3° – 4°
Two Thumbs	4° – 5°
Fist (depth)	6½° – 7½°
Fist (width)	9° – 10½°

Ship Length in Meters (Feet)

Meters	**10**	**20**	**30**	**40**	**50**	**100**	**150**	**200**	**250**	**300**	**350**
Feet	33	65	100	130	165	330	490	650	820	985	1150
1	***573***	***0.62***	0.93	1.24	1.55	3.09	4.64	6.19	7.73	9.28	10.8
2	***286***	***573***	***859***	0.62	0.77	1.55	2.32	3.09	3.87	4.64	5.41
3	***191***	***382***	***573***	***764***	0.52	1.03	1.55	2.06	2.58	3.09	3.61
4	***143***	***286***	***430***	***573***	***716***	0.77	1.16	1.55	1.93	2.32	2.71
5	***115***	***229***	***344***	***458***	***573***	0.62	0.93	1.24	1.55	1.86	2.16
6	***95***	***191***	***286***	***382***	***477***	0.52	0.77	1.03	1.29	1.55	1.80
7	***82***	***164***	***245***	***327***	***409***	***818***	0.66	0.88	1.10	1.32	1.55
8	***72***	***143***	***215***	***286***	***358***	***715***	0.58	0.77	0.97	1.16	1.35
9	***64***	***127***	***191***	***254***	***318***	***635***	0.51	0.69	0.86	1.03	1.20
10	***57***	***114***	***171***	***229***	***286***	***572***	***857***	0.62	0.77	0.93	1.08
11	***52***	***104***	***156***	***208***	***260***	***519***	***779***	0.56	0.70	0.84	0.98
12	***48***	***95***	***143***	***190***	***238***	***476***	***714***	0.51	0.64	0.77	0.90
13	***44***	***88***	***132***	***176***	***219***	***439***	***658***	***878***	0.59	0.71	0.83
14	***41***	***81***	***122***	***163***	***204***	***407***	***611***	***814***	0.55	0.66	0.77
15	***38***	***76***	***114***	***152***	***190***	***380***	***570***	***760***	0.51	0.62	0.72
16	***36***	***71***	***107***	***142***	***178***	***356***	***534***	***712***	***889***	0.58	0.67
17	***33***	***67***	***100***	***134***	***167***	***335***	***502***	***669***	***836***	0.54	0.63
18	***32***	***63***	***95***	***126***	***158***	***316***	***474***	***631***	***789***	0.51	0.60
19	***30***	***60***	***90***	***120***	***149***	***299***	***448***	***598***	***747***	***896***	0.56
20	***28***	***57***	***85***	***113***	***142***	***284***	***425***	***567***	***709***	***851***	0.54
	Gillnetter, Small Troller	*Seiner, Packer, Small Tug, Small Passenger Ferry*	*Medium Tug, Fishing Trawler*	*Mill Bay Ferry, Large Tug*	*Small Car Ferry, Coast Guard Ship, Chip Barge*	*Medium Car Ferry, Log Barge, Small Cruise Ship, Alaska State Ferries*	*Small Container Ship, Large Car Ferry, Car Carrier*	*Medium Cruise Ship (Maasdam, Ryndam)*	*Titanic, Large Cruise Ship, Bulk Carrier*	*Large Container Ship*	*Nimitz Class Aircraft Carrier, Queen Mary II, Supertanker*

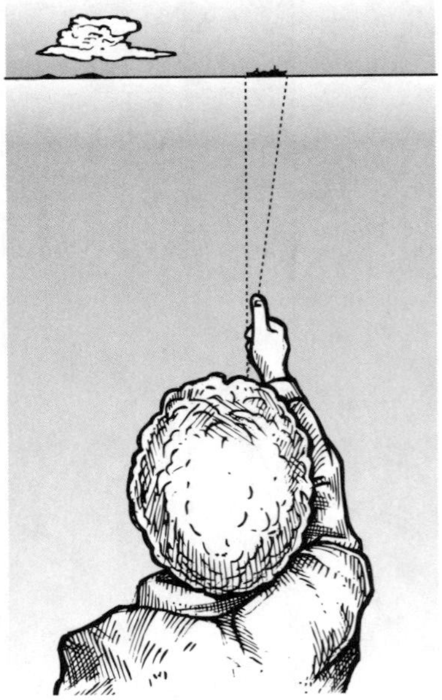

If the angular length of a large car ferry equals the width of the thumb 2°–2½°, the distance is 2.3 Nm.

Table 7-2 — Ship Width in Meters (Feet)
Distances less than 0.5 Nm given in *meters (bold italics)*.

Measured Angular Width of Vessel in Degrees

Index Finger	1½° – 2°
Thumb	2° – 2½°
Index and Mid Finger	3° – 4°
Two Thumbs	4° – 5°
Fist (depth)	6½° – 7½°
Fist (width)	9° – 10½°

Ship Width in Meters (Feet)								
Meters Feet	**3** 10	**6** 20	**10** 33	**20** 65	**30** 100	**40** 130	**50** 164	**75** 246
1	172	344	573	0.62	0.93	1.24	1.55	2.32
2	86*	172	286*	573	859	0.62	0.77	1.16
3	57	115	191	382*	573	764	0.52	0.77
4	43	86*	143	286	430*	573	716	0.58
5	34	69	115	229	344	458*	573	859
6	29	57	95*	191	286	382	477*	716
7	25	49	82	164	245	327	409	613
8	21	43	72	143	215	286	358	536
9	19	38	64	127	191	254	318	477*
10	17	34	57	114	171	229	286	429
11	16	31	52	104	156	208	260	389
12	14	29	48	95*	143	190	238	357
13	13	26	44	88	132	176	219	329
14	12	24	41	81	122	163	204	305
15	11	23	38	76	114	152	190	285
16	11	21	36	71	107	142	178	267
17	10	20	33	67	100	134	167	251
18	9	19	32	63	95*	126	158	237
19	9	18	30	60	90	120	149	224
20	9	17	28	57	85	113	142	213
	Gillnetter, Small Troller	*Packer, Medium Tug, Fishing Trawler, Passenger Ferry*	*Large Tug, Large Fishing Trawler*	*Small Container Ship, Car Ferry, Chip Barge, Log Barge*	*Large Car Ferry, Titanic, Medium Cruise Ship (Maasdam, Ryndam), Medium Container Ship (Panama Canal Max-32m)*	*Queen Mary 2, Large Cruise Ship, Large Container Ship*	*Supertanker (vlcc)*	*Nimitz Class Aircraft Carrier, Supertanker (ulcc)*

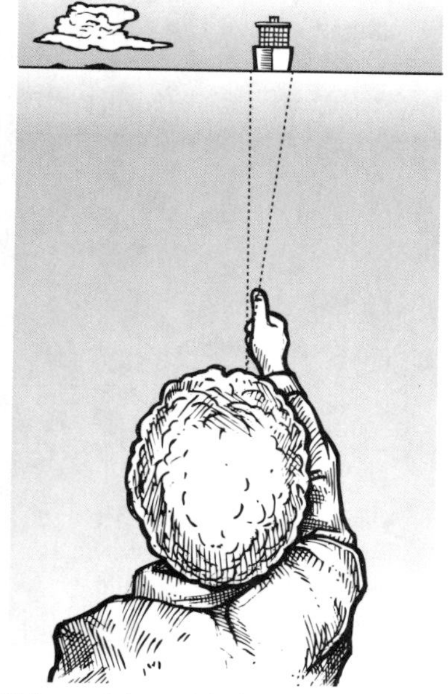
This container ship is approximately 0.5 Nm distant.

Note—Any time you find yourself less than 500 meters directly ahead of a large ship, you are in a hazardous situation. If the commercial vessel is making 25 knots, you have less than 40 seconds to get out of its way. At less than 100 meters you are in extreme danger and have less than eight seconds to get clear.

Table 8 — Relative Size of Ships at Various Chart Scales

	Chart Scale			
	1:5000	1:10,000	1:20,000	1:40,000
Large Car Ferry *Spirit of Vancouver Island* 168 Meters				
Large Cruise Ship *Carnival Destiny* 272 Meters				
Nimitz Class Aircraft Carrier *USS Abraham Lincoln* 333 Meters				

When viewing a large scale marine chart (covering a small area), boaters often regard small constrained channels as being more spacious than they really are. This is especially true in narrow channels that are used by large commercial vessels as well as small craft.

This table will assist boaters in determining the size of various large commercial vessels in relation to the water available in narrow channels, harbours and other waterways, by providing profiles of a few large vessels at various typical chart scales.

If your chart is at 1:5000 scale, you can compare the extent of the waterway to the profile of the ships in the column labeled 1:5000. Similarly, when the chart is at 1:10,000, you may compare it to the vessel profiles in the column labeled 1:10,000.

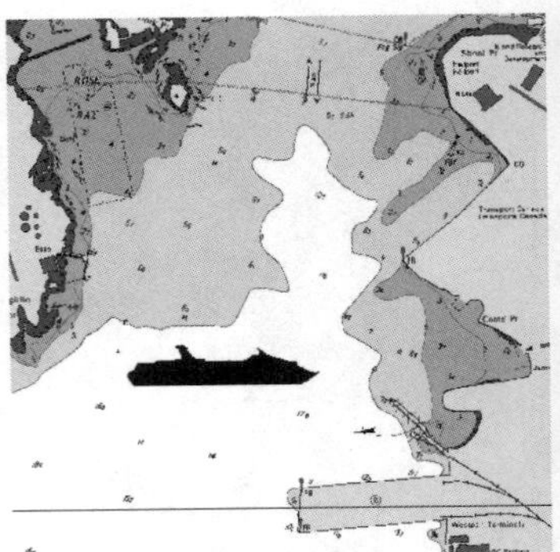

Victoria Harbour entrance and the Carnival Destiny shown at the same scale.

Table 9 — Visible and Radar Horizons at Sea

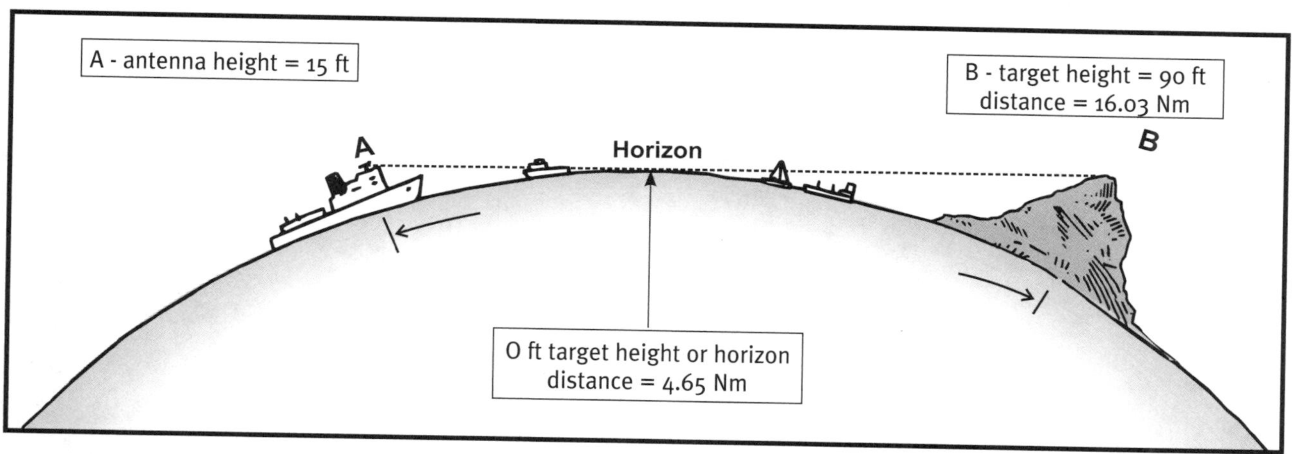
A - antenna height = 15 ft
B - target height = 90 ft
distance = 16.03 Nm
A
Horizon
B
0 ft target height or horizon
distance = 4.65 Nm

Visible Horizon

Where h is the height of eye, the distance to the optical horizon in nautical miles is
$1.15\sqrt{h(f)}$ or $2.08\sqrt{h(m)}$

Maximum Visible Range

The maximum visible range of an object (assuming perfectly clear air), is the maximum distance at which the top of the object (in this case mountain B) shows above your visible horizon.

Radar Horizon

The radar horizon is slightly further away than the optical horizon, because the microwaves are longer and thus more subject to diffraction in the atmosphere than are visible light waves.
Where h is the height of the scanner, the distance to the radar horizon in nautical miles is
$1.22\sqrt{h(f)}$ or $2.21\sqrt{h(m)}$

Table 9-1 — Maximum Detectable Range to a Radar Target in Nautical Miles

Antenna Height in Feet (Meters)	Target Height in Feet (Meters)									
	0 horizon	**10** (3.0)	**20** (6.1)	**30** (9.1)	**40** (12.2)	**50** (15.2)	**60** (18.3)	**70** (21.3)	**80** (24.4)	**90** (27.4)
5 (1.5)	2.68	6.48	8.05	9.26	10.27	11.17	11.98	12.72	13.42	14.07
6 (1.8)	2.94	6.73	8.31	9.51	10.53	11.42	12.23	12.98	13.67	14.32
7 (2.1)	3.17	6.97	8.54	9.75	10.76	11.66	12.47	13.21	13.91	14.56
8 (2.4)	3.39	7.19	8.76	9.97	10.98	11.88	12.69	13.43	14.13	14.78
9 (2.7)	3.60	7.39	8.97	10.17	11.19	12.09	12.90	13.64	14.33	14.98
10 (3.0)	3.79	7.59	9.16	10.37	11.38	12.28	13.09	13.83	14.53	15.18
11(3.4)	3.98	7.77	9.35	10.55	11.57	12.47	13.28	14.02	14.71	15.36
12 (3.7)	4.16	7.95	9.52	10.73	11.75	12.64	13.45	14.20	14.89	15.54
13 (4.0)	4.33	8.12	9.69	10.90	11.92	12.81	13.62	14.37	15.06	15.71
14 (4.3)	4.49	8.28	9.86	11.06	12.08	12.98	13.79	14.53	15.22	15.87
15 (4.6)	4.65	8.44	10.01	11.22	12.24	13.13	13.94	14.69	15.38	16.03
16 (4.9)	4.80	8.59	10.17	11.37	12.39	13.29	14.10	14.84	15.53	16.18
17 (5.2)	4.95	8.74	10.31	11.52	12.54	13.43	14.24	14.99	15.68	16.33
18 (5.5)	5.09	8.89	10.46	11.66	12.68	13.58	14.39	15.13	15.82	16.48
19 (5.8)	5.23	9.03	10.60	11.80	12.82	13.72	14.53	15.27	15.96	16.61
20 (6.1)	5.37	9.16	10.73	11.94	12.96	13.85	14.66	15.41	16.10	16.75

To calculate distances that are beyond the range of this table, use **Table 9-3**. The distance **A-B** is the sum of **(a)** the distance to the horizon for your height of eye (**A**) and, **(b)** the distance from the horizon to the top of the mountain (**B**).

Table 9-2 — Distance of Visible Horizon by Height of Eye

x	y	x	y	x	y	x	y
Height of Eye (Meters)	**Distance to Horizon (Nm)**	**Height of Eye (Meters)**	**Distance to Horizon (Nm)**	**Height of Eye (Feet)**	**Distance to Horizon (Nm)**	**Height of Eye (Feet)**	**Distance to Horizon (Nm)**
1.0	2.08	10.2	6.64	1	1.15	47	7.88
1.2	2.28	10.4	6.71	2	1.63	48	7.97
1.4	2.46	10.6	6.77	3	1.99	49	8.05
1.6	2.63	10.8	6.84	4	2.30	50	8.13
1.8	2.79	11.0	6.90	5	2.57	51	8.21
2.0	2.94	11.2	6.96	6	2.82	52	8.29
2.2	3.09	11.4	7.02	7	3.04	53	8.37
2.4	3.22	11.6	7.08	8	3.25	54	8.45
2.6	3.35	11.8	7.15	9	3.45	55	8.53
2.8	3.48	12.0	7.21	10	3.64	56	8.61
3.0	3.60	12.2	7.27	11	3.81	57	8.68
3.2	3.72	12.4	7.32	12	3.98	58	8.76
3.4	3.84	12.6	7.38	13	4.15	59	8.83
3.6	3.95	12.8	7.44	14	4.30	60	8.91
3.8	4.05	13.0	7.50	15	4.45	61	8.98
4.0	4.16	13.2	7.56	16	4.60	62	9.06
4.2	4.26	13.4	7.61	17	4.74	63	9.13
4.4	4.36	13.6	7.67	18	4.88	64	9.20
4.6	4.46	13.8	7.73	19	5.01	65	9.27
4.8	4.56	14.0	7.78	20	5.14	66	9.34
5.0	4.65	14.2	7.84	21	5.27	67	9.41
5.2	4.74	14.4	7.89	22	5.39	68	9.48
5.4	4.83	14.6	7.95	23	5.52	69	9.55
5.6	4.92	14.8	8.00	24	5.63	70	9.62
5.8	5.01	15.0	8.06	25	5.75	71	9.69
6.0	5.09	15.2	8.11	26	5.86	72	9.76
6.2	5.18	15.4	8.16	27	5.98	73	9.83
6.4	5.26	15.6	8.22	28	6.09	74	9.89
6.6	5.34	15.8	8.27	29	6.19	75	9.96
6.8	5.42	16.0	8.32	30	6.30	76	10.03
7.0	5.50	16.2	8.37	31	6.40	77	10.09
7.2	5.58	16.4	8.42	32	6.51	78	10.16
7.4	5.66	16.6	8.47	33	6.61	79	10.22
7.6	5.73	16.8	8.53	34	6.71	80	10.29
7.8	5.81	17.0	8.58	35	6.80	81	10.35
8.0	5.88	17.2	8.63	36	6.90	82	10.41
8.2	5.96	17.4	8.68	37	7.00	83	10.48
8.4	6.03	17.6	8.73	38	7.09	84	10.54
8.6	6.10	17.8	8.78	39	7.18	85	10.60
8.8	6.17	18.0	8.82	40	7.27	86	10.66
9.0	6.24	18.2	8.87	41	7.36	87	10.73
9.2	6.31	18.4	8.92	42	7.45	88	10.79
9.4	6.38	18.6	8.97	43	7.54	89	10.85
9.6	6.44	18.8	9.02	44	7.63	90	10.91
9.8	6.51	19.0	9.07	45	7.71	91	10.97
10.0	6.58	19.2	9.11	46	7.80	92	11.03

Under abnormal conditions of atmospheric refraction, the visual (and radar) horizons will be either closer or further away than predicted by the table.

Superior Mirage occurs when the air near the sea surface is abnormally colder than the air; an inverted image of an object may appear over the real object. The effect makes objects visible that are normally over the horizon. Ships and small islands may appear to be "floating" in the sky. In Arctic conditions, there have been reported instances of land being visible from more than 200 Nm.

Table 9-3 — Distance of Radar Horizon by Height of Scanner

x	y	x	y	x	y	x	y
Height of Scanner (Meters)	Distance to Horizon (Nm)	Height of Scanner (Meters)	Distance to Horizon (Nm)	Height of Scanner (Feet)	Distance to Horizon (Nm)	Height of Scanner (Feet)	Distance to Horizon (Nm)
1.0	2.21	10.2	7.06	1	1.22	47	8.36
1.2	2.42	10.4	7.13	2	1.73	48	8.45
1.4	2.61	10.6	7.20	3	2.11	49	8.54
1.6	2.80	10.8	7.26	4	2.44	50	8.63
1.8	2.97	11.0	7.33	5	2.73	51	8.71
2.0	3.13	11.2	7.40	6	2.99	52	8.80
2.2	3.28	11.4	7.46	7	3.23	53	8.88
2.4	3.42	11.6	7.53	8	3.45	54	8.97
2.6	3.56	11.8	7.59	9	3.66	55	9.05
2.8	3.70	12.0	7.66	10	3.86	56	9.13
3.0	3.83	12.2	7.72	11	4.05	57	9.21
3.2	3.95	12.4	7.78	12	4.23	58	9.29
3.4	4.08	12.6	7.84	13	4.40	59	9.37
3.6	4.19	12.8	7.91	14	4.56	60	9.45
3.8	4.31	13.0	7.97	15	4.73	61	9.53
4.0	4.42	13.2	8.03	16	4.88	62	9.61
4.2	4.53	13.4	8.09	17	5.03	63	9.68
4.4	4.64	13.6	8.15	18	5.18	64	9.76
4.6	4.74	13.8	8.21	19	5.32	65	9.84
4.8	4.84	14.0	8.27	20	5.46	66	9.91
5.0	4.94	14.2	8.33	21	5.59	67	9.99
5.2	5.04	14.4	8.39	22	5.72	68	10.06
5.4	5.14	14.6	8.44	23	5.85	69	10.13
5.6	5.23	14.8	8.50	24	5.98	70	10.21
5.8	5.32	15.0	8.56	25	6.10	71	10.28
6.0	5.41	15.2	8.62	26	6.22	72	10.35
6.2	5.50	15.4	8.67	27	6.34	73	10.42
6.4	5.59	15.6	8.73	28	6.46	74	10.49
6.6	5.68	15.8	8.78	29	6.57	75	10.57
6.8	5.76	16.0	8.84	30	6.68	76	10.64
7.0	5.85	16.2	8.90	31	6.79	77	10.71
7.2	5.93	16.4	8.95	32	6.90	78	10.77
7.4	6.01	16.6	9.00	33	7.01	79	10.84
7.6	6.09	16.8	9.06	34	7.11	80	10.91
7.8	6.17	17.0	9.11	35	7.22	81	10.98
8.0	6.25	17.2	9.17	36	7.32	82	11.05
8.2	6.33	17.4	9.22	37	7.42	83	11.11
8.4	6.41	17.6	9.27	38	7.52	84	11.18
8.6	6.48	17.8	9.32	39	7.62	85	11.25
8.8	6.56	18.0	9.38	40	7.72	86	11.31
9.0	6.63	18.2	9.43	41	7.81	87	11.38
9.2	6.70	18.4	9.48	42	7.91	88	11.44
9.4	6.78	18.6	9.53	43	8.00	89	11.51
9.6	6.85	18.8	9.58	44	8.09	90	11.57
9.8	6.92	19.0	9.63	45	8.18	91	11.64
10.0	6.99	19.2	9.68	46	8.27	92	11.70

Inferior Mirage occurs when abnormally cool air lies over a warmer sea, or a hot tarred road. The effect is to reduce the distance of the visible horizon. Low-lying islands may be "smeared" vertically and appear to be surrounded by steep cliffs. Far ahead "pools of water" may appear on a hot desert road; but they never get any closer.

To obtain the greatest utility from your radar, you must mount the antenna as high as is practically possible. If you mount the antenna too low, low lying shorelines at medium range will be below your radar horizon. As a result, you will observe the upper parts of buildings and, not being able to see the surrounding land, you may assume they are vessels at sea.

Table 9-4 — Maneuvering Board

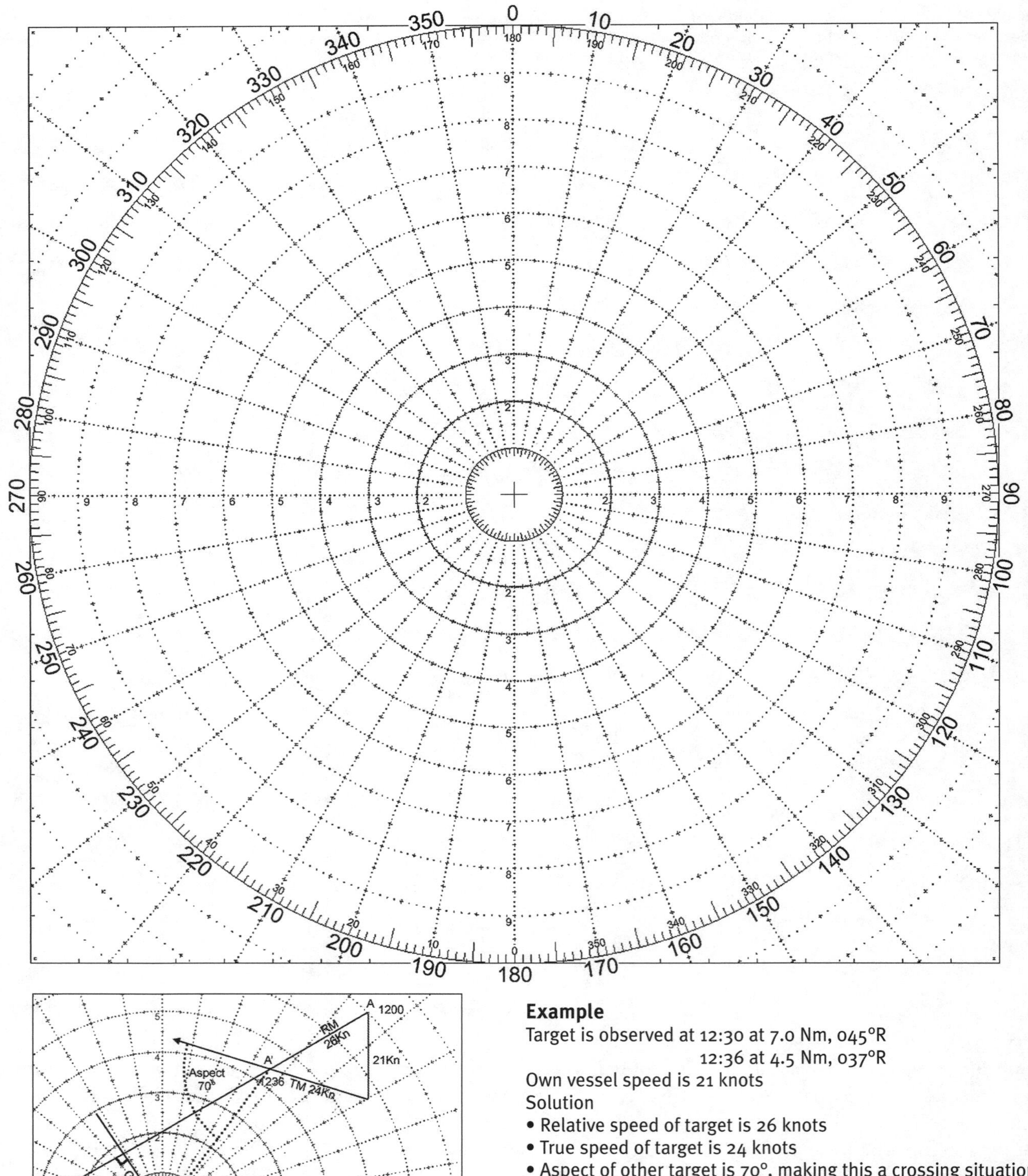
0
10
20
30
40
50
60
70
80
90
100
110
120
130
140
150
160
170
180
190
200
210
220
230
240
250
260
270
280
290
300
310
320
330
340
350

Example

Target is observed at 12:30 at 7.0 Nm, 045°R

12:36 at 4.5 Nm, 037°R

Own vessel speed is 21 knots

Solution

- Relative speed of target is 26 knots
- True speed of target is 24 knots
- Aspect of other target is 70°, making this a crossing situation.
- In this case, the Closest Point of Approach (CPA) is 1.5 Nm and occurs when the target bears 31° to port.

PART II

UNIT CONVERSIONS

Table 10—Knots/Miles per Hour/Kilometers per Hour
Nautical Miles/Statute Miles/Kilometers

Knots/Nautical Miles	Miles per Hour/Statute Miles	Km per Hour/Kilometers
0.1	0.1	0.2
0.2	0.2	0.4
0.3	0.3	0.6
0.4	0.5	0.7
0.5	0.6	0.9
0.6	0.7	1.1
0.7	0.8	1.3
0.8	0.9	1.5
0.9	1.0	1.7
1.0	1.2	1.9
1.1	1.3	2.0
1.2	1.4	2.2
1.3	1.5	2.4
1.4	1.6	2.6
1.5	1.7	2.8
1.6	1.8	3.0
1.7	2.0	3.1
1.8	2.1	3.3
1.9	2.2	3.5
2.0	2.3	3.7
2.1	2.4	3.9
2.2	2.5	4.1
2.3	2.6	4.3
2.4	2.8	4.4
2.5	2.9	4.6
2.6	3.0	4.8
2.7	3.1	5.0
2.8	3.2	5.2
2.9	3.3	5.4
3.0	3.5	5.6
3.1	3.6	5.7
3.2	3.7	5.9
3.3	3.8	6.1
3.4	3.9	6.3
3.5	4.0	6.5
3.6	4.1	6.7
3.7	4.3	6.9
3.8	4.4	7.0
3.9	4.5	7.2
4.0	4.6	7.4
4.1	4.7	7.6
4.2	4.8	7.8
4.3	4.9	8.0
4.4	5.1	8.1
4.5	5.2	8.3
4.6	5.3	8.5
4.7	5.4	8.7
4.8	5.5	8.9
4.9	5.6	9.1
5.0	5.8	9.3
5.1	5.9	9.4
5.2	6.0	9.6
5.3	6.1	9.8
5.4	6.2	10.0
5.5	6.3	10.2
5.6	6.4	10.4
5.7	6.6	10.6
5.8	6.7	10.7

Knots/Nautical Miles	Miles per Hour/Statute Miles	Km per Hour/Kilometers
5.9	6.8	10.9
6.0	6.9	11.1
6.1	7.0	11.3
6.2	7.1	11.5
6.3	7.2	11.7
6.4	7.4	11.9
6.5	7.5	12.0
6.6	7.6	12.2
6.7	7.7	12.4
6.8	7.8	12.6
6.9	7.9	12.8
7.0	8.1	13.0
7.1	8.2	13.1
7.2	8.3	13.3
7.3	8.4	13.5
7.4	8.5	13.7
7.5	8.6	13.9
7.6	8.7	14.1
7.7	8.9	14.3
7.8	9.0	14.4
7.9	9.1	14.6
8.0	9.2	14.8
8.1	9.3	15.0
8.2	9.4	15.2
8.3	9.5	15.4
8.4	9.7	15.6
8.5	9.8	15.7
8.6	9.9	15.9
8.7	10.0	16.1
8.8	10.1	16.3
8.9	10.2	16.5
9.0	10.4	16.7
9.1	10.5	16.9
9.2	10.6	17.0
9.3	10.7	17.2
9.4	10.8	17.4
9.5	10.9	17.6
9.6	11.0	17.8
9.7	11.2	18.0
9.8	11.3	18.1
9.9	11.4	18.3
10.0	11.5	18.5
11	12.7	20.4
12	13.8	22.2
13	15.0	24.1
14	16.1	25.9
15	17.3	27.8
16	18.4	29.6
17	19.6	31.5
18	20.7	33.3
19	21.9	35.2
20	23.0	37.0
21	24.2	38.9
22	25.3	40.7
23	26.5	42.6
24	27.6	44.4
25	28.8	46.3
26	29.9	48.2

Knots/Nautical Miles	Miles per Hour/Statute Miles	Km per Hour/Kilometers
27	31.1	50.0
28	32.2	51.9
29	33.4	53.7
30	34.5	55.6
31	35.7	57.4
32	36.8	59.3
33	38.0	61.1
34	39.1	63.0
35	40.3	64.8
36	41.4	66.7
37	42.6	68.5
38	43.7	70.4
39	44.9	72.2
40	46.0	74.1
41	47.2	75.9
42	48.3	77.8
43	49.5	79.6
44	50.6	81.5
45	51.8	83.3
46	52.9	85.2
47	54.1	87.0
48	55.2	88.9
49	56.4	90.7
50	57.5	92.6
51	58.7	94.5
52	59.8	96.3
53	61.0	98.2
54	62.1	100
55	63.3	102
56	64.4	104
57	65.6	106
58	66.7	107
59	67.9	109
60	69.0	111
61	70.2	113
62	71.3	115
63	72.5	117
64	73.6	119
65	74.8	120
66	75.9	122
67	77.1	124
68	78.2	126
69	79.4	128
70	80.5	130
71	81.7	131
72	82.8	133
73	84.0	135
74	85.1	137
75	86.3	139
76	87.4	141
77	88.6	143
78	89.7	144
79	90.9	146
80	92.0	148
81	93.2	150
82	94.3	152
83	95.5	154
84	96.6	156

Knots/Nautical Miles	Miles per Hour/Statute Miles	Km per Hour/Kilometers
85	97.8	157
86	98.9	159
87	100	161
88	101	163
89	102	165
90	104	167
91	105	169
92	106	170
93	107	172
94	108	174
95	109	176
96	110	178
97	112	180
98	113	181
99	114	183
100	115	185
110	127	204
120	138	222
130	150	241
140	161	259
150	173	278
160	184	296
170	196	315
180	207	333
190	219	352
200	230	370
210	242	389
220	253	407
230	265	426
240	276	444
250	288	463
260	299	482
270	311	500
280	322	519
290	334	537
300	345	556
310	357	574
320	368	593
330	380	611
340	391	630
350	403	648
360	414	667
370	426	685
380	437	704
390	449	722
400	460	741
410	472	759
420	483	778
430	495	796
440	506	815
450	518	833
460	529	852
470	541	870
480	552	889
490	564	907
500	575	926
510	587	945
520	598	963

Knots/Nautical Miles	Miles per Hour/Statute Miles	Km per Hour/Kilometers
530	610	982
540	621	1000
550	633	1019
560	644	1037
570	656	1056
580	667	1074
590	679	1093
600	690	1111
610	702	1130
620	713	1148
630	725	1167
640	736	1185
650	748	1204
660	759	1222
670	771	1241
680	782	1259
690	794	1278
700	805	1296
710	817	1315
720	828	1333
730	840	1352
740	851	1370
750	863	1389
760	874	1408
770	886	1426
780	897	1445
790	909	1463
800	920	1482
810	932	1500
820	943	1519
830	955	1537
840	966	1556
850	978	1574
860	989	1593
870	1001	1611
880	1012	1630
890	1024	1648
900	1035	1667
910	1047	1685
920	1058	1704
930	1070	1722
940	1081	1741
950	1093	1759
960	1104	1778
970	1116	1796
980	1127	1815
990	1139	1833
1000	1150	1852
1010	1162	1871
1020	1173	1889
1030	1185	1908
1040	1196	1926
1050	1208	1945
1060	1219	1963
1070	1231	1982
1080	1242	2000
1090	1254	2019
1100	1265	2037

Table 11—Nautical Miles/Meters

Nautical Miles to Meters

Nm	Meters
0.01	19
0.02	37
0.03	56
0.04	74
0.05	93
0.06	111
0.07	130
0.08	148
0.09	167
0.10	185
0.11	204
0.12	222
0.13	241
0.14	259
0.15	278
0.16	296
0.17	315
0.18	333
0.19	352
0.20	370
0.21	389
0.22	407
0.23	426
0.24	444
0.25	463
0.26	482
0.27	500
0.28	519
0.29	537
0.30	556
0.31	574
0.32	593
0.33	611
0.34	630
0.35	648
0.36	667
0.37	685
0.38	704
0.39	722
0.40	741
0.41	759
0.42	778
0.43	796
0.44	815
0.45	833
0.46	852
0.47	870
0.48	889
0.49	907
0.50	926
0.51	945
0.52	963
0.53	982
0.54	1000
0.55	1019
0.56	1037
0.57	1056
0.58	1074
0.59	1093
0.60	1111
0.61	1130
0.62	1148
0.63	1167
0.64	1185
0.65	1204

Nm	Meters
0.66	1222
0.67	1241
0.68	1259
0.69	1278
0.70	1296
0.71	1315
0.72	1333
0.73	1352
0.74	1370
0.75	1389
0.76	1408
0.77	1426
0.78	1445
0.79	1463
0.80	1482
0.81	1500
0.82	1519
0.83	1537
0.84	1556
0.85	1574
0.86	1593
0.87	1611
0.88	1630
0.89	1648
0.90	1667
0.91	1685
0.92	1704
0.93	1722
0.94	1741
0.95	1759
0.96	1778
0.97	1796
0.98	1815
0.99	1833
1.00	1852
1.10	2037
1.20	2222
1.30	2408
1.40	2593
1.50	2778
1.60	2963
1.70	3148
1.80	3334
1.90	3519
2.00	3704
2.10	3889
2.20	4074
2.30	4260
2.40	4445
2.50	4630
2.60	4815
2.70	5000
2.80	5186
2.90	5371
3.00	5556
3.10	5741
3.20	5926
3.30	6112
3.40	6297
3.50	6482
3.60	6667
3.70	6852
3.80	7038
3.90	7223
4.00	7408

Nm	Meters
4.10	7593
4.20	7778
4.30	7964
4.40	8149
4.50	8334
4.60	8519
4.70	8704
4.80	8890
4.90	9075
5.00	9260
5.10	9445
5.20	9630
5.30	9816
5.40	10001
5.50	10186
5.60	10371
5.70	10556
5.80	10742
5.90	10927
6.00	11112
6.10	11297
6.20	11482
6.30	11668
6.40	11853
6.50	12038
6.60	12223
6.70	12408
6.80	12594
6.90	12779
7.00	12964
7.10	13149
7.20	13334
7.30	13520
7.40	13705
7.50	13890
7.60	14075
7.70	14260
7.80	14446
7.90	14631
8.00	14816
8.10	15001
8.20	15186
8.30	15372
8.40	15557
8.50	15742
8.60	15927
8.70	16112
8.80	16298
8.90	16483
9.00	16668
9.10	16853
9.20	17038
9.30	17224
9.40	17409
9.50	17594
9.60	17779
9.70	17964
9.80	18150
9.90	18335
10.00	18520
10.10	18705
10.20	18890
10.30	19076
10.40	19261
10.50	19446

Meters to Nautical Miles

Meters	Nm
10	0.01
20	0.01
30	0.02
40	0.02
50	0.03
60	0.03
70	0.04
80	0.04
90	0.05
100	0.05
110	0.06
120	0.06
130	0.07
140	0.08
150	0.08
160	0.09
170	0.09
180	0.10
190	0.10
200	0.11
210	0.11
220	0.12
230	0.12
240	0.13
250	0.13
260	0.14
270	0.15
280	0.15
290	0.16
300	0.16
310	0.17
320	0.17
330	0.18
340	0.18
350	0.19
360	0.19
370	0.20
380	0.21
390	0.21
400	0.22
410	0.22
420	0.23
430	0.23
440	0.24
450	0.24
460	0.25
470	0.25
480	0.26
490	0.26
500	0.27
510	0.28
520	0.28
530	0.29
540	0.29
550	0.30
560	0.30
570	0.31
580	0.31
590	0.32
600	0.32
610	0.33
620	0.33
630	0.34
640	0.35
650	0.35

Meters	Nm
660	0.36
670	0.36
680	0.37
690	0.37
700	0.38
710	0.38
720	0.39
730	0.39
740	0.40
750	0.40
760	0.41
770	0.42
780	0.42
790	0.43
800	0.43
810	0.44
820	0.44
830	0.45
840	0.45
850	0.46
860	0.46
870	0.47
880	0.48
890	0.48
900	0.49
910	0.49
920	0.50
930	0.50
940	0.51
950	0.51
960	0.52
970	0.52
980	0.53
990	0.53
1000	0.54
1010	0.55
1020	0.55
1030	0.56
1040	0.56
1050	0.57
1060	0.57
1070	0.58
1080	0.58
1090	0.59
1100	0.59
1110	0.60
1120	0.60
1130	0.61
1140	0.62
1150	0.62
1160	0.63
1170	0.63
1180	0.64
1190	0.64
1200	0.65
1210	0.65
1220	0.66
1230	0.66
1240	0.67
1250	0.67
1260	0.68
1270	0.69
1280	0.69
1290	0.70
1300	0.70

Meters	Nm
1310	0.71
1320	0.71
1330	0.72
1340	0.72
1350	0.73
1360	0.73
1370	0.74
1380	0.75
1390	0.75
1400	0.76
1410	0.76
1420	0.77
1430	0.77
1440	0.78
1450	0.78
1460	0.79
1470	0.79
1480	0.80
1490	0.80
1500	0.81
1510	0.82
1520	0.82
1530	0.83
1540	0.83
1550	0.84
1560	0.84
1570	0.85
1580	0.85
1590	0.86
1600	0.86
1610	0.87
1620	0.87
1630	0.88
1640	0.89
1650	0.89
1660	0.90
1670	0.90
1680	0.91
1690	0.91
1700	0.92
1710	0.92
1720	0.93
1730	0.93
1740	0.94
1750	0.94
1760	0.95
1770	0.96
1780	0.96
1790	0.97
1800	0.97
1810	0.98
1820	0.98
1830	0.99
1840	0.99
1850	1.00
1860	1.00
1870	1.01
1880	1.02
1890	1.02
1900	1.03
1910	1.03
1920	1.04
1930	1.04
1940	1.05
1950	1.05

Meters	Nm
1960	1.06
1970	1.06
1980	1.07
1990	1.07
2000	1.08
2010	1.09
2020	1.09
2030	1.10
2040	1.10
2050	1.11
2060	1.11
2070	1.12
2080	1.12
2090	1.13
2100	1.13
2110	1.14
2120	1.14
2130	1.15
2140	1.16
2150	1.16
2160	1.17
2170	1.17
2180	1.18
2190	1.18
2200	1.19
2210	1.19
2220	1.20
2230	1.20
2240	1.21
2250	1.21
2260	1.22
2270	1.23
2280	1.23
2290	1.24
2300	1.24
2310	1.25
2320	1.25
2330	1.26
2340	1.26
2350	1.27
2360	1.27
2370	1.28
2380	1.29
2390	1.29
2400	1.30
2410	1.30
2420	1.31
2430	1.31
2440	1.32
2450	1.32
2460	1.33
2470	1.33
2480	1.34
2490	1.34
2500	1.35
2510	1.36
2520	1.36
2530	1.37
2540	1.37
2550	1.38
2560	1.38
2570	1.39
2580	1.39
2590	1.40
2600	1.40

Table 12—Meters/Fathoms/Feet

Meters to Fathoms to Feet

Meters	Fathoms	Feet	Meters	Fathoms	Feet	Meters	Fathoms	Feet
0.2	0.1	0.7	21	11.5	68.9	81	44.3	265.7
0.4	0.2	1.3	22	12.0	72.2	82	44.8	269.0
0.6	0.3	2.0	23	12.6	75.5	83	45.4	272.3
0.8	0.4	2.6	24	13.1	78.7	84	45.9	275.6
1.0	0.5	3.3	25	13.7	82.0	85	46.5	278.9
1.2	0.7	3.9	26	14.2	85.3	86	47.0	282.1
1.4	0.8	4.6	27	14.8	88.6	87	47.6	285.4
1.6	0.9	5.2	28	15.3	91.9	88	48.1	288.7
1.8	1.0	5.9	29	15.9	95.1	89	48.7	292.0
2.0	1.1	6.6	30	16.4	98.4	90	49.2	295.3
2.2	1.2	7.2	31	17.0	101.7	91	49.8	298.6
2.4	1.3	7.9	32	17.5	105.0	92	50.3	301.8
2.6	1.4	8.5	33	18.0	108.3	93	50.9	305.1
2.8	1.5	9.2	34	18.6	111.5	94	51.4	308.4
3.0	1.6	9.8	35	19.1	114.8	95	51.9	311.7
3.2	1.7	10.5	36	19.7	118.1	96	52.5	315.0
3.4	1.9	11.2	37	20.2	121.4	97	53.0	318.2
3.6	2.0	11.8	38	20.8	124.7	98	53.6	321.5
3.8	2.1	12.5	39	21.3	128.0	99	54.1	324.8
4.0	2.2	13.1	40	21.9	131.2	100	54.7	328.1
4.2	2.3	13.8	41	22.4	134.5	110	60.1	360.9
4.4	2.4	14.4	42	23.0	137.8	120	65.6	393.7
4.6	2.5	15.1	43	23.5	141.1	130	71.1	426.5
4.8	2.6	15.7	44	24.1	144.4	140	76.6	459.3
5.0	2.7	16.4	45	24.6	147.6	150	82.0	492.1
5.2	2.8	17.1	46	25.2	150.9	160	87.5	524.9
5.4	3.0	17.7	47	25.7	154.2	170	93.0	557.7
5.6	3.1	18.4	48	26.2	157.5	180	98.4	590.5
5.8	3.2	19.0	49	26.8	160.8	190	103.9	623.3
6.0	3.3	19.7	50	27.3	164.0	200	109.4	656.2
6.2	3.4	20.3	51	27.9	167.3	210	114.8	689.0
6.4	3.5	21.0	52	28.4	170.6	220	120.3	721.8
6.6	3.6	21.7	53	29.0	173.9	230	125.8	754.6
6.8	3.7	22.3	54	29.5	177.2	240	131.2	787.4
7.0	3.8	23.0	55	30.1	180.4	250	136.7	820.2
7.2	3.9	23.6	56	30.6	183.7	260	142.2	853.0
7.4	4.0	24.3	57	31.2	187.0	270	147.6	885.8
7.6	4.2	24.9	58	31.7	190.3	280	153.1	918.6
7.8	4.3	25.6	59	32.3	193.6	290	158.6	951.4
8.0	4.4	26.2	60	32.8	196.8	300	164.0	984.2
8.2	4.5	26.9	61	33.4	200.1	310	169.5	1017.0
8.4	4.6	27.6	62	33.9	203.4	320	175.0	1049.8
8.6	4.7	28.2	63	34.4	206.7	330	180.4	1082.7
8.8	4.8	28.9	64	35.0	210.0	340	185.9	1115.5
9.0	4.9	29.5	65	35.5	213.3	350	191.4	1148.3
9.2	5.0	30.2	66	36.1	216.5	360	196.8	1181.1
9.4	5.1	30.8	67	36.6	219.8	370	202.3	1213.9
9.6	5.2	31.5	68	37.2	223.1	380	207.8	1246.7
9.8	5.4	32.2	69	37.7	226.4	390	213.3	1279.5
10	5.5	32.8	70	38.3	229.7	400	218.7	1312.3
11	6.0	36.1	71	38.8	232.9	410	224.2	1345.1
12	6.6	39.4	72	39.4	236.2	420	229.7	1377.9
13	7.1	42.7	73	39.9	239.5	430	235.1	1410.7
14	7.7	45.9	74	40.5	242.8	440	240.6	1443.5
15	8.2	49.2	75	41.0	246.1	450	246.1	1476.3
16	8.7	52.5	76	41.6	249.3	460	251.5	1509.2
17	9.3	55.8	77	42.1	252.6	470	257.0	1542.0
18	9.8	59.1	78	42.7	255.9	480	262.5	1574.8
19	10.4	62.3	79	43.2	259.2	490	267.9	1607.6
20	10.9	65.6	80	43.7	262.5	500	273.4	1640.4

Feet to Fathoms to Meters

Feet	Fathoms	Meters	Feet	Fathoms	Meters	Feet	Fathoms	Meters
1	0.2	0.3	61	10.2	18.6	310	51.7	94.5
2	0.3	0.6	62	10.3	18.9	320	53.3	97.5
3	0.5	0.9	63	10.5	19.2	330	55.0	100.6
4	0.7	1.2	64	10.7	19.5	340	56.7	103.6
5	0.8	1.5	65	10.8	19.8	350	58.3	106.7
6	1.0	1.8	66	11.0	20.1	360	60.0	109.7
7	1.2	2.1	67	11.2	20.4	370	61.7	112.8
8	1.3	2.4	68	11.3	20.7	380	63.3	115.8
9	1.5	2.7	69	11.5	21.0	390	65.0	118.9
10	1.7	3.0	70	11.7	21.3	400	66.7	121.9
11	1.8	3.4	71	11.8	21.6	410	68.3	125.0
12	2.0	3.7	72	12.0	21.9	420	70.0	128.0
13	2.2	4.0	73	12.2	22.3	430	71.7	131.1
14	2.3	4.3	74	12.3	22.6	440	73.3	134.1
15	2.5	4.6	75	12.5	22.9	450	75.0	137.2
16	2.7	4.9	76	12.7	23.2	460	76.7	140.2
17	2.8	5.2	77	12.8	23.5	470	78.3	143.3
18	3.0	5.5	78	13.0	23.8	480	80.0	146.3
19	3.2	5.8	79	13.2	24.1	490	81.7	149.4
20	3.3	6.1	80	13.3	24.4	500	83.3	152.4
21	3.5	6.4	81	13.5	24.7	510	85.0	155.5
22	3.7	6.7	82	13.7	25.0	520	86.7	158.5
23	3.8	7.0	83	13.8	25.3	530	88.3	161.5
24	4.0	7.3	84	14.0	25.6	540	90.0	164.6
25	4.2	7.6	85	14.2	25.9	550	91.7	167.6
26	4.3	7.9	86	14.3	26.2	560	93.3	170.7
27	4.5	8.2	87	14.5	26.5	570	95.0	173.7
28	4.7	8.5	88	14.7	26.8	580	96.7	176.8
29	4.8	8.8	89	14.8	27.1	590	98.3	179.8
30	5.0	9.1	90	15.0	27.4	600	100.0	182.9
31	5.2	9.4	91	15.2	27.7	610	101.7	185.9
32	5.3	9.8	92	15.3	28.0	620	103.3	189.0
33	5.5	10.1	93	15.5	28.3	630	105.0	192.0
34	5.7	10.4	94	15.7	28.7	640	106.7	195.1
35	5.8	10.7	95	15.8	29.0	650	108.3	198.1
36	6.0	11.0	96	16.0	29.3	660	110.0	201.2
37	6.2	11.3	97	16.2	29.6	670	111.7	204.2
38	6.3	11.6	98	16.3	29.9	680	113.3	207.3
39	6.5	11.9	99	16.5	30.2	690	115.0	210.3
40	6.7	12.2	100	16.7	30.5	700	116.7	213.4
41	6.8	12.5	110	18.3	33.5	710	118.3	216.4
42	7.0	12.8	120	20.0	36.6	720	120.0	219.5
43	7.2	13.1	130	21.7	39.6	730	121.7	222.5
44	7.3	13.4	140	23.3	42.7	740	123.3	225.6
45	7.5	13.7	150	25.0	45.7	750	125.0	228.6
46	7.7	14.0	160	26.7	48.8	760	126.7	231.7
47	7.8	14.3	170	28.3	51.8	770	128.3	234.7
48	8.0	14.6	180	30.0	54.9	780	130.0	237.7
49	8.2	14.9	190	31.7	57.9	790	131.7	240.8
50	8.3	15.2	200	33.3	61.0	800	133.3	243.8
51	8.5	15.5	210	35.0	64.0	810	135.0	246.9
52	8.7	15.8	220	36.7	67.1	820	136.7	249.9
53	8.8	16.2	230	38.3	70.1	830	138.3	253.0
54	9.0	16.5	240	40.0	73.2	840	140.0	256.0
55	9.2	16.8	250	41.7	76.2	850	141.7	259.1
56	9.3	17.1	260	43.3	79.2	860	143.3	262.1
57	9.5	17.4	270	45.0	82.3	870	145.0	265.2
58	9.7	17.7	280	46.7	85.3	880	146.7	268.2
59	9.8	18.0	290	48.3	88.4	890	148.3	271.3
60	10.0	18.3	300	50.0	91.4	900	150.0	274.3

Table 12—*(continued)*

Fathoms to Feet to Meters

Fathoms	Feet	Meters	Fathoms	Feet	Meters	Fathoms	Feet	Meters
0.2	1.2	0.4	21	126	38.4	81	486	148.1
0.4	2.4	0.7	22	132	40.2	82	492	150.0
0.6	3.6	1.1	23	138	42.1	83	498	151.8
0.8	4.8	1.5	24	144	43.9	84	504	153.6
1.0	6.0	1.8	25	150	45.7	85	510	155.5
1.2	7.2	2.2	26	156	47.5	86	516	157.3
1.4	8.4	2.6	27	162	49.4	87	522	159.1
1.6	9.6	2.9	28	168	51.2	88	528	160.9
1.8	10.8	3.3	29	174	53.0	89	534	162.8
2.0	12.0	3.7	30	180	54.9	90	540	164.6
2.2	13.2	4.0	31	186	56.7	91	546	166.4
2.4	14.4	4.4	32	192	58.5	92	552	168.3
2.6	15.6	4.8	33	198	60.4	93	558	170.1
2.8	16.8	5.1	34	204	62.2	94	564	171.9
3.0	18.0	5.5	35	210	64.0	95	570	173.7
3.2	19.2	5.9	36	216	65.8	96	576	175.6
3.4	20.4	6.2	37	222	67.7	97	582	177.4
3.6	21.6	6.6	38	228	69.5	98	588	179.2
3.8	22.8	6.9	39	234	71.3	99	594	181.1
4.0	24.0	7.3	40	240	73.2	100	600	182.9
4.2	25.2	7.7	41	246	75.0	110	660	201.2
4.4	26.4	8.0	42	252	76.8	120	720	219.5
4.6	27.6	8.4	43	258	78.6	130	780	237.7
4.8	28.8	8.8	44	264	80.5	140	840	256.0
5.0	30.0	9.1	45	270	82.3	150	900	274.3
5.2	31.2	9.5	46	276	84.1	160	960	292.6
5.4	32.4	9.9	47	282	86.0	170	1020	310.9
5.6	33.6	10.2	48	288	87.8	180	1080	329.2
5.8	34.8	10.6	49	294	89.6	190	1140	347.5
6.0	36.0	11.0	50	300	91.4	200	1200	365.8
6.2	37.2	11.3	51	306	93.3	210	1260	384.1
6.4	38.4	11.7	52	312	95.1	220	1320	402.3
6.6	39.6	12.1	53	318	96.9	230	1380	420.6
6.8	40.8	12.4	54	324	98.8	240	1440	438.9
7.0	42.0	12.8	55	330	100.6	250	1500	457.2
7.2	43.2	13.2	56	336	102.4	260	1560	475.5
7.4	44.4	13.5	57	342	104.2	270	1620	493.8
7.6	45.6	13.9	58	348	106.1	280	1680	512.1
7.8	46.8	14.3	59	354	107.9	290	1740	530.4
8.0	48.0	14.6	60	360	109.7	300	1800	548.7
8.2	49.2	15.0	61	366	111.6	310	1860	566.9
8.4	50.4	15.4	62	372	113.4	320	1920	585.2
8.6	51.6	15.7	63	378	115.2	330	1980	603.5
8.8	52.8	16.1	64	384	117.0	340	2040	621.8
9.0	54.0	16.5	65	390	118.9	350	2100	640.1
9.2	55.2	16.8	66	396	120.7	360	2160	658.4
9.4	56.4	17.2	67	402	122.5	370	2220	676.7
9.6	57.6	17.6	68	408	124.4	380	2280	695.0
9.8	58.8	17.9	69	414	126.2	390	2340	713.2
10	60	18.3	70	420	128.0	400	2400	731.5
11	66	20.1	71	426	129.8	410	2460	749.8
12	72	21.9	72	432	131.7	420	2520	768.1
13	78	23.8	73	438	133.5	430	2580	786.4
14	84	25.6	74	444	135.3	440	2640	804.7
15	90	27.4	75	450	137.2	450	2700	823.0
16	96	29.3	76	456	139.0	460	2760	841.3
17	102	31.1	77	462	140.8	470	2820	859.6
18	108	32.9	78	468	142.6	480	2880	877.8
19	114	34.7	79	474	144.5	490	2940	896.1
20	120	36.6	80	480	146.3	500	3000	914.4

Table 13—Decimal Minutes/Seconds

Decimal Minutes to Seconds—Seconds to Decimal Minutes

Minutes	Seconds	Minutes	Seconds	Seconds	Minutes
0.01	0.60	0.51	30.60	1	0.017
0.02	1.20	0.52	31.20	2	0.033
0.03	1.80	0.53	31.80	3	0.050
0.04	2.40	0.54	32.40	4	0.067
0.05	3.00	0.55	33.00	5	0.083
0.06	3.60	0.56	33.60	6	0.100
0.07	4.20	0.57	34.20	7	0.117
0.08	4.80	0.58	34.80	8	0.133
0.09	5.40	0.59	35.40	9	0.150
0.10	6.00	0.60	36.00	10	0.167
0.11	6.60	0.61	36.60	11	0.183
0.12	7.20	0.62	37.20	12	0.200
0.13	7.80	0.63	37.80	13	0.217
0.14	8.40	0.64	38.40	14	0.233
0.15	9.00	0.65	39.00	15	0.250
0.16	9.60	0.66	39.60	16	0.267
0.17	10.20	0.67	40.20	17	0.283
0.18	10.80	0.68	40.80	18	0.300
0.19	11.40	0.69	41.40	19	0.317
0.20	12.00	0.70	42.00	20	0.333
0.21	12.60	0.71	42.60	21	0.350
0.22	13.20	0.72	43.20	22	0.367
0.23	13.80	0.73	43.80	23	0.383
0.24	14.40	0.74	44.40	24	0.400
0.25	15.00	0.75	45.00	25	0.417
0.26	15.60	0.76	45.60	26	0.433
0.27	16.20	0.77	46.20	27	0.450
0.28	16.80	0.78	46.80	28	0.467
0.29	17.40	0.79	47.40	29	0.483
0.30	18.00	0.80	48.00	30	0.500
0.31	18.60	0.81	48.60	31	0.517
0.32	19.20	0.82	49.20	32	0.533
0.33	19.80	0.83	49.80	33	0.550
0.34	20.40	0.84	50.40	34	0.567
0.35	21.00	0.85	51.00	35	0.583
0.36	21.60	0.86	51.60	36	0.600
0.37	22.20	0.87	52.20	37	0.617
0.38	22.80	0.88	52.80	38	0.633
0.39	23.40	0.89	53.40	39	0.650
0.40	24.00	0.90	54.00	40	0.667
0.41	24.60	0.91	54.60	41	0.683
0.42	25.20	0.92	55.20	42	0.700
0.43	25.80	0.93	55.80	43	0.717
0.44	26.40	0.94	56.40	44	0.733
0.45	27.00	0.95	57.00	45	0.750
0.46	27.60	0.96	57.60	46	0.767
0.47	28.20	0.97	58.20	47	0.783
0.48	28.80	0.98	58.80	48	0.800
0.49	29.40	0.99	59.40	49	0.817
0.50	30.00	1.00	60.00	50	0.833
0.51	30.60			51	0.850
0.52	31.20			52	0.867
0.53	31.80			53	0.883
0.54	32.40			54	0.900
0.55	33.00			55	0.917
0.56	33.60			56	0.933
0.57	34.20			57	0.950
0.58	34.80			58	0.967
0.59	35.40			59	0.983
0.60	36.00			60	1.000

Table 14—Degrees Celsius/Degrees Fahrenheit

Degrees Celsius to Degrees Fahrenheit

Deg C	Deg F
-63	-81.4
-62	-79.6
-61	-77.8
-60	-76.0
-59	-74.2
-58	-72.4
-57	-70.6
-56	-68.8
-55	-67.0
-54	-65.2
-53	-63.4
-52	-61.6
-51	-59.8
-50	-58.0
-49	-56.2
-48	-54.4
-47	-52.6
-46	-50.8
-45	-49.0
-44	-47.2
-43	-45.4
-42	-43.6
-41	-41.8
-40	-40.0
-39	-38.2
-38	-36.4
-37	-34.6
-36	-32.8
-35	-31.0
-34	-29.2
-33	-27.4
-32	-25.6
-31	-23.8
-30	-22.0
-29	-20.2
-28	-18.4
-27	-16.6
-26	-14.8
-25	-13.0
-24	-11.2
-23	-9.4
-22	-7.6
-21	-5.8
-20	-4.0
-19	-2.2
-18	-0.4
-17	1.4
-16	3.2
-15	5.0
-14	6.8
-13	8.6
-12	10.4
-11	12.2
-10	14.0
-9	15.8
-8	17.6
-7	19.4
-6	21.2
-5	23.0
-4	24.8
-3	26.6
-2	28.4
-1	30.2

Deg C	Deg F
0	32.0
1	33.8
2	35.6
3	37.4
4	39.2
5	41.0
6	42.8
7	44.6
8	46.4
9	48.2
10	50.0
11	51.8
12	53.6
13	55.4
14	57.2
15	59.0
16	60.8
17	62.6
18	64.4
19	66.2
20	68.0
21	69.8
22	71.6
23	73.4
24	75.2
25	77.0
26	78.8
27	80.6
28	82.4
29	84.2
30	86.0
31	87.8
32	89.6
33	91.4
34	93.2
35	95.0
36	96.8
37	98.6
38	100.4
39	102.2
40	104.0
41	105.8
42	107.6
43	109.4
44	111.2
45	113.0
46	114.8
47	116.6
48	118.4
49	120.2
50	122.0
51	123.8
52	125.6
53	127.4
54	129.2
55	131.0
56	132.8
57	134.6
58	136.4
59	138.2
60	140.0
61	141.8
62	143.6

Deg C	Deg F
63	145.4
64	147.2
65	149.0
66	150.8
67	152.6
68	154.4
69	156.2
70	158.0
71	159.8
72	161.6
73	163.4
74	165.2
75	167.0
76	168.8
77	170.6
78	172.4
79	174.2
80	176.0
81	177.8
82	179.6
83	181.4
84	183.2
85	185.0
86	186.8
87	188.6
88	190.4
89	192.2
90	194.0
91	195.8
92	197.6
93	199.4
94	201.2
95	203.0
96	204.8
97	206.6
98	208.4
99	210.2
100	212.0
101	213.8
102	215.6
103	217.4
104	219.2
105	221.0
106	222.8
107	224.6
108	226.4
109	228.2
110	230.0
111	231.8
112	233.6
113	235.4
114	237.2
115	239.0
116	240.8
117	242.6
118	244.4
119	246.2
120	248.0
121	249.8
122	251.6
123	253.4
124	255.2
125	257.0

Degrees Fahrenheit to Degrees Celsius

Deg F	Deg C
-56	-48.9
-55	-48.3
-54	-47.8
-53	-47.2
-52	-46.7
-51	-46.1
-50	-45.6
-49	-45.0
-48	-44.4
-47	-43.9
-46	-43.3
-45	-42.8
-44	-42.2
-43	-41.7
-42	-41.1
-41	-40.6
-40	-40.0
-39	-39.4
-38	-38.9
-37	-38.3
-36	-37.8
-35	-37.2
-34	-36.7
-33	-36.1
-32	-35.6
-31	-35.0
-30	-34.4
-29	-33.9
-28	-33.3
-27	-32.8
-26	-32.2
-25	-31.7
-24	-31.1
-23	-30.6
-22	-30.0
-21	-29.4
-20	-28.9
-19	-28.3
-18	-27.8
-17	-27.2
-16	-26.7
-15	-26.1
-14	-25.6
-13	-25.0
-12	-24.4
-11	-23.9
-10	-23.3
-9	-22.8
-8	-22.2
-7	-21.7
-6	-21.1
-5	-20.6
-4	-20.0
-3	-19.4
-2	-18.9
-1	-18.3
0	-17.8
1	-17.2
2	-16.7
3	-16.1
4	-15.6
5	-15.0
6	-14.4

Deg F	Deg C
8	-13.3
9	-12.8
10	-12.2
11	-11.7
12	-11.1
13	-10.6
14	-10.0
15	-9.4
16	-8.9
17	-8.3
18	-7.8
19	-7.2
20	-6.7
21	-6.1
22	-5.6
23	-5.0
24	-4.4
25	-3.9
26	-3.3
27	-2.8
28	-2.2
29	-1.7
30	-1.1
31	-0.6
32	0.0
33	0.6
34	1.1
35	1.7
36	2.2
37	2.8
38	3.3
39	3.9
40	4.4
41	5.0
42	5.6
43	6.1
44	6.7
45	7.2
46	7.8
47	8.3
48	8.9
49	9.4
50	10.0
51	10.6
52	11.1
53	11.7
54	12.2
55	12.8
56	13.3
57	13.9
58	14.4
59	15.0
60	15.6
61	16.1
62	16.7
63	17.2
64	17.8
65	18.3
66	18.9
67	19.4
68	20.0
69	20.6
70	21.1

Deg F	Deg C
71	21.7
72	22.2
73	22.8
74	23.3
75	23.9
76	24.4
77	25.0
78	25.6
79	26.1
80	26.7
81	27.2
82	27.8
83	28.3
84	28.9
85	29.4
86	30.0
87	30.6
88	31.1
89	31.7
90	32.2
91	32.8
92	33.3
93	33.9
94	34.4
95	35.0
96	35.6
97	36.1
98	36.7
99	37.2
100	37.8
101	38.3
102	38.9
103	39.4
104	40.0
105	40.6
106	41.1
107	41.7
108	42.2
109	42.8
110	43.3
111	43.9
112	44.4
113	45.0
114	45.6
115	46.1
116	46.7
117	47.2
118	47.8
119	48.3
120	48.9
121	49.4
122	50.0
123	50.6
124	51.1
125	51.7
126	52.2
127	52.8
128	53.3
129	53.9
130	54.4
131	55.0
132	55.6
133	56.1

Deg F	Deg C
134	56.7
135	57.2
136	57.8
137	58.3
138	58.9
139	59.4
140	60.0
141	60.6
142	61.1
143	61.7
144	62.2
145	62.8
146	63.3
147	63.9
148	64.4
149	65.0
150	65.6
151	66.1
152	66.7
153	67.2
154	67.8
155	68.3
156	68.9
157	69.4
158	70.0
159	70.6
160	71.1
161	71.7
162	72.2
163	72.8
164	73.3
165	73.9
166	74.4
167	75.0
168	75.6
169	76.1
170	76.7
171	77.2
172	77.8
173	78.3
174	78.9
175	79.4
176	80.0
177	80.6
178	81.1
179	81.7
180	82.2
181	82.8
182	83.3
183	83.9
184	84.4
185	85.0
186	85.6
187	86.1
188	86.7
189	87.2
190	87.8
191	88.3
192	88.9
193	89.4
194	90.0
195	90.6
196	91.1

Table 15—Litres/Imperial Gallons/US Gallons

Litres to Imperial Gallons to US Gallons

Litres	Gals (Imp)	Gals (US)	Litres	Gals (Imp)	Gals (US)	Litres	Gals (Imp)	Gals (US)
1	0.22	0.26	110	24.2	29.1	660	145.2	174.4
2	0.44	0.53	120	26.4	31.7	670	147.4	177.0
3	0.66	0.79	130	28.6	34.3	680	149.6	179.6
4	0.88	1.06	140	30.8	37.0	690	151.8	182.3
5	1.10	1.32	150	33.0	39.6	700	154.0	184.9
6	1.32	1.59	160	35.2	42.3	710	156.2	187.6
7	1.54	1.85	170	37.4	44.9	720	158.4	190.2
8	1.76	2.11	180	39.6	47.6	730	160.6	192.8
9	1.98	2.38	190	41.8	50.2	740	162.8	195.5
10	2.20	2.64	200	44.0	52.8	750	165.0	198.1
12	2.64	3.17	210	46.2	55.5	760	167.2	200.8
14	3.08	3.70	220	48.4	58.1	770	169.4	203.4
16	3.52	4.23	230	50.6	60.8	780	171.6	206.1
18	3.96	4.76	240	52.8	63.4	790	173.8	208.7
20	4.40	5.28	250	55.0	66.0	800	176.0	211.3
22	4.84	5.81	260	57.2	68.7	810	178.2	214.0
24	5.28	6.34	270	59.4	71.3	820	180.4	216.6
26	5.72	6.87	280	61.6	74.0	830	182.6	219.3
28	6.16	7.40	290	63.8	76.6	840	184.8	221.9
30	6.60	7.93	300	66.0	79.3	850	187.0	224.5
32	7.04	8.45	310	68.2	81.9	860	189.2	227.2
34	7.48	8.98	320	70.4	84.5	870	191.4	229.8
36	7.92	9.51	330	72.6	87.2	880	193.6	232.5
38	8.36	10.04	340	74.8	89.8	890	195.8	235.1
40	8.80	10.57	350	77.0	92.5	900	198.0	237.8
42	9.24	11.10	360	79.2	95.1	910	200.2	240.4
44	9.68	11.62	370	81.4	97.7	920	202.4	243.0
46	10.12	12.15	380	83.6	100.4	930	204.6	245.7
48	10.56	12.68	390	85.8	103.0	940	206.8	248.3
50	11.00	13.21	400	88.0	105.7	950	209.0	251.0
52	11.44	13.74	410	90.2	108.3	960	211.2	253.6
54	11.88	14.27	420	92.4	111.0	970	213.4	256.2
56	12.32	14.79	430	94.6	113.6	980	215.6	258.9
58	12.76	15.32	440	96.8	116.2	990	217.8	261.5
60	13.20	15.85	450	99.0	118.9	1000	220.0	264.2
62	13.64	16.38	460	101.2	121.5	1010	222.2	266.8
64	14.08	16.91	470	103.4	124.2	1020	224.4	269.5
66	14.52	17.4	480	105.6	126.8	1030	226.6	272.1
68	14.96	18.0	490	107.8	129.4	1040	228.8	274.7
70	15.40	18.5	500	110.0	132.1	1050	231.0	277.4
72	15.84	19.0	510	112.2	134.7	1060	233.2	280.0
74	16.28	19.5	520	114.4	137.4	1070	235.4	282.7
76	16.72	20.1	530	116.6	140.0	1080	237.6	285.3
78	17.16	20.6	540	118.8	142.7	1090	239.8	287.9
80	17.60	21.1	550	121.0	145.3	1100	242.0	290.6
82	18.0	21.7	560	123.2	147.9	1110	244.2	293.2
84	18.5	22.2	570	125.4	150.6	1120	246.4	295.9
86	18.9	22.7	580	127.6	153.2	1130	248.6	298.5
88	19.4	23.2	590	129.8	155.9	1140	250.8	301.2
90	19.8	23.8	600	132.0	158.5	1150	253.0	303.8
92	20.2	24.3	610	134.2	161.1	1160	255.2	306.4
94	20.7	24.8	620	136.4	163.8	1170	257.4	309.1
96	21.1	25.4	630	138.6	166.4	1180	259.6	311.7
98	21.6	25.9	640	140.8	169.1	1190	261.8	314.4
100	22.0	26.4	650	143.0	171.7	1200	264.0	317.0

US Gallons to Imperial Gallons to Litres

Gals (US)	Gals (Imp)	Litres	Gals (US)	Gals (Imp)	Litres
1	0.83	3.8	56	46.6	212.0
2	1.67	7.6	57	47.5	215.8
3	2.50	11.4	58	48.3	219.6
4	3.33	15.1	59	49.1	223.3
5	4.16	18.9	60	50.0	227.1
6	5.00	22.7	61	50.8	230.9
7	5.83	26.5	62	51.6	234.7
8	6.66	30.3	63	52.5	238.5
9	7.49	34.1	64	53.3	242.3
10	8.33	37.9	65	54.1	246.1
11	9.16	41.6	66	55.0	249.8
12	9.99	45.4	67	55.8	253.6
13	10.8	49.2	68	56.6	257.4
14	11.7	53.0	69	57.5	261.2
15	12.5	56.8	70	58.3	265.0
16	13.3	60.6	71	59.1	268.8
17	14.2	64.4	72	60.0	272.5
18	15.0	68.1	73	60.8	276.3
19	15.8	71.9	74	61.6	280.1
20	16.7	75.7	75	62.5	283.9
21	17.5	79.5	76	63.3	287.7
22	18.3	83.3	77	64.1	291.5
23	19.2	87.1	78	64.9	295.3
24	20.0	90.8	79	65.8	299.0
25	20.8	94.6	80	66.6	302.8
26	21.6	98.4	81	67.4	306.6
27	22.5	102.2	82	68.3	310.4
28	23.3	106.0	83	69.1	314.2
29	24.1	109.8	84	69.9	318.0
30	25.0	113.6	85	70.8	321.8
31	25.8	117.3	86	71.6	325.5
32	26.6	121.1	87	72.4	329.3
33	27.5	124.9	88	73.3	333.1
34	28.3	128.7	89	74.1	336.9
35	29.1	132.5	90	74.9	340.7
36	30.0	136.3	91	75.8	344.5
37	30.8	140.1	92	76.6	348.3
38	31.6	143.8	93	77.4	352.0
39	32.5	147.6	94	78.3	355.8
40	33.3	151.4	95	79.1	359.6
41	34.1	155.2	96	79.9	363.4
42	35.0	159.0	97	80.8	367.2
43	35.8	162.8	98	81.6	371.0
44	36.6	166.6	99	82.4	374.8
45	37.5	170.3	100	83.3	378.5
46	38.3	174.1	110	91.6	416.4
47	39.1	177.9	120	99.9	454.2
48	40.0	181.7	130	108.2	492.1
49	40.8	185.5	140	116.6	530.0
50	41.6	189.3	150	124.9	567.8
51	42.5	193.1	160	133.2	605.7
52	43.3	196.8	170	141.6	643.5
53	44.1	200.6	180	149.9	681.4
54	45.0	204.4	190	158.2	719.2
55	45.8	208.2	200	166.5	757.1

Table 15—Litres/Imperial Gallons/US Gallons
(continued)

Imperial Gallons to US Gallons to Litres

Gals (Imp)	Gals (US)	Litres	Gals (Imp)	Gals (US)	Litres
1	1.20	4.5	56	67.3	254.6
2	2.40	9.1	57	68.5	259.1
3	3.60	13.6	58	69.7	263.7
4	4.80	18.2	59	70.9	268.2
5	6.00	22.7	60	72.1	272.8
6	7.21	27.3	61	73.3	277.3
7	8.41	31.8	62	74.5	281.9
8	9.61	36.4	63	75.7	286.4
9	10.8	40.9	64	76.9	290.9
10	12.0	45.5	65	78.1	295.5
11	13.2	50.0	66	79.3	300.0
12	14.4	54.6	67	80.5	304.6
13	15.6	59.1	68	81.7	309.1
14	16.8	63.6	69	82.9	313.7
15	18.0	68.2	70	84.1	318.2
16	19.2	72.7	71	85.3	322.8
17	20.4	77.3	72	86.5	327.3
18	21.6	81.8	73	87.7	331.9
19	22.8	86.4	74	88.9	336.4
20	24.0	90.9	75	90.1	341.0
21	25.2	95.5	76	91.3	345.5
22	26.4	100.0	77	92.5	350.0
23	27.6	104.6	78	93.7	354.6
24	28.8	109.1	79	94.9	359.1
25	30.0	113.7	80	96.1	363.7
26	31.2	118.2	81	97.3	368.2
27	32.4	122.7	82	98.5	372.8
28	33.6	127.3	83	99.7	377.3
29	34.8	131.8	84	100.9	381.9
30	36.0	136.4	85	102.1	386.4
31	37.2	140.9	86	103.3	391.0
32	38.4	145.5	87	104.5	395.5
33	39.6	150.0	88	105.7	400.0
34	40.8	154.6	89	106.9	404.6
35	42.0	159.1	90	108.1	409.1
36	43.2	163.7	91	109.3	413.7
37	44.4	168.2	92	110.5	418.2
38	45.6	172.7	93	111.7	422.8
39	46.8	177.3	94	112.88	427.3
40	48.0	181.8	95	114.09	431.9
41	49.2	186.4	96	115.29	436.4
42	50.4	190.9	97	116.49	441.0
43	51.6	195.5	98	117.69	445.5
44	52.8	200.0	99	118.89	450.1
45	54.0	204.6	100	120.09	454.6
46	55.2	209.1	110	132.10	500.1
47	56.4	213.7	120	144.11	545.5
48	57.6	218.2	130	156.12	591.0
49	58.8	222.8	140	168.13	636.4
50	60.0	227.3	150	180.14	681.9
51	61.2	231.8	160	192.14	727.4
52	62.4	236.4	170	204.15	772.8
53	63.6	240.9	180	216.16	818.3
54	64.8	245.5	190	228.17	863.7
55	66.0	250.0	200	240.18	909.2

Table 16—Millibars/Kilopascals/Inches of Mercury/Millimeters of Mercury

Millibars	Kilopascals	Inches of Mercury	mm of Mercury	Millibars	Kilopascals	Inches of Mercury	mm of Mercury
960	96.0	28.3	720	1015	101.5	29.9	761
961	96.1	28.3	721	1016	101.6	30.0	762
962	96.2	28.4	722	1017	101.7	30.0	763
963	96.3	28.4	722	1018	101.8	30.0	764
964	96.4	28.4	723	1019	101.9	30.1	764
965	96.5	28.5	724	1020	102.0	30.1	765
966	96.6	28.5	725	1021	102.1	30.1	766
967	96.7	28.5	725	1022	102.2	30.1	767
968	96.8	28.6	726	1023	102.3	30.2	767
969	96.9	28.6	727	1024	102.4	30.2	768
970	97.0	28.6	728	1025	102.5	30.2	769
971	97.1	28.6	728	1026	102.6	30.3	770
972	97.2	28.7	729	1027	102.7	30.3	770
973	97.3	28.7	730	1028	102.8	30.3	771
974	97.4	28.7	731	1029	102.9	30.4	772
975	97.5	28.8	731	1030	103.0	30.4	773
976	97.6	28.8	732	1031	103.1	30.4	773
977	97.7	28.8	733	1032	103.2	30.4	774
978	97.8	28.9	734	1033	103.3	30.5	775
979	97.9	28.9	734	1034	103.4	30.5	776
980	98.0	28.9	735	1035	103.5	30.5	776
981	98.1	28.9	736	1036	103.6	30.6	777
982	98.2	29.0	737	1037	103.7	30.6	778
983	98.3	29.0	737	1038	103.8	30.6	779
984	98.4	29.0	738	1039	103.9	30.7	779
985	98.5	29.1	739	1040	104.0	30.7	780
986	98.6	29.1	740	1041	104.1	30.7	781
987	98.7	29.1	740	1042	104.2	30.7	782
988	98.8	29.1	741	1043	104.3	30.8	782
989	98.9	29.2	742	1044	104.4	30.8	783
990	99.0	29.2	743	1045	104.5	30.8	784
991	99.1	29.2	743	1046	104.6	30.9	785
992	99.2	29.3	744	1047	104.7	30.9	785
993	99.3	29.3	745	1048	104.8	30.9	786
994	99.4	29.3	746	1049	104.9	30.9	787
995	99.5	29.4	746	1050	105.0	31.0	788
996	99.6	29.4	747	1051	105.1	31.0	788
997	99.7	29.4	748	1052	105.2	31.0	789
998	99.8	29.4	749	1053	105.3	31.1	790
999	99.9	29.5	749	1054	105.4	31.1	791
1000	100.0	29.5	750	1055	105.5	31.1	791
1001	100.1	29.5	751	1056	105.6	31.2	792
1002	100.2	29.6	752	1057	105.7	31.2	793
1003	100.3	29.6	752	1058	105.8	31.2	794
1004	100.4	29.6	753	1059	105.9	31.2	794
1005	100.5	29.6	754	1060	106.0	31.3	795
1006	100.6	29.7	755	1061	106.1	31.3	796
1007	100.7	29.7	755	1062	106.2	31.3	797
1008	100.8	29.7	756	1063	106.3	31.4	797
1009	100.9	29.8	757	1064	106.4	31.4	798
1010	101.0	29.8	758	1065	106.5	31.4	799
1011	101.1	29.8	758	1066	106.6	31.4	800
1012	101.2	29.9	759	1067	106.7	31.5	800
1013	101.3	29.9	760	1068	106.8	31.5	801
1014	101.4	29.9	761	1069	106.9	31.5	802

Table 17—Useful Conversion Factors

Atmospheric Pressure

millibars	x	0.1	=	kilopascals
	x	0.0295	=	inches of Mercury
	x	0.750062	=	mm of Mercury
kilopascals	x	10	=	millibars
	x	0.2952	=	inches of Mercury
	x	7.50062	=	mm of Mercury
inches of Mercury	x	3.3875	=	kilopascals
	x	33.875	=	millibars
	x	25.4	=	mm of Mercury
mm of Mercury	x	0.13332	=	kilopascals
	x	1.33322	=	millibars
	x	0.03937	=	inches of Mercury

Cubic Measure (Volume)

cubic feet	x	28.31687	=	litres
	x	0.02832	=	cubic meters
	x	0.03704	=	cubic yards
	x	28316.8	=	cubic cm (ml)
cubic meters	x	1000	=	litres
	x	35.3147	=	cubic feet
	x	1.30795	=	cubic yards
	x	1,000,000	=	cubic cm (ml)
litres	x	.001	=	cubic meters
	x	1000	=	cubic cm (ml)
	x	0.03531	=	cubic feet
	x	0.21997	=	Imperial gallons
	x	0.26417	=	US gallons
	x	0.8799	=	Imperial quarts
	x	0.9081	=	US quarts
	x	35.195	=	Imperial fluid ounces
	x	33.81402	=	US fluid ounces
cubic centimeters	x	1	=	Millilitre (ml)
	x	.001	=	litres
	x	0.00022	=	Imperial gallons
	x	0.00026	=	US gallons
	x	0.06102	=	cubic inches
	x	0.03381	=	US fluid ounces
	x	0.03519	=	Imperial fluid ounces
US gallons	x	3.7854	=	litres
	x	3785.41	=	cubic cm (ml)
	x	231	=	cubic inches
	x	0.83267	=	Imperial gallon
	x	4	=	US quarts
	x	8	=	US pints
	x	128	=	US fluid ounces
Imperial gallons	x	4.546	=	litres
	x	4546.09	=	cubic cm (ml)
	x	277.419	=	cubic inches
	x	1.2009	=	US gallon
	x	4	=	Imperial quarts
	x	8	=	Imperial pints
	x	153.722	=	US fluid ounces
	x	160	=	Imperial fluid ounces
	x	10.0092	=	lbs of water

Linear Measure

millimeters	x	0.1	=	centimeters
	x	0.03937	=	inches
	x	0.00328	=	feet
centimeters	x	10	=	millimeters
	x	0.3937	=	inches
	x	0.03281	=	feet
	x	0.01094	=	yards
	x	0.01	=	meters
meters	x	100	=	centimeters
	x	39.3701	=	inches
	x	3.23084	=	feet
	x	1.0936	=	yards
	x	0.54681	=	fathoms
	x	0.001	=	kilometers
	x	0.000621	=	statute miles
	x	0.00053996	=	nautical miles
kilometers	x	3280.84	=	feet
	x	1093.61	=	yards
	x	546.805	=	fathoms
	x	0.62137	=	statute miles
	x	0.53996	=	nautical miles
nautical miles	x	6076.12	=	feet
	x	1852	=	meters
	x	1012.69	=	fathoms
	x	10	=	cables
	x	1.852	=	kilometers
	x	1.15078	=	statute miles
statute miles	x	5280	=	feet
	x	1609.344	=	meters
	x	1760	=	yards
	x	880	=	fathoms
	x	1.609344	=	kilometers
	x	0.86898	=	nautical miles
fathoms	x	6	=	feet
	x	1.8288	=	meters
	x	2	=	yards
	x	0.01	=	cables
	x	0.00098747	=	nautical miles
	x	0.001829	=	kilometers
yards	x	36	=	inches
	x	91.44	=	centimeters
	x	3	=	feet
	x	0.9144	=	meters
	x	0.5	=	fathoms
	x	0.0009144	=	kilometers
	x	0.0005682	=	statute miles
	x	0.0004937	=	nautical miles
feet	x	12	=	inches
	x	30.48	=	centimeters
	x	0.3048	=	meters
	x	0.333333	=	yards
	x	0.1666667	=	fathoms
	x	0.0003048	=	kilometers
feet	x	0.000189	=	statute miles
	x	0.000165	=	nautical miles
inches	x	25.4	=	millimeters
	x	2.54	=	centimeters

Linear Measure *(con't)*

inches	x	0.08333	=	feet
	x	0.0254	=	meters
	x	0.0278	=	yards

Square Measure (Area)

square centimeters	x	0.155	=	square inches
	x	0.001076387	=	square feet
	x	0.0001196	=	square yards
	x	0.0001	=	square meters
square feet	x	144	=	square inches
	x	0.1111	=	square yards
	x	0.0929	=	square meters
square yards	x	9	=	square feet
	x	0.8361	=	square meters
square meters	x	10.7639	=	square feet
	x	1.19599	=	square yards
	x	0.000247	=	acres
	x	0.0001	=	hectares
	x	0.000001	=	square kilometers
acres	x	4046.856421	=	square meters
(216 ft x 216 ft)	x	0.404687	=	hectares
	x	0.00404686	=	square kilometers
	x	0.0015625	=	square miles
hectares	x	10,000	=	square meters
(100m x 100m)	x	2.471	=	acres
	x	0.01	=	square kilometers
	x	0.00386	=	square miles
square miles	x	640	=	acres
	x	258.999	=	hectares
	x	2.58999	=	square kilometers
square kilometers	x	247.1054	=	acres
	x	100	=	hectares
	x	0.3861	=	square miles

Weight (Mass)

tonnes (metric)	x	1000	=	kilograms
	x	1.1023	=	short tons
	x	0.98421	=	long tons
	x	2204.62	=	pounds
tons (short)	x	0.89286	=	tons (long)
	x	0.90718	=	tonnes (metric)
	x	2000	=	pounds
	x	907.185	=	kilograms
tons (long)	x	1.12	=	tons (short)
	x	1.01605	=	tonnes (metric)
	x	2240	=	pounds
	x	1016.05	=	kilograms
kilograms	x	0.001	=	tonnes
	x	0.001102	=	short tons
	x	0.00098	=	long tons
kilograms	x	2.20462	=	pounds
	x	35.27396	=	ounces
	x	1000	=	grams
pounds	x	0.0004536	=	tonnes
	x	0.0005	=	short tons
	x	0.0004464	=	long tons
pounds	x	0.4536	=	kilograms
pounds	x	16	=	ounces
	x	453.59	=	grams
grams	x	0.001	=	kilograms
	x	0.002205	=	pounds
	x	0.03527	=	ounces
ounces	x	0.02835	=	kilograms
	x	0.0625	=	pounds
	x	28.3495	=	grams

Speed

knots	x	1.852	=	kilometers/hour
	x	1.1508	=	miles/hour
	x	0.5144	=	meters/second
kilometers/hour	x	0.53996	=	knots
	x	0.62137	=	miles/hour
	x	0.2778	=	meters/second
miles/hour	x	0.868976	=	knots
	x	1.6093	=	kilometers/hour
	x	0.44704	=	meters/second
meters/second	x	1.94381	=	knots
	x	2.2369	=	miles/hour
	x	3.6	=	kilometers/hour

Power

horsepower	x	0.746	=	kilowatts
kilowatts	x	1.341	=	horsepower

Tonnage

registered tons	x	100	=	cubic feet
	x	2.832	=	cubic meters

Density

Fresh Water	**Specific Gravity = 1.00**			
cubic meters	x	1	=	tonnes (metric)
cubic feet	x	62.43	=	pounds
Imperial gallons	x	10.0092	=	pounds
US gallons	x	8.33436	=	pounds
pounds	x	0.0160184	=	cubic feet
tons	x	32.037	=	cubic feet
Salt Water	**Specific Gravity = 1.025**			
cubic meters	x	1.025	=	tonnes (metric)
cubic feet	x	63.989	=	pounds
Imperial gallons	x	10.25943	=	pounds
US gallons	x	8.54272	=	pounds
pounds	x	0.0156278	=	cubic feet
tons	x	31.2556	=	cubic feet
Gasoline	**Specific Gravity = 0.74**			
Imperial gallons	x	7.4068	=	pounds
US gallons	x	6.1674	=	pounds
cubic feet	x	45.9	=	pounds
litres	x	0.74	=	kilograms
Diesel	**Specific Gravity = 0.84**			
Imperial gallons	x	8.4077	=	pounds
US gallons	x	7.00086	=	pounds
cubic feet	x	52.1	=	pounds
litres	x	0.84	=	kilograms

PART III

WEATHER AND ENVIRONMENTAL TABLES

Table 18 —The Beaufort Wind Scale (to estimate wind speed by the appearance of the land or sea)

Force	Equivalent Speed (*10 m Above Surface*)		Description	At Sea	On Land
	mph	knots			
0	0-1	0-1	Calm	Sea is like a mirror.	Smoke rises vertically.
1	1-3	1-3	Light air	Ripples with the appearance of scales are formed, but without foam crests.	Direction of wind shown by smoke drift, but not by wind vanes.
2	4-7	4-6	Light Breeze	Small wavelets, still short, but more pronounced. Crests have a glassy appearance and do not break.	Wind felt on face; leaves rustle; ordinary vanes moved by wind.
3	8-12	7-10	Gentle Breeze	Large wavelets. Crests begin to break. Perhaps scattered white horses.	Leaves and small twigs in constant motion; wind extends light flag.
4	13-18	11-16	Moderate Breeze	Small waves, becoming larger; fairly frequent white horses.	Raises dust and loose paper; small branches are moved.
5	19-24	17-21	Fresh Breeze	Moderate waves, taking a more pronounced long form; many white horses are formed. Chance of some spray.	Small trees in leaf begin to sway; crested wavelets form on inland waters.
6	25-31	22-27	Strong Breeze	Large waves begin to form; the white foam crests are more extensive everywhere. Probably some spray.	Large branches in motion; whistling heard in wires; umbrellas used with difficulty.
7	32-38	28-33	Near Gale	Sea heaps up and white foam from breaking waves begins to be blown in streaks along the direction of the wind.	Whole trees in motion; inconvenience felt when against the wind.
8	39-46	34-40	Gale	Moderately high waves of greater length; edges of crests begin to break into spindrift. The foam is blown in well-marked streaks along the direction of the wind.	Breaks twigs off trees; generally impedes progress.
9	47-54	41-47	Severe Gale	High waves. Dense streaks of foam along the direction of the wind. Crests of waves begin to topple, tumble and roll over. Spray may affect visibility.	Slight structural damage occurs (chimney-pots and slates blow off).
10	55-63	48-55	Storm	Very high waves with long overhanging crests. The resulting foam, in great patches, is blown in dense white streaks along the direction of the wind. On the whole, the surface of the sea takes on a white appearance. The 'tumbling' of the sea becomes heavy and shock-like. Visibility affected.	Seldom experienced inland; trees uprooted; considerable structural damage occurs.
11	64-72	56-63	Violent Storm	Exceptionally high waves (small and medium-size ships might be lost to view behind the waves for a time). The sea is completely covered with long white patches of foam lying along the direction of the wind. Everywhere, the edges of the wave crests are blown into froth. Visibility affected.	Very rarely experienced; accompanied by wide-spread damage.
12	73-83	64-71	Hurricane	The air is filled with foam and spray. Sea completely white with driving spray; visibility very seriously affected.	Violence and destruction.

Table 19 — Weather Fronts and Frontal Passage

Table 19-1 — About Mid-Latitude (Temperate) Depressions

To the left is a synoptic chart, which graphically depicts the pattern of isobars (lines connecting points of equal barometric pressure) around a temperate depression. The depression is travelling toward the Northeast as indicated by the large arrow.

The cross section through the warm and cold fronts shown on the following page is taken along the line A-B.

Wind direction is indicated by the small arrows. As the system passes, winds shifts clockwise from SE to SW to NW. These shifts can be sudden at frontal passage.

For an observer located north of the system center, the wind shifts counter-clockwise.

The most intense precipitation occurs in the shaded areas.

Actual wind direction at the surface is heavily influenced by surface topography. The Coast Mountains generally deflect near-shore winds to the NW or the SE.

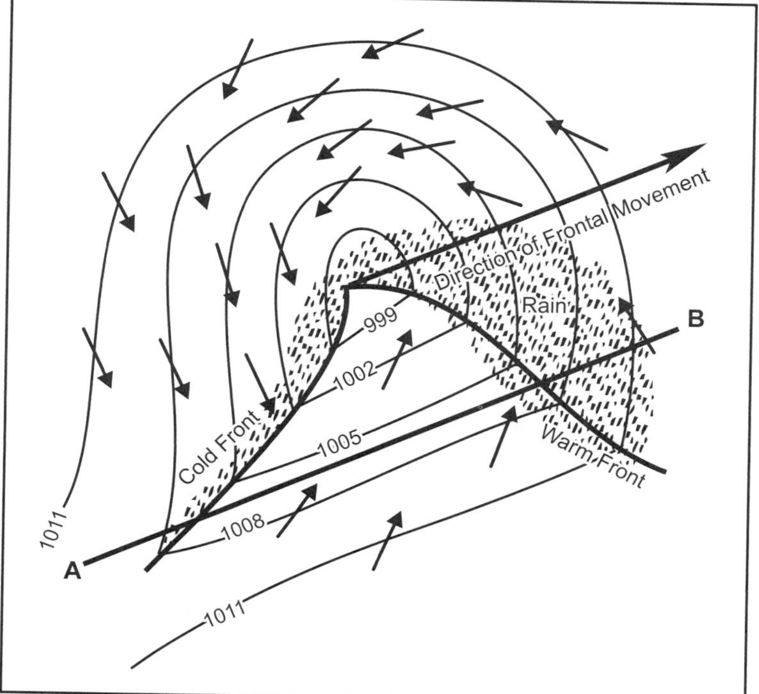
Direction of Frontal Movement
Rain
B
999
1002
1005
1008
1011
1011
Cold Front
Warm Front
A

- Mid-latitude (Temperate) depressions are circulating weather systems centered on a low pressure center. In the northern hemisphere, winds circulate counter-clockwise around a low.
- Temperate depressions in the northern hemisphere generally travel from westerly to easterly. Depressions arriving from the SW are heavily laden with moist air from the central Pacific Ocean. When these systems encounter the Coastal Mountains, heavy precipitation results. In BC, this pattern is sometimes known as the "Pineapple Express".
- The entire system may travel as fast as 35 knots through the region.
- If the barometer fails to rise after the passage of a cold front, and if the sky is mostly overcast, there is probably another system approaching.
- The cold front generally moves faster than the warm front, overtaking it and eventually lifting the warm sector completely off the surface. When the cold front overtakes the warm front, it is known as an "occluded front". The occlusion begins near the low and proceeds to the south. When a low pressure system becomes occluded, with little or no warm sector, it may move erratically or even stall completely.

Red sky at night, sailors delight. Red sky in morning sailors take warning.

Clear skies caused by ridges of high pressure make the sunset or sunrise appear especially red. In temperate latitudes, most weather approaches from the west. Consequently when the clear skies to the west make the sunset red, fair weather is likely. But, when the sky to the east, makes the sunrise red, it may indicate the fair weather has already passed.

Mare's tails and mackerel scales make tall ships take in their sails.

A mackerel sky refers to cirrocumulus clouds, which often precede an approaching warm front (See next page).

"It's best to read the weather forecast before you pray for rain." —*Mark Twain*

Table 19-2 — Cross Section through a Typical Temperate Depression

The descriptions of frontal weather below are generalizations. Every front is different. Some may produce no precipitation while other systems may be very vigorous and produce high winds and torrential rain. When a warm front encounters the seaward side of the Coast Range, the warm air must rise higher and faster, thus producing even heavier rain.

The entire system may travel from West to East at 35 to 40 knots. The entire process outlined below may take up to 48 hours or more.

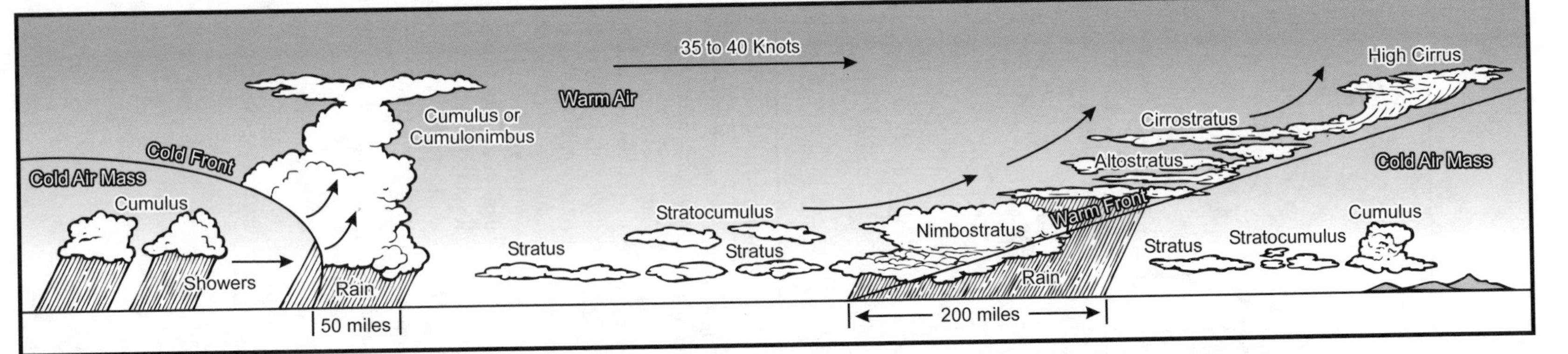
35 to 40 Knots
High Cirrus
Warm Air
Cumulus or
Cumulonimbus
Cirrostratus
Altostratus
Cold Front
Cold Air Mass
Cold Air Mass
Cumulus
Stratocumulus
Warm Front
Nimbostratus
Cumulus
Stratocumulus
Stratus
Stratus
Stratus
Showers
Rain
Rain
50 miles
200 miles

After Cold Front Passage	In the Warm Sector	In Advance of the Warm Front
Cold air mass forces itself under warm air, causing the warm air to rise rapidly and turbulently. The rapid uplift of warm air creates vigorous cumulus and cumulonimbus clouds to form, and precipitation falls in the form of heavy rain or hail. On passage of the cold front, unstable conditions continue, characterized by rain showers with clearing in between. Barometer falls on approach and passage of the front, then rises as weather clears. Wind squally near frontal passage, then backs a little. Temperature drops suddenly at frontal passage, then stabilizes.	After the passage of the warm front, heavy rain stops, and some clearing may occur, but fog and light rain may continue. Barometer steady. Wind veers—typically from SE to westerly. Temperature rises rapidly at warm front passage then stabilizes. In advance of the cold front, breaks in low cloud cover close up, visibility reduces and the temperature begins to fall.	Warm air mass rises over cold air mass. As the warm air rises, it cools and precipitation in the form of rain or snow falls from the rising air. Air on both sides of the front is essentially stable. The first sign of an approaching warm front is high altitude cirrus clouds, possibly forming a halo around the sun/moon, followed by thickening and lowering cirrostratus and altostratus clouds. Usually within 24 hours, the cloud cover becomes uniform stratus and nimbostratus, and moderate to heavy rain falls until the passage of the warm front. Barometer falling. Wind steady. Temperature steady.

When the wind changes direction it is said to veer or to back. The wind veers when its direction changes in a clockwise direction (ie. from southeast to southwest), and backs when its direction changes in a counter-clockwise direction.

Table 20 — Wind and Wave Tables

Use the table which gives the smallest value.

Estimated height in meters (h), length in meters (l), and period in seconds (p) of wind waves for a given duration and force of wind.

Wind Force	Wind Speed (Knots)	Six Hours (h)	Six Hours (l)	Six Hours (p)	Twelve Hours (h)	Twelve Hours (l)	Twelve Hours (p)	Twenty-Four Hours (h)	Twenty-Four Hours (l)	Twenty-Four Hours (p)	Forty-Eight Hours (h)	Forty-Eight Hours (l)	Forty-Eight Hours (p)
5	17-21	1	43	5	1.4	55	7	1.7	85	7.5	2.1	115	8.5
6	22-27	1.5	55	6	1.8	82	8.5	2.4	109	8.5	3	161	10
7	28-33	2.1	76	7	2.4	109	10	3.3	158	10	4.2	222	12
8	34-40	2.7	104	8	3.7	146	11.5	4.6	207	11.5	6.1	305	14
9	41-47	4.6	137	9.5	5.2	192	13	6.4	274	13	8.3	396	16

Estimated height in meters (h), length in meters (l), and period in seconds (p) of wind waves for a given force of wind and fetch.

Wind Force	Wind Speed (Knots)	50 Nm (h)	50 Nm (l)	50 Nm (p)	100 Nm (h)	100 Nm (l)	100 Nm (p)	200 Nm (h)	200 Nm (l)	200 Nm (p)	500 Nm (h)	500 Nm (l)	500 Nm (p)
5	17-21	1.2	37	5	1.4	55		1.7	76		2.1	109	8.5
6	22-27	1.5	43	5	1.8	76		2.1	97		2.7	137	9.5
7	28-33	2.1	55	6	2.4	100		3	122		3.7	152	10
8	34-40	2.7	76	7	3.3	122		3.9	158		5.2	213	11.5
9	41-47	3.6	91	7.5	4.2	152		5.2	198		6.7	274	13

$$\text{Wavelength} = \frac{\text{Speed}}{\text{Period}}$$

Fetch—the distance over which the wind acts on the water to produce waves. The longer the fetch, the larger the waves.

Length—the distance from the crest of one wave to the crest of the succeeding wave.

Height—the vertical distance from the top of a crest to the bottom of an adjacent trough.

Period—the interval in time between the passage of succeeding crests (or troughs).

Duration—the length of time the wind blows.

Fully developed sea—the largest wave size theoretically possible for a specific wind speed, wind duration, and fetch.

Significant Wave Height—equal to the average height of the largest 33% of waves.

One wave in 23 is twice the height of the average wave.

One wave in 1175 is three times the height of the average wave.

One wave in 300,000 is four times the height of the average wave.

The largest wave in recorded history, witnessed in Alaska in 1958, was caused by the collapse of a towering cliff at Lituya Bay. The resulting wave was higher than any skyscraper on Earth and gouged out soil and trees to a height of 500 meters (1640 feet) above sea level.

The largest recorded wind driven wave was observed by the officers of the USS Ramapo in the North Pacific ocean in 1933. The wave was estimated to be 34 meters (112 feet).

Observations taken at Ocean Station Papa, 1000 Nm west of Vancouver Island, indicate that waves 20 meters in height (65 feet) are relatively common.

Table 21 — Cold Water and Wind Chill Effects

Table 21-1 — Hypothermia Field Treatment Guide

Body Temp °C (°F)	Condition	Field Treatment
37 (98.6)	Normal	
	Mild Hypothermia	
36 (96.8) 35 (95.0)	Feels Cold Shivering	Replace wet clothing with dry. Prevent further exposure. Cover neck, insulate whole body including head. Limited exercise. Warm sweet drinks and food (high calories).
	Moderate Hypothermia	
34 (93.2) 33 (91.4)	Clumsy, Irrational, Confused (may appear drunk) Muscle Stiffness	Apply mild heat (hot water bottles etc.) to head, neck, groin and chest. Offer warm sweet drinks only if patient is fully conscious. Plan to keep victim warm for several hours and transfer to hospital.
	Severe Hypothermia	
32 (89.6) 31 (87.8) 30 (86.0)	Shivering stops--patient collapses Semi-conscious Unconscious--no response to pain.	Transfer to hospital as soon as possible--urgent condition. Put patient in pre-warmed sleeping bag, preferably between two people. Skin to skin contact is most effective. Keep victim awake. Apply mild heat to head, neck, trunk, and groin. Nothing by mouth. Monitor pulse and breathing.
	Critical	
29 (84.2)	Slow pulse and breathing.	Nothing by mouth. Warming procedures as above. Slow mouth-to-mouth breathing at patient's own rate. Rough handling may cause cardiac arrest. Avoid rapid re-warming.
28 (82.4)	Cardiac arrest, no obvious pulse or breathing, pupils may be dilated.	CPR, mouth-to-mouth breathing. Avoid re-warming too rapidly.

- Don't give up. Don't assume the situation is hopeless until the patient has been fully re-warmed and still shows no signs of life.
- Handle the patient gently at all times.
- See Table 21-2.
- To prevent post-rescue circulatory collapse (caused by a sudden drop in hydrostatic pressure), keep victim horizontal when recovering from the water.

If you are immersed in cold water, you can significantly extend survival time by raising even a small portion of your body out of the water. If you can't climb out of the water, keep your clothes on and adopt a heat conserving strategy.

Huddle together with other people in the water, or

HELP (Heat Escape Lessening Posture) Arms close to sides of the chest, legs crossed and pulled up closing the groin area."

Table 21-2 — Survival Times in Cold Water due to Hypothermia

Water Temperature Degrees Celsius	Degrees Fahrenheit	Loss of Dexterity with No Protective Clothing	Exhaustion or Unconsciousness	Expected Time of Survival
0.3	32.5	Under 2 minutes	Under 15 minutes	Under 15 to 45 minutes
0.3 to 4.5	32.5 to 40	Under 3 minutes	15 to 30 minutes	30 to 90 minutes
4.5 to 10	40 to 50	Under 5 minutes	30 to 60 minutes	1 to 3 hours
10 to 15.5	50 to 60	10 to 15 minutes	1 to 2 hours	1 to 6 hours
15.5 to 21	60 to 70	30 to 40 minutes	2 to 7 hours	2 to 40 hours
21 to 26.5	70 to 80	1 to 2 hours	2 to 12 hours	3 hours to indefinite
Over 26.5	Over 80	2 to 12 hours	Indefinite	Indefinite

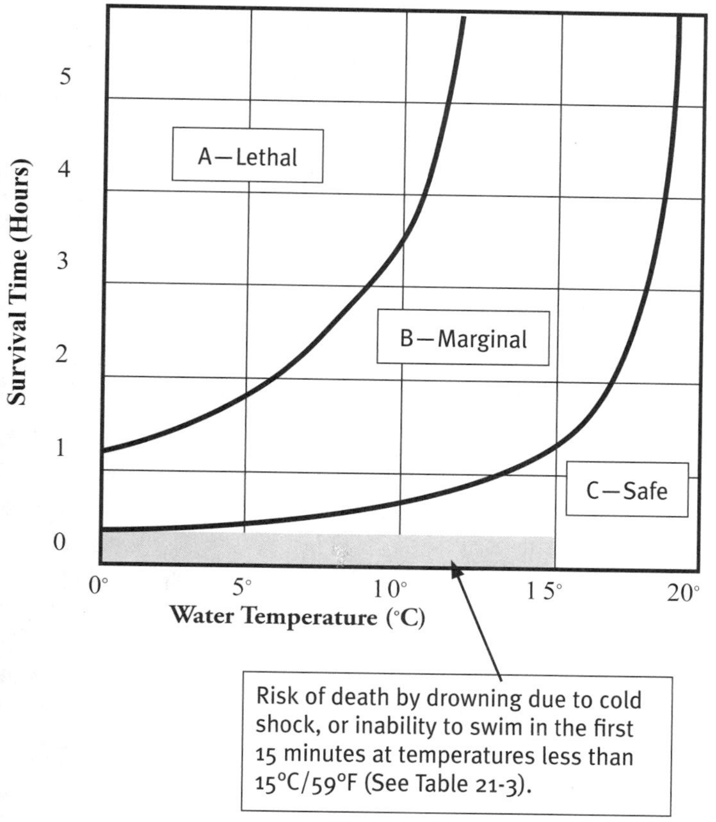
Survival Time (Hours)
0
1
2
3
4
5
A—Lethal
B—Marginal
C—Safe
0°
5°
10°
15°
20°
Water Temperature (°C)

Risk of death by drowning due to cold shock, or inability to swim in the first 15 minutes at temperatures less than 15°C/59°F (See Table 21-3).

Comparison of Survival Times for a lightly clad, reasonably fit person wearing flotation.

A—100% expectation of death

B—50% expectation of unconsciousness which will result in drowning

C—Strong possibility of survival

Barnett, 1962

Note: Tables of survival times due to hypothermia can only indicate trends. Individuals vary widely in their responses to cold water and therefore in survival times as well.

Survival can be greatly extended by wearing thermal protection.

Activity such as treading water and swimming will significantly increase cooling rates and thus decrease survival time.

Water transports heat away from the body 25 times faster than air at the same temperature. This is partly due to the higher conductivity of water and partly due to its density (or specific heat).

If you have the choice, don't get wet at all; try to get into the lifeboat or raft without getting wet. If you cannot avoid immersion, enter the water slowly—Never dive into cold water.

Table 21-3 — Cold Water Immersion

Cold water effects such as cold shock and inability to swim may prove fatal much sooner than is predicted in **Table 21-2.** Recent research suggests that 40% to 60% of people who die in cold water, fail to survive the first 5 to 15 minutes and probably die of drowning rather than hypothermia. (In Alaska, this figure is estimated to be as high as 75%.)

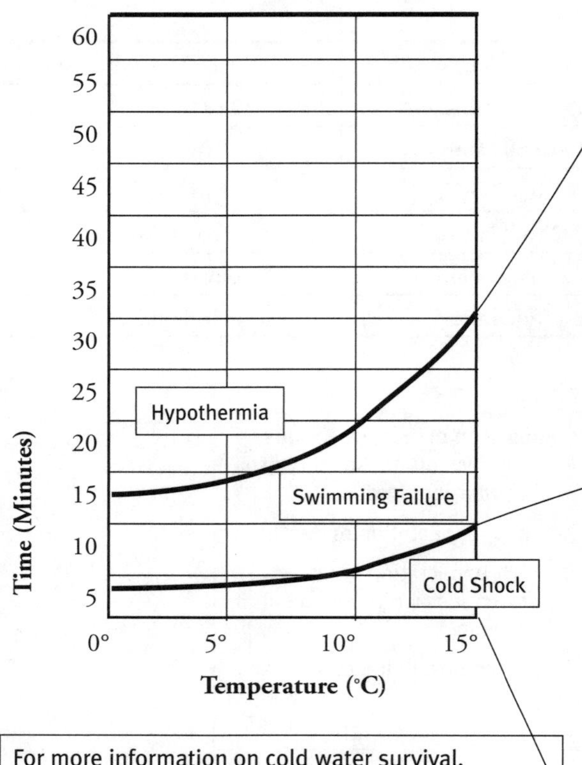
60
55
50
45
40
35
30
25
20
15
10
5
Time (Minutes)
Hypothermia
Swimming Failure
Cold Shock
0°
5°
10°
15°
Temperature (°C)

Stage 3: Hypothermia (40% of cold water fatalities)
(See Tables 21-1 and 21-2)

- Caused by cooling of the body core

Stage 2: Inability to Swim (40% of cold water fatalities)

- Death by drowning occurs within 5 – 30 minutes
- Rapid cooling of the musculature of the arms and legs
- Almost complete loss of coordination, manual dexterity and muscle strength
- Inability to self-rescue using flares or other survival equipment
- Degradation of swimming ability—even short swims may be impossible–many who drown are reported to have been "good swimmers"
- Inability to coordinate swimming stroke and breathing
- Unable to self-rescue
- ***Unable to keep airway clear of water without help***
- Effects increase in severity with time

Stage 1: Initial Immersion or Cold Shock (20% of cold water fatalities)

- Drowning occurs rapidly (within 3 to 5 minutes)
- Cold receptors in the skin cause immediate physiological responses; peak response occurs within 30 seconds
- Large inspiratory gasp upon immersion – may cause drowning
- Uncontrollable hyperventilation and reduced breath-hold ability
- May be unable to get air into lungs—leads to panic
- Massive increase in heart rate and blood pressure may trigger cardiac arrest
- Unable to self-rescue
- ***Unable to keep airway clear of water without help***
- Effects last for just a few minutes, but at the critical stage of ship abandonment or falling overboard

For more information on cold water survival, refer to Transport Canada Publication *Survival in Cold Waters* (TP13822) available at: www.tc.gc.ca/MarineSafety/Tp/Tp13822/menu.htm

- Approximately 55% of open-water drownings occur within about 3 m/10 ft of a safe refuge, and 42% occur within 2 m/6 ft. (UK Home Office Report 1977).
- 41% of those who were boating and drowned were within 10 m of shore. An additional 22% were within 10 to 15 m of shore (Canada SmartRisk Research 2002).
- Many victims are unable to swim even two meters to save themselves.
- Any water less than 15°C/59°F will trigger these physical reactions, though the colder the water, the more severe the response.
- Some studies suggest that these reactions can occur in water as warm as 20°C/68°F.
- If the water is warm enough not to be concerned with cold water responses, it is warm enough for sharks.

Lessons

On sudden immersion in cold water:

- Long before you run the risk of death by hypothermia you can easily die from drowning if you don't have a flotation aid to keep your head airway above water.
- Evidence shows that you will very likely not be able to don a flotation aid once you have entered cold water—**you must be wearing a PFD for it to save your life.**
- Your goal must be to survive the first two stages of Cold Water Immersion—long enough to actually run the risk of hypothermia (20 to 30 minutes)—**almost impossible without a flotation aid.**

Table 21-4 — Wind Chill Tables

Wind Speed in Miles per Hour	Air Temperature in Degrees Fahrenheit											
	30	25	20	15	10	5	0	-5	-10	-15	-20	-25
5	25	19	13	7	1	-5	-11	-16	-22	-28	-34	-40
10	21	15	9	3	-4	-10	-16	-22	-28	-35	-41	-47
15	19	13	6	0	-7	-13	-19	-26	-32	-39	-45	-51
20	17	11	4	-2	-9	-15	-22	-29	-35	-42	-48	-55
25	16	9	3	-4	-11	-17	-24	-31	-37	-44	-51	-58
30	15	8	1	-5	-12	-19	-26	-33	-39	-46	-53	-60
35	14	7	0	-7	-14	-21	-27	-34	-41	-48	-55	-62
40	13	6	-1	-8	-15	-22	-29	-36	-43	-50	-57	-64
45	12	5	-2	-9	-16	-23	-30	-37	-44	-51	-58	-65
50	12	4	-3	-10	-17	-24	-31	-38	-45	-52	-60	-67
55	11	4	-3	-11	-18	-25	-32	-39	-46	-54	-61	-68
60	10	3	-4	-11	-19	-26	-33	-40	-48	-55	-62	-69

Wind Speed in Kilometers per Hour	Air Temperature in Degrees Celsius									
	5	0	-5	-10	-15	-20	-25	-30	-35	-40
5	4	-2	-7	-13	-19	-24	-30	-36	-41	-47
10	3	-3	-9	-15	-21	-27	-33	-39	-45	-51
15	2	-4	-11	-17	-23	-29	-35	-41	-48	-54
20	1	-5	-12	-18	-24	-30	-37	-43	-49	-56
25	1	-6	-12	-19	-25	-32	-38	-44	-51	-57
30	0	-6	-13	-20	-26	-33	-39	-46	-52	-59
35	0	-7	-14	-20	-27	-33	-40	-47	-53	-60
40	-1	-7	-14	-21	-27	-34	-41	-48	-54	-61
45	-1	-8	-15	-21	-28	-35	-42	-48	-55	-62
50	-1	-8	-15	-22	-29	-35	-42	-49	-56	-63
55	-2	-8	-15	-22	-29	-36	-43	-50	-57	-63
60	-2	-9	-16	-23	-30	-36	-43	-50	-57	-64
65	-2	-9	-16	-23	-30	-37	-44	-51	-58	-65
70	-2	-9	-16	-23	-30	-37	-44	-51	-58	-65
75	-3	-10	-17	-24	-31	-38	-45	-52	-59	-66
80	-3	-10	-17	-24	-31	-38	-45	-52	-60	-67

Frostbite Guide

- Risk of frostbite in 30 minutes
- Risk of frostbite in 10 minutes
- Risk of frostbite in 5 minutes or less

Wind Chill

These tables have been produced by the US Weather Service and Environment Canada in an attempt to predict the effect of combinations of low temperature and wind on humans or animals.

These tables do not suggest that a 35 knot wind will actually reduce the temperature from -10F to -41F. After all, if wind speed actually lowered temperature, we wouldn't need refreigerators, we could just use fans.

However, winds do make cold air feel colder, and cause unprotected human skin to lose heat at a faster rate than in calm air. As a result, frostbite and hypothermia will set in sooner, and thus people should act as if the wind chill effects are real.

Sea Spray Icing

During Arctic outbreak conditions, when cold continental air flows out to sea through the mainland inlets, generating gale-force winds, sea spray icing conditions can easily develop.

In southern British Columbia, sea spray icing is unlikely to become a serious hazard, but in the northern B.C. mainland inlets and in Southeast Alaska, during the winter, icing may be a serious concern.

When the air temperature is below -4°C/25° F, and the sea temperature is near 0°C/32°F, sea spray may freeze on deck. This is especially true if the vessel has been in sub-zero conditions for several days and its structure is at the temperature of the air or colder. In gale-force wind conditions, with very low temperature, sea spray icing is almost certain. In these conditions, ice may accumulate very quickly and not only make it difficult to work on deck, but the accumulation of weight above the vessel's center of gravity may seriously reduce the vessel's stability. Icing can be especially dangerous to smaller vessels because sea spray is more likely to come aboard a small vessel and because a relatively smaller amount of ice on board can have devastating effects.

When dangerous icing conditions develop, immediately turn the vessel's head downwind (if possible) to reduce the amount of spray coming on board, and seek shelter. Don't wait for a large amount of ice to accumulate. Once the vessel has accumulated a serious amount of ice, it may be dangerous to turn broadside to the wind and seas. Remove as much ice as possible using wooden mallets, baseball bats, etc. Do not use metal tools because they may damage the vessel's structure, especially at low temperature.

Table 22-1 — Environment Canada's Mariner's Guide

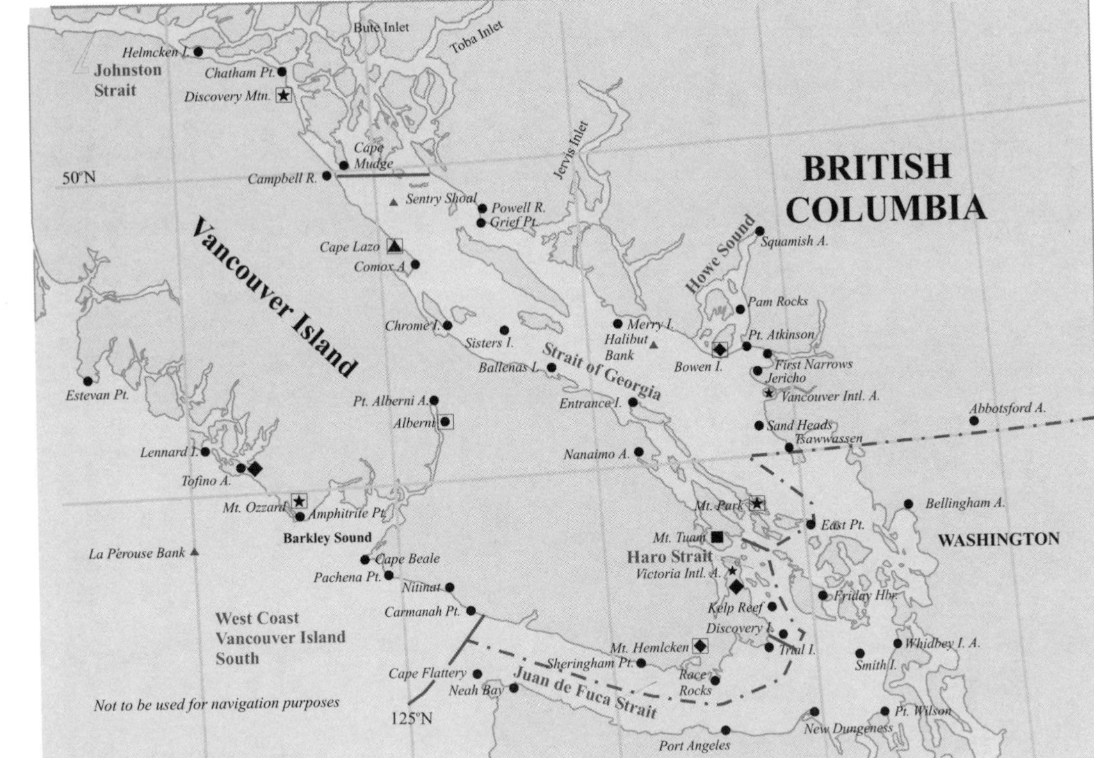
Helmcken I.
Johnston Strait
Chatham Pt.
Discovery Mtn.
Bute Inlet
Toba Inlet
Cape Mudge
50°N
Campbell R.
Sentry Shoal
Powell R.
Grief Pt.
Jervis Inlet
BRITISH COLUMBIA
Vancouver Island
Cape Lazo
Comox A.
Howe Sound
Squamish A.
Pam Rocks
Chrome I.
Sisters I.
Merry I.
Halibut Bank
Strait of Georgia
Ballenas I.
Bowen I.
Pt. Atkinson
First Narrows
Jericho
Vancouver Intl. A.
Estevan Pt.
Pt. Alberni A.
Alberni
Entrance I.
Sand Heads
Tsawwassen
Abbotsford A.
Lennard I.
Tofino A.
Nanaimo A.
Mt. Ozzard
Amphitrite Pt.
Barkley Sound
Mt. Park
Bellingham A.
East Pt.
La Pérouse Bank
Cape Beale
Mt. Tuam
Haro Strait
Victoria Intl. A.
WASHINGTON
Pachena Pt.
Nitinat
Carmanah Pt.
Kelp Reef
Friday Hbr.
West Coast Vancouver Island South
Discovery I.
Trial I.
Whidbey I. A.
Mt. Hemlcken
Sheringham Pt.
Smith I.
Cape Flattery
Neah Bay
Juan de Fuca Strait
Race Rocks
Not to be used for navigation purposes
125°N
Pt. Wilson
New Dungeness
Port Angeles

MARINE WARNINGS

Marine warnings are issued whenever the winds are expected to rise into the following wind speed categories:

Small Craft Warning	**20 - 33 knots**
Gale Warning	**34 - 47 knots**
Storm Warning	**48 - 63 knots**
Hurricane Force Wind Warning	**64 knots or more**

Small Craft Warnings are issued for the southern inner coastal waters beginning in April and continuing until November 11. This warning is **not** based on the size of the vessel but only on the strength of the wind.

The Hurricane Force Wind Warning does **not** imply the presence of a hurricane but only refers to winds of 64 knots or higher.

The text of the wind warning describes the weather systems responsible for the strong winds, the maximum winds expected and when they are likely to diminish.

The warnings are "flagged" in the actual forecast by a statement such as "Gale warning issued". No special message is issued when a warning is canceled but a statement such as "Storm Warning ended" is included in the forecast.

OBTAINING FORECASTS

Free Recordings

Vancouver *(Howe Sound, Strait of Georgia, Haro Strait, Juan de Fuca Strait)*	**604-664-9010**
Victoria	**250-363-6717**
Nanaimo	**250-245-8899**
Comox	**250-339-8044**
Campbell River	**250-286-3575**
Port Hardy	**250-949-7148**
Prince Rupert	**250-624-9009**

For a Fee

WHEN ONSHORE CALL:

Marine Weather 1-900-565-6565 or
1-866-640-6369 (Visa/MasterCard or on account)
To talk to a marine forecaster (fees apply)

WHEN ON or OFFSHORE CALL:

WeatherCall

Speak directly to a marine forecaster
Access phone number provided upon registration,
to register phone 604-664-9033 or fax 604-664-9081

Environment Canada Environnement Canada

MARINER'S GUIDE

46145

MARTHA L BLACK

Canada

WEST COAST MARINE WEATHER SERVICES

For Weather on the Web:

weatheroffice
météo

www.weatheroffice.ec.gc.ca

Table 22-1 — Environment Canada's Mariner's Guide *(continued)*

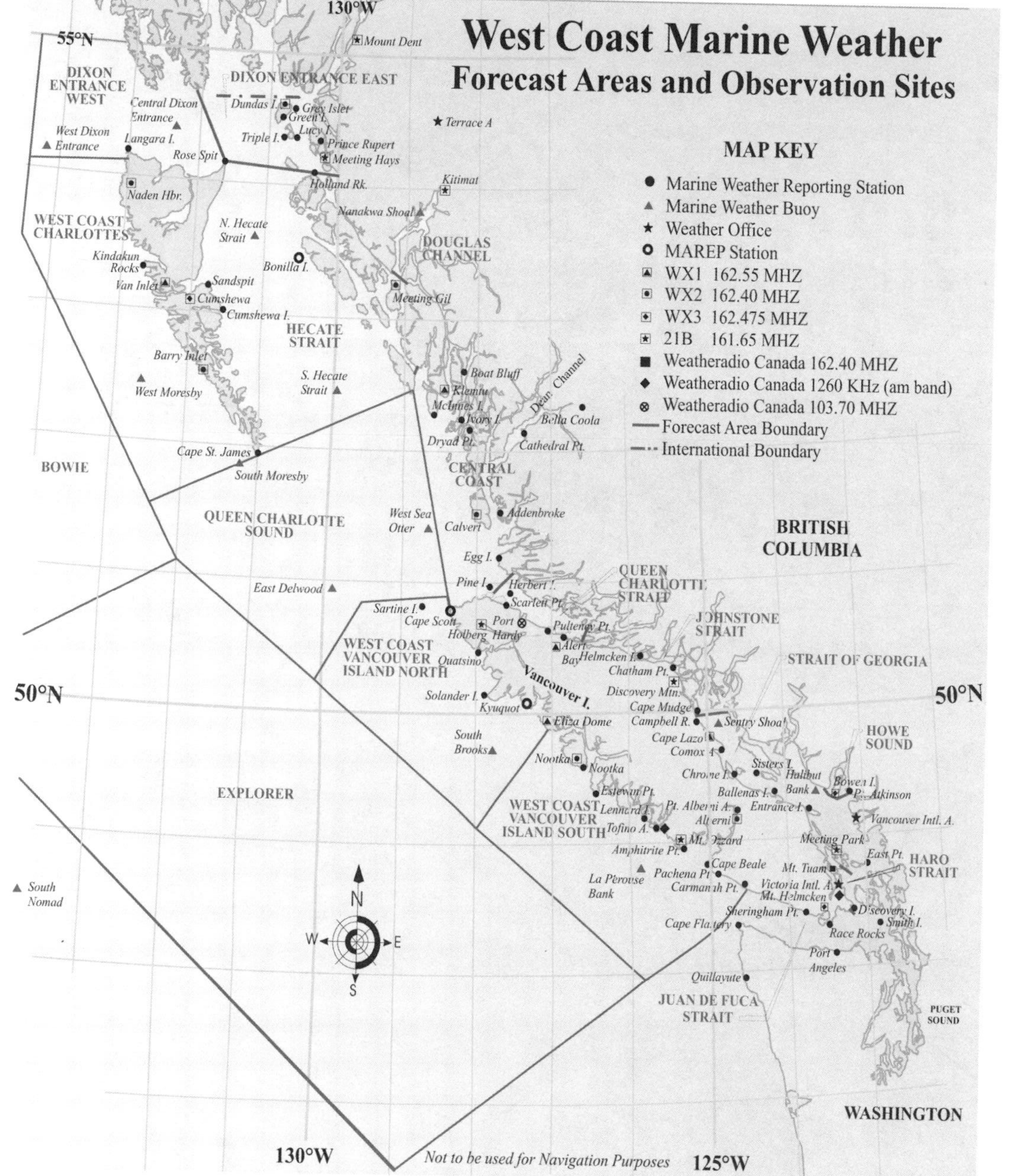
West Coast Marine Weather
Forecast Areas and Observation Sites
MAP KEY
Marine Weather Reporting Station
Marine Weather Buoy
Weather Office
MAREP Station
WX1 162.55 MHZ
WX2 162.40 MHZ
WX3 162.475 MHZ
21B 161.65 MHZ
Weatheradio Canada 162.40 MHZ
Weatheradio Canada 1260 KHz (am band)
Weatheradio Canada 103.70 MHZ
Forecast Area Boundary
International Boundary
55°N
130°W
50°N
125°W
DIXON ENTRANCE WEST
DIXON ENTRANCE EAST
WEST COAST CHARLOTTES
HECATE STRAIT
DOUGLAS CHANNEL
BOWIE
QUEEN CHARLOTTE SOUND
CENTRAL COAST
BRITISH COLUMBIA
QUEEN CHARLOTTE STRAIT
JOHNSTONE STRAIT
STRAIT OF GEORGIA
HOWE SOUND
WEST COAST VANCOUVER ISLAND NORTH
WEST COAST VANCOUVER ISLAND SOUTH
EXPLORER
JUAN DE FUCA STRAIT
HARO STRAIT
PUGET SOUND
WASHINGTON
Vancouver I.
Not to be used for Navigation Purposes

MARINE FORECAST ISSUE TIMES

0400
1030
1600
2130

Issue times remain the same throughout the year.

Marine warnings and amendments are issued as required.

MARINE FORECAST CONTENT

Marine forecasts are valid for 24 hours with an outlook for a further 24 hours.

Synopsis

The Synopsis is located at the beginning of the marine forecast. It describes the location and intensity of the weather systems which will affect the B.C. coastal waters and indicates what their movements will be during the forecast period. In addition, a general description of the present and forecast winds is included.

Wind Speed

The winds in the marine forecast are the average winds that are expected over the open water.

The wind speeds are given in knots.

Gusts or squalls are only mentioned when they are expected to be much higher than the average winds. It should be noted that with the rugged coastline of B.C., considerable local variations from the forecast winds are possible.

Wind Direction

Wind directions refer to the direction from which the wind is blowing and these are based on true north and not on magnetic bearings.

Weather and Visibility

A brief description is given of the sky condition and weather, for example, sunny, cloudy, rain, drizzle, or fog. This is followed by a statement about the visibility if it is expected to be reduced below 1 nautical mile.

Outlook

The outlook describes the winds during the 24 hour period following the main forecast.

Environment Canada's West Coast marine weather books

Brand new in 2003
LIVING WITH WEATHER ALONG THE BC COAST

Marine weather in the Georgia Basin;
THE WIND CAME ALL WAYS
"...highly recommended" as reviewed in The West coast Fisherman.

the ever popular
WEST COAST MARINE WEATHER HAZARDS MANUAL

To order books please phone (604) 664-9077

For information on these or other weather services, contact: **Client Services**
Ph.(604) 664-9355 Fax(604) 664-9081

Environment Canada Environnement Canada

Table 22-2 — Alaska and Washington VHF Weather Forecasts

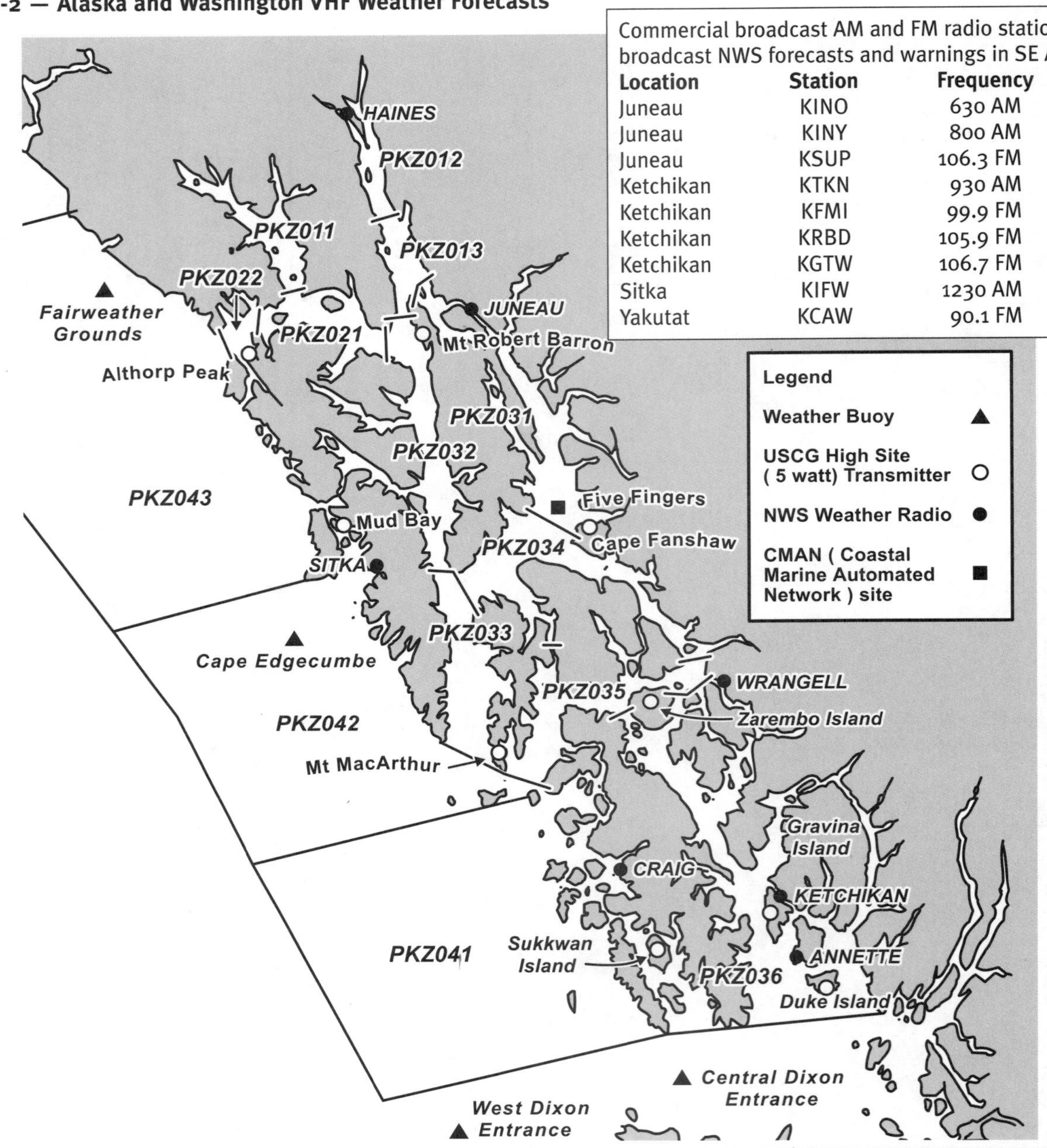
HAINES
PKZ012
PKZ011
PKZ013
PKZ022
Fairweather Grounds
PKZ021
JUNEAU
Mt Robert Barron
Althorp Peak
PKZ031
PKZ032
PKZ043
Five Fingers
Mud Bay
PKZ034
Cape Fanshaw
SITKA
PKZ033
Cape Edgecumbe
PKZ035
WRANGELL
Zarembo Island
PKZ042
Mt MacArthur
Gravina Island
CRAIG
KETCHIKAN
Sukkwan Island
PKZ041
ANNETTE
PKZ036
Duke Island
Central Dixon Entrance
West Dixon Entrance
Legend
Weather Buoy
USCG High Site (5 watt) Transmitter
NWS Weather Radio
CMAN (Coastal Marine Automated Network) site

Commercial broadcast AM and FM radio stations that broadcast NWS forecasts and warnings in SE Alaska.

Location	Station	Frequency
Juneau	KINO	630 AM
Juneau	KINY	800 AM
Juneau	KSUP	106.3 FM
Ketchikan	KTKN	930 AM
Ketchikan	KFMI	99.9 FM
Ketchikan	KRBD	105.9 FM
Ketchikan	KGTW	106.7 FM
Sitka	KIFW	1230 AM
Yakutat	KCAW	90.1 FM

The following Weather Service Offices receive weather observations and broadcast weather forecasts.

VHF

Location	Announce/ Monitor	Broadcast	Times
Annette	16	9	0600, 1550
Yakutat	16	9	1630, 1715

HF/USB 4125 kHz

Location	Time	HF Call Sign
Annette	0700, 1540	KGD58
Yakutat	0515, 1930	KDG91

NOAA Weather Radio

Juneau	WX 1
Sitka	WX 1
Ketchikan	WX 1
Wrangell	WX 2
Haines	WX 2
Yakutat	WX 2
Craig	WX 3

National Weather Service on USCG High Sites*

Sukkwan Island	WX 4
Cape Fanshaw	WX 4
Althorpe Peak	WX 4
Duke Island	WX 5
Mt. Robert Barron	WX 5
Zarembo Island	WX 5
Mud Bay	WX 6
Gravina Island	WX 7
Mt. MacArthur	WX 7

*Five-watt transmitters

National Weather Service Forecast Zones

SE Alaska Inside Waters

PKZ011	Glacier Bay
PKZ012	Northern Lynn Canal
PKZ013	Southern Lynn Canal
PKZ021	Icy Strait
PKZ022	Cross Sound
PKZ031	Stephens Passage
PKZ032	Northern Chatham Strait
PKZ033	Southern Chatham Strait
PKZ034	Frederick Sound
PKZ035	Sumner Strait
PKZ036	Clarence Strait

SE Alaska Outside Waters

PKZ041	Dixon Entrance to Cape Decision
PKZ042	Cape Decision to Cape Edgecumbe
PKZ043	Cape Edgecumbe to Cape Fairweather

Puget Sound and Juan de Fuca Strait

PZZ130	US waters of Juan de Fuca Strait—West
PZZ131	US waters of Juan de Fuca Strait—Central
PZZ132	US waters of Juan de Fuca Strait—East
PZZ133	Northern Inland Waters—Camano Island to Point Roberts
PZZ134	Admiralty Inlet from Admiralty Head to Foulweather Bluff
PZZ135	Puget Sound and Hood Canal

Washington Outside Waters

PZZ150	Cape Flattery to James Island and westward 20 Nm
PZZ170	Cape Flattery to James Island 20 to 60 Nm offshore

The National Bureau of Standards and Technology broadcasts a time and frequency service from stations WWV in Boulder, CO and WWVH in Honolulu, HI.

Included in these broadcasts are hourly voice broadcasts of current high seas storm warnings for the Atlantic, Pacific and Gulf of Mexico, provided by the National Weather Service.

WWV (Boulder, CO)
Frequencies , 2.5,5,10, 15, 20, MHz (AM)
Atlantic warnings 8 min and 9 min past the hour
Pacific warnings 10 min past the hour

WWVH (Honolulu, HI)
Pacific warnings 48 min and 51 min past the hour

NWS Points of Contact in SE Alaska
Continuous Weather Broadcast

Juneau	(907) 586-3997
Sitka	(907) 767-6011
Wrangell	(907) 874-3232
Yakutat	(907) 784-3654

Easy access to land and buoy observations, and coastal marine weather forecasts

Within Alaska	(800) 472-0391
Juneau	(907) 790-6050
Petersburg	(907) 458-3745

NOAA Weather Radio and Canadian Coast Guard Weather Frequencies

162.550 MHz	(WX1)
162.400 MHz	(WX2)
162.475 MHz	(WX3)
162.425 MHz	(WX4)
162.450 MHz	(WX5)
162.500 MHz	(WX6)
162.525 MHz	(WX7)

National Buoy Data Center	www.ndbc.noaa.gov/
Alaska buoys	www.ndbc.noaa.gov/Maps/Alaska.shtml
Washington Buoys	www.ndbc.noaa.gov/Maps/Northwest.shtml
National Weather Service	www.nws.noaa.gov/
Alaska	www.arh.noaa.gov/
SE Alaska forecast areas	www.nws.noaa.gov/om/marine/zone/alaska/ajkmz.htm
Washington	www.wrh.noaa.gov/Seattle/
Washington State forecast areas	www.nws.noaa.gov/om/marine/zone/west/sewmz.htm
Meteorological Service of Canada	www.weatheroffice.ec.gc.ca/canada_e.html
British Columbia Marine forecast	www.weatheroffice.ec.gc.ca/marine/region_03_e.html
Data from BC Lighthouses	www-sci.pac.dfo-mpo.gc.ca/osap/data/SearchTools/Searchlighthouse_e.htm
BC Ocean Buoy Weather Data	www-sci.pac.dfo-mpo.gc.ca/osap/data/newbuoy/buoydatadefault_e.htm
Environment Canada Marine and Ice Warning and Forecast Programs in Radio Aids to Marine Navigation	www.ccg-gcc.gc.ca/mcts-sctm/ramn_arnm/pacific/part_5_e.htm

Dial a Buoy

This service provides wind and wave measurements taken within the last hour at stations located in coastal waters around the United States and in the Great Lakes.

Dial (228) 688-1948, and then enter the five digit station identifier for the station of interest in response to the prompts. A list of station identifiers is available on the internet at http://seaboard.ndbc.noaa.gov

"A great, great deal has been said about the weather, but very little has ever been done about it."—*Mark Twain*

Time Signals in Canada

The National Research Council broadcasts a time signal on CHU (a short wave transmitter located near Ottawa, ON). The signal is transmitted continuously on 3330KHz, 7335KHz and 14670KHz, upper sideband H3E (AM compatible).

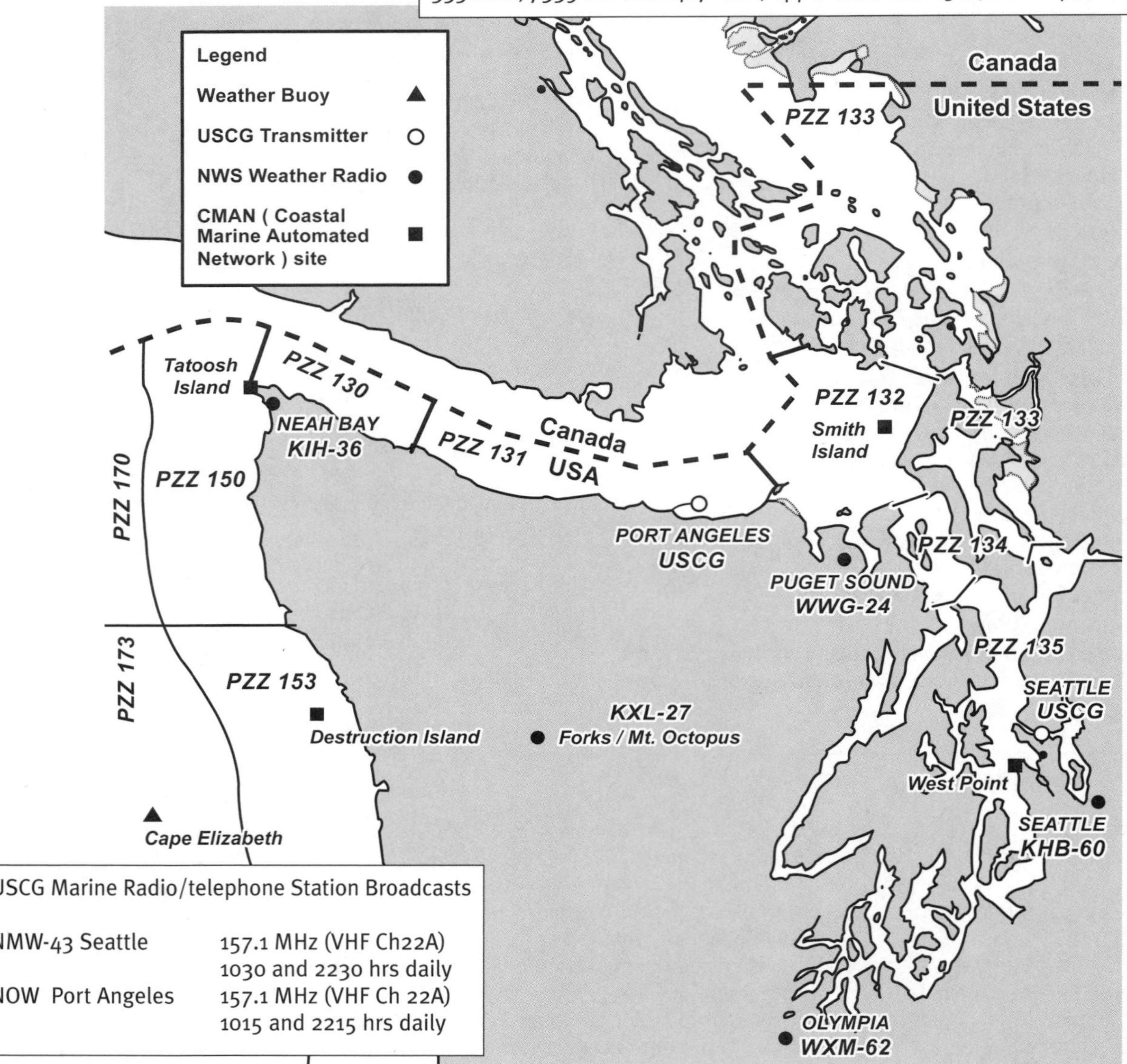
Legend
Weather Buoy
USCG Transmitter
NWS Weather Radio
CMAN (Coastal Marine Automated Network) site
Canada
United States
PZZ 133
Tatoosh Island
PZZ 130
NEAH BAY
KIH-36
PZZ 131
Canada
USA
PZZ 132
Smith Island
PZZ 133
PZZ 170
PZZ 150
PORT ANGELES
USCG
PZZ 134
PUGET SOUND
WWG-24
PZZ 173
PZZ 153
PZZ 135
Destruction Island
KXL-27
Forks / Mt. Octopus
SEATTLE
USCG
West Point
SEATTLE
KHB-60
Cape Elizabeth
OLYMPIA
WXM-62

USCG Marine Radio/telephone Station Broadcasts

NMW-43 Seattle	157.1 MHz (VHF Ch22A) 1030 and 2230 hrs daily
NOW Port Angeles	157.1 MHz (VHF Ch 22A) 1015 and 2215 hrs daily

NOAA Weather Radio in Puget Sound and Juan de Fuca Strait

KHB-60 Seattle	WX 1
KIH-36-Neah Bay	WX 1
KIG-98 Portland	WX 1
WXM-62 Olympia	WX 3
WWG-24 Puget Sound	WX 4

Note: Other weather resources on HF and MF frequencies are available that are not listed here.

All broadcasts are continuous and are updated every three to six hours and amended as required. Broadcasts include:

- Marine forecasts and warnings for coastal waters to 60 miles offshore, including the Strait of Juan de Fuca and the inland waters of western Washington, and Grays Harbor and Columbia River bar forecasts.
- Offshore waters from 60 to 250 miles offshore from Cape Flattery, WA to Point Conception, CA.
- State forecasts and local public forecasts.
- Selected weather observations from Coast Guard buoys, and other stations in western Washington, western Oregon, northern California, and southeastern British Columbia.

PART IV

Anchors, Rope, Wire Rope, and Chain

Table 23 — Safe Working Loads

Table 23-1 — Maximum Safe Working Loads of Rope, Wire Rope and Chain (Pounds)

Rope Diameter (Inches)	Fiber Rope						Wire Rope		
	Manilla	Polypropylene	Nylon (3-Strand Twisted)	Nylon (Double Braided)	Polyester (3-Strand Twisted)	Polyester (Braided)	6 x 19 Improved Plough Steel Fibre Core*	6 x 37 Improved Plough Steel Fibre Core*	Alloy Steel Chain
1/4	100	150	200	440	200	380	1,100	1,000	3,250
5/16	120	250	300	680	300	600	1,650	1,600	
3/8	200	400	500	980	500	840	2,400	2,200	6,600
7/16	270	500	700	1,320	700	1,100	3,200	3,000	
1/2	530	830	1,250	1,700	1,200	1,400	4,400	4,000	11,250
9/16	680	960	1,500	2,160	1,500	1,860	5,300	5,000	
5/8	880	1,300	2,000	2,700	1,900	2,200	6,600	6,400	16,500
3/4	1,080	1,700	2,800	3,880	2,400	3,340	9,500	8,900	23,000
13/16	1,300	1,900	3,200	4,880	2,950	4,200			
7/8	1,540	2,200	3,800	5,260	3,400	4,520	12,800	12,100	28,750
1	1,800	2,900	4,800	6,800	4,200	5,850	16,700	15,800	38,750
1 1/8	2,100	3,000	5,500	9,200	4,900	7,900	21,200	19,600	44,500
1 1/4	2,400	3,750	6,300	10,400	5,600	8,950	26,200	24,400	57,500
1 3/8	2,700	4,200	7,200		6,300		32,400	29,800	67,000
1 1/2	3,000	4,400	8,200	14,800	7,100	12,730	38,400	36,000	79,000
1 5/8	3,700	6,000	10,200	18,000	8,900	15,480	45,200	42,200	
1 3/4	4,500	7,300	12,400	21,200	10,800	18,230	52,000	48,400	94,000
1 7/8	5,300	8,700	15,000		12,900		60,800	56,800	
2	6,200	10,400	17,900	25,200	15,200	21,670	67,600	62,000	

(Safety Factor = 5)

The Cordage Institute specifies that the Safe Working Load (SWL) of a rope shall be determined by dividing the Minimum Tensile Strength by the Safety Factor. Safety Factors range from 5 to 12 for non-critical uses, 15 for life lines.

- For endless or grommet slings multiply SWL by 2.
- When using choker slings reduce SWL by 25%.

*Applies to wire rope with a socket or swaged terminal attachment. For hand-tucked splice attachment, reduce SWL by 15%.

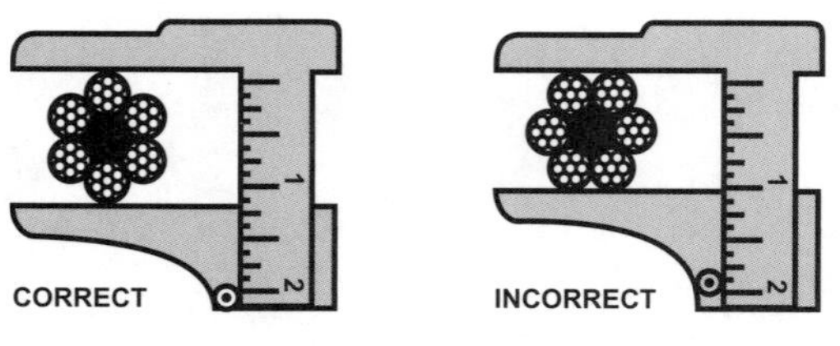
CORRECT
INCORRECT

Correct and Incorrect Methods of Measuring Wire Rope Diameter

Be careful not to oversize your dock lines or your anchor line. Oversized lines will not properly stretch under the imposed loads, and consequently will fail to provide the degree of shock absorbtion of a properly sized line. The result is that oversized lines will actually impose greater shock loads on hull fittings and anchor gear. These loads may result in failure of deck fittings or in breaking out of a well-set anchor; neither is a desirable consequence.

Dock Line Sizing

The diameter of your dock lines depends on the length and weight of your boat. The following is an approximate guide. If your boat is especially heavy for its weight or has a very large wind-sail area, use one size larger.

Boats under 20 ft (6 m)	3/8"	(10 mm)
Boats 20 to 30 ft (6 to 9 m)	1/2"	(13 mm)
Boats 30 to 40 ft (9 to 12 m)	5/8"	(16 mm)
Boats 40 to 60 ft (12 to 18 m)	3/4"	(19 mm)
Boats over 60 ft (18 m)	1"	(25 mm)

Table 23-2 — Rule of Thumb for Estimating Safe Working Load of Fiber Ropes

For SWL in pounds where

D = rope diameter in inches

Manilla	SWL =	$(D \times 8)^2 \times 20$
Polypropylene	SWL =	$(D \times 8)^2 \times 40$
Polyester	SWL =	$(D \times 8)^2 \times 60$
Nylon	SWL =	$(D \times 8)^2 \times 60$

Note:

- Sudden shocks can more than double the instantaneous load on a rope. When working near the SWL, take care to operate rope smoothly.
- When working within its SWL, nylon rope will stretch up to 30%. This results in a tremendous capacity to absorb shocks and avoid peak loads.

Efficiency of Various Knots and Splices

The following knots will reduce the strength of rope to the indicated values. The reduction in the breaking load of the rope must be reflected in a reduction in the Safe Working Load as well.

Clove Hitch	75%
Bowline	50%
Square or Reef Knot	43%
Timber Hitch and Half Hitch	72%
Sheepshank	35%
Short Splice	85%
Long Splice	68%
Eye Splice	85%

Table 23-3 — Loss of Strength for Various Angles of Pull

When lifting with a doubled bridle, the SWL is twice the SWL of a single rope, but because of the angle of pull, the total SWL must be reduced. When lifting with a vertical pull, the bridle is 90° to the horizontal. Any departure from this angle will require a corresponding reduction in the SWL.

- When you are using slings, the greater the angle from vertical, the greater the stress on the sling legs.
- A sling with two legs used to lift a 1,000-pound object will have 500 pounds of the load on each leg when the sling angle is 90 degrees (vertical pull).
- The load stress on each leg increases as the angle decreases; for example, if the sling angle is 30 degrees when lifting the same 1,000-pound object, the load is 1,000 pounds on each leg.
- Try to keep all sling angles greater than 45 degrees; sling angles approaching 30 degrees are considered extremely hazardous and must be avoided.

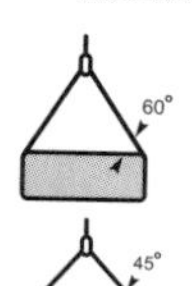
60°
45°

Sling angle **60°**	Reduce total SWL by **15%**
Sling angle **45°**	Reduce total SWL by **30%**
Sling angle **30°**	Reduce total SWL by **50%**

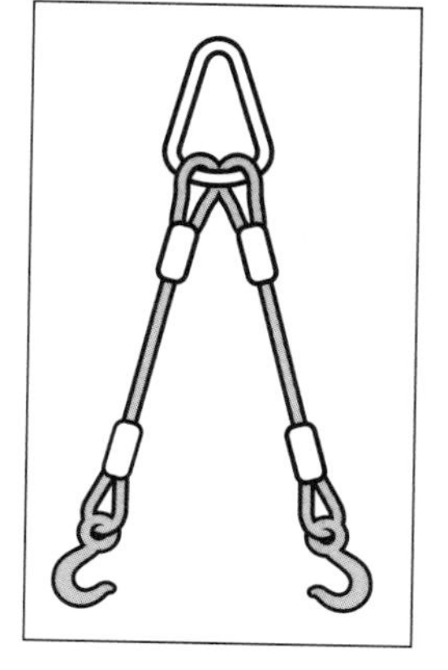

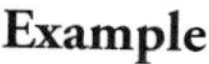

Example

What is the SWL of a double bridle of 1/2 inch 3 strand nylon rope used at an angle of 45°?

From **Table 23-1**

- A sling made from ½ inch 3-strand nylon rope has a SWL of **1,250 lb.**
- If a double bridle is used the total SWL is **1250 lb.** x **2** = **2500 lb.**
- Reduce the SWL by 30% for an angle of pull of 45°.
- Therefore the total SWL of this bridle at this angle is **70%** x **2500 lb.** = **1750 lb.**

Table 24 — Rope, Wire rope, and Chain

Table 24-1 — Weight of Rope, Wire Rope, and Chain

Rope Diameter (Inches)	Polypropylene (lbs/100 ft)	Nylon (lbs/100 ft)	Manilla (lbs/100 ft)	6 x 19 Wire Rope (lbs/ft)	Chain (lbs/ft)
1/4	1.2	1.5	2.0	0.10	0.75
5/16	1.8	2.5	2.9	0.16	1.0
3/8	2.8	3.5	4.1	0.23	1.5
7/16	3.8	5.0	5.3	0.31	2.0
1/2	4.7	6.5	7.5	0.40	2.5
9/16	6.1	8.3	10.4	0.51	3.25
5/8	7.5	10.5	13.3	0.63	4.0
3/4	10.7	14.5	16.7	0.90	6.25
13/16	12.7	17.0	19.5		7.0
7/8	15.0	20.0	22.4	1.23	8.0
1	18.0	26.4	27.0	1.60	10.0
1 1/8	23.8	34.0	36.0	2.03	13.0
1 1/4	27.0	40.0	41.6	2.50	16.0
1 5/16	30.4	45.0	47.8		17.5
1 3/8				3.03	19.0
1 1/2	38.4	55.0	60.0	3.60	23.0
1 5/8	47.6	66.5	74.5		28.0
1 3/4	59.0	83.0	89.5	4.90	31.0
1 7/8					35.0
2	69.0	95.0	108.0	6.40	40.0

Mousing a Hook

Parbuckling

The Gordian Knot

One day, according to ancient Greek legend, a poor peasant called Gordius arrived in the public square of Phrygia, traveling with his wife in an ox cart. As chance would have it, an oracle had previously informed the people of Phrygia that their future king would come into town riding in a wagon. Therefore the people made Gordius king. In gratitude, Gordius dedicated his ox cart to Zeus, tying it up with a highly intricate knot—the Gordion knot. Some years later another oracle foretold that the person who untied the knot would rule all of Asia.

The Gordian knot resisted all attempts to untie it until the year 333 BC, when Alexander the Great cut through it with a sword. Alexander proceeded to conquer all of Asia Minor and even threatened the Indian sub-continent.

Ever since that time, the Gordian Knot has served as a metaphor for insoluble problems that can only be solved by resorting to unconventional solutions.

Table 24-2 — Length of Rope on a Reel

B
A
C

The following formula is used to estimate the number of feet of rope that can be smoothly wound on a drum or reel. (A, B, and C are in inches).

Length of rope in feet = A x (A + B) x C x K

Note—Depending on the stiffness and cross sectional shape of the rope, these values may vary by as much as 20%.

Values of K in the above equation

Diameter of Rope	Value of K	Diameter of Rope	Value of K
1/4	4.19	1 1/8	0.207
5/16	2.48	1 1/4	0.168
3/8	1.86	1 3/8	0.138
7/16	1.37	1 1/2	0.116
1/2	1.05	1 5/8	0.099
9/16	0.827	1 3/4	0.085
5/8	0.670	1 7/8	0.074
3/4	0.465	2	0.065
7/8	0.342	2 1/8	0.058
1	0.262	2 1/4	0.052

Table 25 — Anchor Tables

Table 25-1 — Wind Pressure Table

The wind force is proportional to the square of the wind speed. Therefore, when the wind speed doubles, the force exerted on your boat (and your anchor rode) quadruples.

Theoretical Velocity Pressure of the Wind

Wind Speed Miles/Hour	Wind Speed Knots	Velocity Pressure Pounds/Square Foot
10	8.7	0.50
30	26.1	4.50
35	30.5	6.13
40	34.8	8.00
45	39.1	10.13
50	43.5	12.50
55	47.8	15.13
60	52.2	18.00
65	56.5	21.13
70	60.1	24.50
75	65.2	28.13
100	86.9	50.00
125	108.6	78.00

Rule of Thumb

The approximate force in pounds per square foot is .005 times the square of the wind speed in miles per hour. The resulting actual force exerted on an object is further influenced by the aerodynamic drag of the object and its orientation to the wind.

Table 25-2 below assumes boats of average beam and windage. If your boat has above average beam or windage, refer to loads for the next larger size boat.

Table 25-2 — Wind Speed vs Anchor Loads

Static Load on Anchor in Pounds

Wind Speed (Knots)	Length in Feet							
	20 ft	25 ft	30 ft	35 ft	40 ft	50 ft	60 ft	70 ft
15	90	125	175	225	300	400	500	675
30	360	490	700	900	1,200	1,600	2,000	2,700
42	720	980	1,400	1,800	2,400	3,200	4,000	5,400
60	1,440	1,960	2,800	3,600	4,800	6,400	8,000	10,800

Static Load on Anchor in Kilograms

Wind Speed (Knots)	Length in Meters							
	6m	8m	9m	11m	12m	15m	18m	21m
15	41	57	79	102	136	181	227	306
30	163	222	318	408	544	726	907	1,225
42	327	445	635	816	1,089	1,452	1,814	2,449
60	653	889	1,270	1,633	2,177	2,903	3,629	4,899

- A “Lunch Hook” should be able to hold your boat in a 15 knot breeze.
- A main, or “Working Anchor” should hold up to 30 knots of wind.
- A “Storm Anchor” should hold up to 42 knots.
- Beyond 42 knots, anchor loads increase dramatically.

Table 26 — Holding Power Values for Sizing Anchor Hardware

Maximum Dimensions of Vessel			Holding Power Required				Chain	Rode
Length Overall	Beam: Sail	Beam: Power	Permanent Mooring	Storm Anchor	Working Anchor	Lunch Hook	Diameter*	Diameter* (Nylon)
ft (m)	ft (m)	ft (m)	lbs (kg)	lbs (kg)	lbs (kg)	lbs (kg)	In (mm)	In (mm)
10 (3)	**4** (1.2)	**5** (1.5)	**480** (218)	**320** (145)	**160** (73)	**40** (18)	**3/16** (5)	**5/16** (8)
15 (4.6)	**5** (1.5)	**6** (1.8)	**750** (341)	**500** (227)	**250** (113)	**60** (27)	**3/16** (5)	**3/8** (10)
20 (6.1)	**7** (2.1)	**8** (2.4)	**1080** (491)	**720** (327)	**360** (164)	**90** (41)	**1/4** (7)	**7/16** (11)
25 (7.6)	**8** (2.4)	**9** (2.7)	**1470** (668)	**980** (445)	**490** (223)	**125** (57)	**1/4** (7)	**7/16** (11)
30 (9.1)	**9** (2.7)	**11** (3.4)	**2100** (955)	**1400** (636)	**700** (318)	**175** (80)	**5/16** (8)	**1/2** (13)
35 (10.7)	**10** (3.0)	**13** (4.0)	**2700** (1227)	**1800** (818)	**900** (409)	**225** (102)	**3/8** (10)	**5/8** (16)
40 (12.2)	**11** (3.4)	**14** (4.3)	**3600** (1636)	**2400** (1091)	**1200** (545)	**300** (136)	**1/2** (13)	**5/8** (16)
50 (15.2)	**13** (4.0)	**16** (4.9)	**4800** (2182)	**3200** (1455)	**1600** (727)	**400** (182)	**1/2** (13)	**3/4** (19)
60 (18.3)	**15** (4.6)	**18** (5.5)	**6000** (2727)	**4000** (1818)	**2000** (909)	**500** (227)	**5/8** (16)	**7/8** (22)

(After the American Boat and Yacht Council 2000. Chain and rode specifications from other sources.)

- When using this table by length overall or by beam of the vessel, use whichever gives the highest holding power.
- Once you have determined the holding power required from the table, refer to the manufacturer's specifications for the holding power of a specific anchor.
- Anchor styles and specifications vary significantly so it is not possible to compare all anchors in a single table.
- Manufacturer's specifications of holding power tests generally assume a straight line pull—which does not reflect the real conditions an anchor experiences.

The values in the table above assume that the vessel is anchored with reasonable protection from the sea, fair holding ground and operation at a scope adequate to develop the full holding power of the anchor.

*For length of rode and chain refer to Table 27. Rode and chain diameters are based on the holding power required for a storm anchor for a vessel of the appropriate size (also refer to Table 25-2).

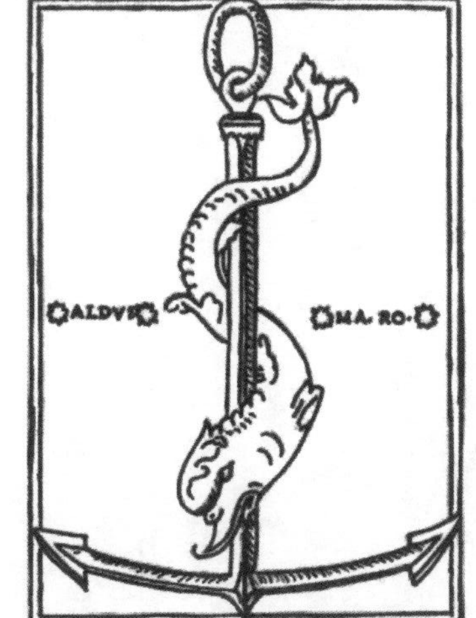
ALDVS
MA. RO.

The famous anchor and dolphin device of Aldus Manutius, one of the greatest early printers

Table 27 — Length of Anchor Rode/Swinging Radius for Various Water Depths

Sudden gusts can impose shock loads that may double or triple the load on the anchor unless the rode is capable of managing the shock. A combination of chain and nylon line works well to absorb shock loads. Nylon line absorbs shock loads by stretching. The chain does so by absorbing energy as it is lifted off the bottom by the strain on the rode. The chain also helps to maintain a horizontal pull on the anchor.

If the shank of the anchor rises 10 degrees off the sea bed, the anchor's maximum holding power is reduced to 60% of its maximum holding power. At 15 degrees it is further reduced to only 40%.

Vessels with all fibre rode should use a 10:1 scope. Vessels with a combination of chain and nylon may use 7:1 scope. Vessels over 50 ft/16 m with an all chain rode may use 5:1 scope. In fair conditions you may reduce the scope. This may also be necessary in crowded anchorages.

The accompanying tables indicate the swinging radius of a vessel when the rode has been fully straightened by the force of the wind. At this time the rode will have lifted almost entirely off the bottom. As a result, when you approach the extreme limits of swinging radius, your anchor may be about to drag; if it hasn't done so already.

The table also indicates the length of rode required in order to maintain a certain scope at various depths both in feet and in meters (next page).

These tables apply only when using a single anchor.

Length of Anchor Rode/Swinging Radius for Various Water Depths (Feet)

Scope	10 : 1		7 : 1		5 : 1		3 : 1	
Water Depth in Feet (Including height of bow roller above the surface)	Length of Rode	Swinging Radius	Length of Rode	Swinging Radius	Length of Rode	Swinging Radius	Length of Rode	Swinging Radius
5	50	49.7	35	34.6				
10	100	99.5	70	69.3	50	49.0		
15	150	149.2	105	103.9	75	73.5	45	42.4
20	200	199.0	140	138.6	100	98.0	60	56.6
25	250	248.7	175	173.2	125	122.5	75	70.7
30	300	298.5	210	207.8	150	147.0	90	84.9
35	350	348.2	245	242.5	175	171.5	105	99.0
40	400	398.0	280	277.1	200	196.0	120	113.1
45	450	447.7	315	311.8	225	220.5	135	127.3
50			350	346.4	250	244.9	150	141.4
60			420	415.7	300	293.9	180	169.7
70			490	485.0	350	342.9	210	198.0
80					400	391.9	240	226.3
90					450	440.9	270	254.6
100					500	489.9	300	282.8
110							330	311.1
120							360	339.4
130							390	367.7
140							420	396.0
150							450	424.3

Anchor drawings from *Nordisk familjebok*, 1878.

Length of Anchor Rode/Swinging Radius for Various Water Depths (Meters)

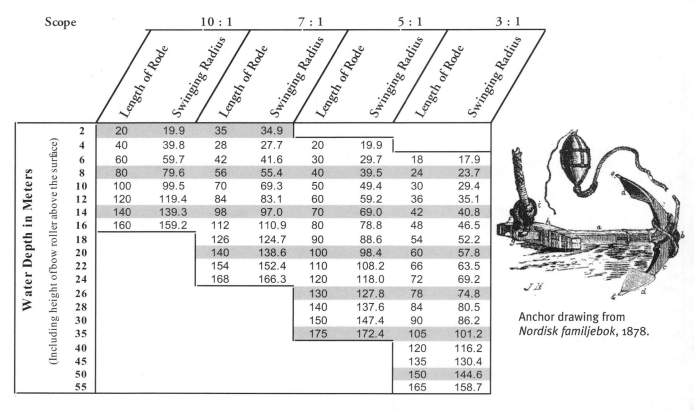

Scope	10 : 1		7 : 1		5 : 1		3 : 1	
Water Depth in Meters (Including height of bow roller above the surface)	Length of Rode	Swinging Radius	Length of Rode	Swinging Radius	Length of Rode	Swinging Radius	Length of Rode	Swinging Radius
2	20	19.9	35	34.9				
4	40	39.8	28	27.7	20	19.9		
6	60	59.7	42	41.6	30	29.7	18	17.9
8	80	79.6	56	55.4	40	39.5	24	23.7
10	100	99.5	70	69.3	50	49.4	30	29.4
12	120	119.4	84	83.1	60	59.2	36	35.1
14	140	139.3	98	97.0	70	69.0	42	40.8
16	160	159.2	112	110.9	80	78.8	48	46.5
18			126	124.7	90	88.6	54	52.2
20			140	138.6	100	98.4	60	57.8
22			154	152.4	110	108.2	66	63.5
24			168	166.3	120	118.0	72	69.2
26					130	127.8	78	74.8
28					140	137.6	84	80.5
30					150	147.4	90	86.2
35					175	172.4	105	101.2
40							120	116.2
45							135	130.4
50							150	144.6
55							165	158.7

Anchor drawing from *Nordisk familjebok*, 1878.

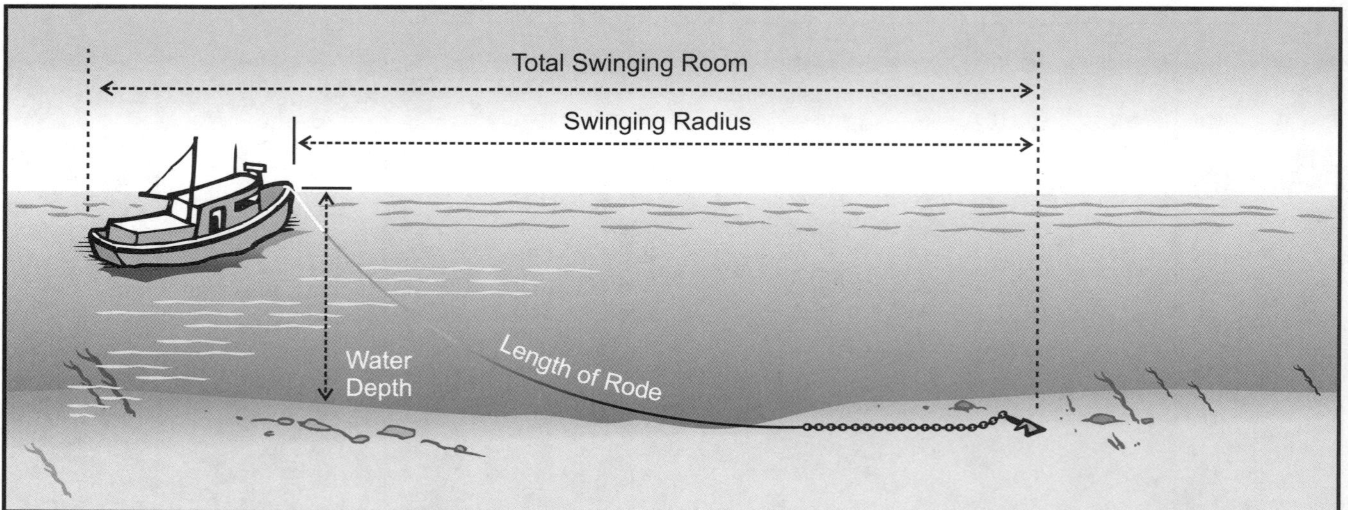
Total Swinging Room
Swinging Radius
Water Depth
Length of Rode

Figure 27-1

- Add the length of your boat to the Swinging Radius to obtain the total Swinging Room required for your boat.
- Add the height of the bow roller to the water depth to obtain the total water depth to enter into the table.

Expert advice varies as to how much chain to use as a minimum. Some advise using a length of chain equal to half the length of your boat, while others advise using 6 ft/2m of chain for every 25 ft/8m of water depth. If you use more chain (up to one third the length of the rode) you will be able to use shorter scope to achieve the same horizontal angle of pull on the anchor.

PART V

COMMUNICATIONS AND COLLISION AVOIDANCE

Table 28 — VHF Channel Assignments in Canada and the United States

Chan	Ship Tx (MHz)	Ship Rx (MHz)	Area	Use
01	156.050	160.650	IC	Public Radio-Telephone
02	156.100	160.700	IC	Public Radio-Telephone
03	156.150	160.750	IC	Public Radio-Telephone
04	156.200	160.800	I	Public Radio-Telephone
04A	156.200		C	CCG
05	156.250	160.850	I	Public Radio-Telephone
06	156.300			Intership—Safety
07	156.050	160.650		Public Radio-Telephone
07A	156.350			Intership-Ship/Shore—Commercial
08	156.400			Intership—Commercial
09	156.450			Intership-Ship/Shore
10	156.500			Intership-Ship/Shore—Commercial
11	156.550			Vessel Traffic Management
12	156.600			Vessel Traffic Management
13	156.650			Bridge to Bridge—Safety of Navigation
14	156.700			Vessel Traffic Management
15	156.750			EPIRB Buoy
16	**156.800**			**Distress/Safety/Calling**
17	156.850			Pilotage—Vessel Docking/Maneuvers
18	156.900	161.500	I	Port Operation
18A	156.900			Intership-Ship/Shore—Commercial
19	156.950	161.550	I	Port Operation
19A	156.950			Port Operation
20	157.000			Port Operation
21	157.050	161.650	I	Port Operation
21A	157.050		A	USCG—Authorized Stations
21B	161.650		C	(CCG Weather Broadcasts)
22	157.100	161.700	I	Port Operation
22A	157.100		CA	USCG/CCG—Public Working Frequency
23	157.150	161.750	IC	Ship/Shore Telephone (Canada)
23A	157.150			Port Operation—USCG
24	157.200	161.800		Public Radio-Telephone
25	157.250	161.850		Public Radio-Telephone
26	157.300	161.900		Public Radio-Telephone
27	157.350	161.950		Public Radio-Telephone
28	157.400	162.000		Public Radio-Telephone
60	156.025	160.625	IC	Public Radio-Telephone
61	156.075	160.675	I	Public Radio-Telephone
61A	156.075		C	Intership-Ship/Shore—CCG
62	156.125	160.725	I	Public Radio-Telephone
62A	156.125		C	Intership-Ship/Shore—CCG
63	156.175	160.775	I	Public Correspondence
63A	156.175		C	Intership-Ship/Shore—Commercial
64	156.225	160.825	IC	Public Radio-Telephone
65	156.275	160.875	I	Public Radio-Telephone
65A	156.275		CA	Port Operation—CCG
66	156.325	160.925	I	Public Radio-Telephone
66A	156.325			Marinas in BC and Washington State
67	156.375			Intership-Ship/Shore
68	156.425			Intership-Ship/Shore—Non-commercial
69	156.475			Intership-Ship/Shore
70	**156.525**			**Digital Selective Calling—Distress/Safety**
71	156.575			Vessel Traffic Management/Pilotage

Area Column

I: Means International only

C: Means Canadian usage

A: American usage—may also be used in Canada for same purpose.

Simplex/Duplex Operation

Duplex channels use separate frequencies for transmitting and receiving; whereas, **simplex** channels do not. Duplex channels are normally reserved for ship-to-shore use.

When operating on channels identified with an "A" suffix (US mode), North American VHF radios both broadcast and receive (simplex operation) on the frequency normally reserved as the ship transmit side of an International duplex channel.

Canada uses a "B" suffix to denote a channel that is limited to one-way broadcast from shore or from official radio stations. Commercially available VHF radios do not transmit on "B" channels; they can only receive.

Phonetic Alphabet

Letters		Numerals
Alpha	November	1—Wun
Bravo	Oscar	2—Two
Charlie	Papa	3—Thu-ree
Delta	Quebec	4—Fo-wer
Echo	Romeo	5—Five
Foxtrot	Sierra	6—Six
Golf	Tango	7—Se-ven
Hotel	Uniform	8—Ait
India	Victor	9—Niner
Juliette	Whiskey	0—Zee-roe
Kilo	X-ray	
Lima	Yankee	
Mike	Zulu	

A decimal is indicated by the word Decimal.

The distress and calling frequency on Medium Frequency SSB is 2182 KHz.

Most modern Emergency Position Indicating Radio Beacons (EPIRB) broadcast on 121.5 MHz and 406 MHz.

Channel	Ship Tx (MHz)	Ship Rx (MHz)	Area	Use
72	156.625			Intership
73	156.675			Intership-Ship/Shore
74	156.725			Vessel Traffic Management
77	156.875			Pilotage
78	156.925	161.525		Port Operation
78A	156.925			Intership-Commercial Fishing
79	156.975	161.575	I	Port Operation
79A	156.975			Intership-Ship/Shore—Commercial
79B		161.575	C	Commercial Fishing—Receive Only
80	157.025	161.625	I	Port Operation
80A	157.025			Intership-Ship/Shore—Commercial
81	157.075	161.675	I	Port Operation
81A	157.075		A	USCG (CCG Anti-pollution)
82	157.125	161.725	I	Port Operation, Ship/Shore Telephone
82A	157.125		A	Port Operation—USCG/CCG
83	157.175	161.775	I	Ship/Shore Telephone—CCG
83A	157.225		A	Intership, Port Operation—USCG
84	157.225	161.825		Public Radio-Telephone
85	157.275	161.875		Public Radio-Telephone
86	157.325	161.925		Public Radio-Telephone
87	157.375	161.975		Public Radio-Telephone
88	157.425	162.025	IC	Public Radio-Telephone
88A	157.425		A	Intership

Weather Channels

Wx1	162.550 MHz
Wx2	162.400 MHz
Wx3	162.475 MHz
Wx4	162.425 MHz
Wx5	162.450 MHz
Wx6	162.500 MHz
Wx7	162.525 MHz
and in Canada	
21B	161.650

Channel 66A was recently assigned by Industry Canada to marina traffic, in order to provide a consistent channel for marina communications throughout the Pacific Northwest. However, many marinas may still use channels 68 or 69, and in Puget Sound some use channel 78A. The Port of Seattle's Shilshole Bay Marina uses channel 17.

Range of VHF Transmissions

In general, VHF frequencies are line of sight. A VHF antenna can only receive from or send to an antenna that is "visible" above the radio horizon. The VHF radio horizon is approximately 15% further away than the visible horizon, and VHF frequencies often reach further than the theoretical horizon distance by a significant amount, because VHF radio waves bend downward in response to atmospheric effects. But antenna height still has a profound effect on transmission range. (Use **Table 9** to estimate the maximum range between two VHF antennas).

Low power hand-held radios broadcasting at three to five watts do not have the power to reach the horizon, so they are limited by broadcast power, not by the horizon. Most radio technicians roughly estimate the practical range of a VHF to be about ***one mile per watt of broadcast power.***

Table 29 — Vessel Traffic Services

Channel Assignments

Vancouver Harbour/Howe Sound	**Channel 12**	*Vancouver Traffic*
Fraser River	**Channel 74**	*Victoria Traffic*
Strait of Juan de Fuca *(East of 124°40'W and north of Nodule Pt, Marrowstone Island)*	**Channel 05A**	*Seattle Traffic*
Puget Sound *(South of Possession Pt, Whidbey Island, or Nodule Pt, Marrowstone Island)*	**Channel 14**	*Seattle Traffic*
Gulf Islands and southern Strait of Georgia *(Southeast of the Merry Island/Ballenas Island line)*	**Channel 11**	*Victoria Traffic*
Northern Strait of Georgia to Cape Caution *(Northwest of the Merry Island/Ballenas Island line)*	**Channel 71**	*Comox Traffic*
West Coast of Vancouver Island *(West of 124°40'W)*	**Channel 74**	*Tofino Traffic*
North Coast of British Columbia	**Channel 11**	*Prince Rupert Traffic*
Chatham Sound (Prince Rupert)	**Channel 71**	*Prince Rupert Traffic*

Table 29-1 — Vancouver VTS Zone Sector 1 and Seattle Traffic

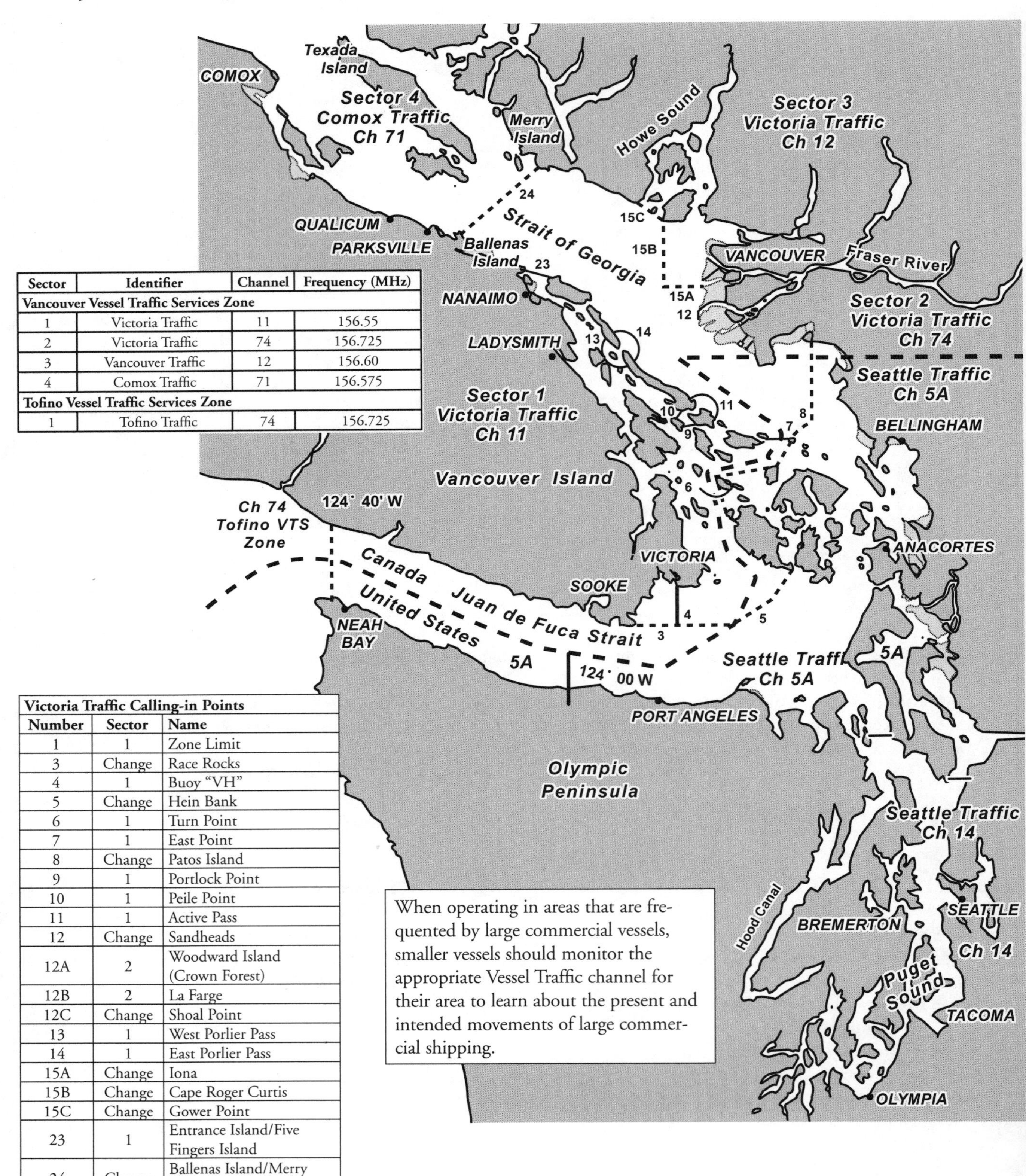
Texada Island
COMOX
Sector 4
Comox Traffic
Ch 71
Merry Island
Howe Sound
Sector 3
Victoria Traffic
Ch 12
24
QUALICUM
PARKSVILLE
Ballenas Island
23
Strait of Georgia
15C
15B
15A
12
VANCOUVER
Fraser River
Sector 2
Victoria Traffic
Ch 74
NANAIMO
LADYSMITH
13
14
Seattle Traffic
Ch 5A
Sector 1
Victoria Traffic
Ch 11
10
11
9
8
7
BELLINGHAM
Vancouver Island
6
Ch 74
Tofino VTS
Zone
124° 40' W
VICTORIA
ANACORTES
SOOKE
Canada
Juan de Fuca Strait
United States
4
5
3
NEAH BAY
5A
124° 00 W
Seattle Traffic
Ch 5A
5A
PORT ANGELES
Olympic
Peninsula
Seattle Traffic
Ch 14
Hood Canal
BREMERTON
SEATTLE
Ch 14
Puget Sound
TACOMA
OLYMPIA

Sector	Identifier	Channel	Frequency (MHz)
Vancouver Vessel Traffic Services Zone			
1	Victoria Traffic	11	156.55
2	Victoria Traffic	74	156.725
3	Vancouver Traffic	12	156.60
4	Comox Traffic	71	156.575
Tofino Vessel Traffic Services Zone			
1	Tofino Traffic	74	156.725

Victoria Traffic Calling-in Points		
Number	Sector	Name
1	1	Zone Limit
3	Change	Race Rocks
4	1	Buoy "VH"
5	Change	Hein Bank
6	1	Turn Point
7	1	East Point
8	Change	Patos Island
9	1	Portlock Point
10	1	Peile Point
11	1	Active Pass
12	Change	Sandheads
12A	2	Woodward Island (Crown Forest)
12B	2	La Farge
12C	Change	Shoal Point
13	1	West Porlier Pass
14	1	East Porlier Pass
15A	Change	Iona
15B	Change	Cape Roger Curtis
15C	Change	Gower Point
23	1	Entrance Island/Five Fingers Island
24	Change	Ballenas Island/Merry Island/Welcome Passage

When operating in areas that are frequented by large commercial vessels, smaller vessels should monitor the appropriate Vessel Traffic channel for their area to learn about the present and intended movements of large commercial shipping.

Table 29-2 — Vancouver VTS Zone Sector 4 and Tofino VTS Zone

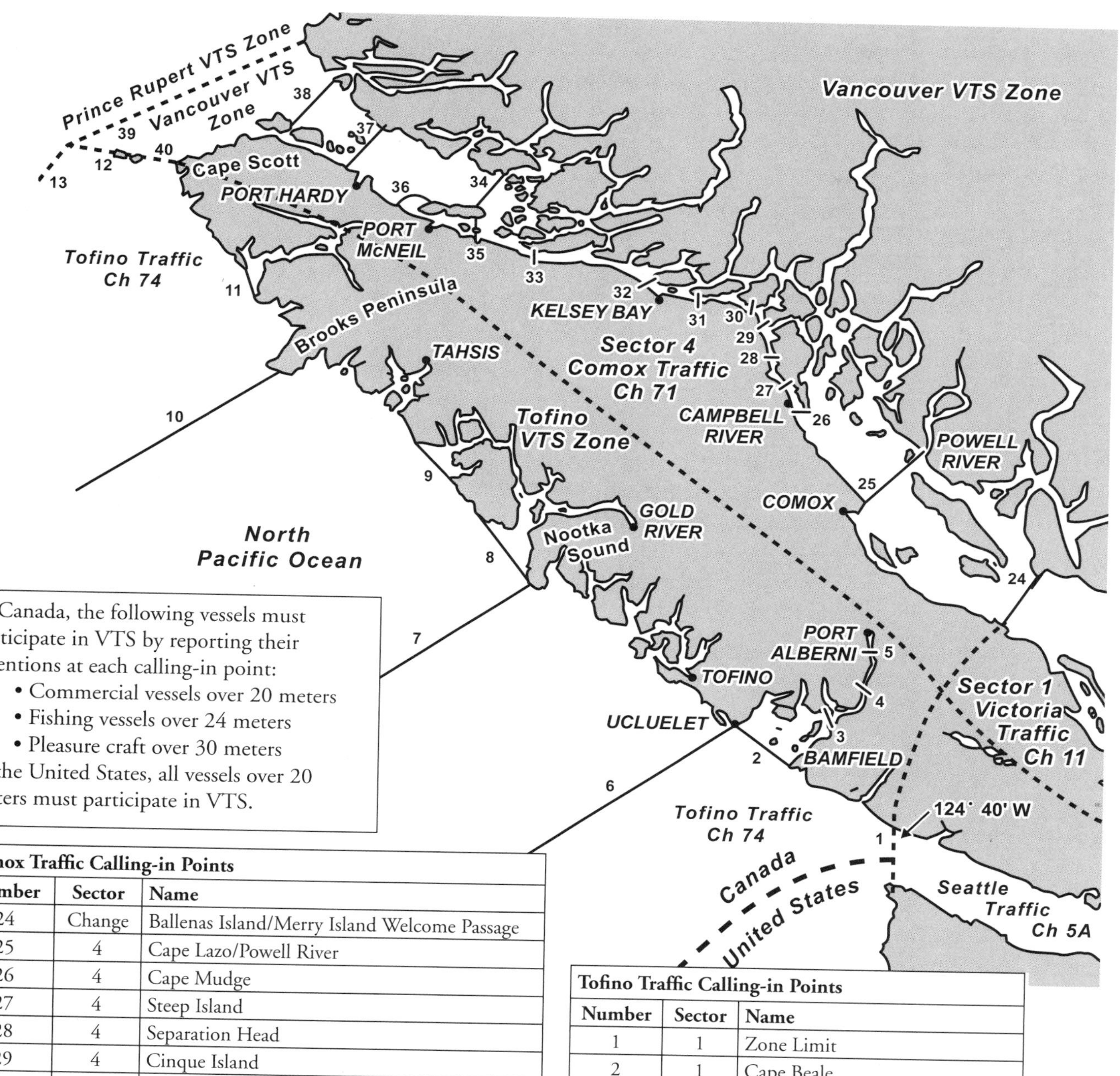
Prince Rupert VTS Zone
Vancouver VTS Zone
Vancouver VTS Zone
Cape Scott
PORT HARDY
PORT McNEIL
Tofino Traffic Ch 74
Brooks Peninsula
KELSEY BAY
Sector 4 Comox Traffic Ch 71
TAHSIS
Tofino VTS Zone
CAMPBELL RIVER
POWELL RIVER
COMOX
GOLD RIVER
Nootka Sound
North Pacific Ocean
PORT ALBERNI
TOFINO
UCLUELET
BAMFIELD
Sector 1 Victoria Traffic Ch 11
124° 40' W
Tofino Traffic Ch 74
Canada
United States
Seattle Traffic Ch 5A

In Canada, the following vessels must participate in VTS by reporting their intentions at each calling-in point:

- Commercial vessels over 20 meters
- Fishing vessels over 24 meters
- Pleasure craft over 30 meters

In the United States, all vessels over 20 meters must participate in VTS.

Comox Traffic Calling-in Points

Number	Sector	Name
24	Change	Ballenas Island/Merry Island Welcome Passage
25	4	Cape Lazo/Powell River
26	4	Cape Mudge
27	4	Steep Island
28	4	Separation Head
29	4	Cinque Island
30	4	Ripple Point
31	4	Vansittart Point
32	4	Fanny Island
33	4	Boat Bay
34	4	Lizard Point
35	4	Lewis Point (Blinkhorne Light)
36	4	Pulteney Point
37	4	Doyle Island
38	4	Pine Island
39	Change	Cape Caution /Triangle Island
40	Change	Cape Scott

Tofino Traffic Calling-in Points

Number	Sector	Name
1	1	Zone Limit
2	1	Cape Beale
3	1	Chup Point
4	1	Ten Mile Point
5	1	Dunsmuir Point
6	1	Amphitrite Point
7	1	Estevan Point
8	1	Nootka Sound
9	1	Esperanza Inlet
10	1	Solander Island
11	1	Kains Island (Quatsino Sound)
12	1	Cape Scott/Triangle Island
13	1	Zone Limit

Table 29-3 — Vancouver VTS Zone Sectors 2 and 3

Vancouver Traffic Calling-in Points		
Number	**Sector**	**Name**
15A	Change	Iona
15B	Change	Cape Roger Curtis
15C	Change	Gower Point
16	3	Halkett Point
17	3	Grace Island
18	3	Cowan Point/Point Atkinson
19	3	Dundarave
20	3	Vanterm
21	3	Berry Point
22	3	Roche Point

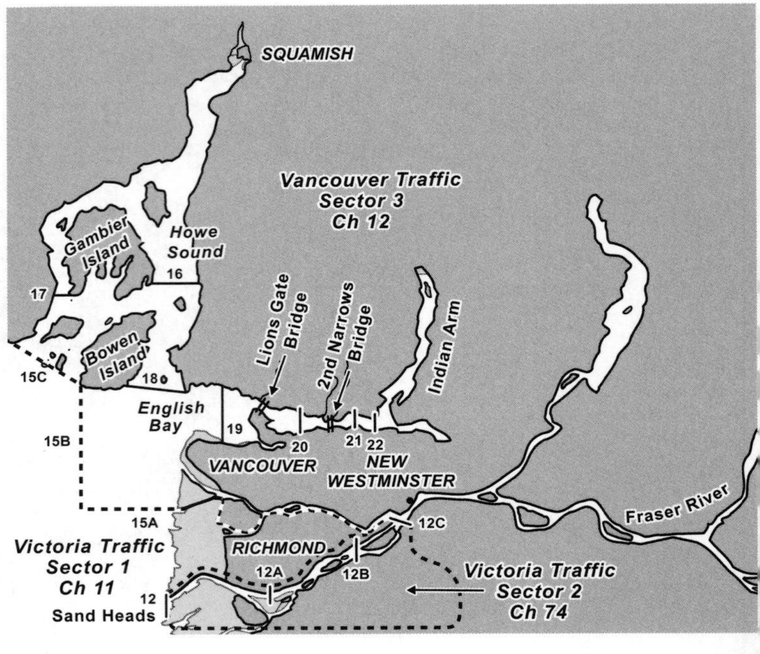
SQUAMISH
Vancouver Traffic
Sector 3
Ch 12
Gambier
Island
Howe
Sound
16
17
Lions Gate
Bridge
2nd Narrows
Bridge
Indian Arm
Bowen
Island
18
15C
English
Bay
15B
19
20
21
22
VANCOUVER
NEW
WESTMINSTER
Fraser River
15A
12C
Victoria Traffic
Sector 1
Ch 11
RICHMOND
12A
12B
Victoria Traffic
Sector 2
Ch 74
12
Sand Heads

Victoria Traffic Calling-in Points		
Number	**Sector**	**Name**
12	Change	Sand Heads
12A	2	Woodward Island (Crown Forest)
12B	2	La Farge
12C	Change	Shoal Point
15A	Change	Iona
15B	Change	Cape Roger Curtis
15C	Change	Gower Point

Table 29-4 — Prince Rupert VTS Zone Sectors 1 and 2

Prince Rupert Vessel Traffic Services Zone—Calling-In Points

Number	Sector	Name	Number	Sector	Name
1A	Change	Cape Caution/Triangle Island	16	2	Lucy Islands
1B	1	Dugout Rocks	17	2	Pillsbury Point
1C	1	Pearl Rocks	18	2	Edye Passage
2	1	Fog Rocks	19	Change	Wales Island
3	1	Walker Island	20A	2	Butterworth Rocks
4	1	Barba Point	20B	Change	Seal Rocks
5	1	Idol Point	21	Change	Rose Spit/Seal Rocks
6	1	Freeman Point	22	2	Rose Spit
7	1	Ditmars Point	23	1	Int'l Boundary/Dixon Entrance
8	1	Griffin Point	24	Change	Langara Point/Point Cornwallis
9	1	Kingcome Point	25	1	Langara Island
10	1	Money Point	26	1	Tasu Sound
11	1	Sainty Point	27	1	Cape St. James
12	1	Pitt Island Light	28	1	McInnes Island/Cape St. James
13A	Change	Baker Inlet	29	1	Cape Mark/McInnes Island
13B	Change	Swede Point	30	1	Bonilla Island/Sandspit
14A	2	Lawyer Islands	31	1	Lawn Point
14B	2	Genn Islands	32	1	White Rocks
15A	2	Petrel Rock	33	1	Duckers Islands
15B	2	Greentop Islet	34	1	Wilson Rock
15C	2	Holland Rock	35	Change	Triangle Island

Table 29-4 — Prince Rupert VTS Zone Sectors 1 and 2 *(continued)*

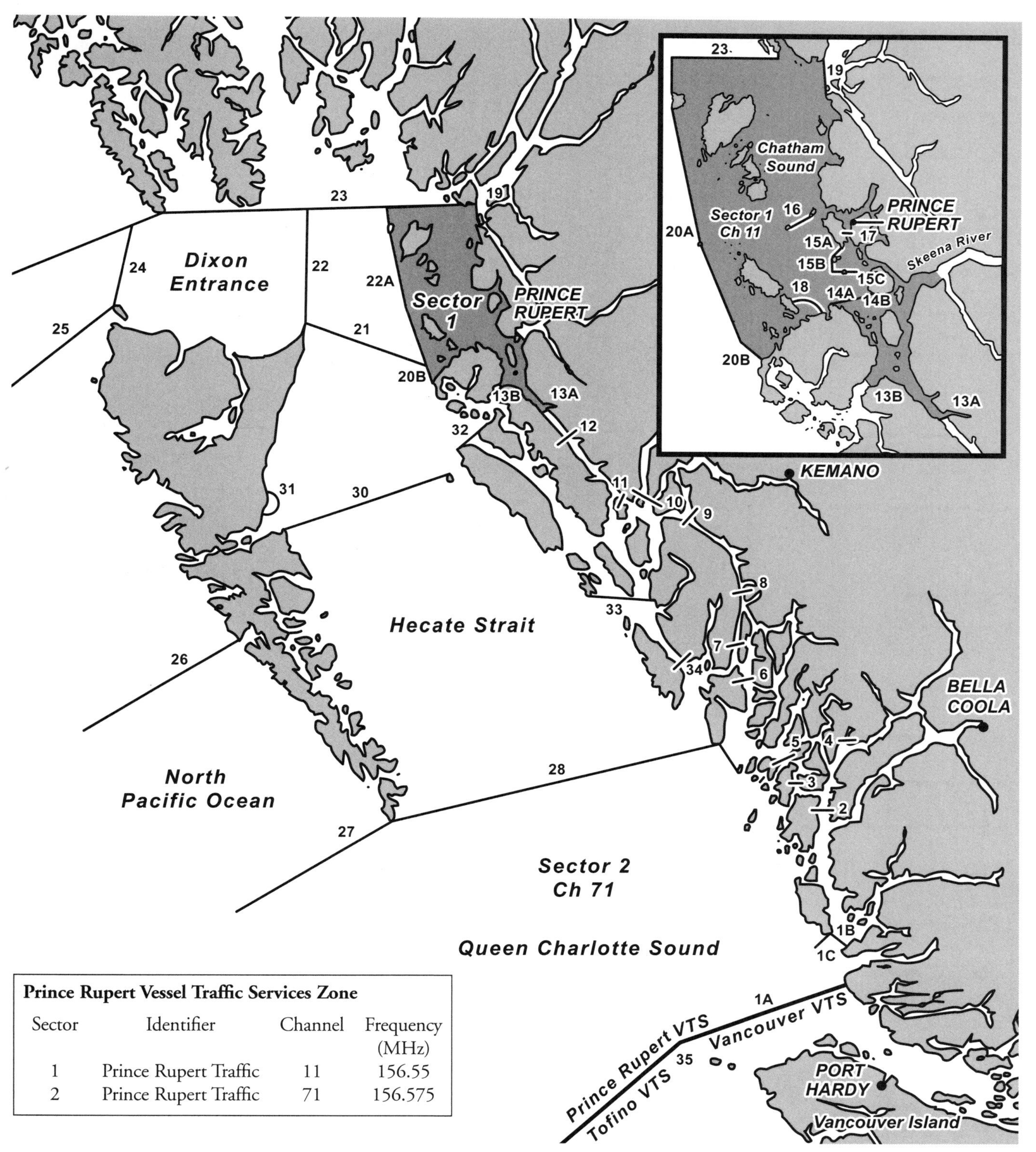
Dixon Entrance
Hecate Strait
North Pacific Ocean
Queen Charlotte Sound
Sector 1
Sector 2
Ch 71
PRINCE RUPERT
KEMANO
BELLA COOLA
PORT HARDY
Vancouver Island
Prince Rupert VTS
Vancouver VTS
Tofino VTS
Chatham Sound
Sector 1
Ch 11
Skeena River
1A
1B
1C
2
3
4
5
6
7
8
9
10
11
12
13A
13B
14A
14B
15A
15B
15C
16
17
18
19
20A
20B
21
22
22A
23
24
25
26
27
28
30
31
32
33
34
35

Prince Rupert Vessel Traffic Services Zone

Sector	Identifier	Channel	Frequency (MHz)
1	Prince Rupert Traffic	11	156.55
2	Prince Rupert Traffic	71	156.575

Table 30 — Whistle Signals
Maneuvering and Fog Signals from the International Collision Regulations

When vessels are in sight of one another

Signal	Meaning
——	Any vessel on nearing a bend
——	Response is the same
——	Power-driven vessel on leaving a berth
	When maneuvering for collision avoidance
–	"I am altering to starboard"
– –	"I am altering to port"
– – –	"I am operating astern propulsion"
– – – – –	"Danger—I do not understand/You are not taking appropriate action"
	When overtaking in a Narrow Channel
—— —— –	"I intend to pass on your starboard side"
—— —— – –	"I intend to pass on your port side"
—— – —— –	"I agree with your proposal"

Fog Signals

Made at two-minute intervals. In restricted visibility, no other sound signals are to be made. Bell and gong signals are to be made at one-minute intervals.

Signal	Meaning
——	Power-driven vessel making way
—— ——	Power-driven vessel not making way
—— – –	Vessel engaged in towing
—— – – –	Last vessel in a tow (if manned)
—— – –	Fishing vessel, sailing vessel, vessel restricted in its ability to maneuver, or not under command
5 seconds or – —— –	Vessel at anchor (if over 100 meters in length, must also sound a gong for five seconds immediately after the bell)
3 strokes 5 seconds 3 strokes or – – ——	Vessel aground (if over 100 meters in length, must also sound a gong for five seconds immediately after the bell)
– – – –	A pilot vessel with a pilot on board

PART VI

Miscellaneous Tables

Table 31 — Galvanic Corrosion and the Galvanic Series

Galvanic Corrosion

Galvanic corrosion occurs when two dissimilar metals are in electrical contact with each other in a conductive environment such as flowing sea water. When corrosion occurs, metal ions actually flow from the cathode to the anode. Over time, this movement of metal ions will result in a wasting away of the anode. Either (or both) metals may or may not corrode by themselves in seawater. But when in contact with a dissimilar metal, the self corrosion rates will change:

- Corrosion of the anode will accelerate.
- Corrosion of the cathode will decelerate or even stop.

In general, ***the further apart the materials are in the galvanic series, the higher the risk of galvanic corrosion, and the greater the rate of corrosion will be.***

Caution: The series does not provide any information on specific rates of galvanic corrosion; it is merely an indicator of the tendency to corrode.

Ignoble (Corroded) End **Anode**

Magnesium
Zinc
Aluminum 5052, 3004, 1100, 6053
Cadmium
Aluminum 2117, 2017, 2024
Mild Steel, Wrought Iron
Cast Iron
Low alloy steel
Austenic Nickel Cast Iron
Naval Brass, Yellow Brass, Red Brass
Aluminum Bronze
Lead-Tin Solders
Lead
Tin
Copper
Manganese Bronze
Silicon Bronze
Tin Bronzes, Naval Bronze
Stainless Steel Type 410, 416
90-10 Copper-Nickel Alloy
80-20 Copper-Nickel Alloy
Stainless Steel Type 430
Nickel-Aluminum Bronze
Monel 400, K500
Silver Solder
Nickel
Nickel-Chromium Alloys
Chrome Iron
Stainless Steel Types 302, 303, 304, 321, 347
Stainless Steel Types 316, 317
Titanium
Silver
Graphite
Gold
Platinum

Noble (Protected) End **Cathode**

Chrome Iron and Stainless Steels *in active mode appear here in the series*

Nickel, Nickel-Chromium Alloys *in active mode appear here in the series*

Movement of Metal Ions ↓

When joining dissimilar metals, make sure that they are close to each other on the galvanic scale. If the two metals to be joined are widely separated, corrosion problems can be reduced by the addition of a spacer between the dissimilar metals that falls between them on the galvanic scale, or by the addition of a sacrificial zinc anode.

Certain alloys in low velocity or poorly aerated water, and at shielded areas, may become significantly more active.

When a sacrificial zinc is installed, ions flow from the zinc to the sea water and consequently, the zinc corrodes instead of the bronze or steel propellor and shaft.

The driving force for corrosion is a difference in the electrical potential between the different metals, discovered in the later 1800th century by Luigi Galvani in a series of experiments on the muscles and nerves of frogs.

The galvanic principle was further developed by Allesandro Volta who built the first wet-cell battery in 1800.

Table 32 — Electrical Tables

Table 32-1 — Lead Acid Batteries

Specific Gravity	Charge Level
> 1.30	overcharged
1.26 to 1.28	100%
1.24 to 1.26	75%
1.20 to 1.22	50%
1.15 to 1.17	25%
1.13 to 1.15	very low
1.11 to 1.12	discharged

Temperature	Charge Efficiency
80°F/27°C	100%
50°F/10°C	82%
30°F/-1°C	64%
20°F/-7°C	58%
10°F/-12°C	50%
0°F/-18°C	40%
-10°F/-23°C	33%
-20°F/-29°C	18%

⚠ DANGER/POISON

SHIELD EYES
EXPLOSIVE GASES
CAN CAUSE BLINDNESS OR INJURY

NO
• SPARKS
• FLAMES
• SMOKING

SULFURIC ACID
CAN CAUSE
BLINDNESS OR
SEVERE BURNS

FLUSH EYES
IMEDIATELY
WITH WATER

GET
MEDICAL
HELP FAST

KEEP OUT OF REACH OF CHILDREN. DO NOT TIP. KEEP VENT CAPS TIGHT AND LEVEL.

Be careful when working around lead-acid batteries. They contain sulphuric acid—a highly corrosive and toxic liquid. Make sure batteries are well ventilated when charging.

Table 32-2 — Wiring Colour Codes for Low Voltage DC Systems

General Wiring

Colour	Use
Green or Green with Yellow Stripe	DC ground
Black or Yellow	DC negative conductors
Red	DC positive conductors

Engine and Accessory Wiring

Colour	Item	Use
Yellow with red stripe (YR)	Starting circuit	Starting switch to solenoid
Brown with yellow stripe (BY) or yellow (Y)	Bilge blowers	Fuse or switch to blowers
Dark Grey (Gy)	Navigation lights Tachometer	Fuse or switch to lights Tachometer sender to gauge
Brown (Br)	Generator armature Alternator charge light Pumps	Generator armature to regulator Generator terminal/alternator terminal to light to regulator Fuse or switch to pumps
Orange (O)	Accessory feed	Ammeter to alternator or generator output and accessory fuses or switches Distribution panel to accessory switch
Purple (Pu)	Ignition Instrument feed	Ignition switch to coil and electrical instruments Distribution panel to electric instruments
Dark Blue	Cabin and instrument lights	Fuse or switch to lights
Light Blue (Lt Bl)	Oil pressure	Oil pressure sender to gauge
Tan	Water temperature	Water temperature sender to gauge
Pink (Pk)	Fuel gauge	Fuel gauge sender to gauge
Green with stripe (except green with yellow)	Tilt down and/or trim in	Tilt and/or trim circuits
Blue with stripe	Tilt up and/or trim out	Tilt and/or trim circuits

Note: If yellow is used for DC negative, blower must be brown with yellow stripe.

Table 32-3 Conductor Sizes for Low Voltage Circuits

12 Volts—3% Voltage Drop

Length of Conductor from Source to Load and Back to Source

Meters	3	4.5	6	8	9	12	15	18	20	25	27	30	33	36	40	43	45	48	52
Feet	10	15	20	25	30	40	50	60	70	80	90	100	110	120	130	140	150	160	170
Total Current in Amps																			
5	18	16	14	12	12	10	10	10	8	8	8	6	6	6	6	6	6	6	6
10	14	12	10	10	10	8	6	6	6	6	4	4	4	4	2	2	2	2	2
15	12	10	10	8	8	6	6	6	4	4	2	2	2	2	2	1	1	1	1
20	10	10	8	6	6	6	4	4	2	2	2	2	1	1	1	0	0	0	2/0
25	10	8	6	6	6	4	4	2	2	2	1	1	0	0	0	2/0	2/0	2/0	3/0
30	10	8	6	6	4	4	2	2	1	1	0	0	0	2/0	2/0	3/0	3/0	3/0	3/0
40	8	6	6	4	4	2	2	1	0	0	2/0	2/0	3/0	3/0	3/0	4/0	4/0	4/0	4/0
50	6	6	4	4	2	2	1	0	2/0	2/0	3/0	3/0	4/0	4/0	4/0				
60	6	4	4	2	2	1	0	2/0	3/0	3/0	4/0	4/0	4/0						
70	6	4	2	2	1	0	2/0	3/0	3/0	4/0	4/0								
80	6	4	2	2	1	0	3/0	3/0	4/0	4/0									
90	4	2	2	1	0	2/0	3/0	4/0	4/0										
100	4	2	2	1	0	2/0	3/0	4/0											

24 Volts—3% Voltage Drop

Length of Conductor from Source to Load and Back to Source

Meters	3	4.5	6	8	9	12	15	18	20	25	27	30	33	36	40	43	45	48	52
Feet	10	15	20	25	30	40	50	60	70	80	90	100	110	120	130	140	150	160	170
Total Current in Amps																			
5	18	18	18	16	16	14	12	12	12	10	10	10	10	10	8	8	8	8	8
10	18	16	14	12	12	10	10	10	8	8	8	6	6	6	6	6	6	6	6
15	16	14	12	12	10	10	8	8	6	6	6	6	6	4	4	4	4	4	2
20	14	12	10	10	10	8	6	6	6	6	4	4	4	4	2	2	2	2	2
25	12	12	10	10	8	6	6	6	4	4	4	4	2	2	2	2	2	2	1
30	12	10	10	8	8	6	6	4	4	4	2	2	2	2	2	1	1	1	1
40	10	10	8	6	6	6	4	4	2	2	2	2	1	1	1	0	0	0	2/0
50	10	8	6	6	6	4	4	2	2	2	1	1	0	0	0	2/0	2/0	2/0	3/0
60	10	8	6	6	4	4	2	2	1	1	0	0	0	2/0	2/0	3/0	3/0	3/0	3/0
70	8	6	6	4	4	2	2	1	1	0	0	2/0	2/0	3/0	3/0	3/0	3/0	4/0	4/0
80	8	6	6	4	4	2	2	1	0	0	2/0	2/0	3/0	3/0	3/0	4/0	4/0	4/0	4/0
90	8	6	4	4	2	2	1	0	0	2/0	2/0	2/0	3/0	4/0	4/0	4/0	4/0	4/0	
100	6	6	4	4	2	2	1	0	2/0	2/0	2/0	3/0	4/0	4/0	4/0				

32 Volts—3% Voltage Drop

Length of Conductor from Source to Load and Back to Source

Meters	3	4.5	6	8	9	12	15	18	20	25	27	30	33	36	40	43	45	48	52
Feet	10	15	20	25	30	40	50	60	70	80	90	100	110	120	130	140	150	160	170
Total Current in Amps																			
5	18	18	18	18	16	16	14	14	12	12	12	12	10	10	10	10	10	10	8
10	18	16	16	14	14	12	12	10	10	10	8	8	8	8	8	6	6	6	6
15	16	14	14	12	12	10	10	8	8	8	6	6	6	6	6	6	6	4	4
20	16	14	12	12	10	10	8	8	6	6	6	6	6	4	4	4	4	4	2
25	14	12	12	10	10	8	8	6	6	6	6	4	4	4	4	2	2	2	2
30	14	12	10	10	8	8	6	6	6	4	4	4	4	2	2	2	1	1	1
40	12	10	10	8	8	6	6	4	4	4	2	2	2	2	2	1	1	1	1
50	12	10	8	8	6	6	4	4	2	2	2	2	2	1	1	0	0	0	0
60	10	8	8	6	6	4	4	2	2	2	2	1	1	0	0	0	2/0	2/0	2/0
70	10	8	6	6	6	4	2	2	2	1	1	0	0	0	2/0	2/0	2/0	3/0	3/0
80	10	8	6	6	4	4	2	2	1	1	0	0	0	2/0	2/0	3/0	3/0	3/0	3/0
90	8	6	6	6	4	2	2	2	1	0	0	2/0	2/0	2/0	3/0	3/0	3/0	4/0	4/0
100	8	6	6	4	4	2	2	1	0	0	2/0	2/0	2/0	3/0	3/0	3/0	4/0	4/0	4/0

Table 33 — Estimating the Weight of Fish

Table 33-1 — To Estimate Weight of Pacific Halibut by Length

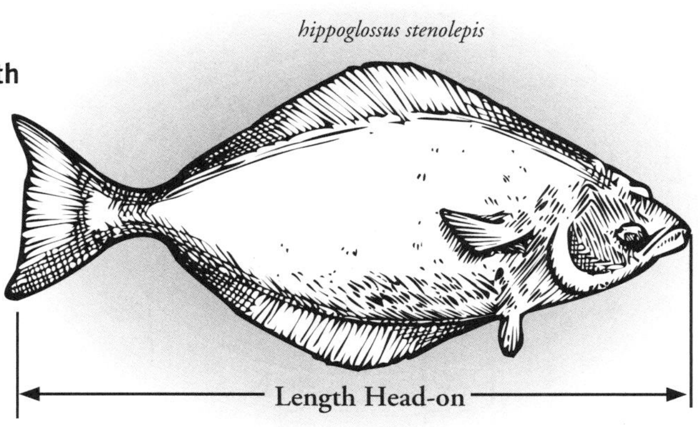
hippoglossus stenolepis
Length Head-on

This table gives the weight of whole uncleaned fish. To estimate head-off, dressed weight multiply the round weight by 75%.

"Don't be in a rush to measure a fish. The longer you wait the longer the fish."

Length (Head On)		Round Weight	
inches	cm	lb	kg
20	51	3.1	1.4
21	53	3.6	1.6
22	56	4.2	1.9
23	58	4.9	2.2
24	61	5.6	2.5
25	64	6.4	2.9
26	66	7.2	3.3
27	69	8.2	3.7
28	71	9.2	4.2
29	74	10.3	4.7
30	76	11.5	5.2
31	79	12.8	5.8
32	81	14.2	6.4
33	84	15.7	7.1
34	86	17.3	7.8
35	89	19	8.6
36	91	21	9.4
37	94	23	10.3
38	97	25	11.2
39	99	27	12.2
40	102	29	13.3
41	104	32	14.4
42	107	34	15.6
43	109	37	16.8
44	112	40	18.1
45	114	43	19.5
46	117	46	21
47	119	49	22
48	122	53	24
49	124	57	26
50	127	60	27
51	130	64	29
52	132	69	31
53	135	73	33
54	137	77	35
55	140	82	37
56	142	87	39
57	145	92	42
58	147	98	44
59	150	103	47
60	152	109	49
61	155	115	52
62	157	121	55
63	160	128	58
64	163	134	61
65	165	141	64
66	168	148	67
67	170	156	71
68	173	163	74
69	175	171	78
70	178	179	81
71	180	188	85
72	183	197	89
73	185	206	93
74	188	215	97
75	191	224	102
76	193	234	106
77	196	244	111
78	198	255	116
79	201	265	120
80	203	277	125
81	206	288	131
82	208	300	136
83	211	312	141
84	213	324	147
85	216	337	153
86	218	350	159
87	221	363	165
88	224	377	171
89	226	391	177
90	229	405	184
91	231	420	190
92	234	435	197
93	236	450	204
94	239	466	211
95	241	482	219
96	244	499	226

Length and weight data provided by the International Pacific Halibut Commission.

Table 33-2 — To Estimate Weight of Pacific Salmon by Length and Girth

This table is based on the formula **Weight = Length x Girth x Girth/775**
Length is measured ***from the nose to the fork of the tail.***
Girth is measured at the thickest part of the fish, ***just in front of the dorsal fin.***

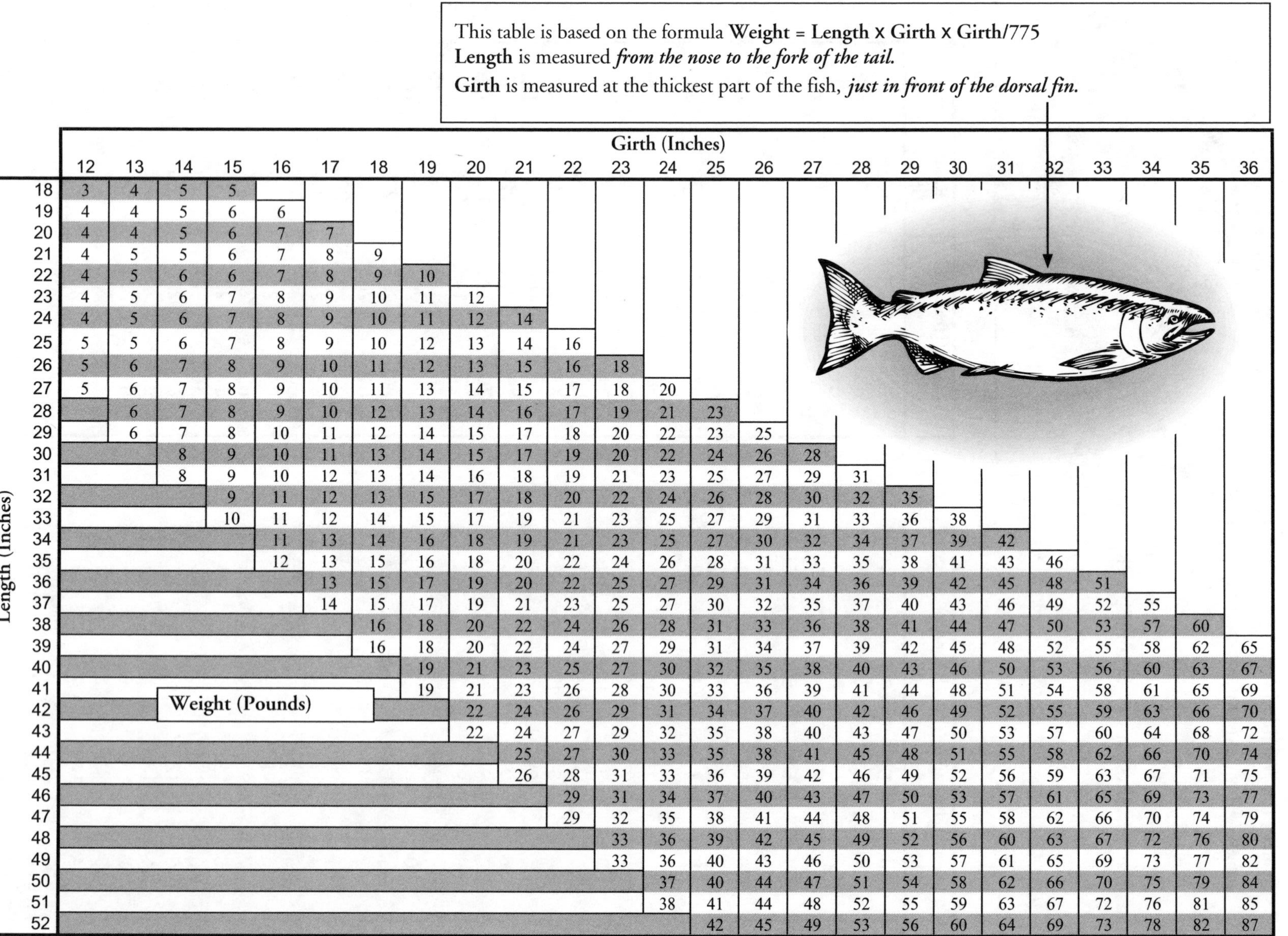

Weight (Pounds)

Length (Inches)	Girth (Inches) 12	13	14	15	16	17	18	19	20	21	22	23	24	25	26	27	28	29	30	31	32	33	34	35	36
18	3	4	5	5																					
19	4	4	5	6	6																				
20	4	4	5	6	7	7																			
21	4	5	5	6	7	8	9																		
22	4	5	6	6	7	8	9	10																	
23	4	5	6	7	8	9	10	11	12																
24	4	5	6	7	8	9	10	11	12	14															
25	5	5	6	7	8	9	10	12	13	14	16														
26	5	6	7	8	9	10	11	12	13	15	16	18													
27	5	6	7	8	9	10	11	13	14	15	17	18	20												
28		6	7	8	9	10	12	13	14	16	17	19	21	23											
29		6	7	8	10	11	12	14	15	17	18	20	22	23	25										
30			8	9	10	11	13	14	15	17	19	20	22	24	26	28									
31			8	9	10	12	13	14	16	18	19	21	23	25	27	29	31								
32				9	11	12	13	15	17	18	20	22	24	26	28	30	32	35							
33				10	11	12	14	15	17	19	21	23	25	27	29	31	33	36	38						
34					11	13	14	16	18	19	21	23	25	27	30	32	34	37	39	42					
35					12	13	15	16	18	20	22	24	26	28	31	33	35	38	41	43	46				
36						13	15	17	19	20	22	25	27	29	31	34	36	39	42	45	48	51			
37						14	15	17	19	21	23	25	27	30	32	35	37	40	43	46	49	52	55		
38							16	18	20	22	24	26	28	31	33	36	38	41	44	47	50	53	57	60	
39							16	18	20	22	24	27	29	31	34	37	39	42	45	48	52	55	58	62	65
40								19	21	23	25	27	30	32	35	38	40	43	46	50	53	56	60	63	67
41								19	21	23	26	28	30	33	36	39	41	44	48	51	54	58	61	65	69
42									22	24	26	29	31	34	37	40	42	46	49	52	55	59	63	66	70
43									22	24	27	29	32	35	38	40	43	47	50	53	57	60	64	68	72
44										25	27	30	33	35	38	41	45	48	51	55	58	62	66	70	74
45										26	28	31	33	36	39	42	46	49	52	56	59	63	67	71	75
46											29	31	34	37	40	43	47	50	53	57	61	65	69	73	77
47											29	32	35	38	41	44	48	51	55	58	62	66	70	74	79
48												33	36	39	42	45	49	52	56	60	63	67	72	76	80
49												33	36	40	43	46	50	53	57	61	65	69	73	77	82
50													37	40	44	47	51	54	58	62	66	70	75	79	84
51													38	41	44	48	52	55	59	63	67	72	76	81	85
52														42	45	49	53	56	60	64	69	73	78	82	87

Bibliography

Admiralty Manual of Seamanship. 1st vol. London: Her Majesty's Stationery Office, 1964.

Bawlf, Samuel. *Sir Francis Drake's Secret Voyage to the Northwest Coast of America, AD 1579.* Salt Spring Island: Sir Francis Drake Publications, 2001.

Burgess, C. R., *Meteorology for Seamen.* Glasgow: Brown, Son, and Ferguson Limited, 1982.

Canadian Hydrographic Service. *Tide and Current Tables, 2004: Discovery Passage and West Coast of Vancouver Island.* 6th vol. Ottawa: Fisheries and Oceans Canada, 2003.

Dugard, Martin. *Farther Than Any Man: The Rise and Fall of Captain James Cook.* New York: Simon and Schuster, 2001.

Fagan, Brian M. *Anchoring.* Camden: International Marine, 1986.

Glover, Thomas J. *Pocket Ref.* Sequoia Publishing Incorporated, Littleton: 1998.

Golden, Frank, and Michael Tipton. *Essentials of Sea Survival.* Windsor: Human Kinetics Books, 2002.

Hilson, Stephen E. *Exploring Alaska and British Columbia, Skagway to Barkley Sound.* Holland: Van Winkle Publishing Company, 1976.

International Building Code. *Uniform Building Code 1997.* 3 vols. Los Angeles: International Code Council, 2003.

Kemp, J. F., and Peter Young. *Notes on Meteorology.* London: Stanford Maritime, 1985.

Lane, Frank W. *Kingdom of the Octopus.* New York: Pyramid Publications Incorporated, 1962.

Lundy, Derek. *The Way of a Ship: A Square Rigger Voyage in the Last Days of Sail.* Toronto: Alfred A Knopf, 2002.

Maloney, Elbert S., and Chapman, Charles Frederic. *Chapman Piloting: Seamanship & Boat Handling.* 63rd ed. New York: Hearst Marine Books, 1999.

Middleton, Robert. *Practical Electricity.* Indianapolis: Theodore Audel & Company, 1975.

Monahan, Kevin, and Don Douglass. *GPS Instant Navigation.* 2nd ed. Anacortes: FineEdge.com, 2000.

Monahan, Kevin, *The Radar Book.* Anacortes: FineEdge.com, 2003.

Newberry, W. G. *Handbook for Riggers.* Revised ed. Calgary: Newberry Investments, 1977.

Phillips, David. *The Canadian Weather Trivia Calendar.* 2004 ed. Calgary: Fifth House Limited, 2003.

Roberts, Charles, and C. E. N. Frankcom. *Maritime Meteorology, A Guide for Deck Officers.* London: Thomas Reed Publications, 1985.

Thompson, Richard E., *Oceanography of the BC Coast.* Canadian Special Publication of Fisheries and Aquatic Sciences 56. Ottawa: Department of Fisheries and Oceans, 1981.

United States Code of Federal Regulations, Title 29, Part 1915, *Standard No. 1915.118, Gear and Equipment for Materials Handling*

Walbran, Captain John T. *British Columbia Coast Names 1592-1906: Their Origin and History.* 1909 ed. Vancouver: J. J. Douglas, Reprint. 1971.

WEBSITES

FineEdge.com LLC, Publishers of this and other fine nautical titles, Anacortes, WA, www.fineedge.com, 2004

Shipwrite Productions, "Marine and Technical Consulting and Publications", the author's web-site, Sidney, BC, www.shipwrite.bc.ca, 2004

The American Boat and Yacht Council, "*Standards & Technical Information Reports—2004,* Edgewater, MD, www.abycinc.org

The Bruce Anchor Group, Douglas, Isle of Man, British Isles, www.bruceanchor.co.uk, 2004

Canadian Coast Guard, Pacific Region, "Marine Communications and Traffic Services", Vancouver, BC, www.pacific.ccg-gcc.gc.ca/mcts-sctm/index_e.htm, 2004

Canadian Coast Guard, "Radio Aids to Marine Navigation", Ottawa ON, www.ccg-gcc.gc.ca/mcts-sctm/docs/ramn_arnm/ramn_arnm_e.htm, 2004

Danforth Marine Anchors, Manufactured by Tie-Down Engineering, Atlanta, GA, www.danforthanchors.com 2004

Discover Vancouver, "The Greater Vancouver Book—Vancouver Stories", Vancouver, BC, www.discovervancouver.com 2004

Douwens, Robert, "Hypothermia Prevention, Recognition and Treatment", Sooke BC, www.hypothermia.org/fieldchart.htm, 2004

Environment Canada, Meteorological Service of Canada, "Canadian Weather Forecasts", Ottawa ON, www.weatheroffice.ec.gc.ca/canada_e.html, 2004

Environment Canada, Meteorological Service of Canada, "Environment Canada's Wind Chill Program", Ottawa ON, www.msc.ec.gc.ca/education/windchill/index_e.cfm, 2004

Fisheries and Oceans Canada, Canadian Hydrographic Service, "Pacific Coast Current Atlas", Otawa ON, http://gp2.chs-shc.dfo-mpo.gc.ca/atlas/, 2004

Intercorr International Ltd., "The One-Stop Materials and Corrosion Information Source", www.corrosionsource.com, 2004

The International Pacific Halibut Commission, "Halibut Length/Weight Chart", Seattle WA, www.iphc.washington.edu/halcom/pubs/bulletin/lenwtmetchart.htm , 1991

The Library and Archives of Canada, Ottawa ON, www.collectionscanada.ca/index-e.html, 2004

The Library of Congress, "Map Collections 1500 – 2004", Washington, DC, memory.loc.gov/ammem/gmdhtml/gmdhome.html, 2004

The McNally Institute, "The Galvanic Series of Metals", Dade City, FL, www.mcnallyinstitute.com/Charts/galvanic-series.html, 2004

The Museum at Campbell River, "The Ripple Rock Story", Campbell River, BC, http://www.crmuseum.ca/exhibits/ripplerock.html, 2004

National Oceanic and Atmospheric Administration, National Weather Service, "The Beaufort Wind Scale", Chicago, IL, www.crh.noaa.gov/lot/webpage/beaufort, 2004

National Oceanic and Atmospheric Administration, National Weather Service, "SE Alaska Forecast Areas", Juneau, AK, www.nws.noaa.gov/om/marine/zone/alaska/ajkmz.htm, 2004

National Oceanic and Atmospheric Administration, National Weather Service, "The United States National Buoy Data Center", Washington, DC, www.ndbc.noaa.gov/rmd.shtml, 2004

National Oceanic and Atmospheric Administration, National Weather Service, "Washington State Forecast Areas", Seattle, WA, www.nws.noaa.gov/om/marine/zone/west/sewmz.htm, 2004

National Oceanic and Atmospheric Administration, National Weather Service, "Wind Chill Temperature Index", Washington, DC, www.nws.noaa.gov/om/windchill/index.shtml, 2004

New England Ropes, "The Leading Manufacturer of Premium Quality Ropes", Fall River MA, www.neropes.com, 2004

Nordisk familjebok, Stockholm, Sweden, www.lysator.liu.se/runeberg/nf/, 1878

Ports and Passes, the complete annual Tide and Current Guide for the Pacific Northwest, Lantzville, BC, www.portsandpasses.com, 2004

rpsoft 2000 software, "Modern Ship Sizes, The Tiny Titanic", www.rpsoft2000.com/shipsize.htm, 2004

Samson Rope Technologies, "The Strongest Name in Rope", Ferndale, WA, www.samsonrope.com/home/newindex.cfm, 2004

United States Coast Guard and Canadian Coast Guard, "Canada/US Cooperative Vessel Traffic Services for the Strait of Juan de Fuca", www.piersystem.com/external/index.cfm?CID=398, 2004

United States Coast Guard, Puget Sound Vessel Traffic Services, Seattle WA, www.uscg.mil/d13/units/vts/psvts.html 2004

United States Coast Guard, "Weather Blanket—USCG High Sites in Alaska", Juneau, AK, www.uscg.mil/d17/Weather_Blanket_Brochure_2003.htm, 2003

United States Geological Service and Microsoft.com, "Microsoft Terraserver Project", www.terraserver.microsoft.com, 2004—the Microsoft aerial photography database.

University of North Carolina, Russ Rowlett, "The Beaufort Scale", Chapel Hill, NC, www.unc.edu/~rowlett/units/scales/beaufort.html, 2004

About the Author

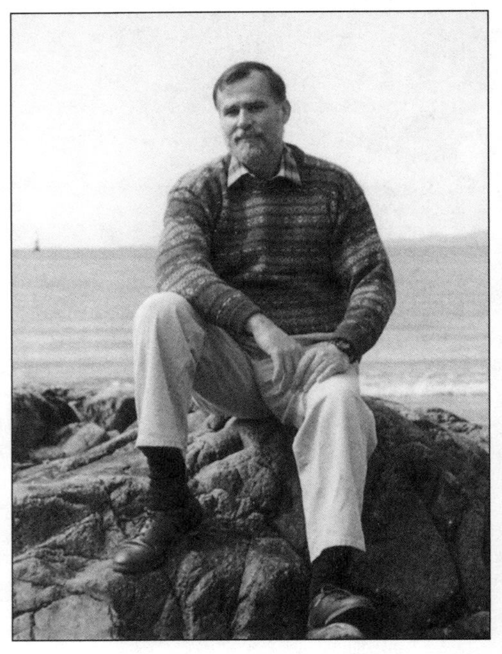

Captain Kevin Monahan is a Canadian Coast Guard officer with over 20 years experience navigating the British Columbia coast as a small-vessel captain. Born in London England in 1951, Monahan—now a resident of Victoria, B.C.—emigrated to Vancouver and attended the University of British Columbia. His articles have appeared in various magazines including *Pacific Yachting, Northwest Yachting,* and the *Fisherman's News* as well as in *West Coast Fisherman* which published a series of his articles on electronic navigation. Captain Monahan was a fisherman for 12 years, after which he worked on ferries and coastal transports, before joining Canada's Department of Fisheries and Oceans as a patrol vessel captain. Captain Monahan is now an officer with the Canadian Coast Guard, having served the last five years in the Office of Boating Safety, first as Chief Investigator and then as Pacific Region Superintendent. He has testified in court as an expert witness in the navigational uses of GPS and is the principal author of *GPS Instant Navigation, 2nd Edition* and *Proven Cruising Routes, Volume 1—Seattle to Ketchikan*, and *The Radar Book.*

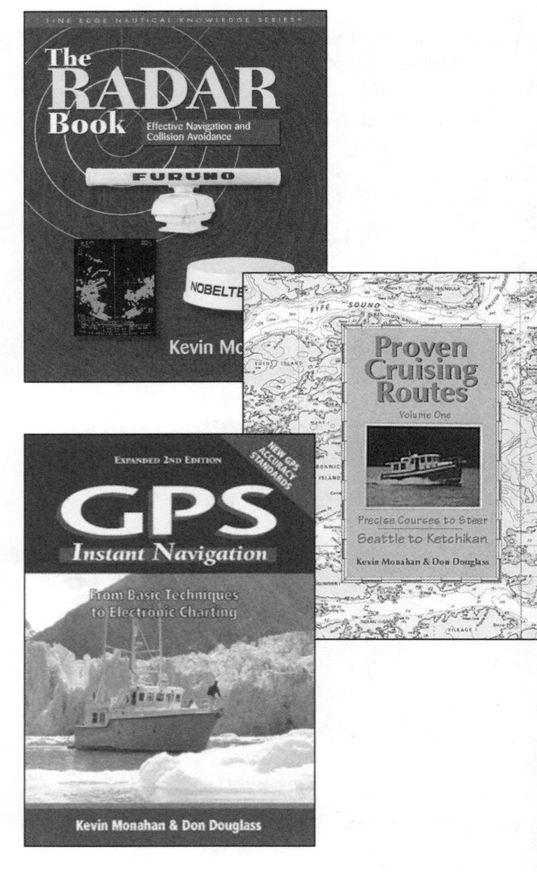
The RADAR Book
Effective Navigation and Collision Avoidance
FURUNO
Proven Cruising Routes
Volume One
Precise Courses to Steer
Seattle to Ketchikan
Kevin Monahan & Don Douglass
Expanded 2nd Edition
NEW GPS ACCURACY STANDARDS
GPS
Instant Navigation
From Basic Techniques to Electronic Charting
Kevin Monahan & Don Douglass

Other Publications by the Author

The Radar Book
Kevin Monahan

The complete picture on how to maximize the use of your marine radar system. By using practical examples, illustrated with screen displays and the corresponding charts, the newcomer to radar as well as the experienced mariner will learn how to tune a radar system, interpret the display in a variety of conditions, take advantage of all of the built-in features and use radar effectively as a real-time navigational tool. Today's next generation radar systems, which combine the chart plotter display and their usage, are described in this comprehensive explanation of marine radar systems.

Proven Cruising Routes, Vol. 1—Seattle to Ketchikan
Kevin Monahan and Don Douglass

With our 34 routes you have the best 100 ways to Alaska! We've done the charting! This route guide contains precise courses to steer, diagrams and GPS waypoints from Seattle to Ketchikan.

Also available: Companion 3.5" IBM diskette to directly download routes into electronic charts.

GPS Instant Navigation, 2nd Edition
A Practical Guide from Basics to Advanced Techniques

Kevin Monahan and Don Douglass

In this clear, well-illustrated manual, mariners will find simple solutions to navigational challenges. Includes 150 detailed diagrams, which illustrate the many ways you can use GPS to solve classic piloting and navigation problems.

Enjoy these other publications from Fine Edge

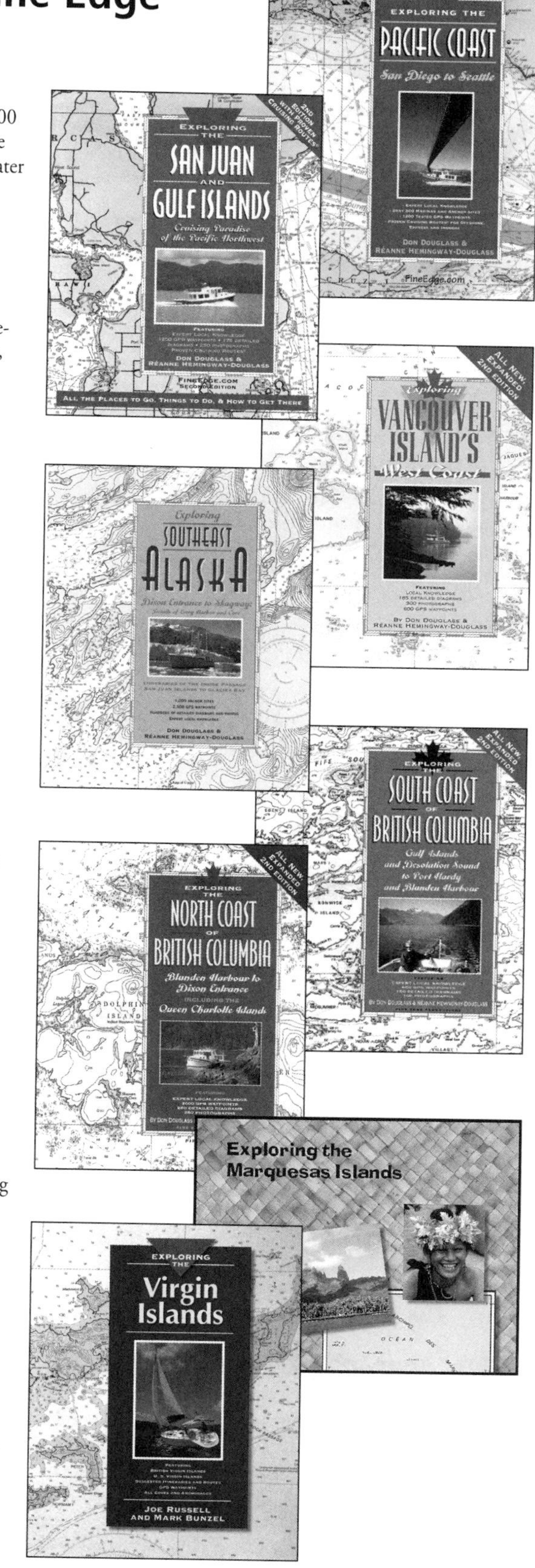

EXPLORING THE
PACIFIC COAST
San Diego to Seattle
EXPLORING THE
SAN JUAN AND GULF ISLANDS
Cruising Paradise of the Pacific Northwest
VANCOUVER ISLAND'S
West Coast
Exploring
SOUTHEAST ALASKA
EXPLORING THE
SOUTH COAST OF BRITISH COLUMBIA
EXPLORING THE
NORTH COAST OF BRITISH COLUMBIA
Exploring the Marquesas Islands
EXPLORING THE
Virgin Islands
JOE RUSSELL AND MARK BUNZEL

Exploring the Pacific Coast—San Diego to Seattle

Don Douglass and Réanne Hemingway-Douglass

All the places to tie up or anchor your boat from the Mexican border to Victoria/ Seattle. Over 500 of the best marinas and anchor sites, starting from San Diego to Santa Barbara—every anchor site in the beautiful Channel Islands, the greater SF Bay Area, the lower Columbia River, and the greater Puget Sound.

Exploring the San Juan and Gulf Islands—2nd Edition

Cruising Paradise of the Pacific Northwest

Don Douglass and Réanne Hemingway-Douglass

Describes the most scenic and accessible marine area in the world—a cruising paradise of 300 tree-covered islets and islands surrounded by well-sheltered waters, comfortable resorts, quaint villages, secure moorings and anchorages.

Exploring Southeast Alaska

Dixon Entrance to Glacier Bay and Icy Point

Don Douglass and Réanne Hemingway-Douglass

Almost completely protected, these waters give access to a pristine wilderness of breathtaking beauty—thousands of islands, deeply-cut fiords, tidewater glaciers and icebergs.

Exploring Vancouver Island's West Coast—2nd Ed.

Don Douglass and Réanne Hemingway-Douglass

With five great sounds, sixteen major inlets, and an abundance of spectacular wildlife, the largest island on the west coast of North America is a cruising paradise.

Exploring the North Coast of British Columbia—2nd Ed.

Blunden Harbour to Dixon Entrance—Including the Queen Charlotte Islands

Don Douglass and Réanne Hemingway-Douglass

Describes previously uncharted Spiller Channel and Griffin Passage, the stunning scenery of Nakwakto Rapids and Seymour Inlet, Fish Egg Inlet, Queens Sound, and Hakai Recreation Area. Includes the beautiful South Moresby Island of the Queen Charlottes, with its rare flora and fauna and historical sites of native Haida culture.

Exploring the South Coast of British Columbia—2nd Ed.

Gulf Islands and Desolation Sound to Port Hardy and Blunden Harbour

Don Douglass and Réanne Hemingway-Douglass

"Clearly the most thorough, best produced and most useful [guides] available . . . particularly well thought out and painstakingly researched." — NW Yachting

Exploring the Marquesas Islands

Joe Russell

Russell, who has lived and sailed in the Marquesas, documents the first cruising guide to this beautiful, little-known place. Includes history, language guide, chart diagrams, mileages and heading tables and archaeology. "A must reference for those wanting to thoroughly enjoy their first landfall on the famous Coconut Milk Run."—Earl Hinz, author, *Landfalls of Paradise—Cruising Guide to the Pacific Islands*

Exploring the Virgin Islands

By Joe Russell and Mark Bunzel

The warm tropical waters and easy sailing make the US and British Virgin Islands one of the most popular cruising destinations in the world. "Exploring the Virgin Islands" provides up to date information on all of the coves and anchorages in both Island chains including many never published before. Many anchorages are illustrated with color aerial photos and diagrams showing the best means for entry and where to anchor. GPS waypoints for each harbor are provide along with the best routing to get there. Local sites, restaurants, beach bars and hiking trails are included along with suggested itineraries and tips on how to prepare for your trip to this Caribbean paradise.

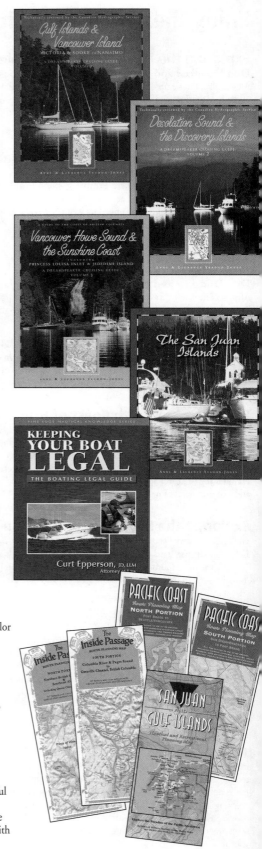